Chaos and Governance in
the Modern World System

Contradictions of Modernity

The modern era has been uniquely productive of theory. Some theory claimed uniformity despite human differences or unilinear progress in the face of catastrophic changes. Other theory was informed more deeply by the complexities of history and recognition of cultural specificity. This series seeks to further the latter approach by publishing books that explore the problems of theorizing the modern in its manifold and sometimes contradictory forms and that examine the specific locations of theory within the modern.

Edited by Craig Calhoun
New York University

Volume 10   Giovanni Arrighi and Beverly J. Silver, *Chaos and Governance in the Modern World System*

Volume 9   François Dosse, *History of Structuralism, Volume 2: The Sign Sets, 1967–Present*

Volume 8   François Dosse, *History of Structuralism, Volume 1: The Rising Sign, 1945–1966*

Volume 7   Patricia Hill Collins, *Fighting Words: Black Women and the Search for Justice*

Volume 6   Craig Calhoun and John McGowan, editors, *Hannah Arendt and the Meaning of Politics*

Volume 5   Gérard Noiriel, *The French Melting Pot: Immigration, Citizenship, and National Identity*

Volume 4   John C. Torpey, *Intellectuals, Socialism, and Dissent: The East German Opposition and Its Legacy*

Volume 3   T. M. S. Evens, *Two Kinds of Rationality: Kibbutz Democracy and Generational Conflict*

Volume 2   Micheline R. Ishay, *Internationalism and Its Betrayal*

Volume 1   Johan Heilbron, *The Rise of Social Theory*

Chaos and Governance in the Modern World System

Giovanni Arrighi and
Beverly J. Silver

with Iftikhar Ahmad, Kenneth Barr,
Shuji Hisaeda, Po-keung Hui, Krishnendu Ray,
Thomas Ehrlich Reifer, Miin-wen Shih,
and Eric Slater

Contradictions of Modernity Volume 10

University of Minnesota Press
Minneapolis
London

Published by the University of Minnesota Press
111 Third Avenue South, Suite 290, Minneapolis, MN 55401-2520
http://www.upress.umn.edu

Library of Congress Cataloging-in-Publication Data

Arrighi, Giovanni.
    Chaos and governance in the modern world system / Giovanni Arrighi and Beverly J. Silver with Iftikhar Ahmad . . . [et al.].
        p. cm. — (Contradictions of modernity ; 10)
    Includes bibliographical references.
    ISBN 0-8166-3151-4. — ISBN 0-8166-3152-2 (pbk.)
    1. World politics. 2. International economic relations. I. Silver, Beverly J.
II. Ahmad, Iftikhar. III. Title. IV. Series.
D299.A75 1999
337—dc21   98-55503

Printed in the United States of America on acid-free paper

The University of Minnesota is an equal-opportunity educator and employer.

10 09 08 07 06 05 04 03 02 01 00 99   10 9 8 7 6 5 4 3 2 1

To Terence K. Hopkins (1928–1997)
Friend, Mentor, and Co-Conspirator

Contents

Preface and Acknowledgments   ix

Introduction
Giovanni Arrighi and Beverly J. Silver   1

1. Geopolitics and High Finance
   *Giovanni Arrighi, Po-keung Hui, Krishnendu Ray,
   and Thomas Ehrlich Reifer*   37

2. The Transformation of Business Enterprise
   Giovanni Arrighi, Kenneth Barr, and Shuji Hisaeda   97

3. The Social Origins of World Hegemonies
   Beverly J. Silver and Eric Slater   151

4. Western Hegemonies in World-Historical Perspective
   Giovanni Arrighi, Iftikhar Ahmad, and Miin-wen Shih   217

Conclusion
Giovanni Arrighi and Beverly J. Silver   271

Bibliography   291

Index   317

Preface and Acknowledgments

This volume originated in a project entitled "Hegemony and Rivalry in the World-System: Trends and Prospective Consequences of Geopolitical Realignments, 1500–2025" funded by the John D. and Catherine T. MacArthur Foundation. One half of the project was coordinated by Terence K. Hopkins and Immanuel Wallerstein and focused on the trajectory of the world-system since 1945. Its results were published in Terence K. Hopkins, Immanuel Wallerstein, et al., *The Age of Transition: Trajectory of the World-System 1945–2025* (London: Zed Books, 1996).

Our half of the project compares the present period of global instability to two earlier (and we argue, analogous) periods in the modern world—the transition from Dutch to British hegemony in the eighteenth century and from British to U.S. hegemony in the late nineteenth and early twentieth centuries. We are very grateful to the MacArthur Foundation, and in particular to Kennette Benedict, for accepting the thesis that, to understand the dilemmas of the contemporary world, we have to investigate processes of social change over centuries.

This book is the outcome of almost a decade of work. Its initial conceptualization and most of the research were undertaken by the Comparative Hegemonies Research Working Group of the Fernand

Braudel Center for the Study of Economies, Historical Systems, and Civilizations of Binghamton University. In addition to those listed as coauthors in the book, Steve Sherman was also a member of the Research Working Group and wrote a chapter on culture that is centrally related to the project. For editorial reasons, the chapter is being published separately as "Hegemonic Transitions and the Dynamics of Cultural Change," *Review* 22, no. 1 (winter 1999).

In April 1993, a group of scholars was invited to Binghamton for a two-day seminar and asked to critique draft chapters of the volume. Their comments and criticisms led us to substantially restructure, expand, and rewrite the volume. We are grateful for their lively participation to Nicole Bousquet, Harriet Friedmann, Victoria de Grazia, Lars Mjöset, Frances Moulder, Ravi Palat, Frances Fox Piven, Mark Selden, Peter Taylor, and Immanuel Wallerstein.

Four years later we submitted the results to Craig Calhoun for this series. His extremely helpful comments together with those of Bruce Fuller and Micah Kleit led to further major revisions in 1997—most notably a complete rewrite of the introduction and conclusion. We would like to thank the able and efficient staff of the University of Minnesota Press for guiding the manuscript through the various production stages, as well as Donna DeVoist of the Fernand Braudel Center, whose assistance throughout has been essential to the completion of the project.

The book is dedicated to the memory of Terence K. Hopkins. As one of the coordinators of the Comparative Hegemonies Research Working Group, he was central in the formulation of the research design. With his characteristic combination of deep insight and generosity, he commented on earlier drafts of the chapters, leaving an indelible mark on the final product. As colleague, mentor, founder, and director of the sociology graduate program in Binghamton, his profound influence on generations of scholars and graduate students is beyond measure. We hope that this book stands as a worthy memorial to him.

Introduction

Giovanni Arrighi and Beverly J. Silver

A sea change of major proportions is taking place in the historical social system forming the modern world. Eric Hobsbawm calls the 1970s and 1980s "decades of *universal* or global crisis," the closing phase of his Short Twentieth Century (1914–91). In his view, the collapse of communist regimes "produced an enormous zone of political uncertainty, instability, chaos and civil war." Worse still, it "also destroyed the . . . system that had stabilized international relations for some forty years . . . and revealed the precariousness of the domestic political systems that had essentially rested on that stability" (1994, 9–10).

> The basic units of politics themselves, the territorial, sovereign and independent "nation-states," including the oldest and stablest, found themselves pulled apart by the forces of supranational or transnational economy, and by the infranational forces of secessionist regions and ethnic groups. Some of these—such is the irony of history—demanded the outdated and unreal status of miniature sovereign "nation-states" for themselves. The future of politics was obscure, but its crisis at the end of the Short Twentieth Century was patent. (Hobsbawm, 1994, 10–11)

Equally patent, was a crisis of the rationalist and humanist assumptions, shared by liberal capitalism and communism, "on which modern society had been founded since the Moderns won their famous battle against the Ancients in the early eighteenth century" (Hobsbawm, 1994, 11). In a similar vein, Immanuel Wallerstein has claimed that the year 1989 marks "the end of a politico-cultural era—an era of spectacular technological achievement—in which the slogans of the French Revolution were seen by most people to reflect inevitable historical truth, to be realized now or in the near future." Like Hobsbawm, Wallerstein situates the upheavals of 1989 in the context of the escalating, self-reinforcing disorder of the preceding two decades. But in contrast to Hobsbawm, he interprets this disorder as a form of systemic chaos caused "by the fact that contradictions of the [world capitalist] system have come to the point where none of the mechanisms for restoring the normal functioning of the system can work effectively any longer" (Wallerstein, 1995a, 1, 268).

As such, the present crisis is taken to mark the end, not just of the particular politico-cultural era launched by the Enlightenment and the French Revolution, but also of the modern world system that came into existence in the "long" sixteenth century. "Just as [the modern world-system] came into existence five centuries ago in Europe as the end point of the unfolding of the 'crisis of feudalism,' so this historical system, which now covers the globe and whose technical-scientific achievements go from triumph to triumph, is in systemic crisis" (Wallerstein, 1982, 11). Starting from different premises, James Rosenau concurs with this assessment. In his view, the parameters that have framed action in the international system for several centuries are being transformed so fundamentally today "as to bring about the first turbulence in world politics since comparable shifts culminated in the Treaty of Westphalia in 1648" (Rosenau, 1990, 10).

Whatever era is thought to be ending—the Cold War era, the longer era of "liberalism" and the Enlightenment, or the even longer era of the system of national states—uncertainty is seen as engulfing the present and the foreseeable future. "As the citizens of the fin de siècle tapped their way through the global fog that surrounded them, into the third millennium," remarks Hobsbawm (1994, 558–59), "all they knew for certain was that an era of history had ended. They knew very little else."

Some even thought that not just an era, but history itself had ended. And they thought it had ended not with the crisis, but with the final triumph of liberal capitalism. With the collapse of Communism, declared Francis Fukuyama, "liberal democracy remains the only co-herent aspiration that spans different regions and cultures around the globe." Two generations ago, "many reasonable people could foresee a radiant socialist future in which private property and capitalism had been abolished. . . . Today, by contrast, we have trouble imagining a world that is radically better than our own, or a future that is not es-sentially democratic and capitalist" (1992, xiii, 46).

Conceived within Reagan's State Department, the original version of this declaration (Fukuyama, 1989) found immediate echo and ap-plication in the vision of a "new world order" that President Bush evoked in confronting Saddam Hussein's invasion of Kuwait. The spectacular U.S./UN victory in the Gulf War gave credence to the idea that a new world order was in the making. Soon, however, that idea came to be seen, in John A. Hall's words, "as a sick joke" in the light of widespread and escalating ethnic violence. The dictum of the Australian historian Geoffrey Bainey that "recurrent optimism is a vital prelude to war" seemed once again to be borne out by the facts (Hall, 1996, xii).

Four Controversies on the Future of the World Political Economy

The purpose of this book is to dissipate at least some of the "global fog" that surrounds us by investigating the dynamics of systemic change in two earlier periods of transformation of the modern world that in key respects resemble the present. If the present period, as we shall argue, is one of decline and crisis of U.S. world hegemony, then it shares important analogies with the two previous periods of world-hegemonic transition—the transition from Dutch to British world hegemony in the eighteenth century and the transition from British to U.S. world hegemony in the late nineteenth and early twentieth centuries. Comparing the similarities and differences between these two completed transitions will shed light on the dynamics of current transformations.

Four interrelated controversies frame our inquiry. The first is the changing balance of power among states, and in particular, whether a new hegemonic state is likely to emerge. The second concerns the balance of power between states and business organizations, and in particular, whether "globalization" has irremediably undermined the power of states. The third concerns the power of subordinate groups, and in particular, whether we are in the midst of an unstoppable "race to the bottom" in conditions of work and life. The fourth concerns the changing balance of power between Western and non-Western civilizations, and in particular, whether we are reaching the end of five centuries of Western dominance in the modern world system.

Each chapter analyzes the two past hegemonic transitions with one of these four issues in mind. We should thus first lay out in some detail the four controversies about the present that inspire our investigation of the past. In the second part of this introduction, we will clarify the central concepts and theoretical framework on which our investigation is based. In the conclusion, we will address these controversial issues with the new insights gained from our journey into the past.

The Geography of World Power

There is widespread debate and uncertainty about whether a new world-hegemonic state is emerging, and if so, which state will play that role. As Robert Gilpin (1996, 2) notes, "[t]here is no consensus on who in fact really won the Cold War, if indeed anyone did." Candidates put forward by different analysts include the United States, a united Europe, and Japan, while still others claim that *all* states have lost power vis-à-vis supranational economic and political organizations.

Assessments of the global power of the United States in the wake of the demise of its Soviet rival vary widely.

> "Now is the unipolar moment," a triumphalist commentator crows. "There is but one first-rate power and no prospect in the immediate future of any power to rival it." But a senior U.S. foreign policy official demurs: "We simply do not have the leverage, we don't have the influence, the inclination to use military force. We don't have the money to bring the kind of pressure that will produce positive results any time soon." (Ruggie, 1994, 553)

Nor does any agreement exist on who, if not the United States, has the leverage, influence, and money to bring the kind of pressure that produces positive results. In 1992, Lester Thurow prognosticated that the integration of the European Common Market on January 1, 1993, would mark the beginning of a new economic contest, in place of the old contest between capitalism and communism. In the new contest, "[a]s the world's largest market, the House of Europe will be writing the rules of world trade in the twenty-first century and the rest of the world will simply have to learn to play their economic game" (1992, 24–25; for a similar assessment, see Burstein, 1991, 11–12).

And yet, come January 1993, Europeans saw things in an altogether different light. Writing in London's *Sunday Times,* Martin Jaques described Europe as "a continent in decline" that "must adjust to a less exalted position" (as quoted in Dicken and Oberg, 1996, 102). Four years later, the very process of European economic integration seemed to bear out the gloomier view.

> With Europe staring at monumental structural economic problems ranging from 20 percent youth unemployment to the escalating costs of supporting an aging population, the timing of monetary union could hardly be worse. At best the political maneuvering over currency integration will serve as a distraction, delaying the wrenching changes needed to make Europe more competitive in the global economy. At worst it will set back the general cause of European unity by creating a huge political backlash against integration if economic conditions worsen soon after the euro is introduced. (Passell, 1997, D2)

The extent of Japanese world power is equally unclear. Japan's influence in world politics seems to have peaked shortly before the collapse of the USSR in the wake of the drastic revaluation of the yen vis-à-vis the U.S. dollar engineered by the Group of Seven (G-7) at the 1985 Plaza meeting. Aimed at containing U.S. trade deficits, the revaluation led instead to a seemingly irresistible ascent of "Japanese money" in financial and real estate markets around the world. Japanese banks came to dominate international asset rankings and Japanese institutional investors set the pace in the U.S. treasuries market. "On Wall Street and in the City of London, and around the seminar tables of the world's finest graduate schools, there was a new, self-confident presence that no one could ignore" (Nakao, 1995, 1). This self-confident presence, along with the takeover of American assets of great symbolic value, such as the Rockefeller Center, Columbia Pictures, the Seattle Mariners, and much of downtown Los Angeles, gave rise in the United States "to dark warnings that decisions about the country's future would be made in Tokyo, not New York and Washington" (Sanger, 1997a). Earlier prognostications of an "emerging Japanese superstate" (Kahn, 1970) or of "Japan as number one" (Vogel, 1979) seemed to be right on the mark.

In the short span of seven years, however, these "dark warnings" appeared "almost laughable." If anything, the Japanese "exerted too little control over their [U.S.] acquisitions" and "took a multi-billion-dollar bath on most of their investments" (Sanger, 1997a). Losses on Japanese foreign investments due to movements in exchange rates were even greater (Hale, 1995, 148). Partly as a result of these losses, at the beginning of 1990 prices on the Tokyo stock exchange collapsed, losing almost 55 percent of their value by the end of 1992 (*Japan Almanac,* 1997). Soon after the crash of 1990,

> the Iraqi invasion of Kuwait sparked the Gulf crisis and exposed Japan's political weakness. Even when war broke out early in 1991, the Japanese government was incapable of taking an independent line and once again fell in behind the leadership of the United States. Japan, it seemed, was a first class economy but third-rate in politics. (Nakao, 1995, 1)

The difficulties involved in identifying an unambiguously "strong state" in the post–Cold War era have led some analysts to argue that the power of *all* states is declining under the impact of intensifying economic integration. This brings us to the second controversy this book will focus on.

The Power of States versus the Power of Capital

The opening salvo in a renewed debate about the relationship between states and capitalism was Charles Kindleberger's claim that the "nation-state" is "just about through as an economic unit" because of the emergence of a system of transnational corporations that neither owe loyalty, nor feel at home in any country (1969, 297; see also Hymer and Rowthorn, 1970, 88–91; Vernon, 1971; Barnet and Muller, 1974, 15–16; Sklar, 1976). It was some twenty years later, however, that the thesis of a general disempowerment of states by supranational economic forces gained widespread currency under the name of "globalization" (see, among others, Dicken, 1992; Ohmae, 1990; Sklair, 1991; Reich, 1992; Barnet and Cavanagh, 1994; Horsman and Marshall, 1994; Waters, 1995). In the intervening period, the expansion of the overseas operations of multinational corporations set off a process of global financial expansion and integration that acquired a momentum of its own and became the strongest piece of evidence in the armory of advocates of the globalization thesis.

According to Fred Bergsten, by the 1995 Halifax meeting of the G-7, the "immense flow of private capital [had] intimidated the officials from any effort to counter them." After quoting Bergsten, Erik Peterson wonders whether those flows can be countered at all and speaks of a "coming hegemony of global markets." As the "competition for global capital" intensifies, deterritorialized market forces (primarily business organizations but also some individuals) place increasingly tighter constraints on the economic policies of even the largest nations, the United States included. "They will also have an impact on the U.S. capacity to carry out effective security and foreign policies abroad and will determine the extent to which Washington can maintain its world leadership role" (Peterson, 1995, 111–13).

To return to our first controversial issue, advocates of the globalization thesis implicitly maintain that no state or group of states really won the Cold War because owners of mobile capital without allegiance to any specific state did. In the emerging situation, private credit-rating agencies like Moody's Investors Services wield an influence that some commentators have compared to that of military superpowers. Commenting on the markdown of Mexico's bonds that precipitated the 1994–95 Mexican financial crisis, Thomas Friedman ventured the hyperbole that we may be living again in a two-superpower world: "There is the U.S. and there is Moody's. The U.S. can destroy a country by leveling it with bombs; Moody's can destroy a country by downgrading its bonds" (quoted in Cohen, 1996, 282).

The globalization thesis of a general disempowerment of states vis-à-vis non-territorial, supranational, or transnational economic forces has not gone unchallenged, even in its less exaggerated forms. Few question the increasing magnitude and speed of capital flows across national boundaries. But many question the idea that this increase constitutes a qualitatively new or irreversible development in state-capital relations.

Some critics have pointed out that states have been active participants in the process of integration and deregulation of nationally segmented and publicly regulated financial markets. Moreover, this active participation occurred under the aegis of neoliberal doctrines of the minimalist state that were themselves propagated by particular states— most notably Britain under Margaret Thatcher and the United States under Ronald Reagan. Since state support and encouragement have been indispensable to the process of globalization, states are said to have the power to reverse the process if they so choose (for different versions of this criticism, see Block, 1990; Sobel, 1994; Helleiner, 1994, 1997; Hirst and Thompson, 1992, 1996; Weiss, 1997).

To be sure, even if it originated in state action, globalization may have acquired a momentum that makes its reversal by states impossible or undesirable because of the costs involved (Goodman and Pauly, 1993; Pauly, 1995). However, there is no agreement among analysts on the extent to which globalization, whether reversible or not, actually constrains state action (Cohen, 1996, 280–93). Some even interpret it as the expression of the further empowerment of the United States. Indeed, various aspects of the seemingly global triumph of Americanism that ensued from the demise of the USSR are themselves widely perceived as signs of globalization. The most widely recognized signs are the global hegemony of U.S. popular culture and the growing importance of agencies of world governance that are influenced disproportionately by the United States and its closest allies, such as the UN Security Council, NATO, the G-7, the International Monetary Fund (IMF), the International Bank of Reconstruction and Development (IBRD), and the World Trade Organization (WTO). Less widely recognized but also significant is the ascendance of a new legal regime in international business transactions dominated by U.S. law firms and Anglo-American conceptions of business law (Sassen, 1996, 12–21; see also Gill, 1990; Sklair, 1991).

The thesis that globalization disempowers states has also been challenged by critics who focus on the longer-term aspects of the phenomenon and see much déjà vu in the alleged novelties of recent changes in state-capital relations. Wallerstein has gone as far as to argue that the basic relationship between states and capital has remained the same throughout capitalist history, with "transnational corporations . . . maintaining today the same structural stance vis-à-vis states as did all their global predecessors, from the Fuggers to the Dutch East India Company to nineteenth-century Manchester manufacturers" (Wallerstein, 1995c, 24–25). More common is the contention that the transformations that go under the rubric of "globalization" originate in the nineteenth century. "If the theorists of globalization mean that we have an economy in which each part of the world is linked by markets sharing close to real-time information," claim Paul Hirst and Grahame Thompson, "then that began not in the 1970s but in the 1870s" (1996, 9–10).

Financial and other major markets were closely integrated once the system of international submarine telegraph cables was in place and in a way not fundamentally different from the satellite-linked and computer-controlled markets of today. Indeed, the difference between an international economy in which market information travelled by sailing ship and one in which it is transmitted by electricity is really one of kind. Commentators sometimes forget that today's open world economy is not unique. (Hirst and Thompson, 1992, 366)

After surveying the evidence, Robert Zevin concludes that "every available description of financial markets in the late nineteenth and early twentieth centuries suggests that they were more fully integrated than they were before or have been since" (1992, 51–52). Indeed, toward the end of this earlier wave of financial globalization, in 1920, Moody's already rated bonds issued by about fifty governments—a number that declined rapidly in the wake of the Great Depression and the Second World War and returned only recently to comparable levels (Sassen, 1996, 43).

These analogies between the present period of globalization and the late-nineteenth and early-twentieth-century period have led some to question whether the present trend toward an unregulated world market economy is as unstoppable as advocates of the globalization thesis maintain. This question has recently been raised by one of the leading figures of cosmopolitan high finance, the Hungarian-born George Soros. In comparing the present age of triumphant laissez-faire capitalism with the similar age of a century ago, Soros finds the earlier age, if anything, more stable than the present, because of the sway of the gold standard and the presence of an imperial power (Britain) prepared to dispatch gunboats to faraway places to maintain the system. Yet the system broke down under the impact of the two world wars and the intervening rise of "totalitarian ideologies." Today, in contrast, the United States is reluctant to be the policeman of the world "and the main currencies float and crush against each other like continental plates," making the breakdown of the present regime much more likely (1997, 48).

Our global open society lacks the institutions and mechanisms necessary for its preservation, but there is no political will to bring them into existence. I blame the prevailing attitude, which holds that the unhampered pursuit of self-interest will bring about an eventual international equilibrium. . . . As things stand, it does not take very much imagination to realize that the global open society that prevails at present is likely to prove a temporary phenomenon. (Soros, 1997, 53–54)

In short, the phoenix of private high finance has undoubtedly risen from the ashes of its destruction in the 1930s and 1940s. But whether it can rule the roost without the support of strong states more effectively than it has in the past—as implied by Peterson's idea of a "coming hegemony of global markets"—remains in dispute. Equally controversial is the question of whether and how globalization and the attendant transformation of relations between states and capital have affected the social, political, and economic power of subordinate groups.

States, Capital, and the Social Power of Subordinate Groups

A staple argument of the literature on globalization is that the increasing geographical mobility and volatility of capital is creating a "race to the bottom" in wages and working conditions as the world's workers are brought into competition in a single labor market. Although workers in low-wage countries may temporarily benefit from the competition, the hyper-mobility of productive and finance capital makes the threat of "capital flight" realistic and palatable everywhere. The result is an overall decline in the capacity of workers to protect and advance their interests (see, among others, Fröbel et al, 1980; Godfrey, 1986, 28; Ross and Trachte, 1990; Brecher, 1994/95; Bonacich et al., 1994, 365–73; Appelbaum, 1996).

Charles Tilly agrees that workers are facing a "devastating reversal" of the secular trend of expanding rights that began in the mid-nineteenth century. But rather than linking the weakening of labor directly to an increase in global economic competition, he emphasizes the intermediate role played by globalization's impact on state capacities. Defining globalization as "an increase in the geographical range of locally consequential social interactions, especially when the increase stretches a significant proportion of all interactions across international or intercontinental limits" (for a similar definition, see Giddens, 1990, 64), he identifies four waves of globalization over the past millennium (in the thirteenth, sixteenth, nineteenth, and late twentieth centuries). He then contrasts the impact on state capacities of the current wave of globalization with that of the previous nineteenth-century wave. Whereas during the nineteenth century states (in fact, European and other Western states on which Tilly's contentions are based) acquired enhanced capacities for action, today states are losing the capacity to monitor and control stocks and flows, and therefore to pursue effective social policies. For Tilly, workers' rights have been enforced by national states; hence, as "states decline, so do workers' rights" (Tilly, 1995, 1–4, 14–22).

Tilly argues that *all* citizens' rights have been guaranteed by states, hence the current weakening of states threatens not only workers' rights, but all democratic rights. John Markoff has similarly identified the increasing power of transnational entities as a major challenge to democracy. "Although more people in the mid-1990s are living under national governments with some claim to democracy than at any other point in the two centuries of modern democratic history, the actual power of those states may be slipping away, passing to . . . emerging transnational structures," which are themselves not particularly democratic. Formally democratic governments in much of the world are likely to make key economic and social policy decisions with "an eye at least as much on pleasing the International Monetary Fund as appealing to an electorate." For Markoff, "the challenge of recreating democracy in the emerging world of transnational decision-making" can only be met by the organization of transnational democratic movements capable of extracting "concessions from the new holders of transnational power" (Markoff, 1996, 132–35). Tilly concurs on the direction of the solution, but is more pessimistic, at least in the short run, that this will happen (1995, 22).

The contention that the weakening of states is the root cause of the weakening of labor and democracy has been challenged on a number of grounds that parallel the debates reviewed in the previous section. Thus, some have argued that the current organization of the international economy is a constructed outcome of political negotiations and conflicts, rather than an independent force. The current "high degree of freedom for international capital flows is not a necessary and inevitable feature of a world economy." If the policies of the politically powerful change, globalization can be reversed (Block, 1990, 16–18). From this point of view, the rhetoric of globalization veils corporate responsibility for massive layoffs (Gordon, 1996, 200–203) or governmental responsibility for the massive redistribution of benefits from labor to capital (Tabb, 1997; see also Piven, 1995; Block, 1996).

Others have challenged the causal link from weakened states to weakened subordinate groups by challenging the degree to which we are in a qualitatively new era of history. Wallerstein advanced his

claim that the basic relationship between states and capital has remained unchanged since the sixteenth century (see above) in direct
response to Tilly's contention that state power is now being undermined by transnational corporations. And Aristide Zolberg has criti-
cized Tilly for disregarding the "dialectical relation" that has linked
national economic policy to the international political economy since
at least the nineteenth century (Zolberg, 1995, 33–34).

For Zolberg, the weakening of labor is not the dependent but the
independent "variable" in explaining the current *labor-unfriendly*
global environment. Building on Polanyi (1957), Zolberg argues that
in the first half of the twentieth century, the "dysfunctional effects of
the [unregulated international] market economy" provoked a series of
disasters, as well as strong movements of self-protection (most importantly, militant labor movements). Drawing lessons from this experience, the leaders of the postwar world order created international
institutions, most notably the Bretton Woods system, that "were designed quite deliberately to be relatively *labor-friendly.*" The effectiveness of state-sponsored efforts to promote social security and welfare
at the national level in the 1950s and 1960s was premised on this "unprecedented benevolent environment" at the global level. But that
benevolent environment was itself created in response to the unprecedented social power of workers in Western countries at the end of the
Second World War (Zolberg, 1995, 33–34).

The post-1970 change from a labor-friendly to a labor-unfriendly
international regime is not due to the weakening of states, Zolberg
maintains, but to the structural weakening of the working class itself
with the advent of "post-industrial society."

> Much as the advent of industrial capitalism brought about condi-
> tions that fostered the creation of the distinctive social formation we
> term "working class," so the waning of these conditions undermines
> its continued existence. . . . [T]he "workers" to whose struggles we
> owe the "rights of labor" are rapidly disappearing and today consti-
> tute a residual endangered species. (Zolberg, 1995, 28)

Despite their disagreement on the causes, both Tilly and Zolberg
agree that labor is being weakened. Yet this contention itself is at odds
with a rapidly growing literature exploring the relationship between
class formation and transformations of the global political economy
(van der Pijl, 1984; Cox, 1987; Gill, 1990, 1993; Gill and Law, 1988;

Gill and Mittelman, 1997; Hettne, 1995; Rupert, 1995; Mittelman, 1996; Robinson, 1996). Most of this literature focuses on the formation of a transnational capitalist class with its own strategic class consciousness. This process is generally interpreted as imposing new constraints on national governments and labor organizations. But the efforts and activities of this transnational capitalist class are themselves conceived as a response to the constraints imposed on capital by strong (not weak) labor movements. Moreover, like Zolberg, some of these studies (most notably Mittelman, 1996; Gill and Mittelman, 1997) invoke Polanyi's contention that global movements toward the creation of a system of self-regulating markets inevitably calls forth spontaneous, global countermovements of resistance against the disruption of established social relations and practices. Unlike Zolberg, however, they see this countermovement coming into action, not just in response to the sway of laissez-faire capitalism in the 1880s, but also in response to its attempted revival in the 1980s.

By Zolberg's own account, it took sixty years—from the 1880s to the 1940s—for the earlier countermovement to produce "labor-friendly" results at the level of the global political economy. What is to prevent the (countermovement) responses to the current revival of laissez-faire from producing comparable results at the global level twenty or thirty years from now? And even now, what are we to make of the fact that in mid-1997 nominally working-class parties—albeit with "foggy" ideas about how to cope with globalization—were in the governing coalitions of thirteen out of fifteen states in the European Union?

The issue of whether or not globalization is disempowering subordinate groups becomes even more controversial as soon as we broaden our horizon beyond the wealthy countries of the West, on whose experience Tilly's and Zolberg's contentions are almost exclusively based. Various studies have contrasted the declining militancy and social power of labor in deindustrializing wealthy countries with the "manufacturing of militance" (Seidman, 1994) in less wealthy but rapidly industrializing countries, such as Brazil, South Africa, and South Korea (see also Silver, 1995; Evans, 1995, 227–29; Markoff, 1996, 20–31; Moody, 1997). In a similar vein, Lourdes Benería (1995, 45–52) has pointed out that the current transformations in the global organization of production may be creating new rights at the same time that old rights are undermined. Even where new labor movements have not emerged, "the sheer fact of rural women's migration to industrial employment [in export-processing zones] may foster their individual rights and autonomy and release them from oppressive patriarchal practices" (Benería, 1995, 48; see also Lim, 1983, 1990; Ong, 1987). Moreover, the creation of a single world labor market is leading to growing "pressures towards recognition of workers' rights" in such forums as the Uruguay Round negotiations of GATT (Benería, 1995, 48).

But whether and to what extent workers' and citizens' rights can continue to expand across time and space is also debatable. Wallerstein contends that the expansion of workers' and citizens' rights since the mid-nineteenth century was itself *premised* on the exclusion of the majority of the world's population from those rights and benefits. The expansion of rights originated in an attempt by Western elites to deal with an increasingly numerous and militant working class within their own countries by means of a strategy of cooptation. A triple package was offered—"the suffrage, the welfare state, and a double nationalism (of the states and of the White world, that is racism)." The strategy "was enormously successful in transforming the 'dangerous classes' [of the West] into a 'responsible opposition' with syndical claims to a share of the pie." But the strategy became too expensive when it was expanded to include the promise of "economic development" in the non-Western world. Allowing the non-Western world "to share in the pie was simply too costly for a capitalist world-economy. One could cut in several-hundred-million Western workers and still make the system profitable. But if one cut in several billion Third World workers, there would be nothing left for further capital accumulation" (1995c, 25).

Indeed, by the 1970s it became clear that world capitalism could not accommodate "the combined demands of the Third World (for relatively little per person but for a lot of people) and the Western working class (for relatively few people but for quite a lot per person)" (Wallerstein, 1995c, 25). The trend toward increasing redistribution and equality was halted. New class divides are being drawn, which in core countries, Wallerstein predicts, will increasingly overlap with racial divides.

> We will have social structures in Europe and North America . . . in which the "working class" will be disproportionately composed of

non-White workers, probably outside the trade-union structures, and even more probably without basic political and social rights. At the same time, the children and grandchildren of today's union members will be "middle class"—maybe unionized, some doing well, and others less well (and thereupon more likely to be engaged in right-wing politics). . . . [W]e will have returned to the pre-1848 situation in which, within the traditional loci of the liberal state . . . the "workers" will be poorly paid and outside the realm of political and social rights. Western workers will once again have become the "dangerous classes," but their skin color will have changed, and the class struggle will be a race struggle. The problem of the *twenty-first* century will be the problem of the color line. (Wallerstein, 1995c, 26–27; emphasis in the original)

A Changing Balance of Civilizational Power

The prediction that "the problem of the color line" would be the problem of the coming century was of course first made by William E. Burghardt Du Bois in 1900 (Du Bois, 1989). Du Bois's prediction concerned the coming revolt of the "darker races" of Asia and Africa against the "lighter races" of the West, which had just completed the military conquest of the world. "It was," in Geoffrey Barraclough's words, "a remarkable prophecy."

When the twentieth century opened, European power in Asia and Africa stood at its zenith; no nation, it seemed, could withstand the superiority of European arms and commerce. Sixty years later only the vestiges of European domination remained. Between 1945 and 1960 no less than forty countries . . . revolted against colonialism and won their independence. Never before in the whole of human history had so revolutionary a reversal occurred with such rapidity. The change in the position of the peoples of Asia and Africa and in their relations with Europe was the surest sign of the advent of a new era, and when the history of the first half of the twentieth century— which, for most historians, is still dominated by European wars and European problems . . . comes to be written in a longer perspective, there is little doubt that no single theme will prove to be of greater importance than the revolt against the west. (1967, 153–54)

In Wallerstein's scheme of things, the impact of this revolt was neutralized in the Cold War era by the promise of a generalized "catching up" with Western standards of wealth and welfare. But the very *failure* of the modernization experience is creating the conditions for a resumption of the revolt in the form of a "racialized" class struggle within the wealthy countries of the West themselves. Starting from altogether different premises, Samuel Huntington (1993, 1996) also anticipates a new revolt against the West in the form, not of a racialized class struggle, but of a "clash of civilizations" brought about by the *success* of modernization in empowering at least some of the peoples and governments of non-Western civilizations.

For Huntington (1993, 39–40), as for Fukuyama, the Cold War has ended in an indisputable triumph of the leading states of Western capitalism, first and foremost the United States. Unlike Fukuyama, however, Huntington sees no final triumph of Western liberal democracy. On the contrary, he sees the nearly absolute Western dominance of international institutions as the onset of a new phase in the evolution of conflict in the modern world. Conflicts among states since the Peace of Westphalia, he says,

> were primarily conflicts within Western civilization, "Western Civil Wars," as William Lind has labeled them. This was as true of the Cold War as it was true of the world wars and the earlier wars of the seventeenth and eighteenth centuries. With the end of the Cold War, international politics moves out of its Western phase, and its centerpiece becomes the interaction between the West and non-Western civilizations and among non-Western civilizations. (Huntington, 1993, 22–23)

Intercivilizational conflicts arise in part because Western dominance of the global political economy fosters resentment, and the more so as it becomes the vehicle of the propagation of Western interests, ideas, and values. But the most important force behind the coming clash of civilizations is the change in the civilizational balance of power entailed by the continuing modernization of the non-Western world. Huntington does not construe this tendency as posing any immediate threat to Western dominance. He nonetheless singles out "the sustained expansion of China's military power and its means to create military power" as "[c]entrally important to the development of counter-West military capabilities." Taken in conjunction with China's disposition to export arms and weapons technology to Middle Eastern states, this tendency is seen as creating a "Confucian-Islamic connection" that can pose a serious challenge to Western dominance. To meet this challenge, Huntington advocates a three-pronged Western strategy aimed at containing and eventually accommodating the growing power of non-Western civilizations: (1) greater cooperation and unity within the West; (2) maintenance of Western military capabilities, as if the Cold War had never ended; and (3) greater attention to the religious and philosophical assumptions underlying other civilizations (Huntington, 1993, 26, 40–41, 47–49).

Huntington's thesis has been subjected to a barrage of criticisms aimed as much at the ill-defined nature of the analytical constructs on which it is based, as at the danger that its predictions will turn into a self-fulfilling prophecy (for early responses, see Huntington et al., 1993; for a critical review of the debate, see Alker, 1995). As John Ikenberry has observed, the image of a Western civilization that separates "us" from the "rest" provides a ready and easily grasped ideological substitute for the "glue" that held together the Atlantic alliance in the Cold War era. Just as the alliance was presented in the Cold War era as a defensive device against communist aggression, so its renewal is now presented as a defensive device against a coming clash of civilizations driven by the success of Chinese modernization. But "to other powers like China and Japan the circling of the Western wagons will look like a declaration of a new Cold War" (1997, 163).

The implication of this criticism is that Chinese modernization poses no significant threat to U.S. and Western interests or, if it does, that there are other, more effective or more desirable means of meeting the threat than declaring a new Cold War on an ill-defined "other." But it is precisely on these two issues that observers and analysts are most divided. To some, the threat posed by the success of Chinese modernization in recent years is far greater than the threat posed by Chinese communism in the Cold War era.

> The irony in Sino-American relations is that when China was in the grip of ideological Maoism and displayed such ideological ferocity that Americans believed it to be dangerous and menacing, it was actually a paper tiger, weak and virtually without global influence. Now that China has shed the trappings of Maoism and embarked on a pragmatic course of economic development and global trade, it appears less threatening but it is in fact acquiring the wherewithal to back its global ambitions and interests with real power. (Bernstein and Munro, 1997, 22)

To others, the real "paper tiger" is the East Asian "economic miracle," of which the Chinese is the latest episode. For Paul Krugman, the most forceful proponent of this claim, the reliance of East Asian economic expansion in the 1980s on heavy investment and big shifts of labor from farms into factories, rather than on productivity gains, makes it resemble the economic expansion of the Warsaw Pact nations in the 1950s. "From the perspective of the year 2010, current projections of Asian supremacy extrapolated from recent trends may well look almost as silly as 1960s-vintage forecasts of Soviet industrial supremacy did from the perspective of the Brezhnev years" (Krugman, 1994, 78).

But a Union Bank of Switzerland (UBS) study finds that "the eight-percent plus average annual income growth set by several [East] Asian economies since the late 1960s is unique in the 130 years of recorded economic history" (Union Bank of Switzerland, 1996, 1). Moreover, what distinguishes most clearly the East Asian economic expansion of the 1980s from that of Warsaw Pact nations in the 1950s is the extraordinary advance of East Asia in global finance. The Japanese share of the total assets of *Fortune*'s top fifty banks in the world increased from 18 percent in 1970, to 27 percent in 1980, to 48 percent in 1990 (Ikeda, 1996). As for foreign exchange reserves, the East Asian share of the top ten central banks' holdings increased from 10 percent in 1980 to 50 percent in 1994 (*Japan Almanac*, 1993 and 1997).

Those who take the East Asian economic miracle seriously, however, strongly disagree on what kind of threat, if any, it poses to U.S. and Western interests. The most influential view, as expressed by Joseph Nye in a Department of Defense report he supervised and in a supporting essay, concurs with Huntington that ultimately the threat is military and that China's economic expansion is the most worrisome development of the post–Cold War era. Like Huntington, Nye's main policy prescription is to maintain U.S. military capabilities in general, and their deployment in East Asia in particular, as if the Cold War had never ended (Nye, 1995, 91–95).

This prescription and the analysis on which it is based have been challenged on the ground that they grossly overestimate China's capacity to match U.S. sea or air power in the foreseeable future (Nathan and Ross, 1997). More fundamentally, Chalmers Johnson and E. B. Keehn (1995) charged that the analysis and prescription disregard the profound decline in the effectiveness of military might as a source of world power. In their view, after Hiroshima and Nagasaki, U.S. military power in the region experienced rapidly decreasing returns and eventual irrelevance. The United States "at best . . . fought to stalemate in the Korean War and lost the one in Vietnam." More recently, the closing of the two largest U.S. overseas bases, Clark Air Base and Subic Bay in the Philippines, "produced not even a shiver of instability," while "[t]he most odious regime in postwar Asia, Pol Pot's Khmer Rouge in Cambodia, was disposed of not by Americans but by Vietnamese communists" (1995, 103–4, 111).

As U.S. military power waned, East Asian economic power waxed. Communist and nationalist militancy in the region, which U.S. militarism energized, began withering away in an embrace with indigenous capitalism. "Despite American whistling in the dark that foreigners' taste for American movies, rock music, blue jeans, and McDonald's hamburgers means that the United States is still their model, this intellectual battle is over. Some version of Asian capitalism lies in most nations' future" (Johnson and Keehn, 1995, 112). According to David Howell, Chairman of Britain's House of Commons Foreign Affairs Committee, even in Europe "Coca-colonization is yesterday's story." On the eve of the 1997–98 financial crisis, which burst the bubble of Western enthusiasm for East Asian economic models, he proclaimed that

> The issue today . . . is not the westernization of the east but the easternization of the West. Europeans are now debating how to draw on the techniques and financial power of Asia in order to shore up their uncompetitive economies and form alliances with the new Asian corporate giants. (1997, 164)

A pull of Eastern civilizations on Europeans is of course what started the formation and expansion of the modern world system some five hundred years ago. As William McNeill has noted, a major problem with Huntington's thesis is that it disregards two basic facts of world history. One is that "contemporary civilizations have always interacted with one another, even across long distances." The other is that, over time, the mutual borrowings and adaptations propagated by these encounters became increasingly pervasive and important in the expansion of human wealth and power.

> At a time when each of the great Asian civilizations sought to minimize disturbing contacts with outsiders, Europeans continued fighting among themselves while exploring the rest of the world with an eager, restless greed for material gain and for intellectual understanding as well. As a result, the West expanded and transformed itself over and over again. (McNeill, 1997, 19, 21)

As McNeill himself underscored in another context, this ceaseless expansion and transformation of the West was embedded in "a self-reinforcing cycle in which [European] military organization sustained, and was sustained by, economic and political expansion at the expense of other peoples and polities of the earth" (1982, 143). Although this cycle was broken by the revolt against the West of the first half of the twentieth century, many of the conceptual frameworks with which we try to apprehend the world tacitly presume that the cycle is still in force. This indeed may be one of the reasons why we find it so difficult to identify the direction(s) of change in the contemporary global political economy. As Janet Abu-Lughod (1990, 281–82) put it, we may have become so fixated on "studying the persistence and evolution of the 'modern' world-system that we are unprepared to understand what we sense may be its break-up or at least its radical transformation."

In concluding her study of the rise and demise of the thirteenth-century Afroeurasian world-trading system, Abu-Lughod suggests that the decline of U.S. military power of the 1970s and early 1980s and the simultaneous rise of East Asian economic power of the 1980s may be a sign that "the old advantages that underlay the hegemony of the West are dissipating." Under the emerging circumstances, "no single player has a spectacular advantage" and the supersession of Western supremacy by a new form of world conquest "is hard to imagine."

> Rather it seems more likely that there will be a return to the relative balance of multiple centers exhibited in the thirteenth-century world system. But that would require a shift to different rules of the game, or at least an end to the rules Europe introduced in the sixteenth century. (Abu-Lughod, 1989, 370–71)

Abu-Lughod does not say what these rules might be and who would make and enforce them. Shortly after she finished her book, the Berlin wall came tumbling down, leading to contradictory claims that the new rules would be made in Washington, or in Brussels, or in Tokyo, or in the secrecy of corporate board rooms, silent electronic networks, and noisy market places, until Huntington came along summoning the circling of the Western wagons lest the Rest under Chinese leadership do to the West what the West has been doing to the Rest. While we wait for the dust to settle, Abu-Lughod's suggestion that the future may bear some resemblance to a premodern past is as good as anybody else's guess.

Hegemonic Transitions: Concepts for Analysis

To paraphrase Hobsbawm, there indeed seems to be little consensus on anything but the fact that an era of history has ended. There is no consensus on which state, if any, benefited most from the confrontation of the Cold War and is now poised to replace the United States as the dominant player in the global political economy. There is no consensus on whether the proliferation in the variety and number of multinational corporations and the formation of global financial markets is undermining state capacities and, if so, how generally and permanently. There is no consensus on whether the world's working class is an endangered species or is simply changing color and the countries of its residence. There is no consensus on whether modernization is shoring up civilizational divides, melting them down, or restoring the intercivilizational balance of power of premodern times. Above all, there is no consensus on what kind of world order, if any, we can expect to emerge from the *combination* of whatever changes are actually occurring in the global configuration of power.

Hegemonic Transitions as Systemic Change

We may take the lack of consensus on the direction and meaning of present changes in the global political economy as a sign that we are in the midst of systemic change—that is, a process of radical reorganization of the modern world system that changes substantively the nature of the system's components, the way in which these components relate to one another, and the way in which the system operates and reproduces itself. In times of systemic change, as Abu-Lughod has pointed out, "small localized conditions may interact with adjacent ones to create outcomes that might not otherwise have occurred, and large disturbances sometimes flutter to an end while minor ones may occasionally amplify wildly, depending upon what is happening in the rest of the system." The "same-cause-yields-same-effects" logic that underlies much of our thinking about the world is ill-equipped to apprehend this kind of change, and we should instead draw inspiration from "chaos theory" (1989, 369).

In a similar vein, Rosenau resorts to the language of chaos theory in conceptualizing present changes in the global political economy as a "bifurcation"—a term coined almost a century ago by Henri Poincaré to designate the emergence of several solutions from a given solution in systems of differential equations (Bergé, Pomeau, and Vidal, 1984, 271). In evoking this image, he underscores how the order that will eventually emerge out of the present turbulence in world politics is not inscribed in the parameters of the order that has broken down. But he also points out that there is an order within chaos. Just as physicists have used the concept of bifurcation "to uncover the order intrinsic to the breakdown of established patterns," so we too should strive "to uncover the underlying patterns of the seemingly chaotic . . . world that has emerged to rival the state-centric world" (1990, 58).

Our investigation has sought clues as to what these underlying patterns might be in the present turbulence by uncovering underlying patterns in comparable past instances of systemic change. The result is a story of the expansion of the modern world system to its present global dimensions through a series of fundamental reorganizations. These reorganizations have occurred in periods of hegemonic transition defined as moments of change both in the leading agency of world-scale processes of capital accumulation and in the political-economic structures in which these processes are embedded.

The formation and expansion of the modern world system is thus conceived as proceeding, not along a single track laid some four to five hundred years ago, but through several switches to new tracks laid by specific complexes of governmental and business agencies. To borrow an expression from Michael Mann (1986, 28), these leading complexes—the Dutch complex in the seventeenth century, the British complex in the nineteenth century, and the U.S. complex in the twentieth century—have all acted as "tracklaying vehicles" (cf. Taylor, 1994, 27). In leading the system in a new direction, they also transformed it. Under Dutch leadership, the emergent system of European states was formally instituted by the Treaties of Westphalia. Under British leadership, the Eurocentric system of sovereign states moved to dominion globally. And under U.S. leadership, the system lost its Eurocentricity to further gain in reach and penetration (Arrighi, 1990b, 1994; Hopkins, 1990).

Leadership by a particular agency and a concomitant systemic transformation are equally essential attributes of the concept of world hegemony on which our investigation is based. As John Ruggie (1983) has pointed out in a critical assessment of Kenneth Waltz's theory of international politics (1979), systemic theories like Waltz's, or for that matter like Wallerstein's, are important correctives of the fallacy involved in attempts to know a totality through the study of its parts. For totalities have properties of their own ("systemic properties") that act, in Waltz's words, "as a constraining and disposing force on the interacting units within it." Systems, therefore, are themselves "productive" and not just the "product" of unit-level processes (as quoted in Ruggie, 1983, 263). In redressing the balance, however, systemic theories can easily go too far and conceive of unit-level processes as all product and not at all productive.

> The problem with Waltz's posture is that, in any social system, structural change itself ultimately has no source *other than* unit-level processes. By banning these from the domain of systemic theory, Waltz also exogenizes the ultimate source of systemic change. . . . As a result, Waltz's theory of "society" contains only a reproductive logic, but no transformational logic. (Ruggie, 1983, 285; emphasis in the original; see also Keohane and Nye, 1987)

Ruggie's criticism of Waltz's conception of international politics can also be leveled almost word for word at Wallerstein's conception of hegemony in the modern system of sovereign states. According to this conception,

> Hegemony in the interstate system refers to that situation in which the ongoing rivalry between the so-called "great powers" is so unbalanced that one power is truly *primus inter pares;* that is, one power can largely impose its rules and its wishes . . . in the economic, political, military, diplomatic, and even cultural arenas. The material base of such power lies in the ability of enterprises domiciled in that power to operate more efficiently in all three major economic arenas—agro-industrial production, commerce and finance. The edge in efficiency of which we are speaking is one so great that these enterprises can not only outbid enterprises domiciled in other great powers in the world market in general, but quite specifically in very many instances within the home markets of the rival powers themselves. (Wallerstein, 1984, 38–39)

In all three instances—Dutch, British, and U.S.—hegemony is the outcome of long periods of "competitive expansion . . . which [result] in a particular concentration of economic and political power." In the course of these competitive expansions, the rising hegemon acquires its decisive edge first in production, then in commerce, and then in finance. But hegemony is firmly secured only through victory in a thirty-year-long climactic "world war"—the Thirty Years' War from 1618 to 1648, the Napoleonic Wars from 1792 to 1815, and the long Eurasian wars from 1914 to 1945. "The winner's economic edge is expanded by the very process of the war itself, and the postwar interstate settlement is designed to encrust that greater edge and protect it against erosion" (Wallerstein, 1984, 39–44).

This postwar settlement consists of one form or another of "global liberalism" aimed at enforcing "the principle of the free flow of the factors of production (goods, capital and labor) throughout the world-economy." Global liberalism serves the double purpose of buttressing the sway of the hegemonic power's competitive edge, and "of delegitimizing the efforts of other state machineries to act against the economic superiority of the hegemonic power." But global liberalism also "breeds its own demise" because it makes it more difficult for the hegemonic power to retard "the spread of technological expertise" to competing states, and because maintaining "uninterrupted production at a time of maximal global accumulation" involves "the creeping rise of real income of both the working strata and the cadres located in the hegemonic power." Over time, these two tendencies undermine the competitive edge of the hegemonic power's enterprises in production, then in commerce, and then in finance. The system thus reverts to a new long period of competitive expansion until another state manages to achieve the triple competitive advantage—in production, commerce, and finance—that defines hegemony (Wallerstein, 1984, 41, 45).

Figure 1 summarizes Wallerstein's model of hegemonic cycles. The model—to paraphrase Ruggie's praise of Waltz's systemic theory—"is a welcome antidote to the prevailing superficiality of the proliferating literature on international transformation, in which the sheer momentum of processes sweeps the international polity along toward the next encounter with destiny" (1983, 285). But it is also vulnerable to the same criticism that Ruggie levels at Waltz, namely, that it exogenizes the ultimate source of systemic change. Particular complexes of governmental and business agencies become hegemonic in the course of competitive expansions by virtue of the efficiency of their actions relative to those of all other competing complexes. But which actions are relatively efficient is a mere reflection of structural properties of the world capitalist system on which they have no impact whatsoever. They are all product and not at all productive.

Whether and to what extent unit-level processes—such as the formation of particular complexes of governmental and business agencies and their actions—simply play out a script dictated by system-level

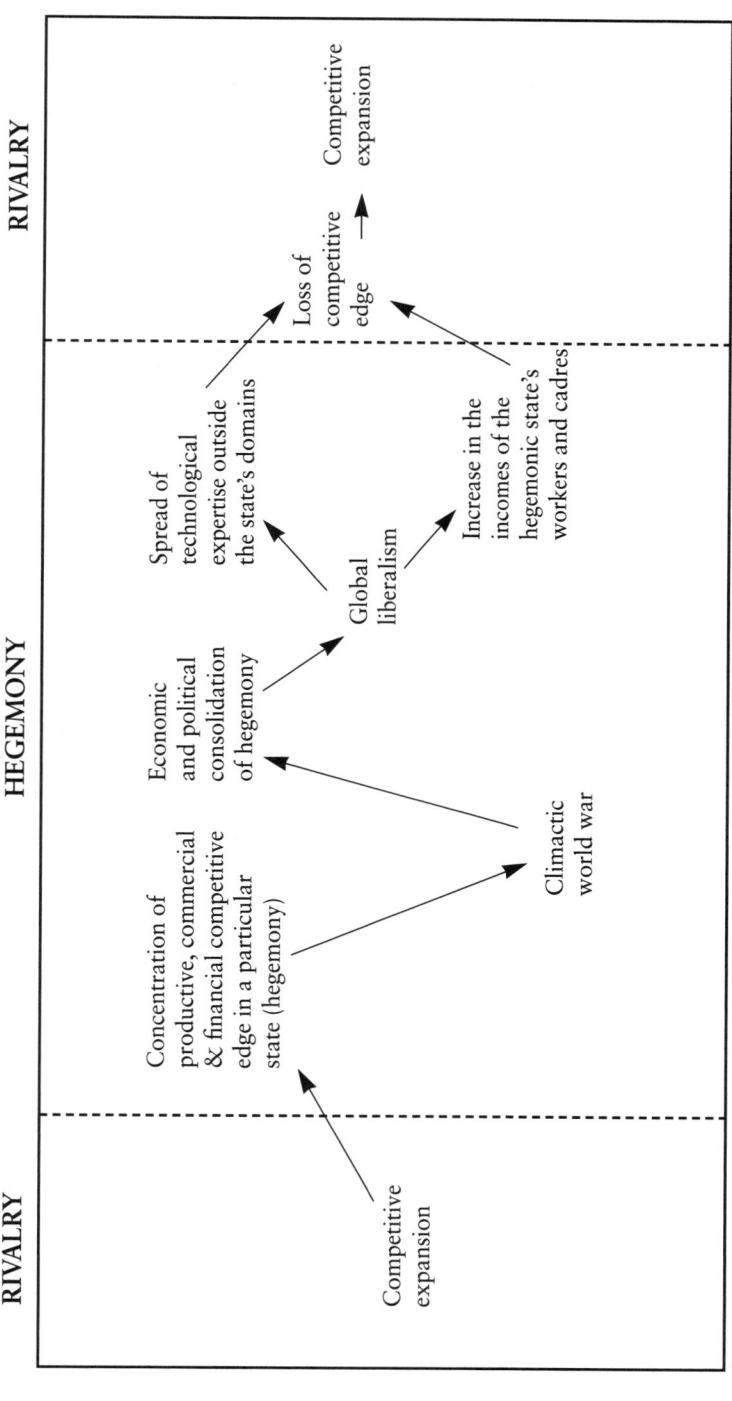

Figure 1. *Wallerstein's hegemonic cycle.*

properties or themselves write the script and thereby form and transform the system, is a question that ultimately can be settled only on empirical-historical grounds. It is indeed on these grounds that we have found Wallerstein's model wanting. For our investigation has revealed that the rise of hegemonic powers in the modern world has not been the mere reflection of systemic properties. Systemic properties do act as powerful constraining and disposing forces on the selection of the states that become hegemonic. But in all instances, hegemony has also involved a fundamental reorganization of the system and a change in its properties.

World Hegemonies as Systemic Leadership and Governance

Like a growing number of students of world politics and society (see, among others, Cox, 1983, 1987; Keohane, 1984a; Gill, 1986, 1993; Gill and Law, 1988; Rupert, 1995; Robinson, 1996), we have derived our concept of hegemony from Antonio Gramsci's idea that

> the supremacy of a social group manifests itself in two ways, as "domination" and as "intellectual and moral leadership." A social group dominates antagonistic groups, which it tends to "liquidate," or to subjugate perhaps even by armed force; it leads kindred or allied groups. (Gramsci, 1971, 57–58)

Whereas domination rests primarily on coercion, the leadership that defines hegemony rests on the capacity of the dominant group to present itself, and be perceived, as the bearer of a general interest.

> It is true that the State is seen as the organ of one particular group, destined to create favorable conditions for the latter's maximum expansion. But the development and expansion of the particular group are conceived of, and presented, as being the motor force of a universal expansion, a development of all the "national" energies. (Gramsci, 1971, 181–82)

Hegemony is thus something more and different than domination pure and simple: it is the *additional* power that accrues to a dominant group by virtue of its capacity to lead society in a direction that not only serves the dominant group's interests, but is also perceived by subordinate groups as serving a more general interest. It is the inverse of the notion of "power deflation" used by Talcott Parsons to designate situations in which governmental control cannot be exercised except through the widespread use or threat of force. If subordinate groups have confidence in their rulers, systems of domination can be governed without resorting to force. But if that confidence wanes, they cannot (1964). By analogy, Gramsci's notion of hegemony may be said to consist of the "power inflation" that ensues from the capacity of dominant groups to present with credibility their rule as serving not just their interests, but those of subordinate groups as well. When such credibility is lacking, we shall speak of "dominance without hegemony" (cf. Guha, 1992a, 231–32).

As long as we speak of leadership in a national context, as Gramsci does, there is little ambiguity about the fact that *society as a whole,* as defined by the jurisdiction of a particular state, is being led in a direction that enhances the power of the dominant group. But when we speak of leadership in an international context, the term is used to designate two quite different phenomena. On the one hand, the term is used to designate the fact that by virtue of its achievements, a dominant state becomes the "model" for other states to emulate and thereby draws them onto its own path of development (see in particular Modelski, 1987; Modelski and Thompson, 1995). This may enhance the prestige and hence the power of the dominant state (Taylor, 1996). But to the extent that emulation is at all successful, it tends to counterbalance and hence deflate rather than inflate the power of the hegemon by bringing into existence competitors and reducing the "specialness" of the hegemon (Gilpin, 1981). This "leadership against the leader's will," as we shall call it, borrowing an expression from Joseph Schumpeter (1963, 89), is always present in hegemonic situations but does not in itself define a situation as hegemonic.

On the other hand, the term leadership is used to designate the fact that a dominant state leads the *system* of states in a desired direction and, in so doing, is widely perceived as pursuing a general interest. Leadership in this sense inflates the power of the dominant state, and is what we shall take as the defining characteristic of world hegemonies. A general interest is, of course, more difficult to define at the level of a system of sovereign states than at the level of individual states. At the latter level, an increase in the power of a state vis-à-vis other states is an important component and in itself a measure of the successful pursuit of a general (that is, "national") interest. But power in this sense cannot increase for the system as a whole, by definition.

A general interest for the system as a whole can nonetheless be identified by recasting in world-systems perspective Parsons's distinction between "distributive" and "collective" aspects of power. Distributive aspects of power refer to a zero-sum-game relationship whereby an agency can gain power only if other agencies lose some. Max Weber's definition of power as "the probability that one actor within a social relationship will be in a position to carry out his own will despite resistance" (1978, 53) focuses on such distributive aspects of power. Collective aspects of power, in contrast, refer to a positive-sum-game relationship whereby cooperation among distinct agencies increases their power over third parties or over nature (Parsons, 1960, 199–225).

The distinction between distributive and collective power drawn by Parsons with reference to social systems bounded by a single political jurisdiction holds also in social systems that encompass multiple political jurisdictions. In the latter systems, the general interest represented by a hegemonic agency cannot be defined in terms of changes in the distribution of power among political jurisdictions. But it can be defined in terms of an increase in the collective power over third parties or nature by the entire system's dominant groups.

Generally speaking, claims to represent a general systemic interest so defined can be expected to become credible and thereby inflate the power of a would-be hegemonic state under two conditions. First, the dominant groups of this state must have developed the capacity to lead the system in the direction of new forms of interstate cooperation and division of labor that enable the system's units to break out of what Waltz (1979, 108–9) has called "the tyranny of small decisions"—that is, to overcome the tendency of the separate states to pursue their national interest without regard for system-level problems that require system-level solutions. In short, there must be an effective "supply" of world-governance capabilities. And second, the system-level solutions offered by the would-be hegemon must address system-level problems that have become so acute as to create among the system's extant or emergent dominant groups a deeply and widely felt "demand" for systemic governance. When these supply and demand conditions are simultaneously fulfilled, the would-be hegemonic state can play the role of "a surrogate of government" in promoting, organizing, and managing an expansion of the collective power of the system's dominant groups (cf. Waltz, 1979, 196).

Our investigation focuses on processes that have recurrently created these two conditions in the modern system of sovereign states since its formal founding under Dutch hegemony in the mid-seventeenth

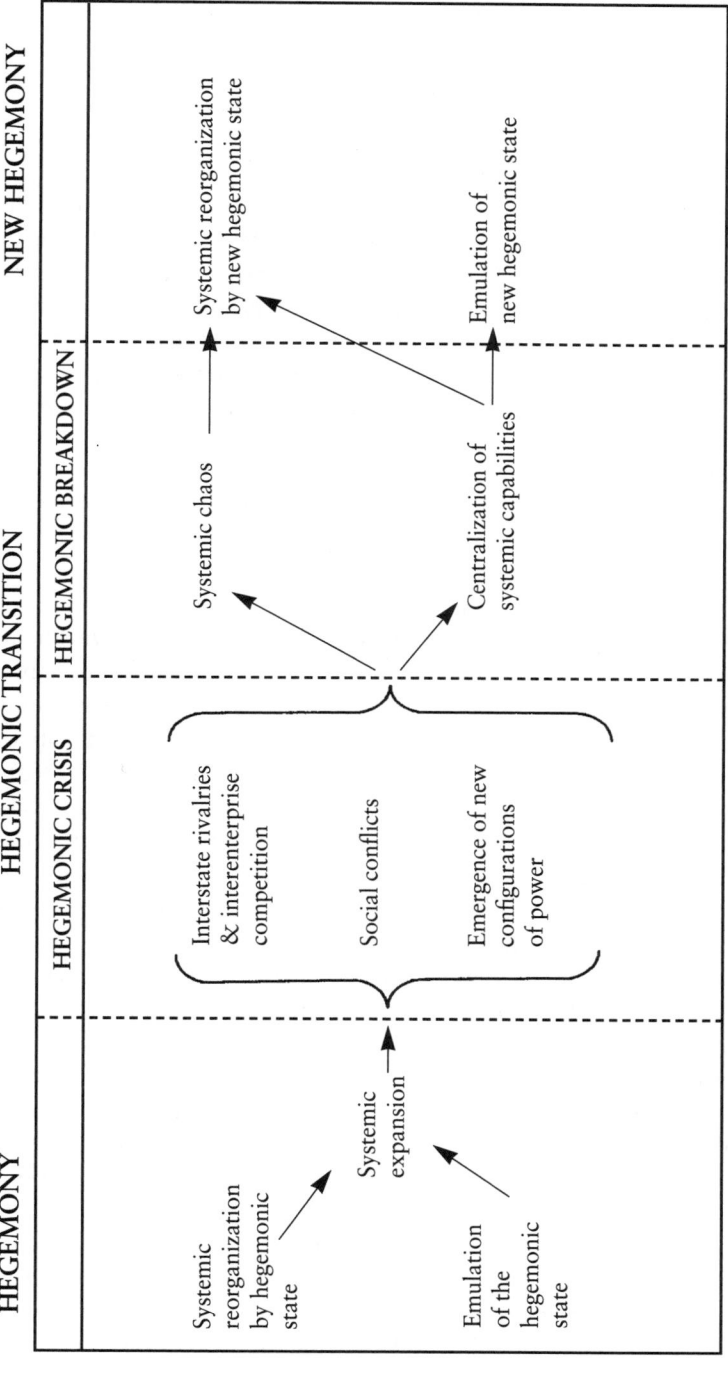

Figure 2. The dynamics of hegemonic transitions.

century. The model of hegemonic transition that has emerged from the investigation is summed up in figure 2. Like Wallerstein's model, our model describes a hegemonic cycle. Unlike Wallerstein's, however, it endogenizes systemic change.

In our model, systemic expansions are embedded in a particular hegemonic structure they tend to undermine. They are the outcome of the interplay of the two different kinds of leadership that jointly define hegemonic situations. Systemic reorganization promotes expansion by endowing the system with a wider or deeper division of labor and specialization of functions. Emulation provides the separate states with the motivational drive needed to mobilize energies and resources in the expansion.

There is always a tension between these two tendencies because a wider and deeper division of labor and specialization of functions involves cooperation among the system's units, while emulation is based on and fosters their mutual competition. Initially, emulation operates in a context that is predominantly cooperative and thereby acts as an engine of expansion. But expansion increases what Emile Durkheim (1964, 115; 1984, 200–205) has called the "volume" and "dynamic density" of the system, that is, the number of socially relevant units that interact within the system and the number, variety, and velocity of transactions that link the units to one another. Over time, this increase in the volume and dynamic density of the system tends to intensify competition among the system's units beyond the regulatory capacities of existing institutions. When that happens, the tyranny of small decisions regains the upper hand, the power of the hegemonic state experiences a deflation, and a hegemonic crisis sets in.

As figure 2 shows, hegemonic crises are characterized by three distinct, but closely related processes: the intensification of interstate and interenterprise competition; the escalation of social conflicts; and the interstitial emergence of new configurations of power. The form these processes take and the way they relate to one another in space and time vary from crisis to crisis. But some combination of the three processes can be detected in each of the two hegemonic transitions completed so far—from Dutch to British and from British to U.S. hegemony—as well as in the present transition from U.S. hegemony to a yet unknown destination. Moreover, differences in form and in spatio-temporal configuration notwithstanding, in all three hegemonic crises—Dutch, British, and U.S.—the three processes have been associated with a pattern we take as the most evident manifestation of the capitalist nature of the modern world system. This pattern is what we shall refer to as a systemwide financial expansion.

Hegemonic Crises and Financial Expansions

Systemwide financial expansions are the outcome of two complementary tendencies: an overaccumulation of capital and intense interstate competition for mobile capital. The first tendency creates what we may call the supply conditions of financial expansions, while the second creates their demand conditions.

The recurrence of financial expansions in the world capitalist system since its earliest origins in the city-states of Renaissance Italy was first noticed by Fernand Braudel, who underscored their supply conditions. Whenever the profits of trade and production accumulated "on a scale beyond the normal channels of investment, finance capitalism was . . . in a position to take over and dominate, for a while at least, all the activities of the business world" (1984, 604). By reaching this stage, "every [major] capitalist development . . . seems . . . to have announced its maturity." Financial expansions are "a sign of autumn" (Braudel, 1984, 246).

Historically, Braudel's financial expansions have always occurred in conjunction with an intensification in interstate competition for mobile capital. Braudel says nothing about such a competition, in spite of Weber's observation that it constitutes "the world-historical distinctiveness of [the modern] era" (1978, 354). Whereas in premodern times the formation of world empires swept away freedoms and powers of the cities that constituted the main loci of capitalist expansion, in the modern era these loci came under the sway of "competing national states in a condition of perpetual struggle for power in peace or war. . . . The separate states had to compete for mobile capital, which dictated to them the conditions under which it would assist them to power." This competitive struggle has created the largest opportunities for modern capitalism, "and as long as the national state does not give place to a world empire capitalism also will endure" (Weber, 1961, 249).

The occurrence of Braudel's financial expansions in periods of particularly intense interstate competition for mobile capital is no mere historical accident. Rather, it is the outcome of a double tendency engendered by particularly rapid, extensive, and profitable expansions of trade and production. On the one hand, capitalist organizations and individuals respond to the accumulation of capital over and above what can be reinvested profitably in established channels of trade and production by holding in liquid form a growing proportion of their incoming cash flows. This tendency creates an overabundant mass of liquidity that can be mobilized directly or through intermediaries in speculation, borrowing, and lending. On the other hand, territorial organizations respond to the tighter budget constraints that ensue from the slowdown in the expansion of trade and production by competing intensely with one another for the capital that accumulates in financial markets. This tendency brings about massive, systemwide redistributions of income and wealth from all kinds of communities to the agencies that control mobile capital, thereby inflating and sustaining the profitability of financial deals largely divorced from commodity trade and production. All systemwide financial expansions, past and present, are the outcome of the combined if uneven development of these two complementary tendencies (Arrighi, 1994, 1997).

The recurrent tendency of capital to regain flexibility by shedding its commodity form in favor of its money form witnesses, in Braudel's words, "a certain unity in capitalism, from thirteenth-century Italy to the present-day West" (1982, 433). Nevertheless, this unity is not at all the expression of a structural invariance of historical capitalism. On the contrary, it is the expression of a basic instability and adaptability. For in each and every financial expansion, world capitalism has been reorganized ever more fundamentally under a new leadership. This has been the case of the earlier financial expansions—when world capitalism was still embedded in a system of city-states and transnational business diasporas—and of the later expansions, when world capitalism came to be embedded in a system of national states and world-encompassing business communities and organizations (Arrighi, 1994, 13–16, 74–84, 235–38, 330–31).

Financial expansions concern us here exclusively as moments of structural transformation of the modern system of sovereign national states. As different chapters of the book will show, they have been an integral aspect of hegemonic crises and the eventual transformation of these crises into hegemonic breakdowns. This transformation is portrayed in figure 2 by the emergence of "systemic chaos" out of the interplay of intensifying interstate and interenterprise competition, escalating social conflicts, and the interstitial emergence of new configurations of power.

By systemic chaos we understand a situation of severe and seemingly irremediable systemic disorganization. As competition and conflicts escalate beyond the regulatory capacity of existing structures, new structures emerge interstitially and destabilize further the dominant configuration of power. Disorder tends to become self-reinforcing, threatening to provoke or actually provoking a complete breakdown in the system's organization.

Financial expansions have a contradictory impact on this tendency. On the one hand, they hold it in check by temporarily inflating the power of the declining hegemonic state. As the "autumn" of major capitalist developments, financial expansions are also the autumn of the hegemonic structures in which these developments are embedded. They are the time when the leader of a major expansion of world trade and production that is drawing to a close reaps the fruits of its leadership in the form of a privileged access to the overabundant liquidity that accumulates in world financial markets. This privileged access enables the declining hegemonic state to contain, at least for a time, the forces that challenge its continuing dominance.

On the other hand, financial expansions strengthen these same forces by widening and deepening the scope of interstate and interenterprise competition and social conflict, and by reallocating capital to emergent structures that promise greater security or higher returns than the dominant structure. Declining hegemonic states are thus faced with the Sisyphean task of containing forces that keep rolling forth with ever renewed strength. Sooner or later, even a small disturbance can tilt the balance in favor of the forces that wittingly or unwittingly are undermining the already precarious stability of existing structures, thereby provoking a breakdown of systemic organization.

Hegemonic breakdowns are the decisive turning points of hegemonic transitions. They are the time when the systemic organization that had been put in place by the declining hegemonic power disintegrates and systemic chaos sets in. But they are also the time when new hegemonies are forged (see figure 2).

Increasing systemic disorganization curtails the collective power of the system's dominant groups. And the greater the curtailment, the more widely and deeply felt the demand for system-level governance. Nevertheless, this demand can be satisfied and a new hegemony can emerge only if increasing systemic disorganization is accompanied by the emergence of a new complex of governmental and business agencies endowed with greater system-level organizational capabilities than those of the preceding hegemonic complex. The breakdown of any given hegemonic order is ultimately due to the fact that the increase in the volume and dynamic density of the system outgrows the organizational capabilities of the particular hegemonic complex that had created the conditions of the systemic expansion. Ultimately, therefore, the ensuing self-reinforcing disorder can be overcome, and the conditions of a new systemic expansion can be created, only if a new complex emerges that is endowed with greater systemic capabilities than the old hegemonic complex.

Historically, the same processes that have generated systemic chaos have also generated the greater concentration of systemic capabilities that, in combination with systemic chaos, eventually resulted in the establishment of a new hegemony. As the rising hegemon leads the system in the direction of greater cooperation among the system's units, while drawing them onto its own path of development, systemic chaos subsides and a new hegemonic cycle begins. But each cycle differs from the preceding one in two main respects: the greater concentration of organizational capabilities wielded by the hegemonic state in comparison with its predecessor, and the higher volume and dynamic density of the system that is being reorganized by the hegemonic state.

Our model thus describes a pattern of recurrence (hegemony leading to expansion, expansion to chaos, and chaos to a new hegemony), which is also a pattern of evolution (each new hegemony reflecting a greater concentration of organizational capabilities and a higher volume and density of the system than the preceding hegemony). This double pattern concerns past hegemonic transitions. To the extent that we can detect it also in present transformations of the global political economy, we gain some insight into their likely future trajectories.

As our account of past hegemonic transitions will show, however, the reproduction of this pattern over the centuries has been as much a matter of historical contingency as systemic necessity. Moreover, the very evolution of the system has made the reproduction of the pattern more problematic than it was in the past. The purpose of establishing analogies between present and past transformations, therefore, is also to identify differences in historical and systemic circumstances that can be expected to make the outcome of present transformations diverge from that of past hegemonic transitions. The more we succeed in specifying these differences, the less indeterminate our speculations about the future will be. But no matter how successful we are, some degree of indeterminacy remains the distinguishing characteristic of systemic change, both past and present.

The four central chapters of this book have a common purpose and format. They all analyze and compare the modern world's two complete hegemonic transitions—from Dutch to British hegemony and from British to U.S. hegemony—as moments of systemic transformation, an understanding of which may throw some light on the dynamics of the present transition from U.S. hegemony to a yet unknown destination. The first part of each chapter analyzes the transition from Dutch to British hegemony; the second part analyzes the transition from British to U.S. hegemony in comparison with the earlier transition; and the concluding section discusses the implications of the analysis for an understanding of present transformations.

What differentiates the chapters are the particular angles of vision from which hegemonic transitions are analyzed. These angles correspond to the four controversial issues about present transformations discussed in the first part of this introduction. Chapter 1 ("Geopolitics and High Finance") focuses on the processes that have led to the displacement of one hegemonic state by another. Chapter 2 ("The Transformation of Business Enterprise") focuses on the changing relationship between the governmental and business organizations of hegemonic states. Chapter 3 ("The Social Origins of World Hegemonies") focuses on the role of social change and conflict in shaping world hegemonies. And chapter 4 ("Western Hegemonies in World-Historical Perspective") focuses on the changes in the intercivilizational balance of power that have been associated with hegemonic transitions.

The common purpose and different angles of vision of the book's chapters have implications that should be borne in mind to avoid misunderstandings. First, the processes analyzed in the different chapters have been selected for their bearing on the dynamics of systemic change, both past and present. Many of these processes are unit-level processes in the sense that they originate in the actions of specific governments, enterprises, and social groups and unfold in specific locations. Our interest in unit-level processes, however, is strictly limited to the role they play as a source of systemic change in hegemonic transitions. Whether our analysis of these processes from this particular perspective has produced any new knowledge in the separate fields of study from which we have drawn our facts and interpretations is up to the specialists of those fields to judge. Our only claim is to have produced an analytical construct capable of shedding new light on system-level structural change in the modern world, both past and present.

Second, all the chapters analyze the same two hegemonic transitions. But each highlights a *different* spatio-temporal feature of these two transitions depending on its particular angle of vision. The processes on which the various chapters focus are interrelated but not synchronous—some start or end earlier than others and they do not all go through the same phases. Nor are their primary locations the same. The most salient processes unfold in some regions of the system but not in others, or they unfold differently in different regions. As a result, the narratives of the different chapters are not fully synchronized, nor are they always focused on the same regions. Our contention is that this spatio-temporal unevenness among processes is itself a property of hegemonic transitions, which deserves as much attention as any other property.

Finally, although each chapter tells a different story about the dynamics of hegemonic transitions, the stories are interrelated and form a totality that has a meaning of its own. These interrelationships are underscored at the beginning and end of each chapter and synthesized in the book's conclusions, where the four controversial issues from which we started are reexamined in the light of the overall dynamic of past hegemonic transitions. This dynamic would, of course, look different had it been reconstructed from a different set of angles of vision. We nonetheless hope that our reconstruction can dissipate some of the global fog that Hobsbawm, with good reason, sees surrounding us as we tap our way into the third millennium.

One

Geopolitics and High Finance

Giovanni Arrighi, Po-keung Hui, Krishnendu Ray, and Thomas Ehrlich Reifer

Our perceptions of the present crisis of state sovereignty are distorted by an overestimation of the actual importance of "nation-states" as the basic units of world politics in the modern era. For one thing, the modern system of sovereign states itself was instituted formally under the leadership of an agency—the United Provinces—that was not quite a nation-state. Rather, it was a semisovereign organization still struggling for juridical statehood and having more features in common with the declining city-states of northern Italy than with the rising national states of northwestern Europe.

After the Peace of Westphalia, national states did become the basic units of politics in the European-centered world system. But in the nineteenth century, the system moved to dominion globally under the leadership of an agency—the United Kingdom—that was no mere national state. Rather, it was an imperial organization whose territorial domains and networks of power encompassed the entire world.

Under the carapace of this imperial organization, industrialization revolutionized the logistics of war- and statemaking, creating the conditions for the emergence in the twentieth century of continent-sized states on Europe's western and eastern flanks. The United States and the USSR dwarfed the typical national state of the European core, which came to be perceived as being "too small" to compete industrially and militarily. The irresistible rise of U.S. power and wealth in the course of the two world wars, and the rise of Soviet power (though not wealth) after the Russian Revolution confirmed the validity of this perception and prepared for the establishment of the "bipolar" Cold War world order under U.S. hegemony.

This evolution of the modern system of sovereign states toward the formation of ever more powerful governmental agencies has occurred through recurrent escalations of the interstate power struggle and competition for mobile capital. Over time, these escalations resulted in a breakdown of the system's organization and a subsequent reorganization under a new and more comprehensive hegemony. In both past transitions, the governmental agencies that emerged as the successful bearers of a new and more comprehensive systemic organization were more powerful than their predecessors, not just militarily, but financially as well. That is, they wielded greater control over globally effective means of violence and universally accepted means of payment.

Many of the difficulties involved in grasping the configuration of power in the global political economy emerging out of the disintegration of the Cold War world order are due to the fact that by historical standards, the present hegemonic crisis is still at an early stage of development. The signs of a coming hegemonic breakdown are few, and whether and when such a breakdown will occur remains an open question. In good part, however, the difficulties arise from the fact that for the time being, the present transition has been characterized not by a *fusion* of a higher order, but by a *fission* of military and financial power. Control over globally effective means of violence has become even more concentrated than it was in the hands of the declining hegemon. But control over universally accepted means of payment is increasingly concentrated in the hands of transnational business agencies or (mostly East Asian) governmental agencies of no politico-military significance and far removed from the traditional (Euro-American) power centers of the modern world system.

This chapter highlights this anomaly of present transformations in comparison with past hegemonic transitions. The first part analyzes the transition from Dutch to British hegemony as a process through which empire-building national states, most notably Britain and France, centralized in their hands systemic capabilities formerly wielded by proto-national states like the United Provinces and city-states like Venice and Genoa. The second part analyzes the analogous process, typical of the transition from British to U.S. hegemony, through which systemic capabilities formerly wielded by Europe's national states came to be centralized in the hands of the two giant, continent-sized states that had formed on Europe's western and eastern flanks—the United States and the USSR, respectively. Finally, the concluding part discusses the implications of the analysis for an understanding of present changes in the configuration of world power.

From Dutch to British Hegemony

Dutch Hegemony and the European Balance of Power

We speak of a Dutch hegemony within the European system of sovereign states primarily because the Dutch played a leading role in the protracted struggles that resulted in the formal founding of that system by the Treaties of Westphalia of 1648. The Treaties replaced the idea of a suprastatal imperial/papal authority with the notion that the European states formed a single political system based on international law and the balance of power—"a law operating between rather than above states and a power operating between rather than above states" (Gross, 1968, 54–55). No effort was made to restrain interstate warfare, which was and remained an essential means in the reproduction of the balance of power among states. Over the next century and a half, however, written and unwritten rules of conduct tended to minimize the disruptive effects of warmaking among sovereigns on the freedom of their subjects to transact their business and interact socially across state boundaries (Carr, 1945, 4).

As Peter Taylor (1994, 27) put it, Dutch hegemony was "a necessary track-laying vehicle" in the creation of the modern system of sovereign states. In the military sphere, the track was laid primarily by demonstrating the limits of the coercive power of Imperial Spain. Confronted with the problem of fighting the Spaniards in the Low Countries, Maurice of Nassau drew on Roman precedents to revolutionize existing defense and siege techniques. By reintroducing the spade, systematic drilling, and small tactical units, he enabled the Dutch to produce a disciplined and effective fighting force, capable of defeating the much larger Spanish forces. And by organizing a military academy for the training of officers, he promoted the spread of the new techniques among actual or potential allies in the struggle against Spain (McNeill, 1982, 127–30, 134).

The importance of Dutch innovations in land-war techniques should not be exaggerated. At best, they helped neutralize Spanish power locally and temporarily. Spanish supremacy in Europe was based primarily on a monopolistic control over extra-European resources—most notably, American silver. If this control were not destroyed or undermined, Dutch resistance would sooner or later have been curbed or bypassed. The main reason it was not is precisely that the Dutch took their struggle to the seas right from the start. They relentlessly harassed Iberian seaborne traffic and simultaneously tightened their own monopolistic control over supplies critical to the war effort by land and sea—most notably, Baltic grain and naval stores (Mahan, 1957, 32–33).

In challenging Iberian sea power, the Dutch drew on a long seafaring tradition in the North Sea. "As the Dutch Commonwealth was born out of the Sea," remarked Sir William Temple, "so out of the same Element, it drew its first Strength and consideration." Gifts of history and geography were used advantageously and in due course supplemented by technological virtuosity in shipbuilding. Mechanical saws, hoists for masts, the manufacture of interchangeable spare parts, and other "high tech" devices enabled Dutch shipyards to produce more massively, at lower costs, and at shorter notice than the shipyards of any rival power. The Dutch seafaring advantage was thereby enhanced and consolidated (Braudel, 1984, 188–191).

The Dutch seafaring advantage was important, not just in undermining Iberian seaborne power, but also in establishing and reproducing the United Provinces' own monopolistic control over Baltic supplies. As Karen Rasler and William Thompson (1989, 89) note, "the earlier winners in the struggle for world leadership owed a significant proportion of their success to their ability to obtain credit inexpensively, to sustain relatively large debts, and generally to leverage the initially limited base of their wealth to meet their staggering military expenses." Of no hegemonic state was this truer than of the Dutch, whose control over Baltic trade was the source of an overabundant liquidity, and whose overabundant liquidity was the single most important source of their competitive edge in the European power struggle.

The profitability of Dutch trade was determined by two main circumstances. One was the intensity of the European power struggle itself. The more intense this struggle became by land and sea, *ceteris paribus*, the greater the demand for Baltic supplies of grain and naval stores and the profits that accrued to the Dutch by virtue of their monopolistic control over those supplies. Ironically, the more obstinate the Habsburgs became in their futile attempts to use American silver to establish a world empire in Europe, the more they unwittingly built the bullion coffers of their Dutch enemies (Arrighi, 1994, 132–52).

The other main determinant of the profitability of Dutch trade was the tendency of the Dutch to keep the large profits of Baltic trade liquid, and to use the liquidity to continue to eliminate competition in the Baltic and to turn Amsterdam into the focal commercial and financial entrepôt of the European-centered world-economy. The more the Dutch succeeded in this endeavor, the more they tightened their control, not just over Baltic supplies, but also over the supplies of silver brought to Europe from the Americas by their Spanish enemies. As Braudel (1984, 209) put it, "Holland's fortune was . . . built on *both* Spain and the Baltic. To neglect either of these would be to fail to understand a process in which wheat on one hand and American bullion on the other played indissociable roles" (emphasis in the original).

Dutch success in turning Amsterdam into the central commercial and financial entrepôt of the European-centered world-economy replicated on a larger scale and under different systemic circumstances the earlier achievements of the Italian city-states, Venice and Genoa in particular. According to Violet Barbour (1950, 13) it was the last time that "a veritable empire of trade and credit could be held by a city in her own right, unsustained by the forces of a modern state." Whether the United Provinces was or was not a "modern state" is a highly controversial issue. Nevertheless, few would dispute Ivo Schoffer's assessment that in the emerging world of absolutist states based upon royal centralization, the Dutch Republic was and remained "an odd variant" in which "an end was made to all centralization" (1985, 103; also Wilson, 1976, 46).

Braudel (1984, 193–95, 205) is among those who find it difficult to decide whether the United Provinces was a state in the modern sense of the word. Eventually, he settled for the ambiguous position that "it certainly cannot be said that the Dutch government was non-existent, though it was not so much a matter of government as of *sheer economic weight*" (emphasis added). And after concurring with Barbour's assessment that with Amsterdam the age of "empire-building cities" came to an end, he saw the Dutch episode as the watershed between two distinct ages of historical capitalism.

The interesting thing about this episode is . . . that it lies between two successive phases of economic hegemony: on the one hand the age of the city, on the other that of the modern territorial state and the national economy, heralded by the rise of London with the backing of the entire English economy. At the heart of a Europe swollen with success and tending, by the end of the eighteenth century, to embrace the whole world, the dominant central zone had to grow in size to balance the entire structure. Cities standing alone, or almost alone, by now lacked sufficient purchase on the neighbouring economies from which they drew strength; soon they would no longer measure up to the task. The territorial states would take over. (Braudel, 1984, 175)

With several important qualifications (spelled out below), these remarks capture the main thrust of the transition from Dutch to British hegemony from the angle of vision of this chapter. In the seventeenth century, "sheer economic weight" was sufficient for a political structure that was more than a city-state, but less than a national state—which is what the United Provinces was—to occupy a commanding position in the European-centered world-economy and to exercise a leading role in the consolidation of the system of sovereign states. But by the late eighteenth century, only empire-building national states were in the running for world hegemony. The only issue that remained open, until Napoleon's defeat settled it, was whether the continental empire-builder France or the maritime empire-builder Britain would come out on top. But in the reorganization of political space that accompanied and followed the Napoleonic Wars, there was no more room for the Dutch Republic, let alone for its Venetian and Genoese predecessors, all of which were erased from the map of Europe not once but twice—first by Napoleon, and then by the Peace of Vienna.

The remainder of the first part of this chapter sketches this metamorphosis in the systemic conditions of world hegemony. We distinguish four phases. In the first phase—typical of the late seventeenth century—the United Provinces lost whatever leverage it had over the European balance of power and became a junior military partner of Britain, which was emerging as the leading Atlantic power. The second phase corresponds to the de-escalation of interstate conflicts in Europe after the end of the War of Spanish Succession (1701–13). As peace set in within Europe, the separate and competing attempts of European states to expand overseas multiplied. Within less than thirty years, intensifying competition resulted in a third phase characterized by a new escalation of the interstate power struggle in Europe.

Throughout the first and second phases, Dutch naval and commercial supremacy was steadily undermined. By 1740, when the third phase began, the United Provinces had long since become a second-rate naval power and was about to become a second-rate commercial power as well. Dutch financial supremacy, in contrast, not only remained virtually unchallenged, but experienced a period of great splendor as soon as the interstate power struggle was renewed. By the 1780s, however, this period of financial efflorescence—and the third phase of the transition from Dutch to British hegemony—came to an abrupt end with the final displacement of Amsterdam by London as the primary center of European high finance.

This displacement did not complete the transition as seen from the angle of this chapter. The establishment of British hegemony required that the French bid for continental imperium be defeated and that the enlarged European-centered world system be reorganized by the arriving hegemon. The fulfillment of these requirements, during and after the Napoleonic Wars, constitutes the fourth and concluding phase of the transition.

From Dutch to British Mastery of the Seas

The Peace of Westphalia marked the apogee of Dutch hegemony. The Peace brought to the Dutch final recognition of their sovereignty after an eighty-year struggle against Spain, and formally instituted the European system of competing national states on which Dutch wealth and power rested. Yet, the Peace also changed the terms of the interstate power struggle and in doing so revealed the limits of Dutch hegemony.

The change was heralded shortly after the signing of the Westphalia Treaties by the three wars the Dutch were forced to fight in rapid succession against the English. "The object of all three Anglo-Dutch Wars," notes John Brewer (1990, 169), "was to destroy Dutch trade and shipping." The first Anglo-Dutch war (1652–54) was fought in response to England's Navigation Acts, which aimed at turning English colonies into a trading area monopolized by English merchants and thereby threatened the Dutch carrying and entrepôt trades. But the Dutch lost the war and were forced to recognize the Navigation Acts, while losing an estimated 1,000 to 1,700 ships to the English in the course of the conflict. In Jonathan Israel's words, this "was unquestionably the greatest single maritime disaster suffered by the Dutch world entrepôt during its great age" (Israel, 1989, 210; Pemsel, 1977, 48; Hugill, 1993, 120).

The second Anglo-Dutch war (1665–67) grew out of the struggle for control of the West African slave trade. In addition to weakening the hold of the Dutch on the most profitable of the Atlantic trades, the war resulted in the transfer from the Dutch to the English of New York, New Jersey, and Delaware. In an attempt to prevent further losses, the Dutch at this point engineered an alliance with Britain and Sweden aimed at countering the growing power of France. In 1670, however, Charles II was "bribed" by Louis XIV into signing a secret treaty of alliance against the Dutch and, two years later, he initiated the third Anglo-Dutch war (1672–74) with the avowed object of curbing Dutch shipping through the establishment of tolls on the Scheldt and the Maas. As envisaged in the secret treaty, Louis XIV followed suit by invading the Netherlands and threatening the very territorial integrity and sovereignty of the United Provinces.

Dutch sovereignty and territorial integrity were saved only by using the waters to flood out the enemy, while England's naval campaign failed mainly because the English Parliament moved to cut off war supplies. By this time the English merchant class was well aware that France posed a greater threat to its interests than the United Provinces. It was not difficult, therefore, for William III to break the Anglo-French alliance and to bring about in its place an Anglo-Dutch rapprochement. Nevertheless, the war between France and Holland dragged on until 1678, sapping the resources of the two contenders, while England reaped the benefits of neutrality, capitalized on its rivals' misfortunes, and extended the reach of its tentacles overseas (Padfield, 1982, 110–17).

The first two Anglo-Dutch wars signaled the fundamental change in the nature of the European interstate power struggle brought about by the Peace of Westphalia. As long as the territorial states of Europe were intent on countering the threat posed to their sovereignty by Imperial Spain, it was easy for the United Provinces to use its money and connections to ensure that other states would carry the main burden of war on land, while concentrating its efforts on the sea war and on becoming the financial and commercial intermediary of the whole of Europe. But once the Spanish threat had been neutralized and state sovereignties consolidated, territorial states sought to incorporate within their respective domains the circuits of capital and the networks of trade that were making the Dutch rich and powerful in the midst of a general European crisis. The Dutch lesson was simple enough: "Trade did engender wealth; wealth, if the government could get at it, could be translated into fleets and armies; fleets and armies, if properly equipped and commanded, did increase state power" (Howard, 1976, 48). The only problem in following the Dutch lead was that the Dutch had monopolized the functions of commercial intermediaries that engendered the greatest wealth. Seventeenth-century European mercantilism, notes H. H. Rowen (1978, 189), "was designed specifically to overcome the Dutch 'mercantile system.'"

The internalization by other states of the sources of Dutch wealth and power through emulation or conquest thus became the primary objective of the European power struggle. The Dutch continued "to lead," in the sense that they were drawing the territorial states of Europe into their path of development. As noted in the introduction, however, this kind of "leadership against the leader's will" deflates rather than inflates the power of the hegemonic state. The significance of the third Anglo-Dutch war is that the English strategy of emulation (based on the construction of an overseas commercial empire in competition with the Dutch) converged with the French strategy of outright conquest of the Dutch Republic as a shortcut to the acquisition of such an empire. As Colbert told Louis XIV, "[if] the king were to subjugate all the United Provinces to his authority, their commerce would become the commerce of the subjects of his majesty, and there would be nothing more to ask" (quoted in Anderson, 1979, 36–37).

The convergence of the English and French strategies revealed the fundamental vulnerability of the Dutch Republic and the Dutch mercantile system to the power pursuits of neighboring territorial states. Caught between the maritime expansionism of the English and the continental expansionism of the French, the Dutch were forced to choose between the lesser of two evils, and threw their lot in with the English. From then on—until Anglo-Dutch hostility flared up again in the wake of the American War of Independence more than a century later—the Dutch would be the faithful and subordinate military ally of the English in the pursuit of the common objective of curbing French maritime and continental power.

French achievements in statemaking and commercial expansion under Louis XIV acted as a powerful catalyst of the Anglo-Dutch alliance. With its functional divisions of the state apparatus, its civilian bureaucracy responsible for the administrative rationalization of the army, and its larger territory and demographic resources, France was the prototype of the "modern" territorial state, as well as the heir of Spain as the dominant land power of Europe. Moreover, by the late 1680s the French navy had managed to achieve momentary superiority over the combined forces of the English and Dutch navies (Williamson, 1922, 333; Thompson, 1992, 141–42; Howard, 1976, 64).

For all their achievements in statemaking, the French were nonetheless incapable of overcoming the constraints imposed on their power in the interstate system by the joint action of the English and the Dutch. France's new bid for continental supremacy during the Nine Years' War (1688–97) strengthened the Anglo-Dutch alliance, which became still firmer in 1689 with William of Orange's accession to the throne of England, Scotland, and Ireland. Under William III, England's "blue water" strategy of countering the military weight of continental powers through control over Europe's seaborne commerce was pursued more systematically and more effectively than ever before. Though England did build up a substantial army, a strategic decision was made to concentrate on the navy, as befitting an island power. By way of contrast, France was caught in a financial crunch due to the war and allied blockade, and was forced to cut the naval budget by roughly 25 percent in 1693 and another 25 percent the following year (Padfield, 1982, 145).

The Nine Years' War demonstrated the success of England's "blue water" strategy. Control of the seas would now be in the hands of the allies, with England at the helm. The English navy went from 173 to 323 ships, while the French declined precipitously. Moreover, not only did the English Parliament guarantee loans for the war, it also specified the number of cruisers needed to protect British trade. Continuous reinvestment in the navy was further ensured by the formation of the Bank of England in 1694 under the aegis of business interests involved in maritime trade. British wealth and power thus became ever more unified in a single strategy, while French sea power was deprived of much-needed funds (Padfield, 1982, 148, 155; McNeill, 1982, 178–184).

In the Treaty of Rijswijk of 1697, France recognized William III as King of England, Scotland, and Ireland and gave up territory on its frontier to provide the Netherlands with a military barrier. Within a few years, however, Anglo-French conflicts took center stage once

again with the War of the Spanish Succession (1701–13), which resulted from the prospect of Spain becoming a client state of France or
Naples and Sicilian bases falling into French hands. In the course of
the war, Britain again stymied Louis XIV, this time by granting subsi-
dies to continental allies and by weaving a net around continental
Europe. Britain did have to land a large expeditionary force onto the
continent, but it concentrated on the sea war, the more so as France's
energies and resources were almost wholly taken up by battles on land
(Dehio, 1962, 83). What's more, under the provisions of a treaty with
the Dutch, the United Provinces supplied three-eighths of the sea
power to Britain's five-eighths and an army of 102,000 versus a British
army of 40,000. This geostrategic division of labor stuck Holland
with the land war, which sapped its strength, leaving Britain to concentrate on building its naval power (Mahan, 1957, 53–54).

Dutch overextension in Flanders and the Iberian peninsula broke
its strength as a naval power and vastly increased the size of the Dutch
national debt. Dutch capital began opting ever more massively for
English investments, thereby keeping British finances in relatively
healthy shape (Braudel, 1984, 261–62, 360). By 1713, then, the Anglo-
Dutch alliance had effected the passing of the baton, with Britain
emerging at the head of the coalition while the Dutch were converted
into a junior partner (Kennedy, 1987, 87–88).

Mercantilism and the Demise of
Dutch Commercial Supremacy

With the signing of the Treaty of Utrecht in 1713, the transition from
Dutch to British hegemony entered its second phase. The British had
eclipsed Dutch sea power, successfully contained French land power,
and put in place a balance of power on the continent that enabled
Britain to dominate the seas and exchanges with the extra-European
world. In the treaty, Britain gained possession of Gibraltar, Minorca,
Port Mahon, Newfoundland, and Hudson Bay Territory, plus the
asiento right to stop in Spanish ports—a right that consolidated the
hold of British merchants on the lucrative Atlantic slave trade. In addition, as anticipated by the Methuen Treaties of 1703, Portugal abandoned its French ally to become a de facto British protectorate. Britain
thus gained privileged access to the resources of the Portuguese overseas empire, including Brazilian gold supplies, which were essential to
the subsequent switch of the British currency from a silver to a gold

standard (cf. Dehio, 1962, 85–86, 107; Israel, 1989, 374–75; Mahan, 1957, 54; Furtado, 1970, 35).

In 1716, the peace process was consolidated by an Anglo-French treaty of "mutual guarantee," which was later widened into the Triple Alliance of Britain, France, and the United Provinces, and later still into the Quadruple Alliance of 1718. As a result of this de-escalation of interstate conflicts in Europe, the United Provinces came to enjoy the longest spell of peace of its entire history. This peace did nothing to slow down the transition from Dutch to British hegemony. It simply changed the mechanisms through which Dutch world power was undermined and British world power strengthened.

In war or peace, the small territorial size and decentralized power structure of the Dutch state were turning into insuperable handicaps in the European power struggle. From the very start, the Dutch had shown an "utter distaste for territorial expansion" (Boogman, 1978, 60); and the province of Holland, Braudel tells us, "always upheld the sovereignty and freedom of the provinces [vis-à-vis the Council of State and the States-General], for if the central authority was weak, Holland would be better placed to impose her will, thanks to her over-whelming economic superiority" (1984, 194). Distaste for territorial expansion and a structurally weak central government were different manifestations of the same underlying strategy of power that consti-tuted both the main foundation and the ultimate limit of Dutch for-tunes in the seventeenth and eighteenth centuries.

As in Venice and Genoa, this strategy conceived of territory and population as mere means in the accumulation of capital—an accumu-lation conceived of as an end in itself. In this sense, the Dutch strategy embodied a strictly "capitalist" logic of power in contrast with the still predominant "territorialist" logic—a logic in which the acquisition of territory and population was an end in itself, and the accumulation of pecuniary wealth mere means (Arrighi, 1994, chapter 1). In the capi-talist logic of power, parsimony in the acquisition of territory and population performed the double function of minimizing both protec-tion costs and social claims to accumulated wealth. In addition, it had the ideological advantage of enabling the United Provinces to present itself—and to some extent to be perceived—as the bearer of a general peace interest. Thus, in a book published in 1662, Peter de la Court likened Holland to a cat in a jungle of wild beasts—the territorial states of Europe: "Lions, Tygers, Wolves, Foxes, Bears, or any other Beast of

Prey, which often perish by their own Strength, and are taken where they lie in wait for others." Although a cat resembles a lion, Holland was and would remain a cat because "we who are naturally Merchants, cannot be turned into Souldiers" and "there is more to be gotten by us in a time of Peace and good Trading, than by War, and the ruin of Trade." As proof that the United Provinces was the only "pacific state" in the world, four years later an anonymous work drew up a list of twenty-one states, all of which, except the Dutch, had outstanding claims on one another's territories (as quoted in Taylor, 1994, 36, 38).

A capitalist logic of power was not necessarily associated with a decentralized state structure and a "weak" central government. Braudel (1984, 35) contrasts Venice, "a strong and independent state" that seized the *Terraferma*, "a large protective zone close at hand," with Genoa, "a mere territorial skeleton" that gave up "all claim to political independence, staking everything on that alternative form of domination, money." His indecision concerning the precise nature of the Dutch state is probably owing to the United Provinces' having combined the features of Venice and Genoa, becoming a fairly strong and independent state whose primary source of power was money. "Money," Braudel (1984, 197) tells us in his discussion of the internal structure of the Dutch state, "was the means by which anyone could be brought to order, but a means which was prudent to conceal."

Money was also the means by which the capitalist "Cat of Holland" could turn to its own advantage the struggles that set the territorialist "Beasts of Prey" of the European jungle against one another. Dutch commercial supremacy depended on this capacity, because the obverse side of Dutch parsimony in territorial acquisitions was a structural deficit of manpower the Dutch could remedy only by tapping the labor resources of foreign countries.

> Holland could only fulfil her role as freighter of the high seas if she could obtain the necessary extra labour from among the wretched of Europe. The wretched of Europe were only too eager to oblige. . . . It was not the laziness of the rest of Europe so much as its poverty which enabled the Dutch to "set up" their Republic. (Braudel, 1984, 1922–33)

As more European states sought to internalize within their own domains the sources of Dutch wealth and power through one variant or another of mercantilism, competition over European labor resources intensified and the small population of the Dutch Republic turned into an increasingly insurmountable handicap. The validity of de la Court's claim that the Dutch had more to gain "in a time of Peace and good Trading, than by War, and the ruin of Trade," was strictly conditional on what war and peace were about. When he was writing, peace was indeed good and war bad for the Dutch, but only because the Dutch were bound to lose from an escalation of armed conflicts designed specifically to overcome the Dutch mercantile system. Half a century earlier, however, the Dutch had gotten far more out of generalized warfare and the ruin of (Iberian) trade than they could have gotten out of peace. The Dutch mercantile system, which required peace after Westphalia, had been built through war before Westphalia.

Moreover, once the Dutch mercantile system had been seriously disrupted by English and French mercantilism—as it had been by the time of the Peace of Utrecht—peace was no longer as good for the Dutch as it might have been in the preceding half century of almost uninterrupted wars. Having laid the foundations of a much larger and denser world-trading system than the Dutch had ever been able or willing to do, the "Lion of England" rather than the "Cat of Holland" was bound to be the main beneficiary of peace and good trading. And so it was. Britain's overabundant supplies of labor and commercial entrepreneurship became powerful instruments in the struggle for the monopolization of Atlantic trade. The Dutch could not compete with the British in settling North America because too few Dutchmen were available for the purpose (Boxer, 1965, 109). As a result, most of the colonial population, and nearly all of the well-to-do merchant, planter, and professional classes were British, accustomed to manufactures from British sources and sales through British factors (Davis, 1969, 115).

English ports began to challenge and then outshine Amsterdam's entrepôt trade. Moreover, while Dutch industries languished, English industries expanded rapidly under the joint impact of Atlantic triangular trade and increasing governmental protection. During the Nine Years' War and the War of Spanish Succession, the English tariff structure had already changed "from a generally low-level fiscal system into a moderately high-level system, which, though still fiscal in its purposes, had become in practice protective" (Davis, 1966, 307). But it was in times of peace and reduced fiscal pressure that the United

Kingdom consolidated and strengthened this system of industrial protection through further restrictions on the import of Indian printed calicoes for domestic consumption in 1721 and Walpole's custom reform of 1722 (Minchinton, 1969, 13).

British success in outcompeting the Dutch in overseas commercial expansion and domestic industrial expansion reduced Amsterdam's share of entrepôt trade and Holland's relative economic weight in the European-centered world-economy. All this undermined the world power of the Dutch and buttressed that of the British, but the greatest blow to Dutch commercial supremacy in this period came less from the successes of British mercantilism in the Atlantic than from the spread of mercantilist practices to the Baltic region itself.

> The basic reason for the decisive decline of the Dutch world-trading system in the 1720s and 1730s was the wave of new-style industrial mercantilism which swept practically the entire continent from around 1720. . . . Down to 1720 countries such as Prussia, Russia, Sweden, and Denmark-Norway had lacked the means and, with the Great Northern War in progress, the opportunity, to emulate the aggressive mercantilism of England and France. But in the years around 1720 a heightened sense of competition among the northern powers, combined with the diffusion of new technology and skills, often Dutch or Huguenot in origin, led to a dramatic change. Within the next two decades most of northern Europe was incorporated into a framework of systematic industrial mercantilist policy. (Israel, 1989, 383–84)

High Finance, the Last Refuge of Dutch Hegemony

With the outbreak of the War of the Austrian Succession (1740–48) the transition from Dutch to British hegemony entered its third phase. The Dutch labor shortage became truly crippling. As Stavorinus deplored, "ever since the year 1740, the many naval wars, the great increase of trade and navigation, particularly in many countries, where formerly these pursuits were little attended to, and the consequent great and continual demands for able seamen, both for ships of war and for merchantmen, have so considerably diminished the supply of them, that, in our own country, where there formerly used to be a great abundance of mariners, it is now, with great difficulty and expense, that any vessel can procure a proper number of able hands to navigate her" (quoted in Boxer, 1965, 109).

The Dutch labor shortage resulting from the new escalation in the European power struggle was the straw that broke the camel's back.

Squeezed between the successes of British maritime mercantilism and the spread of territorial mercantilism to the Baltic region, the Dutch-centered world-trading system finally collapsed. And yet, what was so disastrous for Dutch commerce was not disastrous at all for Dutch capital. On the contrary, the escalation of the power struggle, and the consequent intensification of interstate competition for mobile capital, created the conditions for a financial expansion that temporarily inflated Dutch wealth and power.

The extension of credit to customers had always been an integral "branch" of Dutch commerce. Moreover, "Holland's prosperity led to surpluses which were . . . so great that the credit she supplied to the traders of Europe was not enough to absorb them; the Dutch therefore offered loans to modern states. . . . [and] when the English loan market opened in Amsterdam, from 1710 or so onwards, the 'lending branch' was considerably expanded" (Braudel, 1984, 245–46). The supply conditions of the Dutch-led financial expansion had thus been present long before 1740. As Amsterdam's centrality in European commerce declined, liquidity in Holland "remained abundant . . . with a tendency to transform the financial side of commodity exchange into a foreign banking and investment service" (Kindleberger, 1989, chapter 2). Nevertheless, the de-escalation of the European power struggle after Utrecht tended to generate more "idle" liquidity than actual lending—as witnessed by the dramatic rise of the *Wisselbank*'s stock of precious metals from between seven and eight million guilders in the period 1651–86 to about twenty-five million guilders in 1721–24 (Attman, 1983, 41).

Amsterdam was more than ever the "cash box" of Europe. But for Dutch money to acquire once again the "power of breeding" (Marx's expression) without the necessity of exposing itself to the troubles and risks inseparable from its employment in the commodity trades, interstate competition for mobile capital had to become more intense than it was in the peaceful 1720s and 1730s. When it did in 1740, British borrowing from the Dutch increased rapidly. By 1758, Dutch investors were said to hold as much as a third of the Bank of England, English East India Company, and South Sea stocks. Four years later a well-informed Rotterdam banker estimated that the Dutch held a quarter of the English debt, which then stood at £12 million (Boxer, 1965, 110; cf. Carter, 1975). The British were by no means the only customers of Dutch financiers. "By the 1760s, all the states of Europe were queuing up in the offices of the Dutch money-lenders: the emperor, the elector of Saxony, the elector of Bavaria, the insistent king of Denmark, the king of Sweden, Catherine II of Russia, the king of France and even the city of Hamburg . . . and lastly, the American rebels" (Braudel, 1984, 246–47).

A numerous clientele is not necessarily better for business than a more select clientele. That was certainly true in the case of the Dutch financial entrepôt. As the number of states serviced by the Dutch moneylenders increased, Amsterdam experienced a succession of financial crises that marked its progressive displacement by London as the nerve center of European high finance.

The first crisis broke out at the end of the Seven Years' War (1756–1763). The war had induced the Dutch to overextend themselves in granting credit, which a contemporary observer estimated to be fifteen times the cash or real money in Holland. The bankruptcy of a prominent house in August 1763 touched off the collapse of a system already under severe strain. Suddenly, discounters could no longer discount paper and the whole credit structure came crumbling down, creating a currency shortage that spread from Amsterdam to Berlin, Hamburg, Altona, Bremen, Leipzig, Stockholm, and London. In need of cash, Dutch investors began to recall the capital they had invested in English stocks, paralyzing the Amsterdam Stock Exchange (Braudel, 1984, 269; Kindleberger, 1989, 136–37; Wilson, 1966, 168; Carter, 1975, 63).

The second crisis broke out ten years later in the wake of an English house's bankruptcy in December 1772. Although originating in London, the most serious consequences were felt in Amsterdam. In the earlier crisis, the Bank of England and London private bankers had come to the rescue of their Dutch correspondents by shipping bullion and by delaying presenting bills for payment. Such aid was based on the knowledge that British prosperity was intimately associated with the flow of Dutch capital to Britain. Yet, in 1773 the Bank of England dumped all the pressure of the crisis on Amsterdam by refusing to discount paper (Kindleberger, 1989, 203; 1978, 183).

Left to itself to discount all the paper in circulation, Amsterdam never really recovered from the shock. Braudel (1984, 272) suggests that it was at this time that Amsterdam ceased to be the leading financial center of the European world-economy. If not at this time, Dutch leadership in European high finance was certainly over by the time of the next crisis, which began in 1780 but became particularly devastating for Amsterdam during the fourth Anglo-Dutch war of 1781–84. The war led to the collapse of the *Wisselbank*, which had advanced funds in the emergency of the war to the city of Amsterdam. To make matters worse, Holland suddenly found itself in the throes of the Patriot Revolution and the successful Orangist Counterrevolution, financed by British money and backed by Prussian troops (see chapter 3). A few months after the Prussian troops left Holland, the French default of 1788 terminated once and for all Dutch centrality in European high finance (Kindleberger, 1989; Braudel, 1984, 248, 273–76).

"The outcome of a long and widespread crisis," comments Braudel (1984, 273), "is often that the map of the world is simplified, brutally cutting powers down to size, strengthening the strong and further weakening the weak. Defeated politically [in the War of American Independence] England emerged the economic victor, since from now on the center of the world was in her capital." To this we should add that the "simplification" of the map of the world (the strengthening of the strong and the weakening of the weak) was as much a cause as the outcome of the terminal crisis of Dutch financial supremacy. The United Provinces was indeed "caught between England and France, as the prize of a trial of strength between the two great powers," as Braudel maintains. But it was so caught long before the terminal crisis of the 1780s.

In our account, the United Provinces became a prize shortly after the Peace of Westphalia. The brief alliance between the two emerging great powers against the Dutch in the early 1670s was sufficient to drive the Dutch into the arms of the English as their junior partner in the struggle to contain French power locally and globally. As the mirror image of English sea power, Dutch sea power waned as the former waxed, and the Dutch retreated more and more into the role of financing English state- and warmaking activities.

This process peaked in the Seven Years' War (1756–63). More than on any other occasion, Dutch money was a key ingredient in Britain's decisive victory against France, and as the French consul at Amsterdam remarked in 1760, it was not difficult to understand why the British had been showing increasing respect for the Dutch flag of late (Wilson, 1966, 70–71). The war, however, brought about a fundamental change in the relationship between Dutch money and British power. The victory of the British at Plassey in 1757 initiated a massive transfer of wealth from India, initially as sheer plunder and after 1774 more and more as plunder disguised in commercial forms. Over the next half century or so, Britain received funds variously estimated to total between £100 million and £1,000 million. Whatever the exact amount, "Indian wealth supplied the funds that bought [the] national debt back from the Dutch and others, first and temporarily in the interval of peace between 1763 and 1774, and finally after 1783, leaving Britain nearly free from overseas indebtedness when it came to face the great wars from 1793" (Davis, 1979, 55–56).

This massive transfer of wealth and its long-term effects on the British and Indian economies thoroughly shaped the strategies and structures of British hegemony in the nineteenth century. But its most immediate effect was to make Dutch money redundant in the economy of British power with deleterious results for Dutch financial supremacy. On the one hand, Dutch money lost its most remunerative outlet. For specialized moneylenders whose wealth and power rest on a steady flow of interest, the next worst thing to having their debtors default is having their most solvent debtors pay back the principal. As the British bought back their national debt from the Dutch, Dutch surplus capital began chasing after an increasingly dubious clientele. By the mid-1770s, far from queuing up in the offices of the Dutch moneylenders, "princes had only to snap their fingers and the rich . . . Amsterdammers [along with their Genoese and Genevan competitors] came running to offer their money." It was under these circumstances that the Dutch began subscribing the fateful French loans that sapped and eventually destroyed the residual vitality of the Amsterdam money market (Braudel, 1984, 245–46, 248).

On the other hand, British power began showing less and less respect for the Dutch flag. As Indian plunder became a substitute for Dutch money—and Dutch money began flowing into French coffers—the British interest in keeping the Dutch financial entrepôt alive turned into the opposite interest of making London the one and only center of European high finance. "The great shock for Holland," writes Braudel (1984, 262), "was the violence with which England turned against her in 1782–3 and cast her to the ground." The main reason for this turnabout was not so much that the Dutch had become too dependent on England, as Braudel seems to imply. Rather, it was that British power had finally become independent of Dutch money and it was not prudent to let Dutch money seek alternative outlets among Britain's enemies and competitors. Once the "Lion of England" had laid its paws on the wealth of India, the days of the "Cat of Holland" were numbered. From then on, only "Beasts of Prey" would carry any weight in the European power struggle.

Interregnum

The elimination of the last residues of the seventeenth-century Dutch hegemonic order did not in itself result in the establishment of the nineteenth-century British order. British world hegemony was only established as a result of a final round in the power struggle between Britain and France. This final round constitutes the fourth and concluding phase of the transition from Dutch to British hegemony as seen from the angle of vision of this chapter.

The Seven Years' War did not just create the conditions for the full emancipation of Britain from its previous dependence on Dutch money. As we shall see in chapter 3, it also created an unstable situation in North America that soon materialized in the American Revolution of 1776 and in a temporary revival of French fortunes in the struggle for European supremacy. As in the rebellion of the Dutch against Imperial Spain two centuries earlier, a dispute over taxation provided the catalyst for the American rebellion against British rule. The Seven Years' War had radically changed the relationships of forces in North America. With the French threat gone and their own military capabilities greatly expanded, the British settlers no longer felt any need to "buy" protection through taxes from the British metropolis. On the contrary, they wanted a much freer hand than Britain was willing to grant them in the conquest of a continent there for the taking. As soon as Britain attempted to make them pay for the costs of the Seven Years' War, the settlers rebelled.

France immediately seized the opportunity created by the American rebellion to get back at Britain. In alliance with Spain, France was able for the first time to wage a purely naval and colonial war against Britain. In an attempt to protect their trade, a coalition of seafaring neutrals—which even Portugal and the United Provinces joined—destroyed one of Britain's key weapons in the struggle, privateering. This brief turning of the European balance of power against Britain tilted the scales decisively in favor of the American rebels.

The American colonies gained their freedom. The hub of Britain's world-girdling empire was cut out at the very moment when the idea of an empire had barely taken shape. As guardian of the European balance of power, Britain had humbled her European rivals. Now she was humbled by them, likewise in the name of the balance of power. . . . Yet the jubilation on the mainland over Albion's fall was premature. Britain preserved her direct relationship with the world outside Europe. . . . [Her] strength vis-à-vis the Continent remained unimpaired, the more so as she acquired in the East Indies a substitute for the territories she had lost. (Dehio, 1962, 122–23)

France's main gain in the War of American Independence was the capture of seven of Britain's ten biggest West Indian islands, although France itself lost Saint Lucia to Britain (Duffy, 1987, 3, 18). However, the war left the French in a state of financial bankruptcy that contributed decisively to setting off the French Revolution of 1789 and the subsequent final confrontation between Britain and France (see chapter 3; Skocpol, 1979, 62–64; Addington, 1984, 21–38). When war between the two great powers resumed in 1793, Britain immediately concentrated on winning back control of the West Indies. As Mahan (1957, 226) has pointed out, the West Indies "had a twofold value in war: one as offering military positions for [controlling the Atlantic]; the other a commercial value, either as adding to one's own resources or diminishing those of the enemy." No one was more aware of this twofold value than the British, who spared no loss in human lives to recapture the islands, which they did between 1793 and 1810. Britain's military and commercial hold on the Atlantic was fully reestablished and French maritime strength was dealt a fatal blow (Duffy, 1987, 385–89).

The Battle of Trafalgar (1805) put an end to all French hopes of being in a position to challenge Britain's dominion of the seas, and it forced Napoleon "to fight his maritime enemy indirectly by means of land wars of ever widening scope" (Dehio, 1962, 171). Napoleon's Continental Blockade and Continental System quickly backfired. While Continental states were seriously hurt by their "delinking" from the extra-European world, Britain's island economy easily found overseas both new markets to replace the closed European markets and new resources to use in enticing yet more Continental states to join the anti-Napoleonic coalition (McNeill, 1982, 202–3; Kennedy, 1976, 136–47, 157–58; Goldstein and Rapkin, 1991, 945–46).

After 1812 the struggle drew to a rapid close. Although the attempt by Britain's former colonies to conquer Canada opened up a new war front for Britain; Russia—hard-pressed by the loss of trade with Britain—abandoned the Continental System. Napoleon was left no alternative but the fateful crossing of Niemen. If he did not invade Russia, "his opponent might one day force war upon him at the most inopportune moment. Britain might join up with Russia, start a fire in the east as she had done in the south, in Spain, and roast the Empire at a slow flame" (Dehio, 1962, 171). Instead of being roasted, the Empire was frozen under the Russian winter, and the transition to British hegemony was for all practical purposes completed.

From British to U.S. Hegemony

The Industrial and Imperial Underpinnings of British Hegemony

The Peace of Vienna of 1815 brought to Europe "a phenomenon unheard of in the annals of Western civilization, namely, a hundred years' peace—1815–1914" (Polanyi, 1957, 5). Britain was the main promoter and organizer of this unheard of phenomenon, which therefore well deserves to be called the *Pax Britannica*. As we shall see in chapter 4, the obverse side of Britain's European peace was the endless series of colonial wars that Britain fought throughout the nineteenth century in the non-European world. Here we are exclusively concerned with the making and unmaking of the *Pax Britannica* as an intra-European process.

As Polanyi (1957, 5–7) pointed out, one of the key ingredients in the organization of the nineteenth-century Hundred Years' Peace was the balance-of-power system—the system whereby "three or more units capable of exerting power will always behave in such a way as to combine the power of the weaker units against any increase in power of the strongest." World-historically, however, balance-of-power mechanisms had always maintained the independence of the participating units "only by continuous war between changing partners." The balance-of-power system established by the Treaties of Westphalia, and consolidated by the Treaty of Utrecht, was no exception. Polanyi contrasts an average of sixty to seventy years of major European wars in each of the two centuries preceding 1815–1914 with a mere three and a half years of wars among European powers (including the Crimean War) for the latter period. "The fact that in the nineteenth century the same [balance-of-power] mechanism resulted in peace rather than war is a problem to challenge the historian."

The anomaly can be traced to a basic geopolitical difference between the structures of Dutch and British hegemony. The interstate system established at Westphalia under Dutch hegemony was a truly anarchic system—a system, that is, characterized by the absence of central rule. The interstate system reconstituted at Vienna under British hegemony, in contrast, was not truly anarchic anymore. It was a system in which the European balance of power was transformed, for a while at least, into an instrument of informal British rule.

The British had long been aware of the importance of being the governor rather than a cog of balance-of-power mechanisms, as witnessed by their conception of the balance of power as *policy* rather than *system* (cf. Polanyi, 1957, 259–62). It is not surprising, therefore, that at the end of the Napoleonic Wars, they moved promptly to ensure that the mastery over the balance of power, which they had gained during the wars, would remain in their hands. On the one hand, they reassured and supported the absolutist governments of continental Europe organized in the Holy Alliance by guaranteeing through the newly established Concert of Europe that changes in the balance of power would come about only through consultation with the Great Powers (Weigall, 1987, 58, 111). On the other hand, they created two important counterweights to the power of the Holy Alliance. In Europe, they requested and obtained that defeated France be included among the Great Powers, albeit held in check by being ranked with second-tier powers whose sovereignty was upheld by the Concert (Kissinger, 1964, 38–39). In the Americas, they countered the Holy Alliance's designs to restore colonial rule by asserting the principle of non-intervention in Latin America and by inviting the United States to support the principle. What later became the Monroe Doctrine—the idea that Europe should not intervene in American affairs—was initially a British policy (Aguilar, 1968, 23–25).

By pursuing its national interest in the preservation and consolidation of a fragmented and "balanced" power structure in continental Europe, Britain could thus create the perception that its overwhelming world power was being exercised in the general interest—the interest of former enemies as well as of former allies, of the new republics of the Americas as well as of the old monarchies of Europe. Britain further encouraged this perception by returning parts of the East and West

Indies to the Netherlands and France, and by providing Western governments and merchants with such "collective goods" as the protection of ocean commerce and the surveying and charting of the world's oceans. Thanks to this perception, instead of inspiring challenges, British dominance secured a large measure of willing acceptance among Western states (Kennedy, 1976, 156–64; see also chapter 3).

This state of affairs was consolidated by Britain's *unilateral* liberalization of its trade, which culminated in the repeal of the Corn Laws in 1848 and the Navigation Acts in 1849. Over the next twenty years, close to one-third of the exports of the rest of the world went to Britain—the United States, with almost 25 percent of all imports and exports, being Britain's single largest trading partner, and European countries accounting for another 25 percent (Barratt-Brown, 1963, 63). Through this policy, Britain cheapened the domestic costs of vital supplies and at the same time provided the means of payment for other countries to buy its manufactures. It also drew much of the world into its trading orbit, fostering interstate cooperation and thereby securing low protection costs (Kennedy, 1976, 149–50; Nye, 1990, 53).

In this respect too—as in the mastery of the European balance of power—the nineteenth-century British world order differed radically from the seventeenth-century Dutch world order. In both world orders, the metropolitan territories of the hegemonic power (Amsterdam/ Holland in the seventeenth century, London/England in the nineteenth century) played the role of central entrepôt. But the Dutch mercantile system had hardly become predominant when it began to be disrupted and undermined, first by England's mainly maritime mercantilism, then by France's mainly territorial mercantilism, until it was virtually destroyed by the spread of mercantilism to the Baltic region. Britain's mercantile system, in contrast, survived the long series of wars in the course of which it had been established to buttress British wealth and power in peace.

British mastery of the European balance of power and centrality in world trade were mutually reinforcing elements of the Hundred Years' Peace. The one reduced the chances that any state would have the capabilities to do to the British what the British had done to the Dutch after Westphalia, namely, to initiate the dismantling of their mercantile system before it could be consolidated through "Peace and good Trading." The other "caged" a growing number of states in a world-scale division of labor that strengthened each one's interest in preserving the British-centered world-trading system, the more so as that system became virtually the sole source of critical inputs and the sole outlet for remuneratively disposing of outputs. The more general this interest became, the easier it was for Britain to manipulate the balance of power to prevent the emergence of challenges to its commercial supremacy.

The operation of this virtuous circle was inseparable from a third difference between British and Dutch hegemony. Whereas the Dutch entrepôt was primarily a commercial entrepôt, the British entrepôt was also an industrial entrepôt, the "workshop of the world." England had long been one of the main industrial centers of the European-centered world-economy (Nef, 1943). But as long as Holland remained the central entrepôt of European commerce, it was difficult for England to mobilize its industrial capabilities as an instrument of national aggrandizement. It was only in the course of the eighteenth century that the expansion of England's own entrepôt trade and massive governmental expenditure during the Napoleonic Wars turned British industrial capabilities into such an instrument (Arrighi, 1994, chapter 3).

The Napoleonic Wars, in particular, constituted a decisive turning point. In William McNeill's words,

> government demand created a precocious iron industry, with a capacity in excess of peacetime needs, as the post-war depression 1816–20 showed. But it also created the condition for future growth by giving British ironmasters extraordinary incentives for finding new uses for the cheaper product their new, large-scale furnaces were able to turn out. Military demands on the British economy thus went far to shape the subsequent phases of the industrial revolution, allowing the improvement of steam engines and making such critical innovations as the iron railway and iron ship possible at a time and under conditions which simply would not have existed without the wartime impetus to iron production. (McNeill, 1982, 211–12)

In the course of the nineteenth century, railways and steamships forged the globe into a single interacting economy as never before. In 1848, there was nothing resembling a railway network outside Britain. Over the next thirty years or so, notes Hobsbawm, "the most remote parts of the world [began] to be linked together by means of communication which had no precedent for regularity, for the capacity to transport vast quantities of goods and numbers of people, and above all, for speed." With this system of transport and communication being put in place, world trade expanded at unprecedented rates. From the mid-1840s to the mid-1870s, the volume of seaborne merchandise between the major European states more than quadrupled, while the value of the exchanges between Britain and the Ottoman Empire, Latin America, India, and Australasia increased about sixfold. Eventually, this expansion of world trade heightened interstate competition and rivalries. But in the middle decades of the century, the advantages of hooking up to the British entrepôt so as to draw upon its equipment and resources were too great to be willingly foregone by any European state (Hobsbawm, 1979, 37–39, 50–54).

Unlike the seventeenth-century Dutch world-trading system, which was and remained a purely mercantile system, the nineteenth-century British world-trading system thus became an integrated system of mechanized transport and production that left little room for national self-sufficiency. "All old-established national industries," proclaimed Karl Marx and Frederick Engels (1967, 83–84) at a time when this integrated system was just beginning to develop, "are dislodged by new industries, whose introduction becomes a life and death question for all civilized nations, by industries that no longer work up indigenous raw material, but raw material drawn from the remotest zones; industries whose products are consumed, not only at home, but in every quarter of the globe. . . . In place of the old local and national seclusion and self-sufficiency, we have intercourse in every direction, universal inter-dependence of nations." Britain was both the chief organizer and the chief beneficiary of this system of universal interdependence, within which it performed the double function of central clearinghouse and regulator.

If the function of central clearinghouse was inseparable from Britain's role as the workshop of the world, the function of central regulator was inseparable from its role as the leading empire-builder in the non-European world. To return to Peter de la Court's metaphor, Britain was no mere capitalist "cat"—unlike Holland, which indeed was and remained a "cat." As we shall see in chapters 2 and 4, in the Indian Ocean the "Cat of Holland" behaved more like a beast of prey than a domesticated animal. Nevertheless, its strict adherence to a capitalist strategy of power prevented it from even attempting to conquer a territorial empire through which it might compensate for its meager demographic resources. Britain, in contrast, was and remained a territorialist "beast of prey" whose conversion to capitalism only whetted its appetite for territorial expansion.

"Plassey plunder did not start the Industrial Revolution, but it did help Britain to buy back the National Debt from the Dutch" (Cain and Hopkins, 1980, 471). It actually did much more than that. By enabling Britain to start the Napoleonic Wars nearly free from foreign debt, it facilitated the sixfold increase in British public expenditure in 1792–1815 to which McNeill attributes a decisive role in shaping the capital-goods phase of the industrial revolution. More important, Plassey plunder initiated the process of conquest of a territorial empire in India that would become the principal pillar of Britain's global power.

The unfolding of this process of territorial conquest will be detailed in future chapters. Here, we shall simply mention the two main aspects of its relationship to the enlarged reproduction of British power, one demographic and one fiscal. India's huge demographic resources buttressed British world power both commercially and militarily. Commercially, Indian workers were transformed from major competitors of European textile industries into major producers of cheap food and raw materials for Europe (Barratt-Brown, 1974, 133–36). Militarily, Indian manpower was organized in a European-style colonial army, which throughout the nineteenth century was used regularly, not just on the Indian subcontinent, but also in foreign service in Africa and East Asia. In David Washbrook's (1990, 481) words, this army was "the iron fist in the velvet glove of Victorian expansionism . . . the major coercive force behind the internationalization of industrial capitalism."

The fiscal aspect of the relationship between empire-building in India and British world power was no less important. Even assuming that the empire was acquired in a fit of absentmindedness, as the saying went, it was nonetheless with great rationality that its fiscal assets were exploited to the financial advantage of London. The devaluation of the Indian currency, the imposition of the infamous Home Charges—through which India was made to pay for the privilege of being pillaged and exploited by Britain—and the Bank of England's control over India's foreign exchange reserves jointly turned India into the "pivot" of Britain's world financial and commercial supremacy. India's balance-of-payments deficit with Britain and surplus with the rest of the world enabled Britain to settle its deficit on current account with the rest of the world. Without India's forcible contribution to the balance of payments of Imperial Britain, it would have been impossible for the latter "to use the income from her overseas investment for further investment abroad, and to give back to the international monetary system the liquidity she absorbed as investment income." Moreover, Indian monetary reserves "provided a large *masse de manoeuvre* which British monetary authorities could use to supplement their own reserves and to keep London the centre of the international monetary system" (de Cecco, 1984, 62–63).

In sum, Britain's nineteenth-century hegemony was structured in an altogether different way than seventeenth-century Dutch hegemony had been. Both hegemonies were based on a world-trading system centered on the metropolitan territory of the hegemon. But Dutch hegemony lacked the industrial and imperial underpinnings that endowed British hegemony with far more extensive and complex structures than Dutch hegemony ever had. Europe's Hundred Years' Peace was the most distinctive product of this difference.

Ironically, however, once British hegemony attained its limits—as it did well before the Hundred Years' Peace drew to a close—its more extensive and complex structures crumbled faster than those of Dutch hegemony. The transition from Dutch to British hegemony was a long, drawn-out process that took about one hundred fifty years to run its course. The transition from British to U.S. hegemony took half that long.

In spite of its greater speed, the transition from British to U.S. hegemony followed a pattern that broadly corresponds to that of the earlier transition. The pattern is shown in figure 3, which reproduces our model of hegemonic transitions as perceived from the angle of vision of geopolitics and high finance. In sketching the pattern for the transition from British to U.S. hegemony, we shall distinguish only three phases.

The first phase corresponds to the crisis of British hegemony under the impact of the Great Depression of 1873–96. In the course of the depression, great-power rivalries intensified, military-industrial complexes too powerful for Britain to control through its traditional balance-of-power policy emerged, and a systemwide financial expansion centered on Britain took off. These tendencies came to a head with the outbreak of the First World War, which marks the beginning of the second phase of the transition.

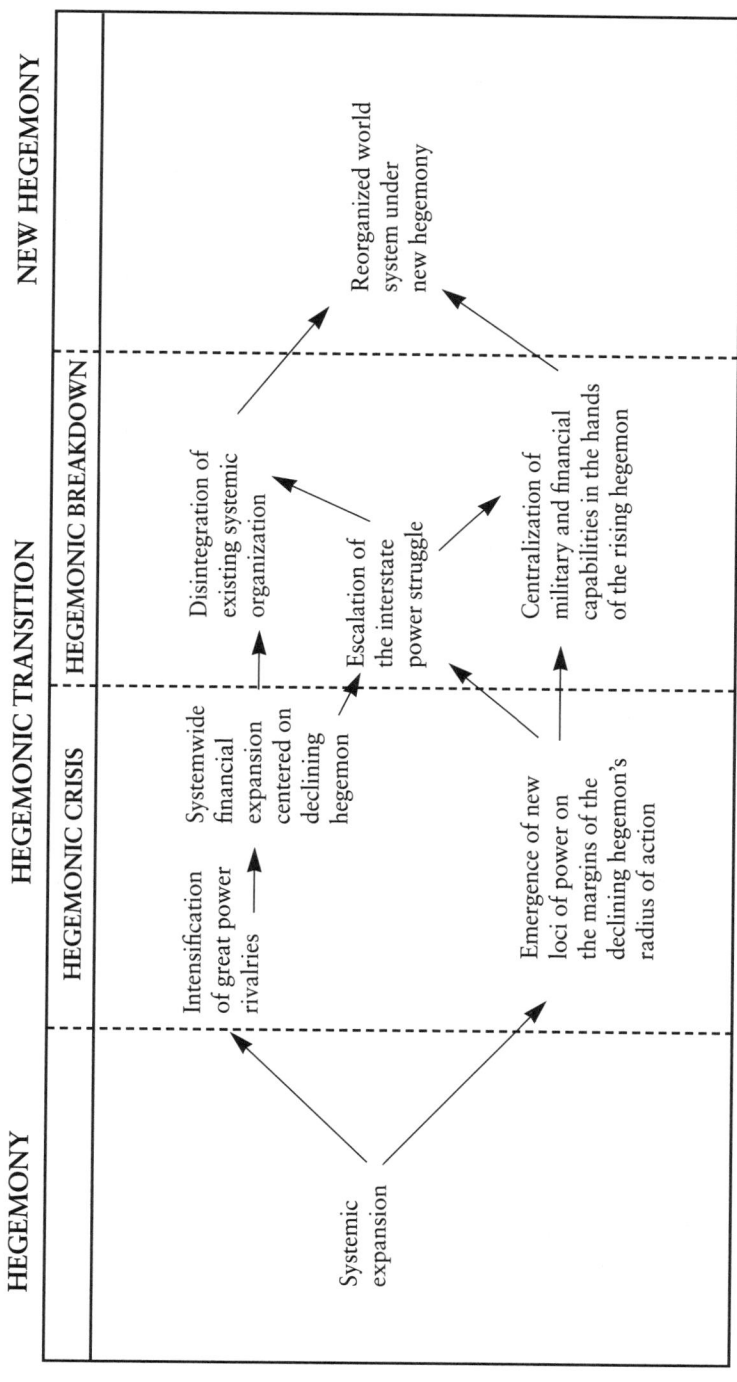

Figure 3. Hegemonic transitions and the interstate power struggle.

The First World War virtually disintegrated the structures of the nineteenth-century world order. The attempt to restore them after the end of the war simply hastened their demise in the early 1930s. As in the transition from Dutch to British hegemony, the breakdown of the old hegemonic order did not translate immediately into the emergence of a new order. The U.S.-centered world order only emerged in the third and concluding phase of the transition. It was in this phase that the Great Depression of the 1930s, the Second World War, and the consolidation of the Soviet Empire in Eurasia created the conditions for the "invention" of the Cold War. Once the structures of the Cold War were in place—as they were by 1950—the transition was complete. The next three sections sketch these three phases of the transition in turn.

The Industrialization of War and the Resurgence of High Finance

"Once the great investments involved in the building of steamships and railroads came to fruition, whole continents were opened up and an avalanche of grain descended upon unhappy Europe" (Polanyi, 1957, 182). The result was the Great Depression of 1873–96—in David Landes's words, "the most drastic deflation in the memory of man." The collapse of commodity prices brought down returns to capital. Profits shrank and interest rates fell so low as to induce economists "to conjure with the possibility of capital so abundant as to be a free good." Only toward the end of the century did prices begin to rise and profits with them. With the improvement in business conditions, the gloom of the preceding decades gave way to a general euphoria. "Everything seemed right again—in spite of rattlings of arms and monitory Marxist references to the 'last stage' of capitalism. In all of western Europe, these years live on in memory as the good old days— the Edwardian era, *la belle époque*" (Landes, 1969, 231).

Underlying this turning of the wheel was a new intensification of great-power rivalries. The "rattlings of arms" was not the harbinger of the "last stage" of capitalism, but it did signal the approaching end of world capitalism as organized under British hegemony. As Hobsbawm (1968, 104) put it, "when the economic sun of inflation once more broke through the prevailing fog, it shone on a very different world." Two things above all had changed: the industrial and the imperial underpinnings of British hegemony had been undermined beyond repair. Britain was no longer the workshop of the world, and the protection costs of its overseas empire had increased dramatically under the impact of the competing imperialisms of European states.

The spread of industrialism and imperialism were closely related responses to the disruptions of the Great Depression. These disruptions shook the confidence of European governments in economic self-healing. Protectionist measures aimed at sheltering national economies from the ravages of the world market became the usual accompaniment of the further expansion of international trade and investment. The spread of industrialism was an integral aspect of national economy-making, and the spread of imperialism was itself primarily the result of "a struggle between the Powers for the privilege of extending their trade into politically unprotected markets." The manufacturing "fever" provoked a scramble for raw material supplies, which reinforced the pressure to export. "Imperialism and half-conscious preparation for autarchy were the bent of Powers which found themselves more and more dependent upon an increasingly unreliable system of world economy" (Polanyi, 1957, 214, 217).

Right up to the First World War, the spread of industrialism and mercantilism did not lessen Britain's role as the central clearinghouse of the world-capitalist system. On the contrary, it was precisely at this time of waning industrial and imperial supremacy that Britain benefited most from being the nerve center of world commerce and finance. "As [Britain's] industries sagged, her finance triumphed, her services as shipper, trader and intermediary in the world's system of payments, became more indispensable. Indeed if London ever was the real economic hub of the world, the pound sterling its foundation, it was between 1870 and 1913" (Hobsbawm, 1968, 125).

As Halford Mackinder pointed out at the turn of the century in a speech delivered to a group of London bankers, the industrialization of other countries enhanced the importance of a single clearinghouse. And the world's clearinghouse "will always be where there is the greatest ownership of capital. This gives the real key to the struggle between our free-trade policy and the protection of other countries—we are essentially the people who have capital, and those who have capital always share in the activity of brains and muscles of other countries" (quoted in Hugill, 1993, 305).

In this respect, Britain's position in the half century preceding the First World War resembled that of Holland in the concluding phase of its hegemony. Like Holland in the seventeenth century, Britain had become a huge "container" of surplus capital—capital accumulating over and above what could be invested profitably in the expansion of trade and production. This surplus found an outlet in moneylending and speculation, both domestically and abroad, and could be used to establish claims on the future revenues of foreign governments and businesses. But for such claims to be effectively established, suitable demand conditions had to obtain. And once again, a sudden escalation of the interstate power struggle took care of that. What the escalation of the mid-eighteenth century did for Dutch capital, the escalation of the late nineteenth and early twentieth centuries did for British capital.

In both situations (to paraphrase Braudel) the financial expansion announced the maturity of processes of capital accumulation as instituted under a particular hegemony. It was "a sign of autumn." In the case of the Dutch, it was a "late autumn," coming as it did when the Dutch world-trading system was at a very advanced stage of disintegration. In the case of the British, it was an "early autumn," coming as it did when the disintegration of the British world-trading system had hardly begun. Either way, autumn it was.

The precocity of the British financial expansion in comparison with the Dutch was due primarily to the impact of the industrial revolution on war- and statemaking activities. While the spread of industrialism left British hegemony in the commercial and financial spheres more or less intact, its effects on the politics of British hegemony were deleterious. German industrialization in particular stands out as "the most important development of the half-century that preceded the First World War—more important even than the comparable growth of the United States, simply because Germany was enmeshed in the European network of power and in this period the fate of the world was in Europe's hands" (Landes, 1969, 326; see also Kennedy, 1987, 209–10).

By the time of the Great Depression and the takeoff of Germany's rapid industrialization, the forecast of the French demographer Messance had finally come true. Back in 1788 he had written: "The people that last will be able to keep its forges going will perforce be the master; for it alone will have arms" (quoted in Landes, 1969, 326). For about sixty years after 1788, geopolitical advantages and organizational innovations continued to be the main determinants of the balance of power among European states. From the mid-1840s onward, however, the application of the products and processes of the industrial revolution to warmaking activities—William McNeill's "industrialization of war" (1982, chapters 7–8)—began turning relative industrial capabilities into the single most important determinant.

The change began in earnest at the height of British hegemony, when the French navy adopted armored steamships carrying large-caliber shell guns, which made wooden warships hopelessly obsolete. As the French navy launched ever more sophisticated armored steamships from the mid-1840s through the 1860s, the British navy had no choice but to follow suit. "Each French breakthrough provoked immediate countermoves in Great Britain, accompanied by public agitation for larger naval appropriations" (McNeill, 1982, 225–27).

As other states entered the race, the industrialization of war acquired a momentum of its own that neither Britain nor France, separately or jointly, could control. Thus the race had just begun when, in 1853, Russian armored ships swiftly destroyed the Turkish navy. Fearing a disintegration of the Ottoman Empire to the primary benefit of Russia, Britain and France joined forces and promptly intervened. Russia backed off, but the Allies decided to land in the Crimea anyway to blow up the Russian navy's installations at Sevastopol. The ensuing Crimean War (1854–56) became a turning point in the industrial transformation of war- and statemaking activities that eventually destroyed from within the nineteenth-century British world order.

The war stimulated a fundamental reorganization of the European armament industry. A first aspect of this reorganization was the introduction of mass-production techniques in European arsenals. In the armament industry, as in most branches of the capital goods industry, around 1850 craft methods of production were still predominant throughout Europe. But between 1855 and 1870, under the initial impact of the Crimean War, these methods were displaced by what was then called the "American system of manufacture"—itself a sign of things to come and a "system" that European governments became aware of at the Great Exhibition held in London in 1851. The key principle was the use of automatic or semiautomatic milling machines to cut interchangeable parts to prescribed shapes. These machines were costly and wasteful of material. "But if a large number of guns were needed, automation paid for itself many times over through the economies of mass production" (McNeill, 1982, 233).

The British government and Belgian gunmakers were the first to import American machinery to speed up gun production for the British army during the Crimean War. By 1870, Austria, France, Prussia, Russia, Spain, Denmark, Sweden, Turkey, and even Egypt had all followed the British example and imported American machinery. As a result, interstate competition in the procurement of small arms was set free from the shackles of artisanal production. Entire armies could be reequipped in a matter of years instead of decades, and this speedup became in itself a factor of incessant innovations in the design of small arms (McNeill, 1982, 234–36).

A second aspect of the reorganization of the European armament industry was the introduction of large-scale private enterprise in the armament race. At the Great Exhibition of 1851, the breech-loading steel artillery design exhibited by the German firm Krupp had already aroused considerable interest. Nevertheless, Krupp's sales and production were held back by technical difficulties in casting guns of uniform and flawless quality. A breakthrough came only with the discovery of the Bessemer process for making steel during the "remarkable outburst of warlike inventiveness" occasioned in Britain by British and French difficulties in the siege of Sevastopol. "Within twenty years, older methods for gun-casting became hopelessly obsolete even though efforts by arsenal officials to cling to traditional gunmetals did not completely cease until 1890" (McNeill, 1982, 237).

By 1890, however, state arsenals had lost out to private enterprise in the production of heavy artillery. Contrary to what had happened in small-gun production—where state arsenals had pioneered changes in the labor process and in product design that enabled them to centralize production in their hands at the expense of private small business—in heavy-artillery production the adoption of new methods and materials was pioneered by big private enterprises, which centralized in their hands activities previously carried out in state arsenals. The leaders of this reorganization were two British firms (Armstrong and Whitworth). Although the Crimean War was over, the Great Rebellion in India (1857–58) and French advances in the construction of armored warships sustained British demand for more powerful artillery pieces. Moreover, both firms profited handsomely by selling guns to the Americans during the Civil War and, once that war was over, to a more diversified clientele that included, among others, Japan and China in East Asia and Chile and Argentina in South America. In the meantime,

Krupp had succeeded in its efforts to improve the quality of its guns thanks to an order from the Prussian government in 1858 and a large Russian order five years later.

> A global, industrialized armaments business thus emerged in the 1860s. . . . Even technically proficient government arsenals like the French, British, and Prussian, faced persistent challenge from private manufacturers, who were never loath to point out the ways in which their products surpassed government-made weaponry. Commercial competition thus added its force to national rivalry in forwarding improvements in artillery design. (McNeill, 1982, 241)

Finally, the Crimean War added a new momentum to the construction of national railway systems throughout continental Europe. The war demonstrated that steamship technology had enhanced the logistical advantages enjoyed by naval powers vis-à-vis land powers. Whereas troops and supplies could be sent from France and England by sea to the Crimea in three weeks, Russian troops and supplies from Moscow sometimes took three months to reach the front. In addition, a British blockade stifled the importation of new weapons into Russia by sea and cut off much of Russia's flow of grain and other exports with which to pay for whatever supplies could be imported overland (Kennedy, 1987, 174).

By expanding the range and freedom of action of sea powers, steamship technology had thus correspondingly reduced the freedom of action of land powers. The land powers could recoup the loss only by "industrializing" their overland transport system and by stepping up their own industrialization. The construction of efficient national railway systems thus came to be perceived as an integral aspect of war- and statemaking activities, not just in Russia, but in central and southern Europe as well, most notably in Prussia/Germany and Piedmont/Italy (McElwee, 1974, 106–10). Although railway construction in continental Europe had begun before, the Crimean War occasioned a true mania for railways spread among European governments. Between 1850 and 1870, 50,000 miles of new line were laid in Europe, as against 15,000 miles in all the years before. The forward and backward linkages of this upsurge in European railway construction, in turn, became the single most important factor in the narrowing of the industrialization gap between Britain and continental European states (Landes, 1969, 201–2).

The mid-nineteenth-century boom of world trade and production thus contained the seeds of the destruction of the world order on which it was premised. As *the* workshop of the world, Britain was uniquely well positioned to take advantage of the spread of industrialism to other countries by supplying means of transport and production in exchange for food and raw materials. These, in turn, cheapened the cost structure and reproduced the competitive edge of British business in world markets. And as Britain ceased to be the only workshop of the world, its superior command over surplus capital still enabled it to profit from the competition for capital among the newly emerging industrial powers. Over time, however, the spread of industrialism eroded British naval supremacy and brought into existence military-industrial complexes too powerful for Britain to control through its traditional balance-of-power policy.

"Britain's new insecurity and growing militarism and Jingoism [toward the end of the century]," notes Andrew Gamble (1985, 58), "arose because the world seemed suddenly filled with industrial powers, whose metropolitan bases in terms of resources and manpower and industrial production were potentially much more powerful than Britain's." The rapid industrialization of unified Germany after 1870 was particularly upsetting for the British, because it created the conditions for the rise of a land power in Europe capable of aspiring to continental supremacy and of challenging Britain's maritime supremacy. This shift in the actual balance of power in Europe "underlay the gradual re-forming of forces that culminated in the Triple Entente and Triple Alliance; it nourished the Anglo-German political and naval rivalry, as well as French fears of their enemy east of the Rhine; it made war probable and did much to dictate the membership of the opposing camps" (Landes, 1969, 327).

The Disintegration of Britain's World Order

When war actually began, the transition from British to U.S. hegemony entered its second phase. The weakening of British hegemony that the industrialization of war implied became manifest. Britain and its allies did succeed in containing Germany. The war even increased the reach of Britain's overseas territorial empire. But the financial costs of these military-political successes sped up the eclipsing of British by U.S. power.

The escalation of governmental expenditures that preceded the First World War had been an essential condition of the continuing strength of London-centered high finance. But once the war came, its astronomical costs destroyed in a few years the foundations of British financial supremacy. "World War I occasioned a considerable liquidation of Britain's external assets, and in the second half of the 1920s the share of new capital issues for overseas borrowers declined from its pre-war range in excess of 50 percent to 37–44 percent before slumping to very much lower levels in the 1930s. . . . In contrast to Britain, America's foreign assets doubled over the course of the war and, after fluctuating in the immediate postwar years, soared in the mid-twenties" (Eichengreen and Portes, 1986, 601–3).

In spite of an increasing use of the U.S. dollar in the settlement of international transactions, especially in Latin America, the weakening of London's world-encompassing financial networks was not associated with the displacement of sterling as the dominant currency in world trade. Even as late as the middle 1940s, perhaps half of world trade was denominated in sterling, as against about 60 percent in the half century preceding the First World War (Cohen, 1971, 71–72; Brown, 1940, 143, 145). By then, however, the two world wars had brought about an almost complete centralization of world liquidity in U.S. hands.

Already in 1910, the United States controlled 31 percent of the world's official gold reserves, while the Bank of England regulated the entire world monetary system with much smaller gold reserves (de Cecco, 1984, 120–21). As long as the United States was heavily indebted to Britain—as it was right up to 1914—this situation did not interfere with the City of London's commanding position in high finance, because British credits toward the United States constituted a claim on U.S. gold reserves and, therefore, were as good as gold. However, as soon as the United States bought back its debt from the British—as it did during the First World War by supplying Britain with armaments, machinery, food, and raw materials far in excess of what the British could pay out of their current incomes—U.S. reserves ceased to supplement colonial sterling reserves as the hidden prop of the British world monetary system. As R. S. Sayers (1990, 295) notes, "[b]etween 1918 and 1925 people had too often said that London's financial strength before 1914 was due to the gold standard. The truth was rather that the strength of the gold standard was due to London's international financial position."

Britain's liquidation of its U.S. assets during the war weakened irremediably London's financial position and left the Bank of England in charge of regulating the world monetary system with wholly inadequate reserves. At the same time, U.S. liquidity was set free for foreign and domestic lending on a massive scale. Within a decade, it became clear that the weakened world monetary system centered on London could not bear the strain of the ebbs and flows of U.S. capital. Between 1924 and 1929, the United States loaned abroad almost twice as much as Britain (Kindleberger, 1973, 56). But already in 1927, the mounting boom on Wall Street began diverting U.S. funds from foreign to domestic investment, acting "like a powerful suction pump." U.S. foreign lending dropped from more than $1,000 million in 1927 to $700 million in 1928, and in 1929—when $800 million of debt service payments on dollar debts came due—it turned negative (Eichengreen and Portes, 1990, 75–76).

Although the first signs of an imminent collapse of the London-centered world monetary system came from the crash on Wall Street and a run on banks in the U.S. southeast, the weakest link of the international financial structure was not in the United States but in Europe. The collapse of the great Credit-Anstalt bank of Vienna in May 1931 led to a run in Germany on the even larger Donatbank, which also collapsed. The London money market began to crack under the strain, and on September 21 Britain went off the gold standard, followed by another twenty-one countries around the world (Marichal, 1989, 209; see also Kindleberger, 1988, 55, 73–82; Drummond, 1987, 40; Fearon, 1979, 36).

In discussing the financial crisis of 1772–73—which began in London but reflected an ongoing shift of world financial supremacy from Amsterdam to London—Braudel advanced the hypothesis that "any city which is becoming or has become the centre of the world-economy, is the first place in which the seismic movements of the system show themselves, and subsequently the first to be truly cured of them." He then went on to suggest that, if at all valid, the hypothesis "would shed a new light on Black Thursday in Wall Street in 1929, which I am inclined to see as marking the *beginning* of New York's leadership of the world" (1984, 272; emphasis in the original). As we shall see in the concluding section of the chapter, this hypothesis also sheds a new light on the collapse of the Tokyo stock exchange in 1990 and the East Asian financial crisis of 1997.

For now let us simply point out that hegemonic transitions in high finance have involved far more than the displacement of one financial center by another in an otherwise stable structure of the world capitalist system, as Braudel seems to imply. Rather, they have involved major reorganizations of the interstate system itself. In the transition from Dutch to British hegemony, the main thrust of such a reorganization was the elimination of proto-nation-states like the United Provinces from the struggle for world hegemony. In the transition from British to U.S. hegemony, it was the turn of the national states themselves to be squeezed out of the great-power game unless they had come to control military-industrial complexes of continental scale.

This new increase in scale of would-be hegemons was closely related to the process that David Harvey (1989, 240–41) has called "time-space compression." Harvey uses the word "compression" to convey the idea "that the history of capitalism has been characterized by speed-up in the pace of life, while so overcoming spatial barriers that the world sometimes seems to collapse inwards upon us." As figure 4 shows, most of this "compression" has actually occurred from the 1840s onward—that is, from the days of the global transport revolution and the takeoff of the industrialization of war.

Time-space compression under the impact of the transport revolution and the industrialization of war—two closely related processes, as we have seen—"revolutionized strategic geography" (Ropp, 1962, 161). The "new navalism" of the 1890s, in particular, destroyed simultaneously British insularity vis-à-vis the European continent and British supremacy of the world's oceans. After 1902, the race in armored steamships with Germany forced Britain to reconcentrate its navy in North Sea home waters, leaving Britain less able to police its global empire. The policy set by Foreign Secretary Lord Castlereagh in 1817 and later codified into the Two-Power Standard of 1889— according to which the British navy had to maintain its superiority by ensuring that its strength be greater than the combined strength of the next two most powerful navies—had to be abandoned (Nye, 1990, 53; Kennedy, 1980, 420–23; Kennedy, 1976, 229; Weigall, 1987, 17, 195–96).

Britain was thus forced to cede unilateral dominion of the oceans and seek instead alliances with regional sea powers such as the United States, France, and Japan. Moreover, the combined land-sea challenge of Imperial Germany led to a renewal of the Continental-Maritime debate discussed earlier with regard to Anglo-French rivalries in the

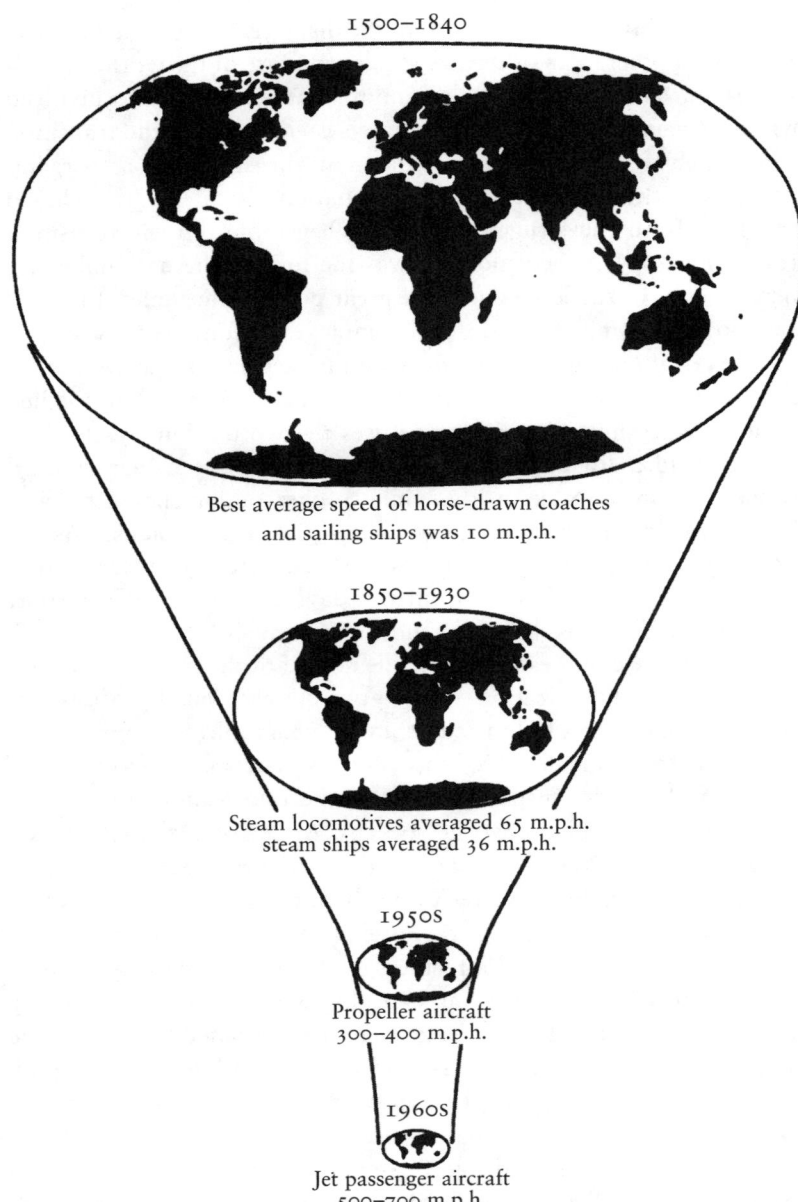

1500–1840

Best average speed of horse-drawn coaches
and sailing ships was 10 m.p.h.

1850–1930

Steam locomotives averaged 65 m.p.h.
steam ships averaged 36 m.p.h.

1950s

Propeller aircraft
300–400 m.p.h.

1960s

Jet passenger aircraft
500–700 m.p.h.

Figure 4. Time-space compression, 1500–1960s. Reprinted with permission of Guilford Press.

transition from Dutch to British hegemony. This time, however, the outcome of the debate was a renewed continental commitment. Britain's chancellor of the exchequer summed up the changed strategic landscape that resulted from the ongoing industrialization of war: "England can no longer give a European ally money, or find soldiers on the continent. A continental ally wants help in men" (quoted in Kennedy, 1976, 233).

Its insularity undermined, Britain had to respond to Germany's invasion of Belgium and France by throwing both men and money in the battle. The deployment of a million troops and heavy casualties were nonetheless not enough to tilt the scales of the European balance of power in Britain's favor. Nor was the most massive deployment of capital in British history. During the war Britain continued to function as the banker and loan-raiser on the world's credit markets, not just for itself, but also by guaranteeing loans to Russia, Italy, and France. This looked like a repetition of Britain's eighteenth-century role as "banker of the coalition." There was nonetheless one critical difference: the huge trade deficit with the United States, which was supplying billions of dollars' worth of munitions and foodstuffs to the Allies but required few goods in return. "Neither the transfer of gold nor the sale of Britain's enormous dollar securities could close this gap; only borrowing on the New York and Chicago money markets, to pay the American munitions suppliers in dollars, would do the trick" (Kennedy, 1987, 268).

When Britain's credit approached exhaustion, the United States threw its economic and military weight into the struggle, tilting the balance to its debtors' advantage. Britain thereby became just another participant in the mechanisms of the European balance of power, the United States becoming the decisive participant. The insularity that the English Channel no longer provided, the Atlantic still did. More important, as innovations in means of transport and communications continued to overcome spatial barriers, America's remoteness became less of a disadvantage commercially and militarily. "Indeed, as the Pacific began to emerge as a rival economic zone to the Atlantic, the USA's position became central—a continent-sized island with unlimited access to both of the world's major oceans" (Goldstein and Rapkin, 1991, 946).

This "continent-sized island" was in part the heritage of a process of territorial expansion that had gained momentum in the concluding phase of the transition to British hegemony in the first half of the nineteenth century (Agnew, 1987). As this continental empire was being assembled, the idea of forging it into a single national economy began to take shape. As David Hounshell (1984, 15) notes, the notion of an "American system" is as closely associated with the protectionist program put forward by Henry Clay in his 1824 tariff speech before the U.S. House of Representatives as it is with the distinctly "American system of manufacture" that emerged in the production of small arms and other machine-produced artifacts. "Internal improvement, and protection of American interests, labor, industry and arts," wrote one of Clay's contemporaries, "are commonly understood to be the *leading* measures, which constitute the American system."

A truly integrated U.S. Continental System, however, was realized only after the Civil War of 1860–65 eliminated all political constraints on the national-economy-making dispositions of Northern industrial interests. As wave after wave of mostly British-financed railway construction swept the continent, internal spatial barriers were overcome; the United States' privileged access to the world's two largest oceans was established; and a full complement of exceptional productive capabilities—not just in industry, but more particularly, in agriculture— was brought into existence. At least potentially, this giant island was also a far more powerful military-industrial complex than any of the analogous complexes being created in Europe. In the 1860s, a practical demonstration of this potential was given in the Civil War, "the first full-fledged example of an industrialized war." The U.S. government's decision to downsize its military establishment after the Civil War froze only temporarily U.S. leadership in industrialized warfare. "The explicit policy and potential military might of the U.S., briefly apparent during and at the close of the Civil War, warned European powers away from military adventure in the New World" (McNeill, 1982, 242–43, 258).

Even before the First World War, therefore, the United States had emerged interstitially as a regional power in the Americas, seriously limiting the global power of hegemonic Britain. The Monroe Doctrine— born as an instrument of Britain's balance-of-power policy—was now wielded by the United States as a highly effective instrument of its own regional supremacy to which Britain itself had to submit. The First World War simply transformed this regional supremacy into an instrument of global dominance, primarily through the massive redistribution of assets from the declining to the rising hegemon brought about by the sale of wartime supplies. The very suddenness of the enrichment, however, left the rising hegemon dependent on the policing capabilities of the declining hegemon to ensure the worldwide security and profitable investment of its newly acquired assets. "We should between us," President Wilson told one prominent British leader, "do the whole of the marine policing of the world. . . . Together, we should have vastly preponderating navies over any forces that could be possibly brought against us" (quoted in McCormick, 1989, 22).

As for land policing—more complex and more costly than marine policing—the United States was quite happy to let Britain carry the burden of stemming the rising tide of nationalism in the non-European world. In spite of President Wilson's proclamation of the right to self-determination (see chapter 3), the United States fully supported Britain's disposition, not just to hold on to, but to expand its colonial empire in the non-European world in exchange for an open door to U.S. enterprise, a strategy that for a short time enabled the United States to enjoy the fruits of imperial power while avoiding the expense (Stivers, 1982, 55, 122, 137, 193). Soon, however, the United States was brought face to face with the fact that it could not have it both ways. When the nineteenth-century world order finally collapsed in 1929–31, Britain abandoned unilateral free trade and turned its far-flung empire into a more protected preserve of its own trade and investment than it already was.

The Making of the Cold War World Order

As world capitalism retreated into its national and imperial preserves, the transition to U.S. hegemony entered its third and concluding phase. On the eve of the crash of 1929, Norman H. Davis, a Wall Street banker and former undersecretary of state, issued an ominous warning to the U.S. government. After arguing that the solvency of Europe in servicing or repaying its debts to the United States was wholly dependent on U.S. leadership in curtailing trade barriers, he went on to paint a highly prescient picture of what might otherwise happen.

> The world has become so interdependent in its economic life that measures adopted by one nation affect the prosperity of others. No nation can afford to exercise its rights of sovereignty without consideration of the effects on others. National selfishness invites international retaliation. The units of the world economy must work together, or rot separately. (Quoted in Frieden, 1987, 50)

Davis's advice fell on deaf ears. The United States did lead Europe but in a direction opposite to that advocated by the Wall Street banker. The Great Crash had yet to occur when, in May 1929, the House of Representatives passed the astronomical Smoot-Hawley Tariff Bill. After the crash, in March 1930, the Senate also passed the bill, which became law in June. The effects on the cohesion of the global economy were devastating. The conference convened to settle the details of a tariff truce—which the United States did not even bother to attend—led to nothing. Worse still, the bill set off a wave of reprisals by nine countries directly, and many more indirectly. Britain's system of imperial preferences established by the Ottawa Agreement of 1932 was itself largely inspired by Canada's reaction to the Smoot-Hawley tariff (Kindleberger, 1973, 131–32, 135).

The signing of the Smoot-Hawley Bill, wrote Sir Arthur Salter in 1932, was "a turning point in world history" (quoted in Kindleberger, 1973, 134). Polanyi (1957, 27) identified such a turning point in 1931, the year of the final collapse of the gold standard. Be that as it may, the two events were closely related aspects of a single breakdown—the final breakdown of the nineteenth-century world order.

> In the early 1930s, change set in with abruptness. Its landmarks were the abandonment of the gold standard by Great Britain; the Five-Year Plans in Russia; the launching of the New Deal; the National Socialist Revolution in Germany; the collapse of the League in favor of autarchist empires. While at the end of the Great War nineteenth century ideals were paramount, and their influence dominated the following decade, by 1940 every vestige of the international system had disappeared and, apart from a few enclaves, the nations were living in an entirely new international setting. (Polanyi, 1957, 23)

The 1940 international setting was in fact not as new as Polanyi claimed. Except for its unprecedented scale, brutality, and destructiveness, the military confrontation that set the great powers against one another resembled the confrontation that led to the establishment of Britain's nineteenth-century world order. This confrontation soon translated into the establishment of a new world order—an order now centered on and organized by the United States. By the time the Second World War was over, the main contours of the new order had taken shape: at Bretton Woods the foundations of a new monetary system had been established; at Hiroshima and Nagasaki new means of violence had demonstrated the military underpinnings of the new order;

and at San Francisco new norms and rules for the legitimization of statemaking and warmaking had been laid out in the charter of the United Nations.

This new world order reflected the unprecedented concentration of systemic capabilities that occurred during the Second World War. To paraphrase Braudel, the war brutally simplified the map of world power. France and Italy were eclipsed early in the struggle. Once the German bid for mastery in Europe and Japan's bid in the Far East and the Pacific failed—as they each did before the war was formally over—the careers of these former Great Powers also ended abruptly. Britain once again was on the winning side but at an even more crippling price than in the First World War. In Perry Anderson's (1987, 47) words, "Washington fine-tuned its aid with more or less cold calculation to shore Britain up as a forward barrier against German domination of Europe, yet whittle it down as an economic competitor in the world at large. As London's financial reserves were expended and its overseas assets liquidated, it was forced to pledge an end to imperial preference, economic autonomy drained away and present alliance became future subordination."

"The bipolar world, forecast so often in the nineteenth and early twentieth centuries, had at last arrived; the international order, in DePorte's words, now moved 'from one system to another.' Only the United States and the USSR counted . . . and of the two, the American 'superpower' was vastly superior" (Kennedy, 1987, 357). In part, this simplified configuration of world power was the outcome of a U.S. strategy that mirrored Britain's strategy in the final confrontation with France 150 years earlier. As Thomas McCormick (1989, 33) has underscored, U.S. leaders fought the Second World War "not simply to vanquish their enemies, but to create the geopolitical basis for a postwar world order that they would both build and lead." In the pursuit of this ambitious end, they were guided primarily by pragmatism but awareness of British precedents during the Napoleonic Wars no doubt helped. In particular,

> Britain entered the main European theater only when the war had reached its final and decisive stage. Its direct military presence acted to inhibit any other continental power from attempting to take France's place in the continental power structure and reinforced the legitimacy of Britain's claim to a dominant say in peace negotiations. In parallel fashion, the United States entered the European theater

only in the last and determinant phase of World War II. Operation Overlord, its invasion of France in June 1944, and its push eastward into Germany similarly restrained potential Russian ambitions in the west and assured America's seat at the head of the peace table. (McCormick, 1989, 34–35)

These analogies reflect the fact that in the concluding phases of both transitions, mastery of the balance of power in the interstate system belonged to the rising hegemon. The new world order that emerged at the end of the Second World War was nonetheless as much the product of the differences as of the similarities between the systemic capabilities of the two rising hegemons. For what concerns the purposes of this chapter, three main differences are particularly significant.

First, the domestic economy of the United States during and immediately after the Second World War was vastly larger in size, and had an altogether different relationship to the world economy, than the domestic economy of Britain during and immediately after the Napoleonic Wars. Britain had long displaced the Dutch as the central entrepôt and clearinghouse of the world's trading system. During the wars, it had also become the workshop of the world. But its clearinghouse role both preceded and outlasted its workshop role. The U.S. domestic economy, in contrast, grew up in the interstices of the U.K.-centered world-trading system as an integrated continental system of production and exchange. It never was, nor would it ever become, the central entrepôt and clearinghouse of the world in the same way that Britain was from the mid-eighteenth century through the early twentieth century. As a result, the relationship of the United States to the world-economic system was one of far greater self-sufficiency and lesser complementarity than that of Britain.

This difference was underscored by a study group established in the early 1950s under the sponsorship of the Woodrow Wilson Foundation and the National Planning Association. In challenging the assumption "that a sufficiently integrated world economic system could be again achieved by means essentially similar to those employed in the 19th century," it pointed out that the United States—although a "mature creditor" like nineteenth-century Britain—had an altogether different relationship to the world than Britain. The latter was "fully integrated into the world economic system and in large measure making possible its successful functioning owing to [its] dependence on foreign trade, the pervasive influence of its commercial and financial institutions, and the basic consistency between its national economic policies and those required for world economic integration." The United States, in contrast, was "only partially integrated into the world economic system, with which it is also partly competitive, and whose accustomed mode and pace of functioning it tends periodically to disturb. No network of American commercial and financial institutions exists to bind together and to manage the day-to-day operations of the world trading system" (Elliott, 1955, 43).

Second, and closely related to the above, the territorial configuration of the United States differed radically from that of nineteenth-century Britain. Unlike the latter, noted the same study group, "the United States . . . is a sovereign national state but with so large an area and population, and with such abundant and balanced resources that it is equivalent to an integrated regional grouping of many national states, a continent in itself. . . . [It] is not simply the largest industrial producer in the world; it is also the world's largest agricultural producer" (Elliott, 1955, 44).

Britain, of course, had territorial domains spread all over the world whose area, population, and resources were also the equivalent of those of many national states. These domains, however, did not constitute an integrated ensemble of contiguous territories. The global dispersion and weak mutual integration of Britain's colonial domains—as opposed to the regional concentration and strong mutual integration, both political and economic, of the territorial domains of the twentieth-century United States—is the most important difference in the spatial configuration of the two hegemonic states. As noted earlier and elucidated in future chapters, Britain's far-flung territorial empire was an essential ingredient in the formation and consolidation of the nineteenth-century British world order. But as soon as interstate competition for "living space" intensified under the impact of the transport revolution and the industrialization of war, the protection costs of Britain's metropolitan and overseas domains began to escalate, and Britain's world-encompassing empire turned from an asset into a liability. At the same time, the overcoming of spatial barriers brought about by these same two phenomena turned the continental size, compactness, insularity, and direct access to the world's two major oceans of the United States into decisive strategic advantages in the escalating interstate power struggle.

This brings us to a third fundamental difference between Britain and the United States at the time of the establishment of their respective world hegemonies—their different relationships to the industrialization of war. When Britain became hegemonic, it had already pioneered the advent of modern industry. But it did not promote the application of the technologies of modern industry to warfare. This application was pioneered by France in Europe and by the United States across the Atlantic. Thanks to its superior industrial and financial capabilities, at the height of its hegemony Britain could easily catch up with any technical advance and surpass its rivals quantitatively each time the basis of competition in weaponry changed. Except in artillery after the discovery of the Bessemer process, however, Britain never became a leader in the industrialization of war.

The United States, in contrast, was such a leader all along—first with France, then with Germany, and eventually by itself until the USSR launched the *Sputnik* in October 1957. More important, unlike all other contenders in the armament race, the United States was in the privileged position of being sheltered by its insularity from the rapid increase in protection costs brought on by that race, again until the USSR launched the *Sputnik*. Once domestic quarrels had been settled in the blood bath of the Civil War, the United States could concentrate on supplying the feuding Europeans with means of war, or with the means to produce them, thereby reaping most of the pecuniary benefit and shouldering little of the cost from the industrialization of war.

Taken jointly, these three differences go a long way in explaining, first, why in the 1930s Norman Davis's exhortations to the U.S. government to lead Europe in the liberalization of trade fell on deaf ears and, second, why in the 1940s the United States led Europe and the world toward an order that differed substantially from Britain's nineteenth-century world order. Norman Davis and other spokesmen for Wall Street were of course highly insightful in foreseeing that the unwillingness of nations to "work together" within the disintegrating world market meant that the nations would soon "rot separately." Nevertheless, it did not follow from this diagnosis that it was in the power or indeed in the interest of the United States to reverse the final demise of the nineteenth-century world order and to prevent the nations of the world from rotting separately.

It is highly doubtful whether the United States or any other government could have saved the system from its own self-destructiveness. The root cause of the crisis was the growing dependence of the great powers of Europe since the end of the nineteenth century on an increasingly unreliable world market system. The ensuing political tension had exploded in 1914. The First World War eased the tension superficially by eliminating German competition, but aggravated its underlying causes by making the world market system even less reliable than it already was (Polanyi, 1957, 22–27).

Under these circumstances, there was little the United States could have done to prevent the final breakdown of the U.K.-centered world system, had its leadership been so inclined. By the 1920s, the United States accounted for over 40 percent of world production but had not "developed into the 'natural' center for intermediation in international economic exchanges that London had been." It remained "an insular giant...weakly integrated into the world economy." Its financial system "could not have produced the necessary international liquidity . . . through a credit-providing network of banks and markets. . . . London had lost its gold, but its markets remained the most important single centre for global commercial and financial intermediation" (Ingham, 1994, 41–43).

At the same time, structural self-sufficiency, continental insularity, and leadership in the industrial production of means of war put the United States in a unique position, not just to protect itself, but to profit even more massively than during the First World War from the escalating interstate violence and systemic chaos that ensued from the final breakdown of the British order. To be sure, initially the breakdown had more devastating effects on the U.S. domestic economy than it did on the British economy. Nevertheless, the social and economic restructuring that occurred under Roosevelt's New Deal in direct response to these effects strengthened further the U.S. position in the final round of the interstate power struggle.

> If before the war America's economy was one among other great economies, after the war it became the central economy in a rapidly developing world economy. If before the war America's military had only sporadic significance in the world's conflicts, after the war its nuclear umbrella backed by high-technology conventional forces terrorized one part of the world and gave security to the other. Above all, the once loosely jointed federal government of the U.S. became a powerful, wealthy, and stable state, the axis on which much of the world's politics, including those of America's enemies, revolved. (Schurmann, 1974, xx)

From this position of strength—already apparent in the closing years of the war—the United States could finally impose on the world an order of its own choice. This new world order was an altogether different construct than the defunct nineteenth-century world order. British hegemony was built from the ground up through mastery of the European balance of power and the strengthening of Britain's world-entrepôt functions. U.S. hegemony, in contrast, was built from the top down as a conscious act of world-government formation aimed at forestalling the destabilizing effects of the final destruction of the European balance of power on the one side, and of the structurally competitive relation that linked the U.S. domestic economy to the global on the other.

As conceived by Roosevelt during the war, the postwar U.S. world order was to be informed by the same ideology of security that had informed Roosevelt's domestic New Deal. In Franz Schurmann's (1974, 66–67) words, "security and fear were symbolic of the major world view that governed the United States at the end of World War II— chaos produced fear which could only be combatted with security." The war had boosted U.S. power and wealth, but it had also revealed the insecure foundations of that power and wealth in an increasingly chaotic world.

> The United Nations would become the nucleus of a world government which the United States would dominate much as the Democrats dominated the American Congress. The essence of the New Deal was the notion that big government must spend liberally in order to achieve security and progress. Thus postwar security would require liberal outlays by the United States in order to overcome the chaos created by the war. (Schurmann, 1974, 67)

This vision implied a fundamental break with the mode of "production" and regulation of world money that had characterized British hegemony. Too narrow a focus on the displacement of London by New York as prime world financial center, and of the British pound by the U.S. dollar as prime world monetary instrument, obscures more than it reveals about this fundamental break—by far the most important facet of the transition from British to U.S. hegemony in the sphere of high finance. Just as the prewar domestic New Deal had been premised on the transfer of control over U.S. national finances from private to public hands, so the postwar global New Deal was premised on an analogous transfer at the world-economic level (cf. Cohen, 1977, 93, 216ff).

As Henry Morgenthau argued at the time of the Bretton Woods Agreements, support for the UN meant support for the IMF because security and monetary institutions were complementary, like the blades in a pair of scissors (cited in Calleo and Rowland, 1973, 87). Indeed, the primary significance of Bretton Woods in the making of U.S. hegemony was neither the gold-dollar-exchange standard envisaged by the agreements, nor the international monetary institutions created by them, but the substitution of public for private regulation in high finance (Ingham, 1994, 40). As Morgenthau himself later boasted, he and Roosevelt "moved the money capital from London and Wall Street to Washington, and [the big bankers] hated us for it" (quoted in Frieden, 1987, 60).

Moving the money capital of the world to Washington was nonetheless not enough to bring about the kind of massive redistribution of liquidity and other resources from the United States to the world at large that was needed to overcome the chaos created by the war. Once the war was over, the only form of redistribution of world liquidity that met no opposition in Congress was private foreign investment. Plenty of incentives were created to increase the flow of U.S. capital abroad. But incentives notwithstanding, U.S. capital showed no disposition to break the vicious circle constraining its own global expansion. Scarce liquidity abroad prevented foreign governments from removing exchange controls; exchange controls discouraged U.S. capital from going abroad; and small flows of U.S. private foreign investment kept liquidity scarce abroad (Block, 1977, 114).

The vicious circle was eventually broken only through the "invention" of the Cold War. What cost-benefit calculations and appeals to *raison d'état* could not achieve, fear of a global communist menace did. As long as surplus capital stagnated within the United States and its regional hinterlands (Canada and Latin America), chaos in Eurasia continued to escalate and to create a fertile ground for the takeover of state power by revolutionary forces. The genius of President Truman and his advisers was to attribute the outcome of systemic circumstances that no particular agency had created or controlled to the allegedly subversive dispositions of the other military superpower, the USSR (Borden, 1984, 23; McCormick, 1989, 77–78).

By so doing, Truman turned Roosevelt's "one-worldist" vision of U.S. hegemony—which aimed at weaving the USSR into the new order—into a "free-worldist" policy of containment directed against the USSR. And yet, the kinds of policies that containment dictated for the free world were essentially those already sketched out in Roosevelt's vision: American military power strategically placed throughout the world, a new monetary system based on the dollar, economic assistance to the destroyed countries, political linkages realized through the United Nations and other international agencies. By the end of the 1940s, a new American world order had clearly emerged. America "lost" Russia in 1945 and China in 1949, but it gained the remainder of the world, which it proceeded to energize, organize, and dominate in a most active way. (Schurmann, 1974, 5)

The result of this energizing and organizing was a new expansion of world trade and production—the so-called Golden Age of Capitalism of the 1950s and 1960s. Like the analogous expansions that had occurred under British and Dutch hegemony, this expansion too ended in a hegemonic crisis. When around 1970 it became clear that the U.S. army was headed toward a humiliating defeat in Vietnam and the U.S.-controlled Bretton Woods monetary system was about to collapse, U.S. hegemony entered a prolonged crisis—a crisis, which in spite of the even greater troubles and eventual collapse of the USSR, has not yet been resolved.

The Bifurcation of Military and Financial Global Power

As discerned from the angle of vision of geopolitics and high finance, the main tendencies that have characterized the crisis of U.S. hegemony since about 1970 share broad similarities with the tendencies typical of past hegemonic crises. As shown in figure 3, past hegemonic crises have been characterized by three main tendencies: an intensification of great-power rivalries, the emergence of new loci of power on the margins of the radius of action of the declining hegemonic state, and a systemwide financial expansion centered on the declining hegemonic state. All three tendencies can also be detected in the crisis of U.S. hegemony, though less distinctly than in past hegemonic crises.

This blurring of the three tendencies typical of past hegemonic crises is due primarily to the fact that one of them—the systemwide financial expansion—has developed far more rapidly and conspicuously than in the past. As we have seen, this has been true also of the British-led financial expansion in comparison with the earlier Dutch-led expansion, and can be taken as a sign of the intensification of the capitalist nature of the system from transition to transition. Underneath the dazzling speed and magnitude of the U.S.-led financial expansion we can nonetheless detect the same combination of tendencies as in past hegemonic crises.

In particular, in the United States, as in the earlier hegemonic crises, an intensification of great-power rivalries has played the role of a necessary intervening condition in transforming an overaccumulation of capital into a financial expansion. As we shall see in chapter 2, in the late 1960s and early 1970s, U.S. multinationals led the way in accumulating surplus capital in extraterritorial money markets that precipitated the crisis of the U.S.-controlled Bretton Woods monetary system. For most of the 1970s, however, this tendency failed to reverse the fall in returns to capital. A turnaround, both for capital and the United States, occurred only when great-power rivalries intensified in the course of what Fred Halliday (1986) has called the Second Cold War. As the U.S. government started to compete aggressively for mobile capital to finance an escalation of the armament race with the USSR and a simultaneous reduction in domestic taxation, returns to capital increased sharply worldwide, the financial expansion gained momentum, and U.S. global power experienced a major reflation (Arrighi, 1994, 316–17).

As seen in the introduction, it was also at this time that the East Asian economic expansion took off and came to be widely perceived as a threat to U.S. global power. As chapter 4 will show, the East Asian economic renaissance has deep roots in the difficulties that both Britain and the United States encountered at the height of their respective hegemonies in subordinating the region to Western domination. But the renaissance itself was an offshoot of the expansion of world trade and production of the 1950s and 1960s and came of age only in the 1970s and 1980s; that is, in the context of the crisis of U.S. hegemony and intensification of rivalries between the two superpowers.

In short, the U.S.-led systemic expansion of the 1950s and 1960s has given rise to the same combination of tendencies typical of the two previous hegemonic crises: an intensification of great-power rivalries resulting in a systemwide financial expansion on the one side, and in a strengthening of the tendency toward the emergence of new loci of power on the other. In past hegemonic crises, this combination was the prelude to a further escalation of the interstate power struggle, a disintegration of existing systemic structures, and a centralization of military and financial capabilities in the hands of an emergent hegemonic state (see figure 3). Can we expect the crisis of U.S. hegemony to unfold the same way? If not, why not? Or, more precisely, what has changed in the structures of the modern world system that may make the future trajectory of the crisis of U.S. hegemony diverge from that of previous hegemonic crises?

Insofar as we can judge from the angle of vision of geopolitics and high finance, the main reason for expecting a divergence has to do with the supersession of balance-of-power mechanisms. In past hegemonic transitions, the escalation of the interstate power struggle that led to the final breakdown of hegemonic structures and the emergence of new ones was associated with the attempt of an aspiring continental hegemon—France in the transition from Dutch to British hegemony, Germany in the transition from British to U.S. hegemony—to unify Europe politically in the face of the joint opposition of western maritime states and eastern continental states. Forced to fight a two-front war against the eastern and western wings of the continent, both of which were directly or indirectly supported by extra-European resources, the successive aspiring continental hegemons soon found themselves bereft of resources. Hemmed in, as they were, on the continent by the superior seapower (and in the second transition by superior airpower as well) of the western maritime states, they found their drives to the east buried under the weight of the land armies of the continent's eastern wings. In the course of these battles, the flanking states increased their power and the maritime nation with the greatest seapower and geostrategic advantage in gaining privileged access to extra-European resources—Britain in the first transition, the United States in the second—emerged as the new hegemonic power.

Each round of the European power struggle, however, altered the spatial configuration of the interstate system on which this recurrent pattern was based. Each round created the conditions of a revolution in the logistics of war and trade, of a further geographical expansion of the European-centered system of sovereign states, of a "migration" of the locus of power further west and east, and of an irreversible mutation in the structure of the enlarged interstate system. As early as 1948, Dehio (1962, 269) presented his study of the mechanisms that had reproduced the European balance of power over the preceding five centuries as dealing "with a structure that has ceased to exist . . . in a manner of speaking, [as] the result of an autopsy."

The balance of power in the Occident was preserved only because new counterweights from territories beyond its frontiers could again and again be thrown into the scale against forces seeking supremacy. . . . In World War II, the forces that had left Europe in successive emigrations . . . unexpectedly turned back toward the region from which they had come. . . . The old pluralistic system of small states was completely overshadowed by the giant young powers which it had summoned to its aid, being less able than ever before to defend itself. . . . Thus the old framework that had encompassed the European scene . . . is breaking up. The narrower stage is losing its overriding importance as a setting for a strong cast of its own, and is being absorbed into the broader proscenium. On both stages the two world giants are taking over the protagonists' role. . . . A divided system of states reverts again and again to a condition of flux. But the old European tendency toward division is now being thrust aside by the new global trend toward unification. And the onrush of this trend may not come to rest until it has asserted itself throughout our planet. (Dehio, 1962, 264–66)

Half a century after this was written, the collapse of one of the two "world giants" (the USSR) in the course of the Second Cold War, and the consequent further centralization of global military capabilities in U.S. hands, make these remarks sound prophetic. As we shall see, U.S. global military capabilities themselves have serious limitations. But whatever these limitations, there can be little doubt that the old European tendency toward the reproduction of a balance of power among a plurality of autonomous and approximately equal military structures has been thrust aside by the tendency toward the concentration and centralization of global military capabilities.

This tendency has been closely associated with a major escalation in the costs and destructiveness of the means deployed in the interstate power struggle. As the scale, technological sophistication, and capital intensity of the military apparatuses engaged in the struggle increased, the number and variety of states that could reasonably aspire to the status of great military power decreased. This tendency was already at work in the transition from Dutch to British hegemony. It became incomparably stronger in the transition from British to U.S. hegemony as a result of the industrialization of war. And it received a new powerful impulse from the development of nuclear weapons during the Second World War, the launching of the Soviet *Sputnik* in 1957, and the U.S. space program in 1961. In spite of General de Gaulle's attempts to keep up with these developments, global military capabilities became an effective "duopoly" of the United States and the USSR.

Under this duopoly, a "balance of terror" rather than a balance of power kept the armament race going. As McNeill notes, "with the discovery of atomic explosives, human destructive power reached a new, suicidal level, surpassing previous limits to all but unimaginable degree." Unimaginable as it was, this degree was surpassed again when the installation of hundreds of long-range missiles in the decade following 1957 empowered the United States and the USSR to destroy each other's cities in a matter of minutes. The signing of a five-year Strategic Arms Limitation Treaty (SALT) in 1972 consolidated the balance of terror between the two superpowers but did not halt the armament race. It simply shifted the race "to other kinds of weapons not mentioned in the treaty for the good reason that they did not yet exist" (McNeill, 1982, 360, 368, 372–73).

In the scientific discovery of new weapons systems—even more than in the industrialization of war—the superpower with greater command over global financial resources could turn the balance of terror to its own advantage by stepping up, or by threatening to step up, its research efforts to levels that the other superpower simply could not afford. This is what the United States did in the Second Cold War, thereby driving the USSR into bankruptcy and bringing the tendency toward the centralization of global military capabilities to its ultimate consequences. In this respect, the Cold War did indeed give way to "the unipolar moment"—the moment, as the triumphalist U.S. commentator quoted in the introduction claimed, when "[t]here is but one first-rate power and no prospect in the immediate future of any power to rival it."

The obverse side of this centralization of global military capabilities in fewer and fewer hands has been a partial evaporation of the substance of the Westphalian principle of national sovereignty. When it was first established under Dutch hegemony, national sovereignty rested on a mutual recognition by European states of each other's juridical autonomy and territorial integrity (*legal* sovereignty), and on a balance of power among the states that guaranteed their *factual* sovereignty against the attempts of any state to become so powerful as to dominate all the others. Violations of legal sovereignty have been countless, and the more so in periods of hegemonic breakdowns. But after each hegemonic breakdown, the principle of legal sovereignty was reaffirmed on an ever expanding scale. Under British hegemony, it was expanded to include the newly independent settler states of North and South America, and under U.S. hegemony, it became universal through the decolonization of Asia and Africa.

Each reaffirmation and expansion of legal sovereignty was nonetheless accompanied by a curtailment of the factual sovereignty that rested on the balance of power. Under British hegemony, the balance continued to operate among the states of continental Europe. Globally, however, privileged access to extra-European resources enabled Britain to manipulate the balance for most of the nineteenth century so as to dominate, informally but effectively, all other states. The very idea of the balance of power as a guarantee of the factual sovereign equality of states had thus already become somewhat of a fiction.

Under U.S. hegemony, the idea was discarded even as fiction. As Anthony Giddens has pointed out, U.S. influence on shaping the new global order both under Wilson and under Roosevelt "represented an attempted incorporation of U.S. constitutional prescriptions globally rather than a continuation of the balance of power doctrine." In an age of industrialized warfare and increasing centralization of politico-military capabilities in the hands of a small and dwindling number of states, that doctrine made little sense either as a description of actual relationships of power among the members of the globalizing inter-state system or as a prescription for how to guarantee the sovereignty of states. The "sovereign equality" upheld in Article Two of the charter of the United Nations for all its members was thus "specifically supposed to be legal rather than factual—the larger powers were to have special rights, as well as duties, commensurate with their superior capabilities" (1987, 258, 266).

The enshrining of these special rights in the charter of the United Nations institutionalized for the first time since Westphalia the idea of a suprastatal authority and organization that restricted juridically the sovereignty of all but the most powerful states (for a comprehensive discussion of the differences between the Westphalia and United Nations systems, see Held, 1995, chapter 4). These juridical restrictions, however, paled in comparison with factual restrictions imposed by the two preeminent state powers—the United States and the USSR—on their respective and mutually recognized "spheres of influence." The restrictions imposed by the USSR relied primarily on military-political resources and were regional in scope, limited as they were to its

Eastern European satellites. Those imposed by the United States, in contrast, were global in scope and relied on a far more complex armory of resources.

The far-flung network of quasi-permanent overseas bases maintained by the United States in the Cold War era was, in Stephen Krasner's words, "without historical precedent; no state had previously based its own troops on the sovereign territory of other states in such extensive numbers for so long a peacetime period" (1988, 21). This U.S.-centric, world-encompassing, politico-military regime was supplemented and complemented by the U.S.-centric world monetary system instituted at Bretton Woods. These two interlocking networks of power, one military and one financial, enabled the United States at the height of its hegemony to govern the globalized system of sovereign states to an extent that was entirely beyond the horizons, not just of the Dutch in the seventeenth century, but of Imperial Britain in the nineteenth century as well.

In short, the crisis of national sovereignty is no novelty of our time. Rather, it is an aspect of the stepwise destruction of the balance of power that originally guaranteed the sovereign equality of the members of the Westphalian system of states. As the system became global in scope under the leadership of ever more powerful governmental complexes, most states lost prerogatives historically associated with national sovereignty. Even powerful states like the former West Germany and Japan have been described as "semisovereign" (Katzenstein, 1987; Cumings, 1997). And Robert Jackson (1990, 21) has coined the expression "quasi-states" to refer to ex-colonial states that have won juridical statehood but lack the capabilities needed to carry out the governmental functions traditionally associated with independent statehood. Semisovereignty and quasi-statehood are the outcome of long-term trends of the modern world system and both materialized well before the global financial expansion of the 1970s and 1980s. During the 1970s and 1980s, the capacity of the two superpowers to govern interstate relations within and across their respective spheres of influence lessened in the face of forces they had called forth themselves but could not control.

These forces will be discussed in the conclusions of the next three chapters. For now let us simply note that the intensification of great-power rivalries that led to the collapse of the USSR left the United States bereft of the financial resources needed to exercise effectively its global military supremacy. The 1991 Gulf War—which restored some of the military self-confidence the United States had lost in Indochina, Iran, and Lebanon—was entirely paid for by other countries. If the war demonstrated that Japan was "third-rate in politics" (see introduction), it demonstrated also that the United States no longer had the resources to finance a war that was over within a matter of days (Hobsbawm, 1994, 242).

As Bergsten (1987, 771) asked even before the Second Cold War was over, "Can the world's largest debtor nation remain the world's leading power? Can a small island nation [Japan] that is now militarily insignificant and far removed from the traditional power centers provide at least part of the needed global leadership?" This double question points to the peculiar spatial configuration of world power that seems to be emerging in the crisis of U.S. hegemony. Whereas previous transitions resulted in a greater *fusion* of world financial and military power under the jurisdiction of the rising hegemon than had been realized by the declining hegemon, the present transition has resulted in a *fission* under different jurisdictions of the two sources of world power. This bifurcation of military and financial power is the true anomaly of present transformations of the global political economy as perceived from the angle of vision of geopolitics and high finance.

The 1990 crash on the Tokyo stock exchange has not eliminated the bifurcation. Just as Braudel drew a parallel between the crisis of 1772–73 and the crisis of 1929–31, so we may draw a parallel between both these crises and the crisis of 1990–92. In all three crises, it was the world financial center that was growing most rapidly—London in the late eighteenth century, New York in the early twentieth century, Tokyo in the late twentieth century—that first experienced "the seismic movements of the system." Braudel sees the crisis in the newly emergent center as part of the growing pains that eventually led it to world dominance. As we have pointed out in partial qualification of this view, past displacements of one dominant world financial center by another were in fact long, drawn-out processes in the course of which the existing systemic organization broke down and a new organization was created under the leadership of the state in which the rising center was located. Since for the time being there are few signs of a systemic breakdown and even fewer of an emergent Japanese systemic leadership, expectations of Tokyo's rise to world financial supremacy are unwarranted. Nevertheless, it remains true that the 1990–92 crisis has all the characteristics of the problems of a world financial center that has not developed the organizational capabilities needed to sustain its phenomenal expansion (very much like New York in 1929), rather than the sign of a reestablished U.S. global financial supremacy.

The crisis has further complicated these problems by strengthening the disposition of Japanese capital to thrust its roots more deeply in East Asia, where its largest profits have been made, rather than spread itself thin in North America, where its largest losses have been made. This disposition has contributed to the consolidation of other financial centers of world significance in the East Asian region, most notably the city-states of Hong Kong and Singapore and the "province" of Taiwan (see introduction). As a result, Bergsten's double rhetorical question still holds and with a vengeance. The world's greatest military power remains the world's largest debtor nation. At the same time, the states that have come to control the largest share of the world's liquidity (except for Japan) are not even national states. They are city-states and a juridically non-sovereign state, all of lesser potential military significance than Japan and farther removed than Japan from the traditional seats of global power.

This dispersal of financial capabilities among multiple competing centers—none of which can remotely aspire to become world hegemonic on its own—has widened the gap between the rapid capital accumulation in the region on the one side, and the capacity of the states that host the centers to sustain organizationally the expansion on the other. This widening gap has surfaced in the devastating financial crisis that swept the entire East Asian region in 1997. For all its devastations, however, this latest (and in all likelihood, not last) East Asian crisis in itself is no more a sign of a rollback of East Asian financial power vis-à-vis the United States than Black Thursday on Wall Street in 1929 (and the devastation of the U.S. economy that ensued) was a sign of a rollback of U.S. financial power vis-à-vis Britain.

Underneath the ongoing turbulence of the global economy, the bifurcation of military and financial power remains in place. In this chapter we have highlighted one aspect of the bifurcation by showing how successive rounds of the interstate power struggle have resulted in an increasing centralization of global military capabilities. In the next chapter, we highlight another aspect by showing how the evolution of state-capital relations has promoted a decentralization, rather than a centralization of global financial capabilities.

Two

The Transformation of Business Enterprise

Giovanni Arrighi, Kenneth Barr, and Shuji Hisaeda

Chapter 1 focused on hegemonic transitions as periods of reorganization of the modern system of sovereign states. In this chapter, the focus shifts onto transformations of the dominant system of business enterprise. From this angle of vision, we shall see how each reorganization of the interstate system has entailed also a fundamental change in state-capital relations.

A recurrent pattern is discernible in each transition. The very success of the leading business enterprises of the hegemonic state in "monopolizing" high-value-added activities draws new competitors into their path of development. As a result, "monopolization" becomes costly or impossible. More important, expansion and intensifying competition along the paths that had made the fortunes of the hegemonic states' enterprises create the conditions for the emergence of new and more profitable paths of development that over time lead to the formation of new systems of business enterprise under new hegemonies. Dutch joint-stock chartered companies in the seventeenth century, English manufacturers in the nineteenth century, and U.S. transnational corporations in the twentieth century were all equally involved in global attempts at "monopolization" backed by state power. But each kind of enterprise did so along a developmental path that departed radically from, and related to state power differently than, the paths of its global predecessors.

Joint-stock chartered companies were half-governmental and half-business organizations chartered by European governments to act on their behalf in the non-European world at a time when European states were still weak by world-historical standards. But as soon as European states became strong—as Britain soon did, thanks, among other things, to the successes of the English East India Company—the chartered companies were phased out and their functions taken over by more specialized governmental and business agencies. Nineteenth-century English manufacturers and the extensive business networks that linked them to suppliers and customers all over the world were among these more specialized business agencies. Their very specialization made them far more dependent on the strong arm of the hegemonic state for the protection and advancement of their global interests than joint-stock chartered companies ever were. But English manufacturers and associated commercial enterprises did less than joint-stock chartered companies to strengthen the state power on which they were so dependent.

Finally, U.S. multinational corporations were even more dependent on the power of the hegemonic state for creating the global conditions of their expansion than their English, let alone Dutch, global predecessors had been. And yet, the very scale and scope of their transnational operations made their expansion far more subversive of the state power on which they depended than their English or Dutch counterparts had been. In no sphere has this contradictory relation between U.S. corporate and U.S. state power been more evident than in high finance. For as soon as U.S. corporations moved to occupy the highly profitable political-economic space that the U.S. government had created for them in Western Europe, the "flight" of their profits to extraterritorial financial markets became the leading force behind the undermining and eventual breakdown of the (largely U.S.-controlled) Bretton Woods world monetary system.

In sum, whereas chapter 1 tells a story of the emergence in the course of each transition of a hegemonic governmental agency more powerful than the preceding one, chapter 2 tells a story of the emergence in the course of these same transitions of business agencies that are ever more dependent on, but also ever more subversive of, the power of the hegemonic state. In the first part of the chapter, we analyze the process whereby the full expansion and eventual disintegration of the seventeenth-century system of joint-stock chartered companies typical of Dutch hegemony created the conditions for the emergence of the system of family business enterprise that came of age with the consolidation of British hegemony. In the second part, we analyze the analogous process whereby the full expansion and eventual disintegration of the nineteenth-century British system of family business enterprise created the conditions for the emergence of the system of vertically integrated, bureaucratically managed, multinational corporations that came of age with the establishment of U.S. hegemony. The stage will thus be set for an assessment of the historical significance and future prospects of present-day tendencies toward the full expansion of the global system of multinational corporations in the light of analogies and differences with the tendencies that have characterized past hegemonic transitions.

The Rise of Corporate Capitalism, Dutch-Style

Corporate Capitalism, Dutch-Style

The magnificence of Dutch capitalism, to paraphrase Braudel (1984, 207; also Aymard, 1982, 8), was supplied first by Europe, and secondly by the world. Magnificence by Europe was supplied primarily through the Baltic—Amsterdam's "mother trade." Magnificence by the world was supplied primarily through the activities of joint-stock chartered companies—first and foremost, the *Verenigde Oost-Indische Compagnie* (VOC) established in 1602. "The VOC," in Charles Boxer's (1979, 51) words, "was a colossal organization, comparable to one of the modern great multinational firms, when due allowance is made for differences in time, space and demography."

For all their similarities, joint-stock chartered companies and twentieth-century corporations differ in one key respect. Unlike the latter, chartered companies were business organizations to which governments granted exclusive trading privileges in designated geographical areas, as well as the right to undertake the war- and statemaking functions needed to exercise those privileges. In its charter, for example, the VOC was granted by the Dutch government a monopoly on all trade east of the Cape of Good Hope and west of the Strait of Magellan, a vast area including the whole of the Indian and Pacific Oceans. It was also granted the right to build a navy, raise an army, construct forts, make war, conclude peace, annex territory, and administer colonial settlements.

In the early seventeenth century, the Dutch were not alone in launching joint-stock chartered companies. The English East India Company was created two years before its Dutch counterpart, and other English trading companies had been chartered even earlier. Within a decade or two, several other states and cities of the Baltic and North Sea followed in the footsteps of the English and the Dutch by chartering their own overseas companies, mostly to engage in trade with the rich markets of the East (Bonassieux, 1969; Blussé and Gaastra, 1981; Tracy, 1990).

In 1621, the Dutch launched the *West-Indische Compagnie* (WIC). Initially, this was more a governmental than a business undertaking, closely related to the resumption of hostilities against Imperial Spain after a twelve-year truce. Facing bankruptcy, the WIC was reorganized in 1674 as a slave-trading enterprise with profitable side activities in contraband trade with Spanish America and sugar production in Surinam. It was the WIC that introduced the Atlantic triangular trade, which was to link manufacturing communities of Europe, slave-procuring communities of Africa, and plantation communities of the Americas to one another in an increasingly massive and profitable circuit of trade and production (Emmer, 1981; Unger, 1982; Postma, 1990). The main beneficiary of this innovation, however, was not the WIC, but French and, above all, English private merchants who centralized in their hands an increasing share of the supply of African slaves (Davies, 1974, 127–28).

In 1664, Colbert organized two fairly substantial companies, the *Compagnie des Indes orientales* and the *Compagnie des Indes occidentales*. After Colbert's death, several smaller companies received charters. The larger and smaller companies were later merged or liquidated and eventually reorganized with the installation of the *Conseil des Indes* in 1723 (Haudrere, 1989, I, 106–14). But mergers and reorganizations notwithstanding, French companies never matched the performance of their Dutch and English competitors (Toussaint, 1966, 126–27).

In light of the small number of success stories among the many joint-stock chartered companies formed in the seventeenth century, Niels Steensgaard's (1974, 1981, 1982) contention that the VOC inaugurated a new era in business history, and indeed in the history of European overseas expansion, may seem questionable. Nevertheless, the epochal significance of this small number of success stories fully justifies his claim. Thus, without the large and steady cash flow generated by the activities of the VOC, Amsterdam might have never become the site of the first stock exchange in permanent session with a volume and density of transactions that outshone all past and contemporary stock markets (Braudel, 1982, 100–106; 1984, 224–27; Israel, 1989, 75–76, 256–58). Without the initial development of Atlantic triangular trade by the WIC and then by the Royal African Company, a principal dynamic element of English industrial expansion in the eighteenth century would have been missing (Wolf, 1982, 199–200). And, as argued in chapter 1, without the prior territorial conquests of the East India Company, Britain in the nineteenth century could never have run persistent trade deficits and still retained, even strengthened, its creditor-nation position vis-à-vis the rest of the world.

The fact that even the most successful of the joint-stock chartered companies went out of business eventually does not in any way diminish their importance as the leading business organizations of their times. It only suggests that the very expansion of any particular system of business enterprise tends to create conditions under which the system can no longer function and is eventually superseded by a different system. In what follows, we shall document the unfolding of this tendency in the transition from Dutch to British hegemony by distinguishing four phases.

The first phase—typical of the late seventeenth century—was characterized by the failure of Dutch attempts to replicate through the WIC in the Atlantic the achievements of the VOC in the Indian Ocean. This failure revealed a major limit of Dutch commercial supremacy, particularly vis-à-vis the English, but left that supremacy more or less intact in Baltic and Indian Ocean trade. Supremacy in these arenas began to be eroded in the second phase of the transition— a phase that spanned the early eighteenth century and was characterized by an increasing diversification of the activities of joint-stock chartered companies.

The escalation around 1740 of the competitive struggle among the chartered companies and their respective chartering states marked the beginning of the third phase of the transition. By the end of the century, this escalating competition had resulted in the common ruin of the vast majority of chartered companies, including the WIC and the VOC (dissolved in 1791 and 1799, respectively). If there was a winner among chartered companies, it was the English East India Company, which attained its maximum expansion at this time. But as events were soon to show, victory in the struggle against its peers did not provide the company with any guarantee of survival once the struggle was over.

Thus, in the fourth and closing phase of the transition, typical of the early nineteenth century, the East India Company came under attack within Britain itself and was progressively deprived of its trade monopolies—of the India monopoly in 1813 and the China monopoly in 1833. In the wake of the Great Rebellion of 1857–58, the company was also deprived of its administrative functions and the Indian subcontinent was formally incorporated into the forming British Empire. As the old structure of accumulation centered on joint-stock chartered companies withered away, a new structure centered on individually owned family enterprises, enmeshed in a dense web of commercial exchanges and operating under the protection of the most extensive and powerful territorial empire the world had ever seen, came into its own, thereby completing the transition to British hegemony.

Strengths and Weaknesses of Corporate Capitalism, Dutch-Style

Steensgaard (1974, 114) attributes the success of the VOC in comparison with, and in relation to, its European predecessor in the Indian Ocean, the Portuguese *Estado da India,* to a reversal of the relationship between "profit" and "power." The *Estado* traded in order to buttress the capabilities of the Portuguese crown to extract tribute through the use of violence. The VOC, in contrast, used violence to establish monopolistic positions in regional and world markets so as to reap high and steady commercial profits.

Within this strategy, the key move was the acquisition of a tight control over the supply of Indian Ocean spices. Fine spices did not find a ready market only in Amsterdam. In the Far East "they were a sought-after exchange currency, the key that opened many markets, just as the grain and ships' masts of the Baltic were in Europe" (Braudel, 1984, 219). But spices were cheap and plentiful throughout the Indian Ocean islands. "If the Dutch company were to become one more among many competing carriers, the result would be to raise prices in Indonesia and probably to glut the European market." This could be avoided "only by doing what the Portuguese had failed to do; by controlling all the main sources of supply" (Parry, 1981, 249–50).

To seize and enforce this control, the VOC had to use as much violence against producers and competitors as the Portuguese had used to extract tribute from the region. After establishing its headquarters in the fortified settlement of Batavia (1619), the VOC seized Malacca (1641); it annexed one after another of the Spice Islands and enslaved their peoples, literally and metaphorically; it settled the Cape of Good Hope (1652), it occupied Ceylon (1658), and conquered Malabar (1663). Formosa, occupied in 1627, was lost in 1661–62. There was nonetheless a fundamental difference between the Dutch and the Portuguese use of violence. Whereas Portuguese violence had raised the protection costs of their own trade in spices and thereby curtailed their profit margins, Dutch violence raised the profit margins of the spice trade and simultaneously centralized it in the hands of the VOC (Lane, 1979, 17–18; Parry, 1981, 250–52; Braudel, 1984, 218).

The reversal of the relationship between "profit" and "power" was thus instrumental in turning the VOC into the source of a large and seemingly inexhaustible cash flow, in bringing extraordinary profits to the promoters of the VOC, and in making the VOC's shares the undisputed "blue chip" of the Amsterdam stock market for more than a century. But the magnificent results of the VOC's strategy were due as much to the peculiarities of the environment in which it was deployed as to the strategy itself.

As Braudel (1984, 496) has observed, the merchant capitalism of Europe could easily lay siege to the markets of the East and "use their own vitality to manoeuver them to its own advantage" because these markets already "formed a series of coherent economies linked together in a fully operational world-economy." Braudel's observation echoes Weber's (1961, 215) remark that it was one thing to undertake commercial expansion in regions of ancient civilization with a well-developed and rich money economy, as in the East Indies, and an altogether different thing to do so in sparsely populated lands where the development of a money economy had hardly begun, as in the Americas. The validity of these observations is borne out by the fact that the Dutch reversal of the relationship between power and profit, which worked wonders in the Indian Ocean, did not work well at all in the Atlantic.

The importance of the WIC and, more generally, of Dutch mercantile activities in the Americas, should not be belittled simply because of their poor returns in comparison with those of the VOC (Emmer, 1981). It is nonetheless true that after some initial successes—due primarily to the highly favorable circumstances for Dutch expansion created by the Thirty Years' War—the WIC ran into trouble and never managed to replicate or capitalize on these initial successes. Launched more to attack the power, prestige, and revenues of Spain and Portugal than to bring dividends to its shareholders, the WIC initially succeeded in doing both things at the same time. Thus, when Piet Heyn captured the Mexican Silver Fleet in 1628, the WIC could declare one of the very few bumper dividends of its history (Boxer, 1965, 49), a capture that also dealt a serious blow to the already war-strained finances of Imperial Spain (Kennedy, 1987, 48). This early success in privateering was soon followed by the conquest of sizeable Portuguese territories in Brazil. But even before the Thirty Years' War was over, the Portuguese reconquered their Brazilian territories from the Dutch, while the escalation of the costs of colonization and land warfare over and above commercial profits weakened irremediably the economic and financial position of the WIC (Boxer, 1957).

On its reorganization in 1674, the WIC was modeled more closely in the image of the VOC. The pursuit of profit was put more firmly in command and the acquisition of control over the most strategic supplies of Atlantic trade was given top priority. Just as the most strategic supplies of Baltic trade were grain and naval stores and those of Indian Ocean trade were fine spices, so the most strategic supplies of the Atlantic trade were African slaves. As previously noted, however, the WIC never reaped the full benefits of its innovative organization of Atlantic triangular trade. Whereas in the Indian Ocean the VOC displaced Portuguese competition and for more than a century kept English competition at bay, in the Atlantic the WIC first lost out to the Portuguese in territorial expansion and colonization, and then lost out to the English in Atlantic triangular trade.

As Kenneth Davies (1974, 127) has pointed out, the defeat of the Dutch in the struggle to monopolize the slave trade can be traced to a combination of three circumstances: (1) the few settlement colonies established by the Dutch, which prevented them from matching the exclusive colonial policies of England and France; (2) the declining military-diplomatic weight of the United Provinces, which prevented the Dutch from holding on to and then reclaiming the *asiento*—the exclusive right to supply slaves to Spain's American colonies; and (3) the continuing reliance of the Dutch on a joint-stock chartered company (the WIC), long after this kind of organization had become obsolete in the slave trade and had been abandoned by England and France.

Each circumstance highlights a different aspect of the limits of the Dutch system of business enterprise. Settlement colonies never were a profitable business proposition, and the strictly capitalist logic of power of the Dutch narrowly limited their disposition to establish such colonies. The WIC did attempt to take over Brazil from the Portuguese, but as soon as the costs of the undertaking rose above the WIC's commercial profits, the Dutch abandoned territorial conquest and colonization in the Americas in favor of greater specialization in commercial intermediation (Boxer, 1965, 49). This left Dutch business hostage to the market-creating activities of the territorialist states of Europe. And once these states decided to support the takeover of trade with their colonies by their own merchant classes—as pioneered by England's Navigation Acts—the role of commercial intermediation in the Atlantic began to slip from Dutch hands.

This tendency was strengthened by the declining military-diplomatic weight of the United Provinces in European politics discussed in chapter 1. The rising power of France and England did not just increase the capabilities of these states to pursue exclusive colonial policies at the expense of the Dutch. In addition, it provided these same states with greater capabilities to outbid the Dutch in securing control over the colonial trade of the now declining Iberian early-comers.

To make things worse for the Dutch, Atlantic trade in general, and the slave trade in particular, were inhospitable environments for joint-stock chartered companies. Much earlier than in the Asian trades, in Davies's (1957, 46) words, "the more flexible system of competitive enterprise emerged triumphant." By the beginning of the eighteenth century, even the Royal African Company—which had displaced the WIC as the main joint-stock company involved in the slave trade—was clearly a doomed enterprise.

At the roots of the companies' problems were the difficulties involved in enforcing their monopolies. The procurement of slaves required the building and upkeep of expensive fortifications on the West African coast, which nonetheless were ineffective means for policing the coast against the competition. The American colonists, whose entrepreneurship was essential to the expansion of Atlantic trade, constantly complained about the price and quantity of supplies, and the debts they owed for slaves bought on credit proved difficult or impossible to collect. Merchants seeking unrestricted entry into the African trade, in alliance with colonial planters seeking cheap slaves and metropolitan manufacturers seeking expanded outlets for their exports, mobilized continually to obtain governmental recognition, which the French and English governments were only too ready to grant. The companies' employees often embezzled goods, traded with interlopers, and neglected the corporate interest. And the mutual competition among the companies chartered by different governments squeezed profit margins, making all the other problems more serious for each one of them (Davies, 1957, 122–135; 1974, 117–31).

"Free trade, then," notes Davies after recounting the downfall of the African Company's monopoly, "won a notable triumph . . . more than sixty years before the publication of the *Wealth of Nations.*" This harbinger of the eventual demise a century or so later of the system of joint-stock chartered companies owed little to theory or ideology. "Free Trade . . . won on merits that were severely practical" (Davies, 1957, 152).

These practical merits were in part due to diseconomies of scale. "Beyond a certain point, the advantages of a large capital and large-scale organization began to be outweighed by the disadvantages of cumbersome administration, inadequate supervision and slow responses to changing needs." In part, however, they were due to "the further handicap of an enforceable responsibility to the public to trade and go on trading whatever the profit might be." The private traders were under no such obligation: "they traded or refrained from trading as they chose." If a private trader encountered a serious loss, "he slipped into the oblivion of bankruptcy, and in time another trader with fresh capital rose to take his place. Individuals were wiped out or deterred; but the system endured" (Davies, 1957, 147–49).

Contradictions of Dutch Commercial Supremacy

The failure of Dutch attempts to replicate through the WIC the successes attained through the VOC constituted a major limit of Dutch commercial supremacy. But it did not mark the end of such supremacy. In the first half of the eighteenth century, however, Dutch commercial supremacy began to be undermined even where it seemed unassailable, and the transition from Dutch to British hegemony in the sphere of world commerce entered its second phase. The tendencies typical of this second phase are best discerned by focusing on the relationship between the VOC and the English East India Company.

The East India Company began rather tentatively as a series of voyages, each trading on separate joint stocks, frequently with different investors, and did not begin operating consistently on a permanent joint stock until the 1660s. The company did make significant gains early on in setting up a number of factories and forts, and even capturing some territory from the Portuguese. Still, in the second quarter of the seventeenth century, it almost went out of business as its shareholders began doubting whether the company could go on trading in the face of an entrenched Dutch monopoly in the most profitable lines of business in the East Indies and an acute shortage of liquidity in London (Chaudhuri, 1965, chapters 2 and 3).

The career of the East India Company was not made any easier by the granting of a charter in 1698 to a rival company, the English Company Trading to the East Indies. However, the merger of the two companies in 1709 into the United Company of Merchants of England Trading to the East Indies marked the beginning of a reversal of fortunes. Within a decade, the new company emerged out of the VOC's shadow and began to assert itself as the dominant collective European actor in Asia (Furber, 1976; Chaudhuri, 1978).

This reversal of fortunes was part of an ongoing shift in the fulcrum of the system of European companies operating in Asia from pepper and spices to piece goods, and from the Malay archipelago to the Indian subcontinent. The beginning of the shift can be traced as far back as the 1680s, but its impact was not felt until half a century later. England's East India Company was both the main agency and the main beneficiary of the shift.

Trade in piece goods was one of the ingredients of the VOC's highly profitable intra-Asian trade. What made this trade highly profitable, however, was not trade in piece goods as such, but the VOC's monopolistic control over the supply of fine spices combined with the strength of the protection-producing apparatus with which the VOC enforced this control. "For the first time in the history of the Indian Ocean trade," observes Om Prakash (1987, 199), "there was a single agency engaged in a large volume of inter-port trade on a multilateral basis under the centralized direction and control of Batavia."

For the English Company, in contrast, homeward and intra-Asian trade in piece goods was the second-best choice, which it was forced into by the VOC's preemption of the more profitable opportunities afforded by the spice trade. The very extent and decentralized structure of the South Asian textile industry made the acquisition of monopolistic positions in the piece-goods trade a far more arduous and risky undertaking than in the spice trade. That's probably why the Dutch left the undertaking open to others. The English Company was the most important among these others. It started out at the beginning of the seventeenth century by concentrating on Surat and Bantam; by the 1680s, it had moved on to Madras and the Coromandel; and by the end of the century, it began to expand its operations in Bengal, Bihar, and Orissa.

In centralizing as much as it could of the Indian supply of piece goods, the English Company used the *dadni,* or contract system. Servants assigned to the company's factories advanced a sum of money to *dadni* merchants or their brokers, who in turn hired *paikars* or rural agents to deliver the money to and receive the cloth from the weavers. Upon delivery to the company's factories, the cloth was sorted and valued, and then penalties were extracted and commissions paid (see Sinha, 1953; also 1965, chapter 2; Chaudhuri, 1978, chapters 11–12; Raychaudhuri, 1982).

These factories were mostly trading posts designed to procure, store, and ship goods. From this point of view, there was no fundamental difference between this regime of factories and that established for its own trade by the VOC, or for that matter by the *Estado* before the VOC. But over time, the networks of procurement and supervision set up by the English far surpassed in volume and density those of their predecessors and competitors.

And yet, volume and density of its trade networks notwithstanding, the English Company continued to experience great difficulties eliminating the competition of other European companies, of European free traders, and of Armenian and other diaspora merchants. This competition brought a constant downward pressure to bear on profit margins in the piece-goods trade and this downward pressure, in turn, was responsible for the precariousness of the company's existence throughout the seventeenth century, as well as for its continual attempts to compensate for low profit margins through the expansion of its operations. It was this expansion that, over time, reversed the fortunes of the English vis-à-vis the Dutch.

This was one of the most fundamental contradictions of Dutch commercial supremacy. The supremacy was built on a highly selective choice of undertakings. Only undertakings that ensured high and steady pecuniary returns and simultaneously preserved the flexibility of Dutch capital in seizing profitable opportunities in the Amsterdam stock and commodity markets were selected. Thanks to this strategy, Amsterdam's commanding position in European commerce and high finance was established and consolidated. But the strategy relied heavily on markets created by the territorialist states of Europe, which pursued objectives of their own and which the Dutch were increasingly unable to subordinate to their own interests. More important, the strategy left plenty of room for rival enterprises to encroach on Dutch trade and to expand turnover in less profitable lines of business. As this happened—first in the West Indies, and then, starting in the early eighteenth century, in the East Indies as well—the contradiction was deepened by the tendency of Dutch surplus capital to flow, via Amsterdam's money market and stock exchange, to foreign governments and businesses, thereby sustaining their expansion (see chapter 1).

By the 1730s and 1740s, the stepping up of the activities not just of the English, but also of the French, Austrian, Danish, and Swedish East India Companies brought the VOC face to face with tougher and more widespread competition than it had been accustomed to in the preceding century (Neal, 1990, 218–23). Since this new situation in the East Indies was paralleled by growing encroachments on Dutch control over Baltic trade (Israel, 1989, 303–4), we may well take it as symptomatic of the fact that around 1740, Dutch commercial supremacy had for all practical purposes come to an end.

The Rise of the English East India Company

The demise of the VOC and the full expansion of the wealth and power of the East India Company were coeval trends of the second half of the eighteenth century. The latter was most important, not just in bringing to a close the era of joint-stock chartered companies, but also in preparing for the subsequent rise of Britain's Free Trade Imperialism. It was simultaneously a commercial and a territorial expansion, but territorial expansion led the way.

At the beginning of the eighteenth century, the territorial acquisitions of the East India Company were still limited to a few coastal settlements. Soon, however, the Mughal empire on the Indian subcontinent began to disintegrate into a multiplicity of autonomous provincial governments, warrior states, and small kingdoms. This disintegration threatened to disrupt the trading operations of the company, but also presented it with an opportunity to replace the Mughal court as the dominant governmental organization of South Asia (cf. Marshall, 1987; Bayly, 1988).

In the 1740s, the size and scope of the company's military forces began to expand and to be reorganized along European lines. On the eve of Plassey (1757), Indian battalions were formed and the company thus came to combine superior European techniques using and controlling violence with an extensive use of local manpower. It was this combination, more than anything else, that accounts for the success of the company in defeating all local rivals in the struggle for Mughal succession (McNeill, 1982, 135; Bayly, 1988, 85).

Initially, the English Company was not alone in bringing European military techniques to bear on South Asian politics. The French Company moved in the same direction, and for a decade or two, French competition was the main obstacle on the road to English political primacy in the region. But once French rivalry was eliminated in the course of the Seven Years' War, the conquest of a South Asian territorial empire by the English East India Company became only a question of time. With the defeat of the combined forces of Mir Kazim, Shah Alam II, and the Wazir of Awadh in the Battle of Buxar in 1764, the company acquired a major territorial foothold in Bengal and began to play a dominant role in the Indian interstate system. From then on, the reach and scope of its commercial operations expanded rapidly under the auspices of an increasingly powerful "company state" (Marshall, 1987).

This expansion was accompanied and sustained by major changes in the strategies and organization of the company in India. Following a practice introduced in Bengal in the 1750s, the *dadni* system was replaced by an agency system. Under the new system, each of the company's factories brought into its organizational domain one or more *arangs*—specialized centers of production in the districts where there were concentrations of artisans (Raychaudhuri, 1982, 282). *Gumashta*s were hired by the chief of each factory to provide the company with greater control over the labor of the weavers in each of the *arangs*. Each *gumashta,* in turn, coordinated the activities of a staff of twenty or so employees responsible for such tasks as overseeing production, appraising cloth, enforcing contracts, keeping the *arang*'s accounts, paying wages, writing correspondence, and bearing goods (Bhattacharya, 1983; Hossain, 1988).

The transformation of the company into an increasingly powerful territorial organization enabled it to deploy its coercive apparatus in support of its intervention in the labor process, as it did through the assignment of military personnel to protect and support the *gumashta*s and their staff, or through the later enactment of legislation requiring weavers to work exclusively for the company. Equally important, the new coercive powers of the company state were used to eliminate the competition of other European companies. Thanks to these actions, the company could continue to expand its trade in piece goods without driving down profit margins for another twenty to thirty years, that is, until the 1780s, when expansion in this line of business began to level off.

By then, however, the company had acquired other, more important sources of revenue, which were rapidly transforming it into a redistributive organization not altogether different from the Portuguese *Estado* of old. Starting with the acquisition of the Bengali *diwani* in 1765, the company had gone into the business of levying and collecting revenue in the form of taxes. As the sovereignty of the company state expanded functionally and spatially, revenues from this source increased massively and the burden of taxation on agricultural producers reached unprecedented heights (Bagchi, 1982, 79–81). Since it was common for weavers to belong to households that engaged in some kind of agricultural production, this meant that they came to be squeezed simultaneously in the fields and in the workshops and were thus pressured into giving up more and more of their labor directly or indirectly to the company (Hossain, 1979).

The company, for its part, used these proceeds to cover various expenses in London and Asia. These included some of the costs of the China trade, the expenses involved in the further expansion of the company's territorial domains in South Asia, and the expenses of wars against rival companies and states. It was one of these wars that in 1795–96 ousted the VOC from Ceylon and precipitated its terminal crisis.

As we shall see, these developments were not without contradictions for the East India Company itself. But first let us underscore how, by the end of the eighteenth century, the system of joint-stock chartered companies had come full circle. Spearheaded by the VOC, the system had begun its career in the early seventeenth century through a reversal of the relationship between power and profit that had been typical of the activities of the *Estado*. By the end of its career two centuries later, this relationship had been reversed once again by the chartered companies themselves. Power was back in command, and the company that proved fittest in effecting this new reversal (the English Company) came out on top (cf. Furber, 1976, 3).

From this point of view, the main difference between the VOC and the English Company lay in the line of business in which they had specialized and in the environment that was most appropriate for this specialization. The spice trade and the Malay archipelago were the line of business and the environment that promised and delivered the highest rate of profit; and their preemptive occupation by the VOC accounts for its extraordinary success as a business enterprise and governmental organization throughout the seventeenth century. The piece-goods trade and the Indian subcontinent, in contrast, promised and delivered a lower rate of profit, but they were also the line of business and the environment best suited for the appropriation of tribute. This difference accounts for the difficulties experienced for more than a century by the English Company in matching the business and governmental performance of the VOC. But it also accounts for the fact that, once the appropriation of tribute became the main source of self-expansion for joint-stock chartered companies, the performance of the English Company began to outshine that of the VOC until the latter was driven out of business.

The Supersession of Joint-Stock Chartered Companies

The victory of the East India Company in the eighteenth century competitive struggle did not guarantee its survival once the struggle was over. Victory itself and the means deployed to attain it became the source of troubles which, over time, led to the demise of the English Company and the final supersession of the system of joint-stock chartered companies by Britain's Free Trade Imperialism. These troubles were in part due to the tendency of the English Company to destroy the main foundation of its own vitality: the existence of rich and well-articulated markets, the vitality of which the company had turned to its advantage. But in exploiting this vitality, the company sapped it and thereby undermined the conditions of continued expansion. As Christopher Bayly (1988, 135) sums up the process, "[t]he East India Company had penetrated the subcontinent by making use of its buoyant markets in produce and land revenue. But the needs of its financial and military machine had tended to snuff out that buoyant entrepreneurship of revenue farmers, merchants and soldiers which kept the indigenous system functioning."

To some extent, this tendency reflected a superexploitation of the human and natural resources incorporated within the company's domains. Too much was squeezed out of labor in the fields or workshops or both for workers to be in a position to reproduce individually and collectively their livelihood and productiveness within and across generations. And the attempts of the laboring classes to procure means of livelihood against all odds often led to a superexploitation of land and other natural resources, which tended to destroy the productiveness of nature as well (Bagchi, 1982, 71, 79–80, 84).

However, the most serious problem was not so much the superexploitation of resources as major dysfunctions in the company's governance of the subject economies. One of these dysfunctions was noted by Marx himself, who was otherwise quite unapologetic about Western rule in Asia.

> There have been in Asia, generally, from immemorial times, but three departments of Government: that of Finance, or the plunder of the interior; that of War, or the plunder of the exterior; and finally, the department of Public Works . . . Now, the British in East India accepted from their predecessors the department of finance and of war, but they have neglected entirely that of public works. (Quoted in Bagchi, 1982, 85)

As Amiya Bagchi notes, by the time Marx was writing, this state of affairs had already changed, because in the 1820s the East India Company had begun to plow some of the tribute exacted from the Indian economy back into restoring and expanding its infrastructure. However, there was another, more fundamental dysfunction in the company's "mode of regulation" of the South Asian economy which, instead of being remedied, got worse over time. Most or all of the tribute exacted by the Mughals and earlier rulers went back into local circulation, not just through public works but through all kinds of ordinary expenditures. The tribute exacted by the company, in contrast, was not only larger—in Bengal twice as large as under the Mughals, according to some contemporary estimates—but was in good part withdrawn from local circulation to be siphoned off to Britain directly or through the China trade (Bagchi, 1982, 80–81, 96–97).

It follows that the predecessors of the company provided the extensive and complex indigenous system of agro-industrial production both with the effective demand necessary for its daily reproduction and the capital necessary to maintain its productiveness over the long haul. The company's management of the Indian economy was instead deficient on both counts, and thus progressively undermined the surplus-yielding capacity of its domains, that is, the very source of its vitality both as company and as state. A first sign of things to come was the tripling of the company's debt between 1798 and 1806, despite a huge acquisition of territory (Bayly, 1988, 84).

This contradiction was aggravated by the tendency of joint-stock chartered companies to contribute with their successful expansion overseas to the emergence of forces at home opposed to their trade privileges. For the liquidity, effective demand, and investments that the company did not return to the circuits of the Indian economy found their way into the circuits of the British economy, thereby contributing to its industrial expansion (see chapter 1). Instead of benefiting the company, however, industrial expansion at home undermined the legitimacy of its privileges. Thus, Birmingham and other provincial manufacturers were in the forefront of the campaign to abolish the company's monopoly of the India trade (Moss, 1976). The monopoly was actually abolished in 1813 with the declared objective of increasing employment and preserving the "tranquillity of the manufacturing population" after the emergence of Luddism (Farnie, 1979, 97).

For about twenty years after the abolition of the India trade monopoly, the company adjusted to the new situation primarily through greater reliance on its continuing monopoly of the China trade. The tea trade with China had been a highly profitable subsidiary activity of the company since the early eighteenth century. Initially, its expansion had been seriously constrained by the lack of demand for European goods in China and the consequent need to ship bullion to purchase tea. The constraint was relaxed when the conquest of Bengal gave the company new means—silver, textiles, and raw cotton—with which to undertake the China trade. But the trade did not enter its golden age until the company began to push sales of opium in China and to monopolize opium production in India. These developments were already under way before the abolition of the company's monopoly of trade with India. But once the monopoly was abolished, the concentration of the company's efforts on this line of business led to an explosive growth of shipments of opium, from 42,527 chests in the decade 1803–13 to 143,123 chests in the decade 1823–33 (Greenberg, 1951, chapter 5, appendix I; Bagchi, 1982, 96–97).

Greater reliance on the China trade helped the company to keep at bay, but not resolve, the underlying contradictions of its mode of operation. The political instability created by the company's territorial expansion in the subcontinent was compounded by the social instability engendered by the loss of its India trade monopoly and the consequent opening of its domains to private merchants who dumped on the weakened structures of the indigenous agro-industrial system the full weight of the competition of British machinofacture. These structures collapsed and the attempt to remedy the situation through expenditures in public works was simply too little too late. Costs of protection escalated beyond the means of the company, and the further curtailment of these means by the abolition in 1833 of the company's trade monopoly with China sounded its death knell. Increasingly, the company appeared to friends and foes alike as incompetent to rule the empire it had conquered, and when this empire was taken over by the British government, few really cared about the company any more.

From Family Capitalism to Corporate Capitalism, U.S.-Style

Industrialism and Family Capitalism

The strategies and structures of the system of family business enterprise that became dominant in the early nineteenth century did not constitute an absolute break with the strategies and structures of the system of joint-stock chartered companies that had been dominant in the preceding two centuries. In key respects, they continued by other means the pursuits of the system they superseded. Joint-stock chartered companies were business organizations empowered by European governments to exercise in the extra-European world statemaking and warmaking functions, both as ends in themselves and as means of commercial expansion. As long as the companies performed these functions more effectively and economically than the governments themselves could, they were granted trading privileges and protection commensurate to the usefulness of their services. But as soon as they no longer did, the companies were deprived of their privileges or dissolved by the governments. Their governmental functions in the extra-

European world, however, were not abolished. They were simply taken over by the metropolitan governments themselves.

This was a strictly pragmatic course of action. As Davies (1957, 152) remarks, in belaboring the African Company in the *Wealth of Nations,* Adam Smith "wrote of the dead." As previously noted, once joint-stock chartered companies had established the Atlantic triangular trade, they could not prevent smaller, unregulated, and more flexible enterprises from growing in the interstices of the companies' formally regulated trade. Nor could they prevent these smaller companies from thriving on and deepening the inefficiencies and contradictions of the companies' bureaucratic structures, and from forming increasingly powerful coalitions opposed to the trade monopolies on which the existence of the companies depended. The very usefulness of the companies in opening up new trade opportunities, in other words, made them obsolete in the subsequent exploitation of those opportunities.

Adam Smith himself—while maintaining that joint-stock chartered companies "have in the long-run proved, universally, either burdensome or useless, and have either mismanaged or confined the trade"— had to concede that "they may, perhaps, have been useful for the first introduction of some branches of commerce, by making, at their own expence, an experiment which the state might not think prudent to make" (Smith, 1961, II, 255). This usefulness was much greater and lasted much longer in the East than in the West Indies. But even in the East Indies, to paraphrase Davies's previously quoted diagnosis of the troubles of the African Company, "[b]eyond a certain point, the advantages of a large capital and large-scale organization began to be outweighed by the disadvantages of cumbersome administration, inadequate supervision and slow response to changing needs." When this point was reached, it became prudent for the British state to step in to govern the territorial conquests of the East India Company in the British national interest, rather than letting the company continue in an undertaking that had outgrown its organizational capabilities.

Smith's influential theories notwithstanding, the abrogation of the company's trade monopolies in the early nineteenth century was no less a pragmatic course of action than the abrogation of the African Company's monopoly in the early eighteenth century. When in the late nineteenth century joint-stock chartered companies appeared to have become useful again, new ones were launched. The most successful specimen of this new breed of joint-stock chartered companies, the

British South Africa Company, combined characteristics of formality and informality.

> What rights it possessed . . . were intended to be the basis for concessions to others rather than the direct activity of its own. Its profits would derive from the work of subcontractors. The company, in short, was a giant concessionaire. (Galbraith, 1974, 122)

Although several of the British South African Company's offsprings thrived in the corporate economy of the twentieth century, the late nineteenth century revival of joint-stock chartered companies was temporary and soon overshadowed by the rise of new and more powerful forms of corporate business. A return to the old system of joint-stock chartered companies was impossible primarily because, in the meantime, the world capitalist system had been thoroughly reorganized.

At the level of means, the nineteenth-century reorganization of world capitalism can be described as a process of diffusion of mechanization. This diffusion occurred through a seemingly endless sequence of related innovations: one, from cotton spinning forward to weaving and finishing and backward to the processing of raw cotton; and two, from extractive and manufacturing activities in general to transport and communications, and from these back to manufacturing (Marx, 1959, 383–84). As David Landes (1969, 2) prefaced his own reconstruction of this sequence of innovations, "[i]n all of this diversity of technological improvement, the unity of the movement is apparent: change begat change."

And yet, change begat change only up to a point. The capitalist nature of the underlying objective of industrial expansion was both its main foundation and its main limit. Just as the commercial expansion of Dutch capital in the seventeenth and early eighteenth centuries was based on, and limited by, a reversal in the relationship between "profit" and "power," so the industrial expansion of British capital in the nineteenth century was based on, and limited by, a reversal in the relationship between "profit" and "livelihood." This reversal had two main aspects. One, underscored by Marx throughout his work, was the subordination of labor to capital in production processes (see especially Marx, 1976). The other, underscored by Polanyi (1957, especially chapter 3), was the subordination of the motive of subsistence to the motive of gain in the regulation of social life.

Machines were expensive and specialized. Their profitable use required that labor's ways of life and work interfered as little as possible with their steady operation at full capacity. At the same time, the mechanized labor process enabled employers to "cage" individual workers into a sequence of operations that tied them all to one another and deprived them all of control over the pace and rhythms of their labors. As Sidney Pollard (1965, 184) underscores, it was "machinery [which] ultimately forced the worker to accept the discipline of the factory."

The use of machines in production processes thus provided capitalist entrepreneurs with both a new rationale and new means for enforcing a more thorough subordination of labor to the commands of capital. The greater the success of capitalist employers in forcing or enticing workers to accept the discipline of the factory, the easier it became for the mechanized factory system to outcompete the artisanal system in procuring inputs and disposing of outputs. Conversely, the greater the success of the factory system in outcompeting the artisanal system, the easier it became for capitalist employers to force displaced artisans and their dependents to put up with the discipline of the machine. A virtuous/vicious circle—virtuous for capitalist employers, vicious for displaced artisans and their dependents—thus came into operation: while workers were being deprived of their established ways of life and work, capitalist employers came to enjoy seemingly unlimited, low-cost supplies of labor power and other primary inputs, as well as seemingly unlimited remunerative outlets for their outputs.

This kind of virtuous/vicious circle was particularly important in sustaining the spread of machinofacture from spinning to weaving in the cotton industry and, more generally, in sustaining processes of capitalist expansion in Britain during the long downswing in commodity prices that followed the end of the Napoleonic Wars. In 1813, there were fewer than 3,000 powerlooms in the British cotton industry; twenty years later there were 100,000, and in 1861 four times as many. Between 1813 and 1833, the spread of powerlooms did not result in the displacement of handloom weavers in the British cotton industry, their numbers remaining in the 200,000–250,000 range throughout the period. Then, from the mid-1830s onward, rapid displacement set in. By 1850, only 40,000 were left. Fifteen years later, weaving in the British cotton industry had been completely taken over by the factory system and handloom weavers had become extinct (Crouzet, 1982, 199; Wood, 1910, 593–99).

The destruction of artisanal textile production was even more massive, if less complete, overseas—especially but not exclusively in India. The abolition of the East India Company's monopoly in 1813 let loose on the already debilitated Indian craft industry the "heavy artillery" of cheap cotton goods from British factories. By the 1860s, India had been "deindustrialized" as thoroughly as it possibly could have been, and the stage was set for its subsequent partial "reindustrialization" on the basis of the factory system (Morris, 1965; 1982; Crouzet, 1982, 194; Bairoch, 1976, 83).

The recovery of capital accumulation in Britain from the postwar depression of the late 1810s and early 1820s was thus closely associated with a progressive destruction of artisanal textile production both in Britain and in India. Destruction in Britain was particularly important in creating seemingly unlimited, low-cost supplies of labor for the expanding Lancashire factory system. Destruction in India was particularly important in creating seemingly unlimited remunerative outlets for its products. An insignificant outlet for British cotton goods up to 1813, by 1843 India had become the single biggest market for such goods, taking up 23 percent of their export in 1850 and 31 percent ten years later (Chapman, 1972, 52).

This process of "creative destruction"—through which profitable opportunities for the spread of mechanization were created by destroying artisanal production—was self-limiting. It could go on only as long as there still were large and unprotected "reserves" of artisanal production that capitalist production could easily outcompete. But as we have just seen, by the early 1860s the expansion of mechanized production had already wiped out the two largest concentrations of artisans within easy reach of the British factory system. From then on, attempts to keep up the expansion would inevitably intensify competitive pressures on the units of the factory system themselves, squeezing the profits of them all.

This same tendency toward an eventual intensification of competitive pressures was inherent in the process of diffusing mechanization from manufacturing to transport and back to manufacturing. Like the diffusion of mechanization from cotton spinning to weaving, this process took off during the long downswing in prices that followed the end of the Napoleonic Wars. As noted in chapter 1, the rapid expansion of government demand during these wars had created a large iron industry in Britain with a capacity well in excess of peacetime needs, as the postwar depression of 1816–20 demonstrated. However, overexpansion created the conditions for renewed growth in the future by giving British entrepreneurs extraordinary incentives to seek new uses for the cheaper products that the new, large-scale furnaces could turn out (McNeill, 1982, 211–12; see also Jenks, 1938, 133–34).

These new uses were soon found in the iron railway and later in iron ships. Combined with the contemporaneous spread of mechanization within the textile industry, these innovations progressively transformed the British capital goods industry into an autonomous and powerful engine of capitalist expansion (Minchinton, 1973, 164–68). Up to the 1820s, enterprises specializing in the production of fixed capital goods had very little autonomy from their customers, be they governmental or business organizations, which, as a rule, subcontracted or closely supervised the manufacture of whatever fixed capital goods they required and did not themselves produce. But as the spread of mechanization increased the number, range, and variety of fixed capital goods in use, the enterprises that specialized in their production actively sought new outlets for their merchandise among actual or potential competitors of their established clientele (Saul, 1968, 186–87).

For about half a century this increasing autonomy of the British capital goods industry, far from intensifying, relieved competitive pressures on British enterprises. British capital goods found a ready demand among governmental and business organizations all over the world. These organizations, in turn, stepped up their production of primary inputs for sale in Britain in order to procure the means necessary to pay for the capital goods or to service the debts incurred in their purchase (Mathias, 1969, 298, 315, 326–28). By mid-century, these joint tendencies resulted in a major boom in world trade and production during which the benefits of expanding supplies of primary inputs and expanding demand for British products more than compensated for the proliferation of nominal competitors due to the worldwide diffusion of British technology and capital goods (Hobsbawm, 1979, 37–54).

This was necessarily a temporary situation. The progressive filling of the vacuum of demand eventually left capitalist enterprises fully exposed to the cold winds of competition. And as profits fell—"squeezed between the upper millstone of price-competition and the lower of increasingly expensive and mechanized plant," as Hobsbawm (1968, 106) put it—the great euphoria of the 1850s and 1860s gave way to the Great Depression of 1873–96.

The Great Depression was as much a turning point in inter-enterprise relations as it was in interstate relations. It marked the beginning of the transition from the British system of family business to the American system of vertically integrated, bureaucratically managed multinational corporations. Like the earlier transition from the Dutch system of joint-stock chartered companies to the British system of family business, this transition was thoroughly embedded in the broader, synchronous processes of the interstate power struggle. In both transitions, the transformation of one dominant system of business enterprise to another did not proceed along some predetermined path inscribed in an invariant structure. Rather, the transformation occurred through a spatial shift of the system's center and a fundamental change in the way business enterprises related to one another and to governments. The governmental and business organizations of the declining center remained trapped in the particular path of development that had made their fortunes, while the opening up of a new path by the governmental and business organizations of the rising center owed as much to the ongoing processes of the interstate power struggle as to the innovations and mutual competition of the enterprises themselves.

The pattern of transformation of the dominant system of business enterprise that we can detect in both transitions is shown in figure 5. In sketching the pattern for the transition from British to U.S. hegemony, we shall distinguish three phases. In the first phase, which encompasses the Great Depression and the subsequent belle epoque of the Edwardian era, the British system attained its maximum expansion but began to be challenged by the emergence of corporate capitalism, not just in the United States, but in Germany as well. In the second phase of the transition, from the outbreak of the First World War to the Crash of 1929, the British system itself underwent major transformations in a corporatist direction but lost ground to the emergent American system. The transition was completed in the third phase, when the restructuring of the American system, under the impact of the Great Depression of the 1930s and the Second World War, prepared it for global dominance in the Cold War era. The next three sections deal with each phase in turn.

The Challenge of Vertical Integration

The corporate economy of the twentieth century is a child of the Great Depression of 1873–96. As Adam Smith had predicted a century earlier,

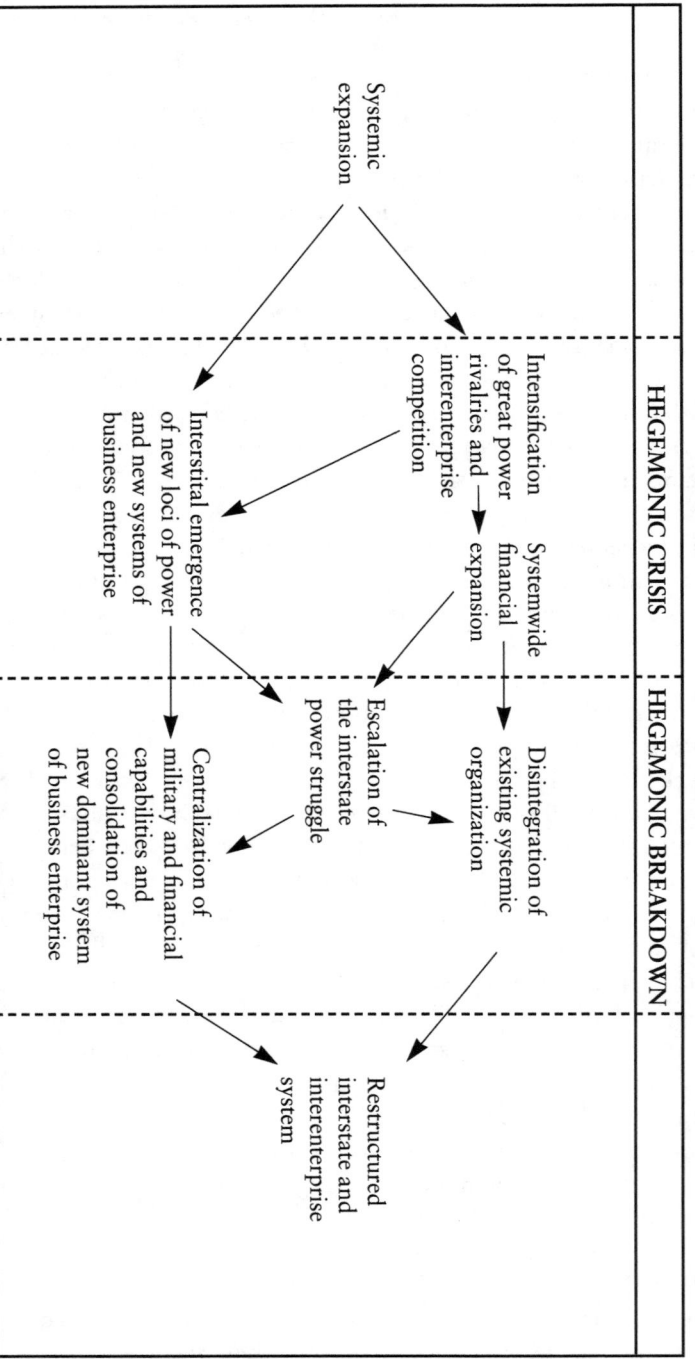

Figure 5. Hegemonic transitions and the transformation of the dominant system of business enterprise.

the intensification of competitive pressures inherent in the process of trade liberalization had resulted in a curtailment of profits to a barely "tolerable" level. That the outcome had been predicted was of little consolation to the entrepreneurs who lived for and by profit. And the fiercer the competition, the harder they struggled to bring it under control. As Edward S. Meade wrote with specific reference to U.S. manufacturers, businessmen were "tired of working for the public." "They want a larger profit without such a desperate struggle to get it" (quoted in Sklar, 1988, 56).

One obvious means in this endeavor was horizontal combination— the fusion through association, merger, or takeover of enterprises using much the same inputs to make much the same outputs for much the same markets. Through combinations of this kind, competing enterprises could reduce market uncertainties for one another; they could set their combined production, purchases, and sales at levels that would guarantee larger profits; and they could pool resources to break into unregulated markets, to develop new technologies, and to organize their operations more effectively. Horizontal combinations, however, were not easy to enforce in overcrowded markets—that is, precisely where they were most needed—especially in the absence of support by governments.

A more roundabout but, where feasible, more effective means of bringing the competition under control was vertical integration—the fusion, that is, of an enterprise's operations with those of its suppliers and customers, so as to ensure supplies "upstream" toward primary production, and outlets "downstream" toward final consumption. The multi-unit enterprises that resulted from this fusion were in a position to reduce the transaction costs, risks, and uncertainties involved in moving inputs/outputs through the sequential subprocesses of production and exchange that linked the procurement of primary inputs to the disposal of final outputs.

> By routinizing the transactions between units, the costs of the transactions were lowered. By linking the administration of producing units with buying and distributing units, costs of information on markets and sources of supply were reduced. Of much greater significance . . . [m]ore effective scheduling of flows achieved a more intensive use of facilities and personnel employed in the process of production and distribution and so increased productivity and reduced costs. In addition, administrative coordination provided a

more certain cash flow and more rapid repayment for services rendered. (Chandler, 1977, 7)

As the large and steady cash flows ensured by this kind of centralization were plowed back into the creation of hierarchies of top and middle managers specialized in monitoring and regulating markets and labor processes, the vertically integrated enterprises acquired decisive competitive advantages vis-à-vis single-unit enterprises or less specialized multi-unit enterprises. Once established, these hierarchies became a far more imposing barrier than technology to new entry into the industries that had been successfully reorganized through vertical integration (Chandler, 1977, 299).

The tendencies toward horizontal combination and vertical integration set off by the intense, widespread, and persistent competition of the last quarter of the nineteenth century developed very unevenly among the business communities of the three main industrial countries of the time—Britain, the United States, and Germany. The German business community moved most rapidly and successfully in both directions, giving rise to that cohesive system of business enterprise that Rudolf Hilferding (1981) later turned into the paradigm of "organized capitalism." The British business community, in contrast, moved most slowly and least successfully in either direction—particularly in the direction of vertical integration. Finally, the U.S. business community fell somewhere in between, being less successful than the German in its early attempts to move in the direction of horizontal combination, but eventually emerging as the most successful of all in practicing vertical integration (Chandler, 1990).

The German pattern was thoroughly embedded in the state- and warmaking activities of the newly established German *Reich*. When the slump of 1873–79 hit Germany, the spread of unemployment, labor unrest, and socialist agitation, combined with a crippling fiscal crisis of the *Reich,* induced Chancellor Bismarck to intervene to protect German society, lest the ravages of unfettered market competition destroy the imperial edifice he had just built. At the same time, the growing convergence of agrarian and industrial interests in pressing for governmental protection from foreign competition provided Bismarck with unique opportunities to use the political power vested in the *Reich* executive "to secure a new balance of power between the *Reich* and the states . . . and to complete the national unification by cementing it with unbreakable economic ties" (Rosenberg, 1943, 67–68).

In cementing the unity of the German domestic economy and endowing the German state with a powerful military-industrial apparatus, the German government actively sought the assistance of enterprises in the forefront of the ongoing industrialization of war (see chapter 1) and, above all, six large banks. These *Grossbanken* had emerged out of the personal and interfamilial structure of German banking, still prevalent in the 1850s, primarily through the promotion and financing of railway companies and heavy industrial enterprises involved in railway construction (Tilly, 1967, 174–75, 179–80). Their dominance in German finance increased further during the slump of the 1870s. When a large proportion of their entrepreneurial and pecuniary resources were released by the nationalization of the railways in the 1880s, they moved swiftly to take over, integrate, and reorganize German industry in collusion with a small number of powerful industrial firms (Henderson, 1975, 178).

Whereas on the eve of the Great Depression family capitalism was still the norm in Germany as in Britain, by the turn of the century it had become a subordinate component of a highly centralized corporate structure. Over the next two decades centralization increased further, mostly through horizontal integration. To the extent that small and medium-sized enterprises survived, as many did, they lived on as subordinate members of a private command economy controlled by a closely knit group of financiers and industrialists acting through increasingly extensive and complex managerial bureaucracies. The German domestic economy, to paraphrase Engels (1958), was indeed beginning to look like "one big factory."

In sharp contrast with trends in Germany, in Britain "there was little movement toward the differentiation of management from ownership, toward the elongation of organizational hierarchies." In most industries, family businesses remained as dominant as they had been throughout the nineteenth century, so that the eventual domination of the nation's economic structure by the corporate enterprise can hardly be perceived in Britain before the First World War. At the end of the nineteenth century, very large mergers occurred in several industries. But the resulting giant businesses remained under the control of the vendors, with disastrous consequences for the effectiveness and efficiency of the combinations. Thus, the Calico Printers' Association, formed in 1899 by the amalgamation of fifty-nine firms, was described eight years later as "a study of disorganization." As the vice-chairman of another giant concern suffering from similar dysfunctions remarked, "it was an awful mistake to put into control of the various businesses purchased by the company the men from whom the businesses were purchased, because these men have got into one groove and could not get out of it" (Payne, 1974, 20–23).

In fact, it was much more than individual entrepreneurs who had gotten into one groove and could not get out of it. The entire British system of business enterprise was trapped into a particular path of development, which it could not abandon except at costs that far exceeded calculable benefits (cf. Ingham, 1995, 353). This was the path of a highly extroverted economic system that drew its raw materials from the whole world and depended critically on foreign outlets for the profitable disposal of its industrial production. As argued in chapter 1, Britain's role as the "workshop of the world" further increased its capacity to function as the commercial and financial entrepôt of the world economy. This enhanced capacity, in turn, provided British business with relatively well-protected market niches within which to specialize once its competitiveness in industrial production began to wane (Rubinstein, 1977; Ingham, 1984).

It is highly doubtful that it would have been more profitable for Britain to compete with the rising industrial nations through a fundamental restructuring of its industries than to specialize more fully, as it did, in its role as world commercial and financial intermediary. In any event, the capacity of British business to move toward the kind of reorganization that was sustaining rapid industrial expansion in Germany and the United States was strictly limited by the highly decentralized and specialized structure inherited from its earlier industrial expansion. For throughout the nineteenth century, British industry in general, and the textile industry in particular, showed a strong tendency toward the *fission* rather than the fusion of sequential subprocesses of production and exchange—that is, toward vertical "disintegration" rather than integration. From about 1780 to the end of the Napoleonic Wars, leading London and provincial industrialists had ventured into overseas trade, often beginning in the United States and the West Indies, where most of the raw cotton for the English textile industry was procured. During the economic depression that followed the end of the war, however, the phenomenon was reduced to insignificance. As export markets became more dispersed and the supplies on which the competitiveness of British industries depended came to be procured more economically through volume cash purchases, British manufacturers lost the capacity to compete, and indeed the interest in competing, in overseas trade. Their competitive edge came to reside ever more firmly in specialized production in domestic market niches. The procurement of supplies and the disposal of outputs, in contrast, was left safely and profitably in the hands of equally specialized accepting houses, which promoted the formation and financed the growth of truly global networks of commission agents and small general merchants (Chapman, 1984, 9–15; 1992, 116; see also Farnie, 1979, 83).

The rapid spread of machinofacture from spinning to weaving in the second quarter of the nineteenth century was associated with some vertical integration of these two subprocesses. But after 1850 the tendency was reversed. Spinning, weaving, finishing, and marketing became the separate and specialized domains of different enterprises, often highly localized and specialized even within each branch. As a result, in the last quarter of the nineteenth century, the British system of business enterprise was more than ever an ensemble of highly specialized medium-sized firms held together by a complex web of commercial transactions—a web that was centered on Britain but spanned the entire world (Hobsbawm, 1968, 47–48; Gattrell, 1977, 118–20; Crouzet, 1982, 204–5, 212).

The main disadvantage of this extroverted, decentralized, and differentiated business structure was high transaction costs. "A pound of cotton arriving in Liverpool," noted Melvin Copeland (1966, 371), "frequently . . . will pay tribute to two Liverpool brokers, to a yarn agent and merchant, to a cloth agent, converter, and merchant, and finally to a wholesaler and retailer. During its course it may also have been the property of a spinner, a doubler, a weaver, and a printer." Nevertheless, the high transaction costs involved in this fragmented structure were more than compensated for by the advantages of being located in the "dense network of specialists" that had developed in the Lancashire industrial district—"a development which can hardly be matched elsewhere in the industrial world"—and of being connected to the markets of the entire world by a highly flexible commercial network (Copeland, 1966, 327–29).

The tentacles of the Manchester trade reach out to all corners of the world, and whatever form of manufactured cotton is sought, whatever accommodation is desired, some one can be found in Manchester ready to accept the commission. Of all the assets which make it possible for the cotton industry to attain its largest dimensions in a country which does not produce the raw material, and which consumes only ten or twenty per cent of the yarn and cloth manufactured in its mills, none is more significant than the adaptability of the commercial organization. (Copeland, 1966, 371)

The more British industrial enterprises specialized locally in processing world supplies for world markets, the more dependent they became upon commission agents and large-scale merchant importers, who were not as aggressive as the salesmen of much larger American and German enterprises. But even if they wanted to, they were "too small to afford a vigorous selling effort in world markets by means of a salaried force of commercial travellers" (Payne, 1974, 54). As foreign competition intensified, they had little choice but to specialize further within the global commercial network that supported and "caged" them at the same time. Thus, under the impact of the Great Depression of 1873–96, the tendency toward vertical *dis*integration, far from being reversed, became stronger. In 1884 firms combining spinning and weaving still accounted for 57.3 percent of the looms and 39 percent of the spindles in Lancashire, but by 1911 these shares were down to 33.7 and 20.5 percent respectively (Tyson, 1968, 119).

Further specialization within a global commercial network was neither the oniy nor indeed the main response of British entrepreneurs to the intensification of competitive pressures that ensued from the mid-nineteenth century world trade expansion. The rerouting of cash flows from production to moneylending and speculation, and from domestic to foreign investment, was far more important in determining the eventual outcome of the incipient crisis of the British system of business enterprise. For now, however, let us underscore that the British system of business enterprise did not generate from within its national core the tendency toward the vertical integration of subprocesses of production and exchange that was to become the dominant characteristic of business organization in the twentieth century. Just as the switch from the corporate to the family business form in the eighteenth and early nineteenth centuries was closely associated with a spatial shift of the epicenter of systemic processes of capital accumulation from the United Provinces to the United Kingdom, so the switch from the family to the corporate form of business in the late nineteenth and early twentieth centuries was closely associated with an analogous spatial shift from the United Kingdom to the United States.

It was in the United States that the tendency toward vertical integration developed most fully and successfully. Initially, the attempt to bring the competitive pressures of the late nineteenth century under control caused the United States to go in the same direction as Germany, that is, toward the formation of horizontal combinations in restraint of competition and toward an increasing dominance of a small group of private financial institutions that had grown through investments in railway companies and related industrial enterprises. In the United States, however, these nationwide associations of manufacturers mostly failed to attain their objectives long before they were declared illegal in 1890 by the Sherman Antitrust Act. And the dominance of financial institutions never went far beyond the construction and operation of railroad systems (Chandler, 1977, 317, 335, 187).

In the 1880s and 1890s, the changing structures of German and U.S. business began to diverge radically. In both countries the centralization of capital gained momentum. In Germany opportunities to pursue vertical integration were rapidly exhausted and the main thrust of the centralization of capital became horizontal combination (Landes, 1966, 109–10). In the United States, by contrast, the main thrust of the centralization of capital became vertical integration. As underscored by Alfred Chandler (1977, 1978, 1990), ineffectual, unpopular, and eventually illegal horizontal combinations were abandoned. Business enterprises in branches ranging from cigarettes and canned meat to office and agricultural machinery moved toward integrating within their organizational domains the sequential subprocesses of production and exchange. All phases, from the procurement of primary inputs to the disposal of final outputs, were linked within the single firm.

The greater speed at which primary inputs could be turned into final outputs by the vertically integrated enterprises enabled these enterprises to lower costs and increase production per worker and per machine faster and to a greater extent than single-unit enterprises or less specialized multi-unit enterprises. And as the large and steady cash flows generated by these "economies of speed" were plowed back into the creation of hierarchies of top and middle managers specialized in monitoring and regulating markets and labor processes, the competitive advantages of vertically integrated enterprises increased further. The result was a swift growth and diffusion of the new organizational structure. "Almost nonexistent at the end of the 1870s, these integrated enterprises came to dominate many of the most vital [U.S.] industries within less than three decades" (Chandler, 1977, 285).

Growth was not limited to the U.S. domestic market. U.S. corporations became multinational almost as soon as they had completed their continental integration (Hymer, 1972, 121). By 1902 Europeans were already speaking of an "American invasion"; and by 1914 U.S. direct investment abroad amounted to 7 percent of U.S. GNP—the same percentage as in 1966, when Europeans once again felt threatened by an "American challenge" (cf. Wilkins, 1970, 71, 201).

The Demise of the British System of Business Enterprise

In seeking an explanation for the triumph in the early twentieth century of the U.S. paradigm of mass production, Charles Sabel and Jonathan Zeitlin (1985, 164) advocate a reinterpretation of economic developments in the United States and Western Europe in the nineteenth century "as concurrent and competing attempts to elaborate a distinct variant of industrial technology suited to the particularities of national circumstances." While they have no difficulty identifying major national industrial variants, they nonetheless find that the origins of these variants remain obscure and the evidence of their clash in international competition too fragmentary to weigh heavily in defense of what they call the "many-worlds view" (Sabel and Zeitlin, 1985, 164–71).

The analysis here shows that the evidence supporting such a view is much stronger if we focus on systems of business enterprise, rather than on technological paradigms, as Sabel and Zeitlin do. Thus, the branching of nineteenth-century family capitalism into three distinct directions during the Great Depression of 1873–96 can be seen as originating in the different responses of the British, German, and U.S. business communities to the challenges posed by the intensifying competitive pressures typical of the time. Differences in response, in turn, largely correspond to differences in the national circumstances under which the three business communities operated.

The world-entrepôt function exercised by the British economy was the single most important factor conditioning the British response.

As competition in agro-industrial production intensified, British business specialized further in global commercial and financial intermediation, supported by the British government's more activist role in world politics. German business—unable to compete in global commercial and financial intermediation with British business, or in agricultural production with U.S. business and other overseas producers—moved instead in the direction of national-economy formation. Actively encouraged by the German government, it pushed vertical integration as far as it could and combined horizontally to generate that highly centralized state economy that became the model of Marxist theories of state monopoly capitalism. The U.S. business community, taking advantage of the continental size and natural self-sufficiency of the domestic economy, moved in a direction as distinct from the British as from the German: it did not go very far in the creation of a comprehensive system of horizontal combinations, but it created in most industries elongated managerial hierarchies through vertical integration.

This ramification of nineteenth-century family capitalism into several national developmental paths is indeed aptly described by the metaphor of a branching tree that Sabel and Zeitlin (1985, 163) derive from Stephen J. Gould. Right up to the First World War, family capitalism, supported by Free Trade Imperialism, remained the central and dominant form of business enterprise at the level of the world capitalist system. It continued, so to say, to constitute the "trunk" of the branching tree. The U.S. and German variants of corporate capitalism (along with lesser national systems of business enterprise), in contrast, were and remained just "branches" of the British "trunk," whose vitality and centrality they did not yet threaten seriously.

To be sure, sectors of British business did perceive U.S. and German advances in industrial production as a challenge to their continuing dominance in domestic and world markets. Alarm for "the American invasion" around the turn of the century was first vented in Britain—at this time the primary location of the overseas transplant of U.S. corporations (Wilkins, 1970, 70–71). Fear of German competition was no less acute (Landes, 1969, 328).

British fears were nonetheless grossly exaggerated. Speaking of the engineering industry, S. B. Saul (1968, 201) claims that the scare over the American invasion "was entirely artificial." For the first and only time since the 1830s, British railways had bought American engines;

but the purchase was due to "a dearth of home orders in the United States and booming order books for the British makers," hardly a sign of declining British competitiveness. Even when challenges were real, they were mostly limited to specific industries and British business could meet them easily (1) by taking over the new technologies through the purchase of machinery, as it did in the small arms and shoe industries (see Fries, 1975; Church, 1968); (2) by specializing more fully in the high-value-added activities associated with Britain's world-entrepôt functions; and (3) by establishing claims on the value added produced in other countries through foreign lending and investment.

The extent to which British business managed to keep at bay the German challenge in processes of capital accumulation without itself undergoing a major restructuring of the U.S. or German kind can be gauged by the discrepancy between the German "catching up" with Britain in industrial production on the one side, and in value added on the other. As David Landes (1969, 329) notes, "Where British output of manufactured commodities . . . slightly more than doubled from 1870 to 1913, against a German increase of almost sixfold, the ratio between the rising incomes of the two countries, whether calculated in aggregate or *per capita,* was of the order of 0.7 or 0.8 to 1." In other words, Germany had to expand industrial output almost three times faster than Britain to make a relatively small gain in value added. As underscored in chapter 1, the rise of German industrial might did pose a serious threat to British national security and world power. But until that threat materialized in a military confrontation, British supremacy in global processes of capital accumulation remained unchallenged.

Even then, it was not German but U.S. corporate capitalism that began unseating British family capitalism from its position of global dominance. In the half century preceding the First World War, the United States, unlike Germany, had caught up and surpassed Britain not just in industrial production, but in aggregate and per capita income as well. Nevertheless, the explosive growth of British foreign investment in this same period had mortgaged to British residents a significant and growing share of the increase in incomes generated in the United States. Thus, between 1870 and 1914, foreign investment and long-term lending to the United States amounted to $3 billion. But during this same period, the United States made net payments of interest and dividends, mostly to Britain, amounting to $5.8 billion. The consequence was an increase in the U.S. foreign debt from $200 million in 1843 to $3,700 million in 1914 (Knapp, 1957, 433). Britain, in contrast, at the beginning of the First World War had nearly one-half of its assets overseas and received about 10 percent of its national income in the form of interest on foreign investment (Cairncross, 1953, 3, 23).

As Peter Mathias (1969, 329) has pointed out with specific reference to British investment in the United States, "this was not just 'blind capital' but the 'blind capital' of *rentiers* organized by financiers and businessmen very much with a view to the trade that would be flowing when the enterprise was under way." British railway building in the United States and, a fortiori, in countries like Australia, Canada, South Africa, and Argentina, "was instrumental in opening up these vast land masses and developing export sectors in primary produce . . . for Britain" (see also Chapman, 1992, 233 ff). Capital lending was no less "blind" in creating outlets for Britain's own exports.

> The complex of activities into which capital lending fitted can be most clearly seen in such a case as China where the British firm Jardine Mathieson was in the lead. They organized the raising of loans to Chinese provincial governments (on which they took the margin). They supplied the railways at a profit, sometimes shipped the equipment on their own shipping lines, which brought in freight charges, and supplied equipment and arms to the contestants in the wars whose strategy was being shaped by the railways. Such a pyramid of activities . . . makes it difficult actually to work out a rate of profit on the loans for parties that were hoping to profit from them in so many interrelated ways. (Mathias, 1969, 328)

In short, the overabundant liquidity that accumulated in, or passed through, British hands was a powerful instrument in the competitive struggle that ensued from the growing "industrialization" of the world capitalist system. What eventually destroyed the centrality and vitality of British family capitalism was not market competition, but military confrontation.

> A world war could simply not be combined with "business as usual." By 1918 the government had taken over the running of several industries, controlled others by requisitioning their output or licensing, organized its own bulk purchases abroad, restricted capital expenditure and foreign trade, fixed prices and controlled the distribution of consumer goods. Fiscal policy was used—clumsily—to divert more resources to the war effort than people were willing to forgo, largely

by indirectly induced inflation. One part of this fiscal war-effort, the so-called McKenna duties of 1915 . . . made the first *de facto* breach in the wall of Free Trade. . . . In fact between 1916 and 1918 Britain was forced to evolve a first incomplete and reluctant sketch of that powerful state-economy of the Second World War. (Hobsbawm, 1968, 203)

The First World War and its aftermath thus played a decisive role in precipitating the demise of the British system of family business enterprise and the corresponding rise of the U.S. system of corporate business. In business as in government, however, the destruction of an old regime does not in itself bring into existence a new regime. The First World War and its aftermath destroyed the vitality and centrality of the British system of business enterprise, but it took another great depression and another world war before the emergent U.S. system acquired the capabilities necessary to become dominant on a world scale.

As long as vertically integrated, multi-unit enterprises remained the exception rather than the rule in the U.S. domestic economy, and the U.S. domestic economy itself enclosed only a fraction of world purchasing power, the expansion of such enterprises was sustained by the takeover of single-unit enterprises and the diversion of purchasing power from the rest of the world to the United States. By the end of the First World War, these two sources of exogenous support began to wane. The war brought about a major redistribution of purchasing power from the rest of the world to the United States, so that much less remained to be diverted to the U.S. economy. Moreover, by 1919 the process of displacing the structures of family capitalism in the United States was nearly complete. Out of thirty-eight "key" industries, only four were not dominated by the hundred largest corporations. Moreover, even in non-key industries, which by and large remained unconcentrated, the large enterprises of the key industries exercised a growing influence over the flow and prices of goods through their purchases from, and sales to, the smaller single function, single-unit enterprises (Chandler, 1978, 120).

By the end of the First World War, in other words, the emergent U.S. system of corporate capitalism had come to stand or fall on its own. It could no longer expand by sapping the residual vitality of family capitalism domestically and internationally. It could expand only on the basis of its own vitality.

The Rise to Global Dominance of
Corporate Capitalism, U.S.-Style

To cope with the new situation, U.S. corporate business underwent a major reorganization characterized by product diversification and the consequent adoption of a multidivisional organizational structure—a structure, that is, "consisting of autonomous and integrated operating divisions and a general office, that appraised and planned the work of the divisions and the corporation as a whole" (Chandler, 1978, 121). As William Lazonick (1991, 32) has noted, the multidivisional organizational structure that emerged in the 1920s and spread rapidly in the 1930s and 1940s arose out of the need for already dominant enterprises "to move into new product lines and regional markets in order to continue to transform the high fixed costs inherent in . . . past investments into low unit costs as old product lines and markets became saturated or outmoded." And yet, "to move into new products and regions required even more fixed costs for ongoing research and development facilities as well as for the plant, equipment, and personnel required to produce the new products and service the new markets." The multidivisional structure, in other words, continually recreated at an ever higher level of organizational complexity the need to diversify operations out of which it had originated.

As it moved in the direction of product and market diversification, U.S. corporate capitalism moved also in the direction of "manufacturing" customers. Consumerism, writes Stuart Ewen (1976, 54), "emerged in the 1920s not as a smooth progression from earlier and less 'developed' patterns of consumption, but rather as an aggressive device of corporate survival." Under the impact of a sharp contraction in market share, Ford Motor Company itself was forced to introduce significant style and equipment changes, thereby relaxing its fixation with standardized mass production (Hounshell, 1984, 275–76). New fashions had to be invented to keep plants running once the original market had been supplied.

> Within the ideal of a "scientifically" managed industry, raw materials and consumers were both viewed as malleable. They both would have to be shaped by the demands of the production line, pecuniary interests, and the newly emergent managerial tools of capital. (Ewen, 1976, 25–26)

Advertising became the main weapon in the struggle of U.S. corporate business against "puritanism in consumption," as Leverett Lyon in 1922 branded all patterns of life that resisted domination by the needs of industrial machinery. The need to influence human conduct, "encoded within the rhetoric of some businessmen a revealing idiom; 'human conduct' or the 'consumer's dollar' became equivalent to industrial discoveries, more valuable to manufacturing 'than the uses of electricity or steel'" (Ewen, 1976, 26, 56–57).

The extent to which advertising could overcome "puritanism in consumption" was nonetheless limited by the imperatives of capital accumulation in the context of a disintegrating world market. "Despite rhetorical calls among business people for 'higher wages' as a tactic of social integration," observes Ewen (1976, 57), "wages among the vast number of working people remained too low and the desire for expanding profits among business too high to create a high level of material participation by workers in the commodity market." Backed by insufficient purchasing power, the new needs created by advertising did not translate into an increase of *effective* demand large enough to sustain the profitable expansion of mass production. After 1921, the expansion of mass production in the United States occurred under conditions of profitability inferior to those of 1900–1920 (Duménil, Glick, and Rangel, 1987, 354ff). And when foreign outlets for U.S. business collapsed in the wake of the Crash of 1929 and the tariff war triggered by the Smoot-Hawley Tariff Bill (see chapter 1), mass production experienced the most serious crisis of its history.

The emergent U.S. system of corporate business had come to stand or fall on its own and had failed the test. As the banker Paul Mazur put it in the columns of the *New York Times*, "the power of production . . . has been so great that its products have multiplied at geometric rates . . . at the same time the power of consumption—even under the influence of stimuli damned as unsocial and tending toward profligacy [for example, advertising and built-in obsolescence]—has expanded only at a comparatively slow arithmetic rate." The result had been "overproduction and the disastrous discontinuity of industry that comes as a consequence" (quoted in Hounshell, 1984, 322).

The Great Depression of the 1930s did not reverse the tendency to stimulate consumption through advertising and built-in obsolescence. But its main effect was to induce big business to multiply its efforts to regain some flexibility in adjusting to market conditions through subcontracting to outside suppliers (Hounshell, 1984, 299–300). This strategy was no more successful in sustaining the profitable expansion of U.S. corporate business than the strategy of product and market diversification and the adoption of the multidivisional form of organization. What eventually pulled U.S. big business out of the depth of the Great Depression of the 1930s was not its own strategies of survival, but massive government expenditure during and after the Second World War. As Lewis Mumford (1934, 93–94) had noted, "Quantity production must rely for its success upon quantity consumption; and nothing ensures replacement like organized destruction. . . . War . . . is the health of the machine." The Second World War fully confirmed the validity of this diagnosis (Hounshell, 1984, 330).

As the French Regulation School (Aglietta, 1979; Boyer, 1988; 1990) has underscored, already before the war the New Deal had inaugurated the conscious intervention of the U.S. government in creating aggregate demand conditions favorable to the expansion of mass production. But as the new economic collapse of 1937–38 demonstrated, the intervention had failed in its objective. Robert Brenner and Mark Glick (1991, 92) say that "The New Deal, in itself, had little or nothing to do with the end of the depression." This is an exaggeration, because increasing government expenditures do stimulate effective demand even when they are balanced by increased taxation, as they were under the New Deal. Without this stimulus, the depression might have become much worse than it actually was, thereby making the subsequent recovery more problematic. It remains nonetheless true that, as they conclude, "In so far as a rise in demand helped pull the economy from the depression . . . the impetus came . . . from massive deficit spending on armaments."

After the war, massive deficit spending on armaments was institutionalized in what James O'Connor (1973, chapter 6) has aptly characterized as the U.S. "warfare-welfare state." Military expenditures without precedent in periods of peace (DeGrasse, 1983, 20–21), combined with the U.S. federal government's commitment under the Employment Act of 1946 to maintaining maximum employment and the largest possible aggregate demand, finally brought to fruition the strategic and structural innovations introduced by U.S. corporate business in the 1920s and 1930s. The multidivisional form of organization, which had failed to rescue U.S. big business from the Great Depression, now turned into a key instrument in meeting the demand of the U.S. federal government for military and advanced scientific hardware.

> During the years of the Cold War, the government required a wide variety of weapons, ranging from aircraft, carriers, missiles and submarines to conventional guns and tanks, as well as nuclear reactors for the Atomic Energy Commission and the spaceships with all their accoutrements for the National Aeronautics and Space Administration. To handle these markets, the companies merely added a separate division or group of divisions for atomic energy weapons or for government business in general. (Chandler, 1978, 127)

Similarly, under the aegis of the warfare-welfare state, the struggle of U.S. corporate business to overcome "puritanism in consumption" through advertising and built-in obsolescence finally succeeded in creating steady and expanding mass markets for its mass production lines and bureaucratic structures.

> Coming out of the Second World War, state consumption and the financial seeding of foreign markets . . . created apparently stable employment for wide sectors of the population whose lives had been chronically characterized by the instability and disquietude of deprivation. Government loans to G.I. families and others helped erect suburban communities which would prove fertile soil for the cultivation of a consumer Eden. . . . The mass marketing of television . . . carried the consumer imagery into the back corners of home life. The vision of the *modern family* informed a suburban migration which dwarfed (five fold) even the massive European migration to these shores in the first decade of the century. The shift of work and commercial activity into arenas of bureaucracy, service and communications further minimized the notion of popular self-sufficiency. (Ewen, 1976, 205–6; emphasis in the original)

From this domestic base of strong governmental support for the establishment and reproduction of the demand conditions of integrated mass production and distribution sprang a new wave of multinational expansion. As previously noted, U.S. corporations became multinational almost as soon as they had completed their continental integration. Many had done so before the First World War. A few more followed in the 1920s. In the 1930s and 1940s, however, depression and war dampened the tendency (U.S. Department of Commerce, various years; Dunning, 1983, 91–93).

> Then in the 1950s and early 1960s, particularly after the opening of the European Common Market, there was a massive drive for for-

eign markets. Direct American investment in Europe alone rose from $1.7 thousand million in 1950 to $24.5 thousand million in 1970. This "American challenge" was spearheaded by the 200 firms that accounted for more than half of the direct investment made by United States companies abroad. These 200 were nearly all in the capital-intensive, technologically advanced industries and were those that had adopted the multidivisional form of organization. (Chandler, 1978, 127–28)

The multidivisional structure thus helped to capture not just governmental demand at home for military and advanced scientific hardware, but foreign markets and resources as well. As Chandler notes, the large integrated corporations could simply add to their existing divisions one or more international divisions to supervise and coordinate overseas activities and to advise their top management on investment decisions; or they could put their product divisions in charge of the overseas lines of business they already handled domestically. Either way, the scale, scope, and reach of the corporations increased further, adding to their power vis-à-vis markets and governments alike.

The U.S. government played as decisive a role in fostering the transnational expansion of U.S. corporate capital as it did in creating the conditions of its domestic consolidation. It provided U.S. corporations operating abroad with tax incentives and insurance schemes, as well as political and military protection (cf. Commission on International Trade and Investment, 1971). Most important, it contributed decisively to turning western Europe into the primary arena of U.S. direct foreign investment. As John Foster Dulles had declared in 1948, "a healthy Europe" could not be "divided into small compartments." It had to be organized into a market "big enough to justify modern methods of cheap production for mass consumption." To this end, the new Europe had to include a reindustrialized Germany. Without German integration into the European economy, remarked General Motors Corporation chairman Alfred P. Sloan, "there is nothing that could convince us in General Motors that it was either sound or desirable or worthwhile to undertake an operation of any consequence in a country like France" (both quotations from McCormick, 1989, 79–80).

The U.S. government spared neither money, nor energies to create in Europe a political-economic space large enough to enable U.S. corporate capital to experience a second youth across the Atlantic.

Through the skillful use of economic inducements (most notably, the Marshall Plan), it fostered European cooperation and the reduction of intra-European economic barriers. Through U.S. and European re-armament under the North Atlantic Treaty Organization (NATO), it provided further inducements for European economic integration and for U.S. direct foreign investment. In these and other ways, it provided essential backing for the establishment of a European Payments Union and the European Coal and Steel Community, thereby initiating the process that culminated in the formation of the European Economic Community in 1957.

As Gilpin underscores, "the fundamental motivation for support-ing the economic unification of Western Europe was political—the se-curity of the West against the Soviet Union." In this pursuit, the U.S. government was willing to tolerate some discrimination against the import of U.S. goods in the newly created Common Market. But it was not willing to tolerate discrimination against the transplant of U.S. corporations within the walls of that market. U.S. support of the Rome Treaty was conditional upon a European guarantee "that an American-owned subsidiary would be treated equally with national firms of European countries. The importance of this policy, and of subsequently negotiated bilateral commercial treaties, for the Euro-pean expansion of American corporations cannot be overemphasized" (Gilpin, 1975, 108).

As U.S. corporate capital seized the opportunities for domestic and transnational expansion created by the U.S. government, world capitalism came to operate under an entirely new system of business enterprise. For about twenty-five years after the end of the Second World War, the U.S. multidivisional, multinational corporation be-came the model that businesses worldwide sought to imitate. As Servan-Schreiber (1968, 10–11) put it, the "American challenge" was not primarily financial or technological but organizational, "the ex-tension to Europe of an *organization* that is still a mystery to us." And yet, by the time Servan-Schreiber was writing, a growing number of European firms had found effective ways to meet the challenge, be-coming challengers themselves of the long-established U.S. corpora-tions, even in the U.S. market (Chandler, 1990, 615–16). The stage was thus set for a new major intensification of interenterprise compe-tition and a new metamorphosis of the dominant system of business enterprise.

The Double Crisis of Corporate Capitalism, U.S.-Style

From the angle of vision adopted in this chapter, past hegemonic transitions appear as moments of fundamental transformation of the dominant system of business enterprise. As figure 5 sums up, the intensification of great-power rivalries and the interstitial emergence of new loci of power that ensued from each major expansion of world trade and production were intertwined with an intensification of inter-enterprise competition and the emergence of new systems of business enterprise. This combination of tendencies laid bare the weaknesses and contradictions of the previously dominant interstate and inter-enterprise systems, while creating the conditions for their reorganization under a new hegemony.

In both transitions, the displacement of one hegemonic structure by another was accompanied by a spatial shift of the system's center. The business enterprises and the government of the declining center tended to remain trapped in the particular path of development that had made their fortunes. Continued adherence to the old path of development protected the declining center from many of the challenges of intensifying competition; but it could not prevent new centers that were particularly well positioned to exploit the greater growth potential of alternative paths from outshining the wealth and power of the declining center.

Aspects of this pattern can also be detected in present transformations of the global political economy. As many observers have pointed out, the very expansion of the U.S. system of multinational corporations has precipitated a crisis, not just of states, the United States included (see introduction), but of the corporations themselves. In the words of Manuel Castells and Alejandro Portes (1989, 29–30),

> The large corporation, with its national vertical structure and the separation of its functions between staff and line, does not appear any more as the last stage of a necessary evolution toward rationalized industrial management. Networks of economic activities, networks of firms, and coordinated clusters of workers appear to comprise an emergent model of successful production and distribution.

The main feature of this emergent model is its "informality," in sharp contrast with the "formality" of the previously dominant model of corporate capitalism based on the regulatory powers of big business, organized labor, and big government (Castells and Portes, 1989,

27–29; on the different meanings of "informality" and "informaliza-tion," see Portes, 1994).

In a similar vein, Michael Piore and Charles Sabel have argued that we are in the midst of an "industrial divide," one of those rare his-torical moments in which the path or paradigm of technological devel-opment itself is at issue. In their view, the triumph of mass production, undertaken in bureaucratically managed, giant corporations, over the "flexible specialization" of small-batch craft production, carried out in small and medium-sized business units coordinated by market rela-tionships of cooperation and competition, was neither complete nor irreversible. Indeed, the triumph may now be in the process of being reversed (Piore and Sabel, 1984, 4–5, 15, 19–20).

Integral to the claim that we may be in the midst of a reversal of the century-long tendency toward the formation of centralized, for-mally regulated, and rigidly specialized business structures has been a revival of interest in Alfred Marshall's (1919, 283–88) notion of "industrial districts" as the locus of "external economies" (external, that is, to individual business units). Thanks to these economies, small business was said to be able to survive and prosper without any need to exploit the "internal economies" of scale and scope available to big business (Becattini, 1989, 1990; Brusco, 1982, 1986). Magnified and publicized by Piore and Sabel's influential book, this rediscovery of Marshallian industrial districts quickly caught the imagination of scholars, media, and policy makers. Silicon Valley was conceptualized as a quintessential Marshallian district (Gilder, 1989; Saxenian, 1990, 1993); small machine and electronics manufacturing enterprises were hailed as the "true" source of Japan's international competitive advan-tage (Friedman, 1988); and, conversely, Britain's international com-petitive disadvantage was attributed to the absence of comparable networks of small businesses (Best, 1990). "The trend of a century is being reversed," editorialized the *Economist* in 1989. "Now it is the big firms that are shrinking and small ones that are on the rise. The trend is unmistakable—and businessmen and policy makers will ig-nore it at their peril" (quoted in Harrison, 1994).

The large corporation, notes Bennett Harrison (1994, 12), thus began to be portrayed as "something of a dinosaur, increasingly unable to compete in a 'post-industrial' world characterized by continually fluc-tuating consumer demands, heightened international competition, and the need for more 'flexible' forms of work and interfirm interaction."

The world described by an earlier generation of scholars—Raymond Vernon, John Kenneth Galbraith, and Alfred Chandler—was thought to be collapsing before our eyes. Now it was the turn of the small, agile companies to drive technological progress, according to writers of every ideological persuasion and academic discipline. (Harrison, 1994, 12–13)

After surveying the evidence, Harrison concludes that this is a grossly distorted image of actual trends. Before we turn to actual trends, however, let us notice how present arguments about the competitive advantages of decentralized, informal, and flexible structures of business enterprise vis-à-vis corporate capitalism, U.S.-style, are reminiscent of the arguments advanced two centuries ago about the advantages of the "free" trade of small, private business vis-à-vis the formally regulated trade of corporate capitalism, Dutch-style. Could it be that the withering away of corporate capitalism, Dutch-style, of the late eighteenth and early nineteenth centuries is about to be replicated by an analogous withering away of corporate capitalism, U.S.-style? Are present tendencies toward market coordination of world-scale processes of production and distribution the harbinger of the emergence of a new dominant system of business enterprise more akin to the nineteenth-century British system than to the twentieth-century U.S. system? Or is U.S.-style corporate capitalism so different from its Dutch predecessor as to make us expect a different prospective outcome to its alleged crisis?

Our analysis has indeed shown that the recurrent transformation of the dominant system of business enterprise is inseparable from the constant evolution of the system from transition to transition. Thus, joint-stock chartered companies were surrogate agencies in the opening up and penetration of distant markets in place, and for the benefit, of the states that had chartered them. Eventually, the companies were driven or phased out of existence. But the pioneering activities of the WIC and the African Company in establishing Atlantic triangular trade, and of the VOC and the English East India Company in laying the foundations of European imperialism in Asia, prepared the ground on which British family capitalism waxed rich and powerful. Without Atlantic triangular trade, the dense networks of family business enterprise that constituted the backbone of Britain's future industrial districts may have never come into existence. And without the unprotected markets and tribute of Britain's Indian empire, these same networks might have withered before they developed fully during and after the great mid-nineteenth-century world trade expansion.

The rise of twentieth-century U.S. corporate capitalism, in turn, was based as much on the realization of the full potential of Britain's nineteenth-century family capitalism as on its limits and contradictions. It was this system that under the carapace of Free Trade Imperialism promoted the rapid diffusion of mechanization from one branch of industry to another, from industry to transport and communications, and from country to country. Without this diffusion of mechanization in all directions, and without the formation of mass markets for agricultural and industrial products that went with it, U.S. business would have had neither the stimulus, nor the means to integrate vertically, to create powerful managerial hierarchies, and to expand across industries and political jurisdictions.

It follows that the corporate capitalism of giant multinational corporations rose and became dominant worldwide under radically different world-historical circumstances than the corporate capitalism of joint-stock chartered companies. Joint-stock chartered companies were precursors in the process of world-market formation that became irreversible with the mid-nineteenth century industrial revolution in long-distance transport and communications. Multinational corporations are a by-product of that process. Joint-stock chartered companies were half-business, half-governmental organizations that specialized territorially in the monopolization of trade opportunities in the extra-European world. Multinational corporations are strictly business organizations that pursue profit by specializing functionally across the territorial jurisdictions of sovereign states. Joint-stock chartered companies depended for their very existence on exclusive trading privileges granted by their metropolitan governments. Multinational corporations have established and reproduced themselves primarily on the basis of the competitiveness of their managerial hierarchies. Joint-stock chartered companies were the outgrowth and instrument of states that were fundamentally weak by world-historical standards. Multinational corporations have been the outgrowth and instrument of the most powerful military-industrial apparatus the world has ever seen.

Taken jointly, these differences point to fundamental changes in the dynamic of interenterprise competition and state-capital relations. For what concerns the dynamic of interenterprise competition, the most striking change is the phenomenal increase in the number of relevant units in the system. Owing to their territorial specialization and exclusiveness, viable joint-stock chartered companies of all nationalities were few in number, probably no more than a dozen or so at any given time. And as soon as their mutual competition intensified, their number decreased further to one or two specimens in each major arena of commercial expansion. Owing to their trans-territoriality and functional specialization in a greatly expanded world market, in contrast, the number of multinational corporations that have operated under U.S. hegemony has been incomparably larger, always being in the three rather than in the two digits. Moreover, the intensification of their mutual competition in the 1970s and 1980s has been associated, not with a decrease, but with an explosive growth in that number. By 1980, it was estimated that there were over 10,000 multinational corporations, and by the early 1990s three times as many (Stopford and Dunning, 1983, 3; Ikeda, 1996, 48).

Partly related to this phenomenal increase in the number of relevant units in the interenterprise system is a fundamental change in the relationship between government and business. In underscoring the overlapping and complementary interests that have linked the U.S. government to U.S. corporations, Gilpin (1975, 141–42) has noted how this relationship "is not unlike that between the British government and the mercantile enterprises which dominated the world economy in the seventeenth and eighteenth centuries. . . . The American multinational corporation, like its mercantile ancestor, has performed an important role in the maintenance and expansion of the power of the United States." We concur with Gilpin in maintaining that the U.S. government saw in the unfettered expansion of U.S. corporations in Western Europe a key instrument of its own world hegemony. As it turned out, however, multinational corporations proved to be far less malleable instruments of world power than joint-stock chartered companies.

Nothing illustrates this difference better than comparing the incorporation of Western Europe after the Second World War into U.S. networks of power with the late eighteenth and early nineteenth century incorporation of the Indian subcontinent into British networks of power. As we have seen, the latter incorporation was the work of a joint-stock chartered company (the East India Company). As soon as the company had fulfilled its task of opening up South Asia to British commercial and territorial expansion at its own risk and expense, it was phased out through the progressive revocation of its trading privileges. The incorporation of Western Europe within the power networks of the United States, in contrast, was undertaken by the U.S. government itself. Once governmental action had prepared the terrain for the profitable transplant of U.S. corporations, the latter invaded Europe in large numbers, contributing to the consolidation of U.S. hegemony. Soon, however, the transplant developed a dynamic of its own, which backfired on U.S. world power.

For one thing, the claims on foreign incomes established by the subsidiaries of U.S. corporations did not translate into a proportionate increase in the incomes of U.S. residents and the revenues of the U.S. government. On the contrary, precisely when the fiscal crisis of the U.S. "warfare-welfare state" became acute under the impact of the Vietnam War (see chapter 3), a growing proportion of the incomes and liquidity of U.S. corporations, instead of being repatriated, fled to offshore money markets (Mendelsohn, 1980). In the words of Eugene Birnbaum of Chase Manhattan Bank, the result was "the amassing of an immense volume of liquid funds and markets—the world of Eurodollar finance—outside the regulatory authority of *any* country or agency" (quoted in Frieden, 1987, 85; emphasis in the original). This massive flight of U.S. capital to offshore money markets precipitated the collapse of the U.S.-controlled Bretton Woods system and the still unresolved fiscal crisis of the U.S. government (Ingham, 1994, 44–46).

Equally important, the consolidation of U.S. hegemony and the concomitant new wave of transnationalization of U.S. business created favorable conditions for the transnationalization of Western European and East Asian business as well. As the ranks of multinational corporations were swollen by these new arrivals, a global system of production, exchange, and accumulation came into existence that was subject to no state authority and had the power to subject to its own "laws" even the most powerful states, the United States included. This is probably the most important difference between the present supersession of corporate capitalism, U.S.-style, and the supersession two hundred years ago of corporate capitalism, Dutch-style. The legacy of the system of joint-stock chartered companies established under Dutch hegemony was a major centralization of world power in the hands of European states in general, and of Britain in particular. This centralization, in turn, provided Britain's nineteenth-century Free Trade world order with a solid political foundation. The legacy of the system of multinational corporations established under U.S. hegemony, by contrast, has been a major weakening of the regulative capacities of even the most powerful states, not just at the level of the global economy as a whole, but also at the level of their own domestic economies.

This weakening of the regulatory capacities of states is both the most distinctive outcome of U.S. hegemony and a major contributing factor of the present tendency toward informalization in the organization of business enterprise. As discussed above, U.S. big business became dominant worldwide only when it was rescued from the depth of the Great Depression of the 1930s by the U.S. government, which was itself made "big" and powerful by the Second World War and the institutionalization of the U.S. warfare-welfare state in the Cold War era. And yet, once the U.S. government had created the conditions for the global expansion of U.S. big business, this very expansion and the competitive responses it elicited from Western European and East Asian business undermined the centralization of world financial and economic power within the U.S. that had made possible the institutionalization and enlarged reproduction of the U.S. warfare-welfare state. As in the interwar period, therefore, U.S. big business faced once again a situation in which it had to stand or fall on its own. In comparison with the interwar period, however, the self-expansion of U.S. big business over the last twenty-five years has been far more dependent on foreign markets and resources and far more exposed to foreign competition.

To cope with this new situation, U.S. corporations have been forced to cut their managerial hierarchies and subordinate workforce and to enter into all kinds of informal alliances and deals with other corporations, both U.S. and foreign, with governments at all levels, and with small businesses all over the world, to which they subcontract activities previously carried out within their own organizations. The tendency toward the bureaucratization of business through vertical integration and product diversification, which had made the fortunes of U.S. corporate business since the 1870s, thus began to be superseded one hundred years later by a tendency toward informal networking and the subordinate revitalization of small business. In acknowledging this tendency, Harrison (1994, 7, 244–45) finds that it "looks more like the lopping off of the tip of an iceberg than a meltdown of the old prevailing structure." He interprets this "lopping off" of the tip of the iceberg of corporate power as the expression of what he calls "the emerging principle of concentration without centralization."

> [R]ather than dwindling away, concentrated economic power is changing its shape, as the big firms create all manner of alliances, short- and long-term financial and technology deals—with one another, with governments at all levels, and with legions of generally (although not invariably) smaller firms who act as their suppliers and subcontractors. . . . [M]anagers first divide permanent ("core") from contingent ("peripheral") jobs. The size of the core is then cut to the bone—which, along with the minimization of inventory holding, is why "flexible" firms are often described as practicing "lean" production. These activities, and the human beings who perform them, are then located as much as possible in different parts of the company or network, even in different geographical locations. (Harrison, 1994, 8–11)

Large corporations, in other words, have themselves resorted to networking as a highly effective way to decentralize production outside their organizational domains, without reducing, and often increasing, their control over markets and technological and financial resources. Under these circumstances, Marshallian industrial districts have tended either to lose their vitality as manufacturing centers or to lose their autonomy vis-à-vis big business (Blim, 1990; Harrison, 1994, chapters 4–5; Braczyk, Schienstock, and Stefensen, 1995). "In the context of a global system populated by big companies on the perpetual prowl for new profitable opportunities," comments Harrison (1994, 37), "the very success of the district itself can bring about changes which give rise to their opposite, and we observe the recreation of hierarchical organization."

The strategy of big business, operating transnationally, to turn the advantages of small business into an instrument of the consolidation and expansion of its own power has been in evidence everywhere. But nowhere has it been pursued more consistently and successfully than in East Asia. Without the assistance of multiple layers of formally independent subcontractors, notes JETRO (Japan's External Trade Organization), "Japanese big business would flounder and sink" (Okimoto and Rohlen, 1988, 83–88). Close relationships of cooperation between large and small firms are buttressed by informal arrangements among the parent companies themselves in the form of semipermanent trade agreements and intergroup shareholding that enable management to concentrate on long-term rather than short-term performance (Eccleston, 1989, 31–34). Starting in the early 1970s, the scale and scope of this multilayered subcontracting system increased rapidly through a spillover into a growing number and variety of East Asian states (Arrighi, Ikeda, and Irwan, 1993, 55ff).

As we shall see in chapter 4, the spillover made a major contribution to the economic expansion of the entire East Asian region and strengthened the competitiveness of Japanese big business in the global economy at large. It contributed also to the revitalization of the overseas Chinese business diaspora, a powerful network of medium-sized, family-owned enterprises stitched together by ethnic ties, marriages, joint ventures, political connections, and a common culture and business ethic. Informal though pervasive throughout the maritime and coastal regions of Northeast and Southeast Asia, the diaspora's networks quickly became the dominant business organization in the region and the main intermediary in the reintegration of Mainland China into the global economy (So and Chiu, 1994, chapter 11; Arrighi, 1996, 33–37; Katzenstein, 1997, 13–14, 37–41. For a comparative analysis of East Asian business organizations, see Orrù, Biggart, and Hamilton, 1997).

It is too early to tell what kind of dominant system of business enterprise will emerge out of this highly diversified tendency toward "concentration without centralization." We may nonetheless expect with some confidence that such a dominant system will be characterized by greater informality and marketlike coordination than the system of vertically integrated and bureaucratically managed corporations that became dominant under U.S. hegemony. But we may just as confidently expect that this greater informality and marketlike coordination will not resurrect the kind of market capitalism that prospered in the nineteenth century under British hegemony.

Three differences seem most likely to materialize. First, the proliferation in the number and variety of transnational corporations in the present transition (in contrast to the almost complete extinction of joint-stock chartered companies in the transition from Dutch to British hegemony) makes safe the prediction that the emergent system will be characterized more by a synthesis of corporate and family business forms than by the prevalence of the family form, as in the nineteenth-century British system. Second, the weakening of the regulative capacities of even the most powerful states in the present transition (in contrast to the strengthening of the regulative capacities of

European states, Britain in particular, in the transition from Dutch to British hegemony) makes equally safe the prediction that the emergent system of business enterprise will not be able to rely on the strong arm of an imperial state, as the nineteenth-century system did on the strong arm of Imperial Britain. Finally, to the extent that East Asia is indeed best positioned to realize the full potential of present tendencies toward concentration without centralization, the emergent system will bear the social and cultural imprint of a non-Western civilization.

This brings us to the issue of the social and civilizational foundations of world hegemonies. So far we have been almost exclusively concerned with hegemonic transitions as moments of reorganization of the modern world system under the impact of intensifying interstate rivalries and interenterprise competition. In the next two chapters, we broaden our angle of vision to examine the interplay between these rivalries and competition on the one side, and conflicts among social groups and civilizations on the other.

Three

The Social Origins of
World Hegemonies

Beverly J. Silver and Eric Slater

The focus of this chapter is on the social foundations of world hege-monies. The central argument is that the systemwide expansions in trade and production that have characterized each period of hege-mony have been based on social compacts between dominant and sub-ordinate groups. Periods of hegemony have been characterized by a "virtuous circle," with social peace and material expansions in trade and production reinforcing one another. Periods of hegemonic tran-sition, in contrast, have been characterized by a "vicious circle" in which intensifying interstate and interenterprise competition interacts with mounting and increasingly dysfunctional social conflict, leading to periods of systemwide rebellions, state breakdowns and revolutions.

This chapter builds on the previous two chapters by showing how the intensification of competition among states and capitalist enter-prises during each of the hegemonic transitions undermined the condi-tions necessary for the reproduction of established social compacts. In particular, we describe how the growing "financialization" of pro-cesses of capital accumulation during each transition was associated with a rapid and extreme polarization of wealth, which in turn under-mined the "middle class" consent upon which the world-hegemonic order rested. Part of the force behind the growing social conflict of the transition periods comes from the efforts of these "middle" strata to defend the privileges they had enjoyed under the hegemonic social compact.

The chapter also emphasizes how the systemic expansions themselves undermined the social foundations of successive world hegemonies by transforming the world-scale balance of class forces. During periods of systemic expansion, new social groups and classes—excluded from the benefits of the established hegemonic social compact—grew in size and disruptive power. The struggles of these groups to expand their rights have been both causes and consequences of the escalating interstate and interenterprise competition.

Finally, periods of hegemonic transition have been characterized by growing intra-elite conflict, in reaction to the intensification of interstate and interenterprise rivalry on the one hand, and to increasing social unrest from below on the other. The result of these combined processes has been long periods of social turbulence stretching for a half a century or more in past transitions. These periods have played a decisive role, not just in destroying the strained social foundations of the collapsing hegemonic order, but in shaping the nature of the new world-hegemonic order.

The consolidation of each world hegemony presupposed the establishment of new "historical compromises" capable of bringing social conflict under control. The cooptation of rising groups was pivotal—the settler bourgeoisies of the Americas and the propertied middle classes of Europe in the transition from Dutch to British hegemony, and the Westernized elites of the non-Western world and the working classes of the Western world in the transition from British to U.S. hegemony. But in both transitions, the widening of the social foundations of the hegemonic bloc was accompanied by, indeed, premised on a de jure or de facto exclusion of the majority of the world's population from access to the same rights and privileges.

The two main parts of the chapter analyze the interplay of interstate rivalries, intercapitalist competition, and social conflict during the transition from Dutch to British hegemony and from British to U.S. hegemony, respectively. For each transition we describe the unraveling of the old order under the impact of escalating social conflict and the emergence of a new social order capable of bringing the conflict under control through a combination of cooptation and repression. The two transitions taken together describe a pattern of evolution: the social unrest with which the rising hegemon must come to terms is of far greater geographical scope and social depth in the transition to U.S. hegemony than in the transition to British hegemony. Thus, in telling the story of the transition from Dutch to British hegemony, we focus on rebellion and revolution in Europe and the Americas. In describing the transition to U.S. hegemony, our story becomes *global*.

The concluding part examines present tendencies toward the breakdown of the social compacts that undergird U.S. hegemony. Our examination of past hegemonic transitions allows us to see patterns of both recurrence and evolution. As in past hegemonic transitions, we are in the midst of a systemwide financial expansion that has led to an increasing polarization of wealth and to the squeezing-out of some of the "middle" strata that had been incorporated into the U.S. hegemonic bloc. The mass-production working class of the core, in particular, has lost power and privileges with the increasing "financialization" and mobility of capital. At the same time, new classes and groups emerged and were strengthened in the course of the systemwide expansion and in the early stages of the transition. A new world hegemony—if there is to be one—will have to come to terms with the growing size and centrality of women and people of color among the workers of the world.

The Rise of the Propertied Classes

The Social Foundations of Dutch Hegemony

The social foundations of Dutch hegemony were forged during the period of systemwide political and social upheavals known as the "general crisis of the seventeenth century." The republic that emerged from the long war of Dutch independence against the Hapsburgs quickly became an admired model of social relations that others sought to emulate. The "northern Netherlands was the first European country to reject the Renaissance Court," which had grown in lavishness throughout Europe, supporting its extravagance through the sale of offices, and thus spawning parasitic bureaucracies that "sent their multiplying suckers . . . deep into the body of society" (Trevor-Roper, 1967, 93–102). Emulation of the Dutch republic—that is, the elimination of princely states in favor of streamlined mercantile states—was carried forward with varying degrees of success in the second half of the seventeenth century throughout Europe. In Britain, the post-1688 settlement "asserted the political power of a capitalist landowning and mercantile oligarchy," but it "clothed oligarchic rule" with a constitutionally constrained monarchy that became a symbol of cross-class consent (Blackburn, 1988, 69, 72). In France, the "unbridled violence" of the peasant insurrections and repressions of the seventeenth century gave way to "a social and political order, authoritarian in character, yet accepted and acceptable" (Braudel, 1990, 391–92).

The Dutch also led the way in establishing new rules for interstate relations that guaranteed the safety of private enterprise, while dampening the religious impetus to revolution by making official religious tolerance an international norm. The Treaties of Westphalia (1648) established the principle that civilians were not party to the quarrels between sovereigns, while subsequent agreements introduced rules to protect the property and commerce of noncombatants (see chapter 1; see also Taylor, 1996, 109–10; Carr, 1945, 4). By the early eighteenth century, treaties among the European powers had also reduced the uncertainties dogging commercial expansion in the Atlantic. With the Peace of Utrecht in 1713, favorable conditions were established for both plantation development and the organization of large-scale slave trafficking (Blackburn, 1988, 11). In the seventeenth century, communities of buccaneers and pirates had flourished in the Caribbean. By the early eighteenth century, transatlantic commerce was flourishing and "anarchy gave way to slavery" (Curtin, 1990, 86–96). Wars peppered eighteenth-century Atlantic life, but at least up through the Seven Years' War, they proved to be far more a boon than a disruption for profitable transatlantic commerce and production.

A "virtuous circle" thus came into operation in the early eighteenth century. By reducing the weight of parasitic classes and leading to the establishment of the Westphalia system, the political upheavals and revolutions of the seventeenth century had created favorable conditions for a renewed expansion of trade and production. A widening "middle class" shared in the prosperity, thus contributing to the continuation of social and political stability. At the same time, the commercial expansion provided rulers with the means to establish the coercive apparatus (and elite unity) needed to secure the compliance of the prosperity's victims—most notably the millions of African slaves who toiled in the booming plantations of the Americas.

Among the big beneficiaries of the eighteenth-century expansion were large European landowners with a marketable surplus (Wallerstein, 1989, 64), as well as manufacturers and mine operators throughout Europe. But "the true economic victors of the age" were the colonial planters, and the merchants and shippers of such "splendid ports" as Bordeaux, Bristol, and Liverpool, together with the "great officials and financiers who drew their wealth from the profitable service of the state" (Hobsbawm, 1962, 36).

Transatlantic commerce created fabulous fortunes. To be sure, these fortunes were not shared equally, and there were significant intra-elite tensions—between merchants and planters in the Atlantic, between planters and metropolitan governments, between nobility and wealthy commoners, and among European states vying for a larger share of the pie. Slaveholding planters, for one, were prone to an "intimate antagonism toward metropolitan merchants and their local agents" (Blackburn, 1988, 3, 15). With few local sources of credit, colonial planters frequently found themselves indebted to merchant-shippers who charged high rates of interest on colonial loans (Curtin, 1990, 140–41). Resentments toward merchants tended to spill over into resentments toward the colonial governments who put the planters at a disadvantage vis-à-vis the merchants and shippers by granting trading monopolies to the latter. For Virginia tobacco planters, this meant they had to sell at low prices to British merchants who proceeded to re-export four-fifths of the tobacco crop to consumers in continental Europe. Likewise, sugar planters in the French Caribbean, in addition to finding themselves "chronically in debt" to merchant companies with "home offices in Nantes or some other Atlantic port," received no benefit from mercantilist protection of the home market since their plantations produced the world's cheapest sugar (Curtin, 1990, 140; Blackburn, 1988, 77, 87, 163).

However, for as long as the commercial expansion lasted, these intra-elite tensions remained under control and did not escalate into the kind of open rift that would become crucial to the detonation of the revolutionary upheavals of the late eighteenth century. The actual system of colonial trade was in fact much more "flexible" than official policy implied. There was a yawning gap between mercantilist theory and the everyday reality—the century from 1680 to 1780 has been dubbed "the golden age of smuggling" (Rediker, 1987, 72; see also Curtin, 1990, 132). Moreover, some colonial planters did benefit from the metropolitan connection. Protected access to the fast growing British market translated into a sizable subsidy for British West Indian planters, as their sugar was more costly than that of their French Caribbean neighbors (Mintz, 1989, 39). And empirewide free trade allowed them to buy cheap North American and Irish supplies as well as cheap English metal implements and textiles (Blackburn, 1988, 4, 14–16).

These profit-loss calculations were reinforced by social and political considerations. Over half of the West Indian proprietors lived in Britain, and wealthy colonial merchants and proprietors were able to purchase influence or representation at Westminster. North American notables even played a part in helping to devise the settlement of 1688–89, through their representatives in London and through the parallel action of colonial assemblies (Nash, 1986, 21–22; Blackburn, 1988, 78). Thus, even where there were economic tensions between planters and merchants, these were "not automatically translated into friction between colony and metropolis" (Curtin, 1990, 140–41). At the same time, well-established representative assemblies existed in the British and French colonies. While formally owing allegiance to the metropolitan authorities, in practice they had considerable autonomy. "White colonists," notes Blackburn (1988, 11) "enjoyed a measure of freedom unknown in the Old World while blacks were subjected to a more systematic and ferocious system of enslavement than had ever been seen before."

Indeed, it was this contrast between the freedom of white settlers and the subjugation of black slaves that ultimately provides the most important explanation for why the latent tensions between settlers and mother country did not explode for most of the eighteenth century. Until the 1760s, no group in the colonies had the commercial and financial facilities, much less the military capacity, to survive on its own. British West Indian planters were well aware of the fact that, with slaves composing a majority of the population, British troops were needed to guarantee the colonial order. In Saint Domingue, while planters chafed under the metropolitan government's trade restrictions, they were also aware of the role played by colonial garrisons in restraining the majority slave population, as well as in maintaining the roads, ports, and systems of irrigation that made the colony so productive. The survival of the North American settlers (not to mention their expansionist ambitions) was only possible if the Royal Navy protected them from the French and the Indians (Blackburn, 1988, 16–17, 84). In other words, settlers in the Americas could see their "tax dollars at work" in the coercive forces defending and extending the plantation system and slavery.

The benefits of the eighteenth-century expansion of trade and production did not accrue only to the political and economic elite of the Atlantic world. The expansion led to the emergence of "great middle-class societies" in the urban centers that serviced this mushrooming trade and commerce. Plantations were excellent customers for the finished goods of artisans and manufacturers. During the eighteenth century, combined English exports to the North American and West Indian colonies expanded by 2,300 percent (Mintz, 1985, 42, 56). Planters were also good customers for local farmers and manufacturers, and they engaged the services of overseers, bookkeepers, lawyers, doctors, and the like (Blackburn, 1988, 15). Finally, the slave trade itself was "financed by a highly democratic pooling of the modest resources of 'attorneys, drapers, grocers, barbers, and tailors'"; the profits thus trickled down to the middle rungs of the class structure (Williams, 1964, 37; Mintz, 1985, 168).

This incorporation (co-optation) of a broadening "middle class" strengthened the social and political stability of the Atlantic system by further isolating those in the bottom rungs of the productive system. Planters promoted white racial solidarity by extending political concessions to less prosperous whites. In Virginia, for example, any white man who owned fifty acres with a house could vote (a criteria, which given the easy access to land, was not beyond reach of many white men). In the French Caribbean, while the franchise was more narrow, "[n]early all free males between sixteen and sixty were armed" and were members of colonial militias that acted as auxiliaries to the regular garrisons (Blackburn, 1988, 85–87, 163).

Moreover, territorial conquest in the Americas strengthened cross-class cohesion among whites on both sides of the Atlantic by creating easy access to land for the surplus population of Europe. The Caribbean Islands—although closed to smallholders with the switch to large-scale slave-based sugar production in the eighteenth century—became an important outlet for surplus members of already wealthy families. This kind of safety valve was by no means unimportant: colonization "was added to war and privateering as a gentleman's occupation," suitable for landless younger sons (Davis, 1973, 125–42; see also Mintz, 1985, 168–69 and Pares, 1950).

The North American mainland, in contrast, became "the small

man's refuge." The flow from Europe broadened in the eighteenth century as the mid-Atlantic colonies eliminated restrictions on foreign
landholdings and encouraged the migration of European farmers and
artisans facing economic or political dislocation. Restless youth, dislo-
cated families, religious dissidents, and war refugees were removed as
a burden not just from England and France, but also from Scotland,
Ireland, Germany, and Switzerland (Davis, 1973, 125–42). They arrived in an environment characterized by "widespread opportunity for
almost two generations before the end of the Seven Years' War." It was
in this environment—where "[h]ard work and frugality had led to material success, not only for merchants, professionals, and extraordinary
lower-class sons such as Benjamin Franklin, but also for scores of artisans" and farmers—that Whig political theory became dominant
(Nash, 1986, 212–13).

With an Atlantic ruling class united around the defense of property
in general, and slaveholding in particular, and with the "middle classes"
effectively co-opted as junior partners in the hegemonic bloc, there was
no space for successful general slave uprisings. Throughout the seventeenth and most of the eighteenth century, open slave resistance led
either to "bloody defeat and heroic sacrifice of life" or to the establishment of maroon societies in the hinterlands beyond colonial society
(Genovese, 1979, xix). Slaves faced short life expectancies (an average
of seven to ten years for the newly arrived Caribbean slave) and a "ferocious and integrated apparatus of coercion and control." The only two
slave rebellions prior to the 1790s that threatened to engulf a whole
colony (the Danish island of Sainte Croix in 1733 and the Dutch Berbice
in 1763) were crushed with the help of troops from more powerful
slaveholding neighbors (Blackburn, 1988, 57–58; Genovese, 1979, 21).

Localized slave revolts did take place often enough to give planters
nightmares. But where and when the Atlantic economy was booming,
slaves found successful revolt almost impossible: "Colonies that were
growing and prosperous attracted settlers and could afford the upkeep
of patrols, militia units and garrisons." Even autonomous maroon
communities of escaped slaves were "more of a problem at the periphery of the slave systems or in colonies that were stagnating" (Blackburn, 1988, 58; see also Genovese, 1979, 51–68; Mintz, 1989, 78).

The highly successful slave colonies on the North American mainland were particularly secure. The objective conditions for rebellion
were extremely unfavorable. In contrast to the Caribbean, slaves consti-

tuted a minority of the population—about one-quarter of the population in British North America in 1770. Moreover, they tended to live on farms rather than plantations; the average slaveholding unit contained only twenty slaves. The hinterlands were inhospitable for the establishment of maroon communities. Meanwhile, the white population—which "constituted one great militia," "fully and even extravagantly armed"—was united around defending the privileges that came from slaveholding or racism or both (Genovese, 1979, 12–17). This lack of space for slave resistance explains in large measure why North Americans would be the first to risk an open display of intra-elite disunity with a bid for independence. They correctly sensed that they could challenge the colonial relationship without precipitating an uncontrollable revolt from below (Blackburn, 1988, 58).

Plantation slaves were not the only coerced labor force upon which the Atlantic economic prosperity was built. Transatlantic commerce required approximately half a million tons of shipping and employed more than a hundred thousand seamen and dockers (Blackburn, 1988, 6). Physical force supplemented market forces in creating an interracial and international maritime working class composed of poor whites, indentured servants, and slaves. At times of war, when the "simultaneous mobilization of the Royal Navy and of enormous privateering forces generated furious competition for the skills and strength of Jack Tar," press gangs would roam the poorer quarters of port cities and kidnap unwilling participants for adventure on the high seas—a dangerous adventure as almost half of all of those pressed into service in the seventeenth and eighteenth centuries died at sea (Rediker, 1987, 12–13, 31–33, 62, 67, 290).

In sum, the creation of "great middle-class societies" during the Atlantic boom (i.e., the eighteenth century "cycle of rights establishment") was premised on the exploitation of millions of African slaves and hundreds of thousands of coerced maritime workers. Unity at the top, combined with the wealth generated by slave labor on conquered lands, provided the resources necessary for the broadening of the "middle class," as well as the resources necessary to put down any rebellion from those upon whose backs the prosperity had been built.

The First Wave of Rebellion and Revolution

The American Revolution was the first major event to signal a change in the "virtuous circle" of expansion and social cohesion. It had a resounding impact in both Europe and in the Americas, helping to set off a chain of rebellions and revolutions that enveloped the Atlantic world.

What changed? On the one hand, the balance of class forces was transformed in the course of the long economic expansion. In particular, the settler elites began to feel strong enough to force a renegotiation of the colonial relationship. On the other hand, the expansion itself began to sputter. A commercial depression combined with financial speculation led to growing social polarization and a withering of middle-class support for the political status quo. With the breakdown of intra-elite unity and the alienation of the "middle classes," the space was opened for revolts from below by the excluded and exploited.

For the North American colonies, the Seven Years' War was the decisive turning point—and the start of the hegemonic transition as seen from the angle of vision of this chapter. The impact of the Seven Years' War on the North American colonies was both "traumatic and paradoxical." On the one hand, the "war convinced the American colonies of their growing strength and maturity." On the other hand, "it rendered them unusually sensitive to the disadvantages of the British mercantile connection" and "exposed in stark detail the social costs of the transition to a capitalistic economy" (Nash, 1986, 147).

The strengthening effects of the war were both economic and political. The early war years lifted the northern commercial centers out of a business depression and, with the exception of Boston, created "flush times." Employment expanded and fortunes were made provisioning the British troops stationed in North America. Even greater fortunes were made by merchants engaged in privateering. At first, "the rush to scoop up French riches from an English dominated sea" was congruent with British war strategy; but by 1759 the privateers "had so thoroughly cleared the seas of French vessels" that they began to turn to smuggling, in particular provisioning the "island-bound enemy" at extraordinary prices (Nash, 1986, 147–52). Thus, the war led to an unprecedented, and most profitable, flaunting of British mercantile regulations.

On the political front, a new degree of unity among the colonies was achieved as Britain encouraged "the formerly localistic and fragmented colonies [to coordinate their actions] in a common military effort." The resounding victory against France, to which the colonies contributed considerable human and material resources, boosted their confidence in their military self-defense capacities. Perhaps most important, the British victory, by ejecting the French from the North American continent, "was too sweeping for its own good"; it "emancipated the colonists" from their need for British protection (Blackburn, 1988, 19, 82–84).

The destabilizing effects of the war were felt mainly in its aftermath, when the wartime boom came to "a shuddering halt": war contracts evaporated, and the withdrawal of the British army and navy "meant that English shillings no longer clanked into the tills of tavern-keepers and shopowners." The flow of credit from London was tightened, while an "invigorated British customs service cracked down on American smugglers." The severe dislocation caused by the London-centered financial crisis of 1772 (see chapter 1) "was felt from the top to the bottom of the social scale." As London tried to shift a greater share of the costs of empire onto the colonies themselves through such measures as the Stamp Act of 1765 and the Tea Act of 1773, many local merchants felt aggrieved and found common ground in anti-British protests with planters, manufacturers, artisans, and the laboring poor (Nash, 1986, 155–56, 204–6; Wallerstein, 1989, 198–99, 209–10).

Further compounding difficulties for the settlers was the growing armed resistance by Native Americans to the westward push of the colonists, thus blocking the usual outlet for the renewed postwar inflow of Irish and German immigrants (Nash, 1986, 156–57). The Pontiac uprising, which was crushed by British troops at the settlers' behest, was followed by British efforts to economize on military expenses by limiting the westward expansion of the settlers and by turning to "trans-Appalachia as a source of extraction via peaceful trade with secure indigenous populations" (Wallerstein, 1989, 202–3). This British strategy threatened to close the frontier and thereby eliminate one of the main devices by which social cohesion among the white settlers had been maintained in North America. The policy thus became another major source of metropolitan-settler tensions.

The postwar depression was not only deeper and longer than previous cyclical downturns of the eighteenth century; it was also accompanied by a wide and increasing polarization of wealth. This polarization was already visible during the war, but when "everyone believed he could be a winner in the wartime sweepstakes, the ground for political contention all but disappeared" (Nash, 1986, 167). The depression led to the "rapid growth of a class of truly impoverished persons in the port towns" and "struck hard at many in the middle sector," such as established craftsmen and small shopkeepers. The implications for maintaining social cohesion were significant as these "middling town dwellers" tended to be "politically conscious" and to figure importantly in Boston's town meeting, New York's common council, and Philadelphia's voluntary militia (Nash, 1986, 159, 161–62).

The emergence of a class of desperately poor people and the growing insecurity of the middle classes was paralleled by the emergence of a class of "fabulously wealthy" people:

> [T]own dwellers . . . could see the urban mansions built during the 1760s, the sharp rise in the number of four-wheeled coaches and carriages imported from London, and the burst of newspaper advertising by those who served the urban rich—wigmakers, silk dryers, retailers of expensive furniture, instructors of music and dancing. . . . (Nash, 1986, 163)

The political impact of this polarization was explosive, as "hostility toward men of great wealth intensified and the cultural hegemony of the elite, never firmly established, tottered precariously" (Nash, 1986, 166). The wealthy merchants and lawyers who attempted to lead the resistance movement knew they could not resist the Stamp Act and other British imperial pretensions without mobilizing the lower classes, "but they were also becoming fearful of the awful power of the assembled artisans and their maritime compatriots . . . [For] once the genie was out of the bottle, how could it be imprisoned again?" (Nash, 1986, 184–99).

In the end, the genie was kept under control. The respectable leadership of the American Revolution of 1776 successfully channeled radical sentiment and action into attacks against the British and their supporters, rather than against oligarchic wealth in general (Nash, 1986, 176, 220–47). And crucially, all sides shrank from making abolitionist appeals to the slave population in exchange for their active support—an element that would be important in the slave emancipations that would take place in the Caribbean and South America over the next several decades. The constitutional compromise on taxation and representation (whereby slaves were counted as three-fifths of a person) held the United States together as a flourishing slaveholding power (Blackburn, 1988, 104, 112–14, 123–26). And the compromise reserving the northwest for family farming held the United States together as an aggressively expansionist power, violently displacing the indigenous population in the southwest and northwest with slaveholding plantations and settler-farmers, respectively.

Revolution in Europe

Toward the end of the century, the center of political and social upheaval moved across the Atlantic. Europeans were experiencing transformations and dislocations similar to those that had precipitated unrest in North America. At the same time, "globalization" processes had advanced to the point where words and deeds in the Americas could have a rapid and resounding impact on Europe (and vice-versa).

Despite its limitations, the new American Republic was perceived in Europe as an inspiring model of democracy and liberty. "When the Declaration of Independence insisted that 'all men are created equal' and endowed with an inalienable right to 'life, liberty, and the pursuit of happiness' it took a historic leap beyond the particularistic notion of the 'rights of Englishmen.'" "Resounding slogans had been launched on the world; the fine print of the Constitution made less of an impression" (Blackburn, 1988, 111, 126).

The first and greatest effect of the American Revolution on Europe, according to R. R. Palmer (1959, 239–40), was to make Europeans feel "that they lived in a rare era of momentous change." The American Revolution was seen as "a lesson and an encouragement for mankind." There was "an expectancy of change, a sense of great events already begun, a consciousness of a new era, a receptivity to . . . attempt[s] at world renewal."

For both the rising and declining hegemonic states, the American Revolution called into question their status as the most advanced models for state-society relations. The American Revolution "dethroned England, and set up America, as a model for those seeking a better world" (Palmer, 1959, 282). Britain's political and military defeat "at the hands of a patriot rabble was an intimate and lasting wound." It inspired opponents of the regime to seek "radical, democratic alternatives to oligarchy and corruption," while waking the ruling classes to the fact that "fundamental reforms were necessary if the contagion of revolutionary democracy was not to spread" (Blackburn, 1988, 133).

Likewise, the widely admired Dutch Republic, long seen as "a byword for political stability," was increasingly seen by its inhabitants as an intolerable system of "nepotism and oligarchy." In the early 1780s, "politics in Holland . . . exploded from the realm of a politely circumscribed elite to a chaotic and impulsive mass activity." The Dutch Patriots called for the recapturing of "the imagined vigor of [the Republic's] origins" through radical reform, including a "democratic system of direct and frequent elections" (Schama, 1989, 248–50). The Dutch Patriots saw the American Revolution as "virtually a repeat performance of their own republican epic, complete with tyrannical empire, citizen militias and a taciturn hero as the 'father' of the nation." The American Revolution was euphorically associated with "the past of Dutch freedoms and their impending rebirth" (Schama, 1992, 60).

For France as well, "the Revolution began in America." The consequences of French involvement in the revolutionary wars were "profoundly subversive and irreversible." Apart from the disastrous fiscal impact on the French state, there were important ideological consequences. The American rebels were enormously popular among sections of the enlightened aristocracy in France; the latter's "flirtation with armed freedom," in the process of which they scored spectacular military successes against the British, boosted their self-confidence and led them to equate patriotism with liberty (Schama, 1989, 24, 40, 47).

In Europe, as had been the case for North America, revolutionary language caught on in a time of extreme polarization of wealth associated with a combination of commercial depression and wild financial speculation. This, in turn, led to a situation in which the middle and lower classes felt increasingly squeezed by and resentful of their social "superiors." In Holland, the final flowering of Amsterdam as the center of European high finance (see chapter 1) coincided with widespread processes of "deindustrialization" (most clearly reflected in shipbuilding) and with a contraction of working-class incomes. "The merchant-bankers and the wealthy rentiers might never have 'had it so good,'" notes Charles Boxer (1965, 293–94), but as an eyewitness reported at the end of the period, "'the well-being of that class of people who lead a working life [was] steadily declining.'"

The resulting "contrasts between luxury and penury" sharpened political animosities, especially as it was not just the poor who were becoming poorer. Many in the "middle classes" were feeling the effects of industrial and commercial decline. As their economic difficulties increased, "the attitude of the small burgher—the shopkeeper, guildsman, or artisan—toward the periwigged oligarchs became decidedly more ambivalent" (Schama, 1992, 43–47; see also Boxer, 1965, 302–31).

In this environment of deindustrialization and economic polarization, political hostility was directed at "allegedly self-satisfied and short-sighted rentiers and capitalists, who preferred to invest their money abroad rather than in fostering industry and shipping at home and thus relieving unemployment" (Boxer, 1965, 328). Resentment of the financial elite and the ruling elite went hand in hand. The Dutch regent-oligarchs were thoroughly involved in long-distance trade and high finance, and access to many of the most lucrative activities was denied to those without the right political, family, and religious connections (Palmer, 1959, 326–27). True, fabulously wealthy or fabulously loyal commoners might be granted regent status by the prince, thus opening a path into a closed hereditary oligarchy. But "the admission of new regents on the strength of either their great wealth or their partisanship (or both) was almost calculated to alienate" those who possessed neither attribute. Thus, a section of well-off, albeit not fabulously rich burghers came to support Patriotic politics (Schama, 1992, 50–52; see also Palmer, 1959, 326).

As we shall see, this combination of social polarization and "middle-class" political alienation has characterized all declining hegemonic powers during their decline and final flowering as centers of finance. In Kevin Phillips's words,

> Finance cannot nurture a [large middle] class, because only a small elite of any national population—Dutch, British, or American—can share in the profits of bourse, merchant bank and countinghouse. Manufacturing, transportation and trade supremacies, by contrast, provide a broader national prosperity in which the ordinary person can man the production lines, mines, mills, wheels, mainsails and nets. Once this stage of economic development yields to the next, with its sharper divisions from capital, skills, and education, great middle-class societies lose something vital and unique, just what worriers believe was happening again to the United States in the late twentieth century. (Phillips, 1993, 197)

We shall return to this theme in discussing both the transition to U.S. hegemony and the current crisis. At this point we will only note that although Phillips limits his argument to a comparison of trends within the hegemonic powers, the processes of financialization, polarization, and political alienation were widespread during each hegemonic transition. We have already discussed their interrelationship with regard to North America. The same processes were visible in France in the last decades before the Revolution. In the French countryside, financialization and polarization took the form of an "offensive by landed proprietors" (the so-called seignorial reaction) in which landed property was touched by a "general mania for speculation." The "seigniorial reaction," writes Braudel

> was determined not so much by a return to tradition as by the spirit of the times, the climate, new to France, of financial racketeering, stock exchange speculation, investment bubbles, as the aristocracy began to take an interest in overseas trade or mining, in short, what I would describe as capitalist temptation as much as a mentality. (1982, 295)

The sustained effort by "both tenant-farmers and proprietors to restructure [modernize] large estates . . . aroused panic and resentment among the peasants" (Braudel, 1982, 295–97; see also Le Roy Ladurie, 1974, 1975). Spectacular new wealth went hand in hand with the creation of "streams or rather oceans of beggars" (Braudel, 1990, 395). Moreover, speculation in grain went hand in hand with renewed fears of famine and shortages. As a result, peasant revolts leading up to and through the Revolution were increasingly directed at the *seigneur* in modernizing regions ("against the enclosers, the irrigators, the modernizers," Wallerstein, 1989, 48–49), rather than against the traditional noble or the state, as had been the case in the seventeenth century (Braudel, 1982, 297; Braudel, 1990, 387–99).

Likewise, with the Revolution itself, political rhetoric was increasingly directed against merchant-capitalists and financiers as well as the nobility. "The radical thrust behind the Revolution based on the *sans-culottes* and sections of the peasantry was explicitly and strongly anticapitalist" (Moore, 1966, 69). This anticapitalist reflex, visible already in the North American and Dutch revolutions, would intensify in France as a large-scale flight of capital between 1789 and 1791 led to a collapse of the French currency and the domestic economy. "On 25 November 1790, the comte de Custine fulminated from the rostrum of the National Assembly: 'Will this Assembly, which has destroyed all kinds of aristocracy, flinch before the aristocracy of capitalists, these cosmopolitans whose only fatherland is the one in which they can pile up their riches?'" (Braudel, 1982, 236–37).

In North America the genie of social revolution was kept in the bottle as the settler elite (north and south) remained unified and successfully directed the protests of poor whites against the British, while excluding the slave population from active participation in the revolution. In the United Provinces, the bottle was recorked by (British-backed) Prussian troops just as the genie was about to escape. The Dutch state *did* collapse in the face of the Patriot Revolution, but the "Free Corps dissolved in the face of Prussian regular forces in 1787" (Palmer, 1959, 338). In France, the genie finally made it out of the bottle and spread across the European continent and back across the Atlantic to Haiti and South America.

The French state was left with little room to maneuver in resolving intra-elite tensions. French intervention in support of the American rebels had left France drowning in "oceans of red ink" (Schama, 1989, 61–62). While Britain could use its income from plundering the Asian subcontinent to pay back its national debt (beginning with Plassey in 1757; see chapters 1 and 2), the French state had to squeeze additional resources from within France or the settler-colonies. Moreover, the immunity of the nobility and clergy to direct taxes—a cornerstone of aristocratic and clerical privilege—placed a major roadblock in the path of resolving the monarchy's fiscal crisis. Aristocratic tax exemption resulted in a major loss of revenue, especially as the more dynamic members of the hereditary nobility were "important participants" in the most lucrative activities of the era, including those related to the booming Atlantic economy. Attempts by the monarchy to reduce or eliminate aristocratic privilege met with wide resistance. As the number of newly ennobled families grew—six thousand families were ennobled during the eighteenth century alone—"those who stood to lose status as well as cash" if privileges were reduced or eliminated "constituted an ever-broadening coalition" (Schama, 1989, 69, 103, 117–18; see also Chaussinand-Nogaret, 1985).

The French notables, like their Dutch and American counterparts, were aware of the dangers of playing with the revolutionary fire. Indeed, "most members of the Constituent Assembly were more frightened of the populace and of the hazards of democratic experiment than they were of counter-revolution" (Blackburn, 1988, 189). Nevertheless, perhaps because of the small maneuvering space available for resolving intra-elite differences, this time the notables lost control of the revolution and began to turn against each other to save their own skins:

> It is only as of the moment that the popular forces enter the scene for reasons that have nothing to do with the revolution desired by the notables that a fault appears which will eventually widen the ditch between nobility and bourgeoisie. For it now became a question of saving one's hide, and to that end any maneuver is legitimate. Threatened just as much as the nobility, the bourgeoisie played a major trump card, the comedy of scandalized virtue; it shouted alongside the people and displaced onto the 'aristocracy' the tempest which threatened to sweep them away. (Chaussinand-Nogaret, as quoted in Wallerstein, 1989, 52)

The Spread of Revolution Back to the Americas

Saint Domingue and the other slave colonies were immensely profitable for France and for the free population of the colonies, thus providing a strong incentive for keeping a lid on factional strife among the free population and between colony and metropolis. Nevertheless, fierce intra-elite divisions in the metropolis inflamed intra-elite divisions in the colonies. The fault lines widened between maritime bourgeoisie and colonial planters, between whites and free coloreds, and between *petits blancs* and *grands blancs*. All these intra-elite and elite-middle-class rifts, in turn, opened the space for a full-scale slave insurrection in Saint Domingue.

The class and caste power structure of Saint Domingue was extremely complex. The *grands blancs* elite was composed of large sugar planters and merchants (some with strong ties to the metropolis, some with strong autonomist leanings). There was also a large group of free coloreds who owned coffee plantations and slaves or were professionals or both. The *petits blancs* were prone to resent the success of the free coloreds and strived to make race rather than wealth the criteria for status and political power. All had an interest in ensuring that the majority slave population remained under firm control.

At first, the Revolution brought colony and mother country closer together: "The events of 1789 aroused great enthusiasm among the colonists of the French Caribbean. The storming of the Bastille had an electric effect on the opponents of 'ministerial despotism' in the colonies" (Blackburn, 1988, 175). Metropolitan merchants and colonial proprietors were for a time united in Jacobin Clubs. The colonists were prepared to support the Third Estate in its bid for majority rule, and the Third Estate was willing to support the colonists' bid for political representation in France. Moreover, in 1790 the Assembly guaranteed that the fundamentals of the slave order (that is, the slave trade, slavery, and metropolitan resources for the repression of slave uprisings) would not be touched.

But colonial planters and local merchants took advantage of the weakening grip of the mother country to evade the *exclusif*. In France, the anger of the port cities at lost trade coalesced with the frustration of the urban population at rising prices for plantation produce, as sugar, coffee, and cacao were diverted from the French entrepôts by the higher prices in New York, Amsterdam, and London. The disruption of colonial trade also fueled the major revolt in the *Vendée* (Blackburn, 1988, 222). French efforts to bring smuggling under control stimulated growing calls for autonomy by colonial planters and local merchants.

The open rift (and spark for civil war) would come over the issue of the franchise. The initial franchise adopted by the Assembly (for mother country and colonies alike) was restricted to property owners and taxpayers—a law that had the effect of enfranchising many of the free coloreds while disenfranchising poor whites. The white population of the colonies resisted implementation of the law. In May 1791 the Assembly passed a law explicitly enfranchising free coloreds born of free parents who met other qualifications. Despite the small number who actually met all the criteria—only four hundred in Saint Domingue—the decree provoked open resistance by white colonists. Fearing that they would lose their most profitable colony, the Constituent Assembly quickly withdrew its support for the implementation of mulatto rights. But by now, the free colored population had determined to take matters into their own hands: "Armed, mulattos sought to enforce their rights" (Blackburn, 1988, 189).

The fateful move in the factional strife in Saint Domingue was the arming of some slaves—a move assiduously avoided in the North American revolt. Factional strife among the elite issued into a full-scale slave revolt in August 1791.

[A]bout 20,000 former slaves left their estates and formed encampments in the foothills surrounding the Northern plain and at Ounaminthe near the border . . . The planters or their managers acknowledged changed conditions by making concessions to their

slaves—an extra day per week, or more extensive cultivation rights—
and in this way retained their work-force. (Blackburn, 1988, 193)

All contenders for power (including the free people of color and
the black generals) had remained committed to the defense of slavery.
But as slave rebellions spread in 1793 and 1794, it became clear that
the slaves themselves held the balance of power: no force could triumph without their support. Touissaint Louverture and Sonthonax
(the Commissioner for the French Republic in the North of Saint
Domingue) both came to understand that "the slaves were the key to
the future of the colony and that victory would belong to whoever was
accepted by them as the bearer of their will to freedom." In August
1793, Sonthonax issued a decree freeing all slaves in his jurisdiction,
and in September, the Commissioner in the South backed Sonthonax's
decree. In February 1794 the Convention in Paris decreed emancipation in all the French colonies, and the Committee of Public Safety assembled an expedition to the New World with instructions to undertake a revolutionary war of liberation of the slaves. In April 1794,
Touissant, who had already begun giving shelter to slave rebels, broke
with Spain and allied with revolutionary France and the spreading
slave rebellions. "For a brief but vital period the programme of radical
abolition was fuelled by slave rebellion and sponsored by a major
power" (Blackburn, 1988, 206, 215–21, 223–26).

The slave rebellion's power was in part rooted in the rapid growth
of the African population in the Americas. Despite appalling mortality
rates, the slave population of the Americas had grown from about
400,000 in 1700 to 2,400,000 in 1770. In the Caribbean region, slaves
composed the majority of the population (Genovese, 1979, 13–14;
Blackburn, 1988, 5; Mintz, 1985, 53). Apart from numerical dominance, two separate roots nourished the power of the slave revolt. On
the one hand, the revolution in the Caribbean drew strength from
the "proto-peasant" aspirations of the slaves (Mintz, 1989, 146–56).
"[T]here can be little doubt that many of St. Domingue's former slaves
saw emancipation principally in terms of their opportunity to cultivate
a plot of land, and raise a family, unmolested by their former overseers." On the other hand, a disciplined and organized labor force had
developed in the plantations.

Localistic, 'proto-peasant' resistance largely thwarted [the various
local and foreign attempts] to recreate a plantation regime. But para-

doxically those who had been formed by the plantations played a major part in sustaining the new Republican political order. Ultimately it was the discipline and coherence of the army, echoing that of the plantations, which defeated the partisans of re-enslavement. (Blackburn, 1988, 236; see also James, 1989, 85–86)

The former slaves were able to hold back a series of restorationist invasions, first by Britain and Spain in 1794, then by Britain again in 1796, and finally by France in 1802. The 1802 French invasion received tacit support from Britain and the United States, which saw the elimination of the black government as essential to the preservation of their own slaveholding societies. Despite the capture of Toussaint Louverture and the wholesale massacre of noncombatants by French forces, a united front of blacks and mulattoes successfully resisted French attempts to restore slavery. On January 1, 1804, the independent Republic of Haiti was proclaimed (Blackburn, 1988, 249–51).

The ability of an army of former slaves to successfully defeat the major European powers of the era had an enormous impact on all actors in the Atlantic world. The example of Haiti inspired slave conspiracies and maroon rebellions throughout the Americas, and a second wave of abolitionist and reform mobilizations in Europe.

Black rebels in Cuba in 1812, in the United States in 1820, in Jamaica and Brazil in the 1820s, found inspiration in Haiti. British, French, and North American abolitionists all wrote books about Toussaint Louverture and the drama of the Haitian revolution. The example of St Domingue lived on in the fears of planters and colonial authorities. (Blackburn, 1988, 257)

Haiti gave material support as well as inspiration to the liberation struggles in Spanish America. The radical and emancipationist turn that Simon Bolivar would take in 1815 was directly linked to the support he received from Haiti. After experiencing a series of defeats from 1811 to 1815, Bolivar appealed to the president of Haiti for help. President Pétion agreed to provide substantial help, but only if Bolivar would undertake to free the slaves in all the lands he liberated. Bolivar's emancipationist policy radicalized the independence struggle and brought him into conflict with many slaveholding Republicans. In the end, the social-political legacy of the struggle, like those throughout the revolutionary epoch, was mixed. Rebellions by Indian and mestizo peasants, such as the Tupac Amaru in 1780–82 or the Hidalgo and Morales uprising in Mexico in 1810, were heavily repressed and elicited few gains. Emancipationist gains were slow and uneven. Nevertheless, the independence movements put slavery on the road to extinction (Blackburn, 1988, 345, 372–73; Wallerstein, 1989, 250).

In the United States, the revolutions in France and Haiti inspired a second wind of abolitionist sentiment, leading to the passage of emancipation laws in New York (1799) and New Jersey (1804), and to the abolition of the slave trade in 1807. But it also led national leaders such as Jefferson to take measures designed to consciously head off any potential for slave rebellion, including supporting the ban on the slave trade as part of an effort to ensure that slaves remained a minority population in the southern states. In addition, Jeffersonians sought to strengthen cross-class alliances between planters and the "common man" (farmers and artisans) based on whiteness, and to design federal structures around "states' rights," so as to preclude the chance that nonslaveholding states might interfere in the southern slaveholding regime. "Jefferson's Republican success . . . brought white American men closer to their government . . . but . . . riveted more securely the chains of southern blacks" (see Blackburn, 1988, 268–86).

Restoration and Hegemonic Consolidation

Britain emerged from the Napoleonic Wars as the most powerful state in the world, both militarily and economically (see chapters 1 and 2). In the aftermath of the wars, Britain used its world power to implement a conservative and restorationist agenda. The Congress of Vienna established a program of monarchical and colonial restoration, including the restoration of slave regimes that had been overthrown as a direct or indirect consequence of the French Revolution and the Napoleonic Wars. For Castlereagh, Britain's foreign secretary from 1812 to 1822, the "only perfect security against the revolutionary embers more or less existing in every state of Europe . . . [was for the European Powers] to stand together in support of the established social order" (quoted by Hobsbawm, 1962, 126). Moreover, after "more than twenty years of unbroken war and revolution . . . it was evident to all intelligent statesmen that no major European war was henceforth tolerable, for such a war would almost certainly mean a new revolution, and consequently the destruction of the old regimes" (Hobsbawm, 1962, 126–28).

British support for restorationist repression abroad was matched by a policy of repression and resistance to reform on the homefront.

Britain was not immune to the spread of revolutionary processes throughout the Atlantic world. The loss of its North American colonies was shortly made up for by major acquisitions in Asia. But the American Revolution and the early years of the French Revolution inspired a first wave of mobilization in support of political reform in Britain itself. Haiti's victory against France in 1804 inspired a second wave of reform mobilization. The 1807 ban on the slave trade was passed during this period of activism. But the mobilizations were cut short by political repression in 1792, and again in the aftermath of the Napoleonic Wars. Unlike in France, intra-elite unity remained strong (despite strains). Imperial success brought prosperity, and prosperity ensured the basic loyalty of the middle classes to an unreformed, corrupt, and unrepresentative political system. The coercive apparatus of the British state remained solid and reliable in the face of popular discontent.

The postwar repression was particularly harsh. The war itself ended amidst riots as thousands of disbanded soldiers and sailors returned to find unemployment in their villages. Middle class reformers—alarmed at this mobilization of the "rabble"—set aside their own grievances (e.g., the 1815 Corn Law) and again sided with the oligarchy. The Coercion Acts of 1817 suspended habeas corpus and gave the government power to ban meetings. The Peterloo massacre of peaceful demonstrators in Manchester in August 1819 was followed by the passage of the Six Gag Acts in December. This further curtailment of civil rights marked the launching of "the most sustained campaign of prosecutions in the courts in British history" (Thompson, 1966, chapter 15).

Yet, the prewar status quo could not be fully restored in intrastate or interstate relations. Something *had* changed as a result of the struggles of the revolutionary epoch. According to Perry Anderson (1980, 36) "the whole ideological world of the West was transformed." The undefeated revolution in Saint Domingue, the ongoing slave revolts in the Caribbean, and the liberation struggles in South America had a profound impact on perceptions of human freedom and democracy. While reform sentiment in Britain had been a novelty in the 1790s, after 1815 "the claims of *Rights of Man*" were "*assumed*" (Thompson, 1966, 603).

By the early 1830s, it was increasingly clear that the revolutionary genie had not been put back in the bottle. By 1831, political mobilization in Britain had again reached the point of a prerevolutionary crisis as the wages and living conditions of laborers deteriorated. There were huge working-class demonstrations in mining and manufacturing districts, Captain Swing riots in the countryside, and "the marches and drilling of Political Unions demanding parliamentary reform" (Thompson, 1966, 808–9; Blackburn, 1988, 446). Moreover, mass mobilization in Britain fed and was fed by simultaneous uprisings on the Continent (e.g., the 1830 Revolution in France) and slave revolts in the West Indies (such as the 1831 mass uprising on Christmas Day in Jamaica). Again, events in the Americas inspired renewed reform and radical political activity in Europe, which in turn furthered the struggles in the Americas (Blackburn, 1988, 432, 436).

Faced with widespread revolutionary ferment, King William gave his support to a limited reform enfranchising one-tenth of the adult male population. The British Reform Bill passed in June 1832. In August 1833, the reformed Parliament passed a slave emancipation bill that generously compensated slaveowners for almost the full value of their slaves. The same parliament then proceeded to pass a new Poor Law in 1834, which eliminated all outdoor relief for the unemployed (Polanyi, 1957, 224). As E. P. Thompson put it, in 1832 "blood compromised with gold to keep out the claims of *egalité*." The 1832 reform represented an "accommodation between landed and industrial wealth, between privilege and money" (1966, 819–20).

The political dynamic of the 1840s confirmed the solidity of the 1832 alliance, albeit with the growing strength of "gold" vis-à-vis "blood" in the partnership. In 1846 the Corn Laws were repealed, thanks in part to working-class mobilizations. But the powerful Chartist movement—with its demand for universal manhood suffrage—was roundly defeated as "all those with a property stake in the country" closed ranks (Saville, 1987, 227; see also Mann 1993, 529–30). Keeping the poor away from political power came to be seen as a fundamental precondition for the functioning of laissez-faire and the protection of private property. "It would have been an act of lunacy," Karl Polanyi notes, "to hand over the administration of the New Poor Law with its scientific methods of mental torture to the representatives of the self-same people for whom that treatment was designed." Indeed, Britain's political leaders saw the Charter's call for universal manhood suffrage as an attack on the Constitution, revealing that "constitutionalism [had] gained an utterly new meaning" in the nineteenth century. Instead of a primary concern with acquiring protection from interference by the state, capitalists now sought protection "not against the Crown but against the people" (Polanyi, 1957, 225).

Following the 1832 parliamentary reform, Britain reassumed the role of symbolic leader for middle-class reformist currents on the Continent, and began presenting itself as the model for how reform should be achieved. Britain's policy of publicly supporting the repressive measures of the Holy Alliance had already begun to change in 1822, when "the flexible Canning replaced the rigid reactionary Castlereagh." Britain came out in support of independence for the Latin American states, and when revolts broke out in Spain, Italy, Greece, and Portugal, Britain finally spoke out against the Holy Alliance's efforts to repress them, making Britain the beacon for continental liberals (Adams, 1940, 84–85; Hobsbawm, 1962, 131).

James Adams (1940, 99), in a passage that seems steeped in hegemonic ideology, contrasts the British reform movement with the continental upheavals of 1830: "It was typical of the British, as contrasted with their Continental neighbors, that their revolution, if we may call it so, of 1830–32 was comparatively peaceful, as well as constitutional, and lasting." Likewise, of Britain in 1848, Priscilla Robertson (1967, 406) claims that "the spirit of conciliation of classes [was at work], each one eager to render justice to the others, each one contributing by its good will to the common welfare." Peaceful compromise and limited reforms became the organizing myth of British hegemony—as a description of its own history and as a prescription for others.

The Continent would indeed emulate the "British model" in the aftermath of the 1848 revolutions, although the path to get there was far from "peaceful." Faced with the threat of social revolution, the bourgeoisies of Europe called a halt to *their* revolution, set aside their demands for more commercial and intellectual freedom, and embraced reaction (as the British bourgeoisie had done in the immediate postwar years). When faced with a choice between "order" and "freedom," the middle classes chose "order." In the aftermath of 1848, symbiotic alliances between old landed wealth and new industrial elites were established. The working-class movements were isolated and crushed; the propertyless and the poor were firmly excluded from political power. Even the franchise for the propertied classes was often

temporarily sacrificed. But in the alliance that resulted, the bourgeoisies were able to gain their most vital demands as capitalist principles were advanced through "reforms from above" (Kocka, 1986,
288–91; Robertson, 1967, 140).

In sum, British hegemony came to symbolize an increased political
role for the propertied, but non-noble classes (the bourgeoisies) of
Europe. The social power of the propertied middle class was to be
slowly but surely recognized in the West. But universal suffrage remained the demand of radicals. The various reforms were largely agreements among the old elite and the emerging middle classes designed to
head off more radical and democratic concessions to the emerging
working classes. There was a major expansion of the Westphalia system as the newly independent national bourgeoisies in the former
American colonies were recognized and incorporated as full members
in the system of states. But Haiti was ostracized. Slavery, overthrown in
much of the Atlantic world, continued to thrive (with tacit British support) in Brazil, Cuba, and the southern United States. Finally, the rights
of non-Western peoples to self-determination were trampled upon, as
Britain proceeded to build the Second Empire in Asia as the main pillar
of its hegemony in the Western world (see chapter 4).

The Rise of Labor and National Liberation Movements

From Vicious to Virtuous Circle and Back

With the emergence of autonomous working-class militancy in the
most industrialized areas of Europe, the revolutions of 1848 can be
seen as harbingers of the rebellions and revolutions that marked the
transition from British to U.S. hegemony in the first half of the twentieth century. But given the complete and bloody defeat of the working-
class uprisings, 1848 is more fruitfully seen as the final round of the
struggles leading up to the firm establishment of British hegemony.

The decisive defeat of the working-class movements in 1848, together with the reforms won by capitalist interests, created favorable
social conditions for the systemwide expansion of trade and production of the 1850s and 1860s—what Hobsbawm (1979) dubbed the
"Age of Capital" (1848–1875). This British-led expansion was analogous in several ways to the earlier Dutch-led expansion. First, it was a
period of relative political stability and social peace. Just as the social
and political turbulence that had characterized much of the seventeenth

century subsided toward the end of the century, so the revolutions and state breakdowns that had spread throughout the Atlantic world during the transition to British hegemony virtually disappeared in the decades following 1848.

At the root of both these shifts from turbulence to quiescence was a "virtuous circle": the wealth generated in the course of the system-wide expansions in trade and production allowed for the establishment of intra-elite peace—that is, class compromises among the big and small beneficiaries of the prosperity. This intra-elite peace, in turn, fostered the conditions for continued material expansion. In the early eighteenth century, as we have seen, this meant that settlers and planters in the Americas accepted their subordinate status within the hegemonic bloc. In the third quarter of the nineteenth century, this meant that the national bourgeoisies in sovereign states outside of Britain accepted British world hegemony and eagerly hooked up to the British industrial entrepôt as suppliers of raw materials and consumers of capital goods. Britain was at the center of a rapidly growing world-capitalist system that brought the greatest fortune and power to Britain, but whose benefits trickled down to embrace a far-flung global elite. As a result, peace and prosperity reinforced one another (see chapter 1; also Carr, 1945, 11).

Moreover, during both the Dutch-led and British-led expansions of world trade and production, benefits from the expansion trickled down as far as the upper strata of the laboring classes, including artisans and farmers. In contrast to the growing polarization between rich and poor that characterized the periods of financial expansion, "middle classes" grew in size with the expansion of trade and production, and consensual rule widened its embrace. In the decades after 1848, in various European countries, a distinction was gradually made between the "respectable" working class (the artisanal elite) and the rabble, with the former cautiously welcomed as junior partners into the hegemonic bloc through judicious extensions of the adult male franchise.

This intra-elite and cross-class peace was underwritten by territorial conquest and racial oppression in both periods of hegemony. Slavery and the conquest of the Americas had been central to the social underpinnings of Dutch hegemony. Likewise, the "opening" of the entire North American continent for farmer-settlers and slave plantations in the wake of the Mexican-American War (1846–48) and the expanding opportunities for settler-farmers and civil servants in the colonial bureaucracies in conquered territories in Asia and Africa were crucial to the social underpinnings of nineteenth-century British hegemony.

Moreover, British Free Trade Imperialism contributed to a decline in the tax burden—especially significant, as taxation had been one of the central grievances feeding social unrest in the late eighteenth and early nineteenth centuries. Unilateral free trade lowered Britain's military costs (and hence per capita taxation) by encouraging peaceful interstate commerce in the West. At the same time, the formation of the British empire in India shifted a good part of the financial and human costs of the *Pax Britannica* onto the peoples of Asia themselves through, among other things, an increase in *their* tax burden (see chapters 1, 2, and 4). The result was "tax relief" on a European-wide scale in the mid-nineteenth century. Mann (1993, 533) maintains that "regressive war finance had caused most class politicization since the 1760s," and that as the tax burden on consumption declined from the 1840s onward, so working-class politicization also declined. "In the late nineteenth century, new forms of class politicization would arise, but [in the decades following 1848] there came a lull."

Common to both hegemonies, thus, was the building of cross-class cohesion through the exacerbation of the racial divide on a world scale. Moreover, in both periods, intra-elite unity and widening support from the world's "middle classes" left little opportunity for effective rebellion by the victims of the world trade expansion—in the nineteenth century, those who failed to escape the dreaded fall into the proletariat, and the victims of European expansion in Asia, Africa, and the Americas. Thus, the high point of British hegemony corresponded not only to a lull in working-class mobilization and politicization in Europe, but to the repression of popular uprisings in China (the Taiping Rebellion of 1850–64) and in India (the Great Rebellion of 1857), as well as to the final defeat of all North American Indian resistance to their forcible removal from the land (Brown, 1971).

Finally, while both the Dutch-led and British-led booms in world trade and production created a virtuous circle of expanding profitability and social peace in the short run of a generation or two, in the medium run they led to an intensification of intercapitalist competition, a shift to financial speculation, and growing social-economic polarization. They also both transformed the world-scale balance of class forces. In other words, one by-product of the material expansions was the eventual undermining of the social bases of the world hegemonic order and the setting of the stage for a renewed period of widespread rebellion and revolution. In the late eighteenth century, as we have seen, financialization and social-economic polarization eroded cross-class cohesion within countries and widened rifts between colonial settler populations and mother countries. Moreover, these rifts grew within a social-structural context that had been greatly transformed by the material expansion of the preceding decades—that is, the numbers and resources of the junior partners of the hegemonic bloc (e.g., the colonial settlers) had been greatly strengthened, as were the numbers and the strategic power of some of the excluded and exploited (e.g., the Caribbean slaves).

British hegemony followed an analogous denouement. The explosive growth of world trade and production in the "Age of Capital" (1848–1873) brought about two major transformations that impacted social relations worldwide. On the one hand, by 1873 it had provoked a sharp intensification of intercapitalist competition, followed by the British-led financial expansion of the Edwardian belle époque (see chapter 1). On the other hand, it transformed the world-scale balance of class forces—creating, enlarging, and strengthening the social forces that would challenge the established world order. As in the transition from Dutch hegemony, the economic polarization and social disruptions that accompanied the financial expansion combined with the structural transformations in the balance of class forces to produce a major world-scale wave of rebellions and revolutions. Escalating social conflict combined and interacted with intensifying interstate conflict, leading to the destruction of the old world order and contributing to the shaping of the social foundations of a new world order.

Figure 6 provides a graphic summary of the processes at work in both transitions as seen from the angle of vision adopted in this chapter. However, as we shall see below, the waves of social conflict that mark the transition from British to U.S. hegemony were not a simple repeat of the previous transition. As a result of the transformations of the world capitalist system that took place under British hegemony, the agencies of social conflict would be different. Moreover, the speed, scale, and scope of the social conflict, as well as its impact on interstate power struggles, would be far greater.

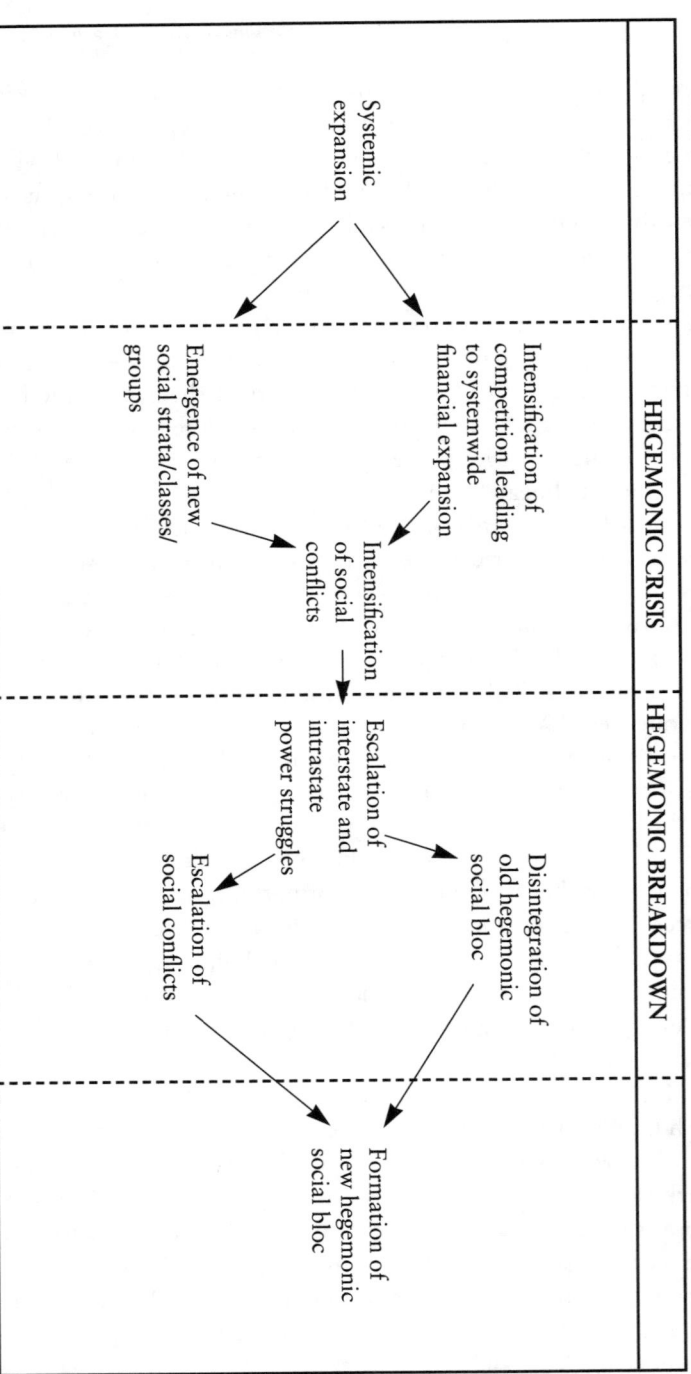

Figure 6. Hegemonic transitions and social conflict.

The Great Depression and the Rise of Workers' Movements and Mass Parties

The Great Depression of 1873–1896 was a decisive turning point for British hegemony from the angle of vision of the interstate power struggle (see chapter 1) and of interenterprise competition (see chapter 2). Closely related were the first signs of the undermining of the social bases of British hegemony in the 1880s and 1890s. For most of its duration, the Great Depression was primarily a depression for capitalists, not for workers. In Britain, for example, real wages grew steadily during the depression, while unemployment did not increase significantly (Saul, 1969, 28–34). Nevertheless, by the 1890s capitalists had succeeded almost everywhere in shifting much of the burden of the new competitive environment onto their workers through various restructuring strategies. The Great Depression, writes David Montgomery (1987, 56) was "the cradle in which scientific management was born." As the earnest efforts of management to tighten control over the pace and style of work met the equally earnest efforts of workers to resist, class tensions in the workplace escalated. Moreover, by the last decade of the century, financialization, along with horizontal and vertical integration (see chapter 2), succeeded in transforming the deflationary pressure on capitalists into inflationary pressures on workers— that is, prices began to rise faster than wages (Gordon, Edwards, and Reich, 1982, 95–99; Boyer, 1979; Phelps Brown and Browne, 1968). Workers responded by combining their efforts in defense of their wages and working conditions. Trade unions and working class parties proliferated throughout Europe and the Americas. The final years of the Depression saw the reestablishment of the (Second) International, the appearance of a significant number of socialists in parliaments, and a mushrooming in union membership and strike activity. This was the first major upsurge in labor militancy since 1848 (Abendroth, 1972, chapter 3; Hobsbawm, 1987, 130).

In sharp contrast to 1848, however, this upsurge could not be easily repressed. The size and scope of the industrial working classes had grown enormously in the course of the preceding expansion. In Germany, while only 600,000 workers (or about 4 percent of the total labor force) were employed in mining or manufacturing in 1850, by 1873 the number had tripled, and by 1900 it had reached 5.7 million workers (or 22 percent of the total labor force) (Kocka, 1986, 296–97).

In the United States, between 1840 and 1870 employment in manu-facturing increased fivefold. In Boston, the numbers employed in major industries doubled between 1845 and 1855, and again between 1855 and 1865. In the three decades after the Civil War, the advances in industrial output and employment, the emergence of giant factories, and the disappearance of artisanal establishments were even more rapid (Gordon, Edwards, and Reich, 1982, 82–83; Shefter, 1986, 199–200; Bridges, 1986, 173).

The attacks on craft standards chipped away at the "consent" of the "labor aristocracy" and induced skilled workers to reach out to unskilled workers. In Britain the discontent of the artisanal elite and the growing size and power of unskilled workers was signaled by the "new unionism" of the late 1880s. In only four years following 1888, union membership doubled to 1.5 million and union density jumped from 5 to 11 percent, with industrial unions in mining and transport leading the way. An employer offensive in the late 1890s was followed by another forward burst of unionism in the decade prior to the world war, with membership jumping to over 4 million and union density reaching 25 percent. Trade unionism became more aggressive and po-litical and *less sectional,* "absorbing unskilled, semiskilled, and skilled workers alike" (Mann, 1993, 601–9).

This trend toward greater unity of action and purpose across skill levels was visible wherever the old craft elite felt threatened while the new industrial workforce mushroomed in size. In France this period saw not only a "second great burst of socialist ferment and organiza-tion," but the first time that "factory workers and artisans were in-tegrated into a common class-conscious movement" (Sewell, 1986, 67–70). In the United States union membership increased fourfold be-tween 1880 and 1890, while strike activity swelled in the 1890s and the first decade of the twentieth century. Strikes in this period were often sparked by craft workers resisting "deskilling." However, they tended to spread quickly and envelop the full labor force in large fac-tories. Cooperation between skilled and unskilled workers (and men and women) could also be seen in the widespread community support in manufacturing towns that striking workers received. Late-nineteenth-century strikes were frequently accompanied by marches from factory to factory, and through working-class neighborhoods, calling for sup-port. Non-striking members of the working-class communities com-monly participated in these marches and open-air meetings (Shefter,

1986, 217–18; Brecher, 1972; Gordon, Edwards, and Reich, 1982, 121–27; Montgomery, 1979).

Gordon, Edwards, and Reich attribute this growing tendency toward multioccupational (and community) solidarity to the increasing homogenization of the labor force: the attack on craftworkers brought their conditions of work closer to the unskilled and fostered a natural solidarity. Moreover, the mushrooming size of the unskilled workforce and its concentration in downtown factory districts and working-class neighborhoods facilitated both the rapid spread of protest across categories of workers and plants, and a growing common class consciousness. Protests launched in one plant or neighborhood quickly spread, leading contemporary observers to use the epidemiological metaphor of "contagious diseases" to describe the diffusion of protest. "This density and intensity of 'communicable' protest," write Gordon et al., "both took root in the increasingly homogeneous working conditions of masses of wage workers and helped contribute to these workers' spreading consciousness of common problems and conditions" (1982, 126).

While the most spectacular trade union growth took place in Britain, and the most violent class warfare erupted in the United States, the most stunning example of working-class party growth was in Germany. The German Social Democratic Party (SDP) quickly became the largest political party after the abrogation of the antisocialist laws in 1890. The electoral strength of the SDP doubled from 10 percent of the vote in 1887 to 23 percent in 1893. They attracted "nearly one and a half million votes in 1890, over two millions in 1898, three millions out of an electorate of nine millions in 1903, and four and a quarter millions in 1912." The German case was the most striking example of a general process. While mass working-class parties barely existed in 1880, by 1906 they were "the norm" in industrializing countries wherever they were legal. In Scandinavia and Germany they were already the largest party (although still not a majority) (Barraclough, 1967, 135; Piven, 1992, 2).

If keeping the poor away from political power was a fundamental precondition for the functioning of the British-centered world capitalist system, then the rise of working-class parties and the general agitation for universal manhood suffrage presented a profound challenge. In Polanyi's words: "Inside and outside England . . . there was not a militant liberal who did not express his conviction that popular democracy was a danger to capitalism" (1957, 226). A common response to the challenge was repression (the German Social Democratic Party was outlawed in 1879), but pure repression was no longer a sufficient response. In 1890 the ban on the German SDP was removed, and major extensions of the franchise were won throughout most of Europe around the turn of the century. To be sure, as suffrage rights were broadened, various tactics, such as limiting the constitutional powers of directly elected bodies and gerrymandering, were introduced as safeguards (Hobsbawm, 1987, 85–99, 116–18). Nevertheless, the emergence of politically organized working classes was a profound transformation and required more than a modification of tactics; a fundamental change in ruling class strategies was required (Therborn, 1977, 23–28).

The night-watchman state would be sacrificed in an attempt to diffuse working-class protest from below. Social insurance schemes (old-age pensions, health and unemployment insurance) were introduced in the last decade of the nineteenth century and first decades of the twentieth century as part of an effort to take the steam out of socialist agitation. Germany was precocious with the first moves in the 1880s; Britain followed with a series of measures in 1906–1914 (Abbott and DeViney, 1992).

However, the new legitimation of state activism was not a reaction to working-class demands alone. The intense competition that characterized the Great Depression prompted clamors for "protection" from all segments of the class spectrum. The agrarian classes in continental Europe were especially hard hit by the massive inflow of imported grains as the steamship and railroads (and free-trade policies) allowed cheap American and Russian supplies to flood the continental market (Mayer, 1981). Even in the United States, repeated overproduction crises in agriculture led to vigorous demands from farmers for government action aimed at expanding their markets and providing them with cheap railroad transportation (LaFeber, 1963, 9–10; Williams, 1969, 20–22).

Moreover, the national bourgeoisies of continental Europe, which had tended to see international free trade as being in their own as well as Britain's interest during the mid-nineteenth century, changed their tune by the 1878 Congress of Berlin. They joined agrarian elites in demanding that government action be oriented toward obtaining exclusive spheres of influence, protected markets, and privileged sources of supply. In the United States, the depression of 1893 (the first crisis to hit manufacturing harder than agriculture) cemented the alliance between agriculturalists and industrialists in favor of aggressive overseas expansion. The fact that this depression was accompanied by widespread social unrest contributed to the sense of urgency. As William A. Williams (1969, 41) notes: "The economic impact of the depression [of 1893], and its effect in producing a real fear of extensive social unrest and even revolution," led U. S. business and government leaders to finally accept "overseas expansion as the strategic solution to the nation's economic and social problems." One immediate outcome was the U.S. government decision to fight Spain on two fronts in 1898—a war in large measure designed to expand U.S. access to the markets of Asia.

Thus, by the end of the depression "all western countries . . . irrespective of national mentality or history" moved toward the implementation of policies designed to protect citizens against the disruptions caused by a self-regulating world market (Polanyi, 1957, 216–17). But protection of domestic markets from foreign competition and high-pressure colonial tactics required military might to conquer colonies and to fend off the growing number of imperialist rivals pursuing similar strategies. By the end of the Great Depression, a vicious circle linking domestic and international conflict was engaged.

Great Power Rivalries and Revolution: The First Wave

Starting in the 1880s, the escalation of the armaments race among European powers and their mutual competition for mobile capital inflated profits and brought a belle epoque for the European bourgeoisie (see chapter 1). But the belle epoque did not signify a new stabilization of the social foundations of British hegemony; rather, the depression for capitalists was overcome by tightening the squeeze on workers. Thus, the Edwardian era (like the first phase of the transition from Dutch hegemony) was one of growing economic and social polarization.

In the previous transition, the conspicuous consumption of elites side by side with mass (and middle-class) misery had been an important ingredient provoking growing social conflict in the late eighteenth century, from the American Revolution through the Dutch and French Revolutions. Analogous processes emerged in the late nineteenth century and fed into the rising socialist and labor agitation. Moreover, just as Dutch elites were particularly embarrassed by the wide divergence between their puritan self-image and their gluttonous reality, so members of the British bourgeoisie were hard pressed to make the same leadership claims that might have seemed credible earlier in the nineteenth century. If, as Hobsbawm (1987, 127, 168–69) claims, "a common front had united those who laboured and produced, workers, artisans, shopkeepers, bourgeois against the idle and against 'privilege'" and was "largely responsible for the earlier historical and political force of liberalism," by the late nineteenth century this common front had crumbled. The bourgeoisie became "more visibly integrated into the undifferentiated zone of wealth, state power and privilege. It joined the 'plutocracy' which . . . increasingly flaunted itself, visibly and through the new mass media."

The increasing polarization between rich and poor was also intimately tied to the intensification of rivalries among the great powers. Although the intensification was in part rooted in an effort to contain domestic conflicts through a strategy of fusing national and social protection, its effects were not unambiguously favorable for the promotion of national social cohesion. As in the transition from Dutch to British hegemony, conflict over distributing the costs of war-financing inflamed social conflict. In the previous transition the main contention was the distribution of the tax burden. In the transition from British to U.S. hegemony, inflationary deficit spending by governments was the main source of financing the arms buildup. Like direct taxes, inflation contributed to the squeeze on real wages, but it created a less visible target in the state. Or perhaps more accurately, it increased the visibility of the "triple alliance" of governments, finance capital, and heavy industry—so-called monopoly capital—as the culprit and target at which protest was directed.

If we judge from the direction of mass protest in the decades leading up to the First World War, it would appear that national hegemonic projects fusing national and social protection were not containing social tensions. As figure 7 shows, a rapid escalation of labor militancy took place in the 1890s, and then again from 1905 until the outbreak of the war. Working classes continued to grow rapidly throughout the capitalist world during the belle epoque and they were increasingly located in strategic concentrations. Moreover, they took advantage of this size and strategic location (in an increasingly planned and conscious fashion) to launch mass strikes in the sectors that were

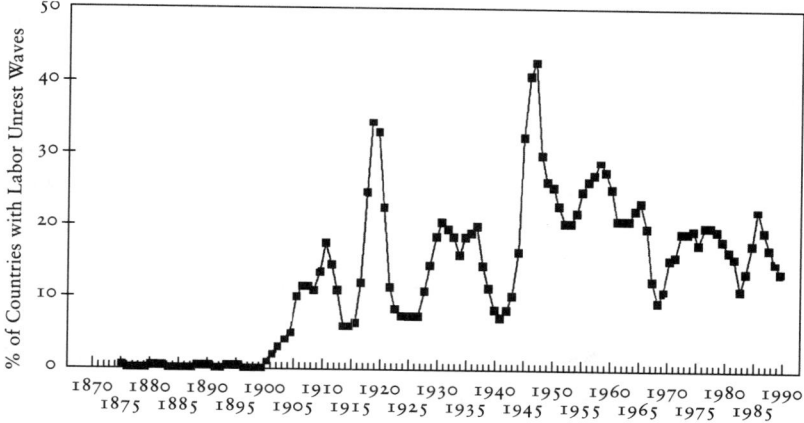

Figure 7. *Labor unrest waves in the world-system (three-year moving average). Figures from 1870 to 1905 based on* New York Times: *figures from 1906 to 1990 based on maximum of* New York Times *and* Times (London). *Source:* WLG *Database.*

the lifeblood of the world capitalist system: especially coal mining, maritime transport, and railways.

Given the militancy of European working classes in the decades leading up to the war, it surprised most contemporary observers when European citizens (including most of the working class) went to war in 1914 with apparent enthusiasm. It now appeared that the ruling elites had successfully fashioned national hegemonic projects that brought cross-class allegiance to the state. Indeed, once the masses were in a position to make demands on their respective states for social and economic protection, working-class internationalism was on shaky ground. As E. H. Carr put it:

> In the nineteenth century, when the nation belonged to the middle class and the worker had no fatherland, socialism had been international. The crisis of 1914 showed in a flash that, except in backward Russia, this attitude was everywhere obsolete. The mass of workers knew instinctively on which side their bread was buttered . . . International socialism ignominiously collapsed. (Carr, 1945, 20–21; see also Haupt, 1972)

The masses in European states supported their flags. To the surprise of the war planners, draft evasion was virtually nonexistent. Labor militancy and socialist agitation declined precipitously during the first years of the war (see figure 7). To be sure, this decline in part had coercive roots (Tilly, 1989, 441–42), but it was also rooted in active government efforts to secure the consent and cooperation of trade unionists. Tripartite agreements between trade unions, employers, and governments secured no strike pledges from union leaders in exchange for government and employer recognition of trade unions and the establishment of collective bargaining and grievance procedures. For the union movement in many countries (e.g., the United States) the First World War marked the first time that employers relaxed their implacable hostility to trade unions (Hibbs, 1978, 157; see also Feldman, 1966; Brody, 1980; Dubofsky, 1983; Davis, 1986; Giddens, 1987).

However, a central characteristic of the early twentieth century was the extremely unstable nature of all these national hegemonic compacts. The brutality of the war would disabuse many of the idea that a successful formula for protecting citizens had been found. This sentiment was registered loud and clear by the major wave of rebellions and revolutions that exploded in the midst of the war and continued in its aftermath. By 1916 mushrooming strikes, desertions, and revolts gave lie to the conclusion that new stable national hegemonies had been formed. By the time of the 1917 Russian Revolution, antiwar feeling among the populations of Europe was probably a majority sentiment. And in 1918 it seemed like socialist revolution would spread throughout Europe.

If the strikes in the 1905–1914 period revealed the vulnerability of capital to labor agitation in transport and mining industries, during the war itself it was the vast armaments industries that proved most vulnerable to labor militancy. The industrialization of war (see chapter 1) meant massive private and public investments in weapons manufacture. Workers in the metalworking industries became critical cogs in the war machine, supplying the soldiers at the front. But the industrialization of war also meant a confrontation with craftworkers, as efforts to mechanize arms production were pushed forward. It was in the metalworking industries that the Tripartite Agreements first floundered, for it was here that "the traditional force of labour organization, the skilled workers . . . with stubborn craft unions met the modern factory." The vast armaments industries—in Britain, Germany, France, Russia, and the United States—became the centers of industrial and antiwar militancy by both skilled and unskilled workers. The metalworkers in the factories turned to revolution during and after the war, as did "the new high-tech navies" or "floating factories" at Kronstadt and Kiel (Hobsbawm, 1994; 1987, 123–24; Cronin, 1983, 33–35).

Thus, from the beginnings of the belle epoque through the aftermath of the First World War, a vicious circle of escalating social and interstate conflict can be clearly seen. A link between interstate conflict and domestic social conflict can also be seen in the transition from Dutch to British hegemony. As was argued in the first part of this chapter, the dislocations and boom-bust cycle caused by the Seven Years' War in North America were important in detonating the American Revolution. The immense costs of France's intervention in the American Revolutionary War were crucial in bringing about the final collapse of the French monarchy and the French Revolution. However, contrary to the transition from British to U.S. hegemony, there is no evidence that the reverse relationship also obtains—that is, neither the Seven Years' War nor the French intervention in the American Revolutionary War seem to have been motivated by efforts to quell social unrest on the home front. The escalation of interstate conflict precedes the escalation of intrastate conflict, with geopolitical considerations (discussed in chapter 1) as the main driving force behind the initial escalation of military confrontations.

In the transition from British to U.S. hegemony, the relationship between intrastate and interstate conflict is far more intertwined. Class and nationalist agitation is clearly escalating on the eve of the First World War. Even the colonialist adventures in the late 1890s follow (and attempt to divert) increasing class antagonisms. Little victorious wars could be popular and bolster governments. The Spanish-American War (in the United States) and the South African War (in the United Kingdom) were two such examples. However, the danger that lost (or otherwise unpopular) wars represented was also well known. This was one of the lessons rulers learned from the revolutionary upheavals that shook the Russian Empire in 1905 in the wake of its defeat by Japan.

In sum, if prior to the nineteenth century rulers seemed to fight wars with little concern for "public opinion," by the end of the century domestic politics and international politics were intimately intertwined. Indeed, by the time of the First World War, military strategists were well aware of this close relationship. New military strategies, such as naval blockades aimed at cutting off food supplies and raising the threat of mass starvation among noncombatants, were designed to create domestic instability on the enemies' homefront. Such strategies recognized the importance of retaining popular loyalty (and the danger of losing mass support) for success in war (Offer, 1985).

A first premonition of this link was visible during the Napoleonic Wars. Indeed, part of the restoration that took place in the early nineteenth century involved ending experimentation with citizen armies and returning to old-style armies—that is, armies of paid professionals, mercenaries, and "gentlemen." As McNeill has pointed out, the experience of warfare in the age of revolution had convinced Europe's rulers that "the fierce energy of the French conscripts in 1793–95, and the nationalist fervor of some German citizen soldiers in 1813–14, could challenge constituted authority as readily as it could confirm and strengthen it" (1982, 221). By restoring the old-style armies, Europe's rulers "refrained from tapping the depths of national energies that the revolutionary years unveiled." But they also kept "the specter of revolutionary disorder at bay."

In the early nineteenth century, the genie could be put back in the bottle since the nationalization and democratization of the state had only just begun. By the time of the outbreak of the First World War, however, states had gone far in developing nationalism and patriotism as the new civil religion. Soldiers would once again be mobilized as "citizens" fighting for a just cause (Tilly, 1990). If European rulers hoped in 1914 for a popular little war, they badly misjudged the changed conditions that the industrialization and nationalization of warfare had brought about. Once the wheel turned from nationalist to revolutionary fervor, the arms used to defend the constituted order were used to challenge it. Demobilized and deserting soldiers returned to their towns and villages from the battleground, carrying both the message of revolution and the guns with which to fight for it (Wolf, 1969).

This volatile admixture resulted in a speeding up of social history: great power rivalries and social conflict were far more intertwined, and systemic chaos was unleashed far more quickly than in the first transition. A second and related difference was the widening of the geographical space in which revolutionary processes were diffused. If revolutionary contradictions largely diffused within an "Atlantic space" during the first transition, the second transition had become a global affair.

This globalization of revolutionary processes was linked to the globalization of the world capitalist system in the nineteenth century. With the spread of railroads and steamships, the intensification of competition that marked the late nineteenth century Great Depression shook local class relations from South America to Asia and Africa. From the sugar plantations of Morelos in Mexico to the vineyards of western Algeria and the rubber plantations of southern Vietnam, the new opportunities to sell cash crops in the world market initiated a race by capitalist entrepreneurs to grab land, labor, and other resources. Sometimes local, sometimes foreign capitalist classes, sometimes backed by local oligarchic rule, sometimes backed by foreign imperial power, the result nevertheless was a crisis of livelihood for the peasantry and a crisis of legitimacy for existing social contracts upon which political stability had been based.

We have emphasized the impact that the intensification of capitalist competition had on labor-capital relations. On a world scale—and even in much of Europe itself—the greatest disruptions (with the most important political consequences) took place in the agrarian sector (Mayer, 1981). Eric Wolf (1969, 280–81) argues that the rapid commodification of land and labor in the periphery in the late nineteenth century brought on an ecological crisis of the peasantry. "Where in the past the peasant had worked out a stable combination of resources to underwrite a minimal livelihood, the separate and differential mobilization of these resources as objects to be bought and sold endangered that minimal nexus." The commercialization of land threatened access to pasture, forest, and other common lands; and the "outright seizure of land by foreign colonists and enterprises drove the peasants back upon a land area no longer sufficient for their needs." Peasant resistance to the destruction of traditional ways of life by domestic and foreign capital was crucial to the major revolutions of the twentieth century, from Mexico and Russia to China, Vietnam, and Algeria.

The Mexican Revolution in Morelos provides one example of this general process. The extension of the railroads in the 1870s and 1880s in Mexico opened new opportunities for turning haciendas into capitalist enterprises oriented toward the world market. Beckoning profits motivated a "race . . . to grab land, water, and labor" through whatever means necessary. Villages began to disappear, swallowed up by plantations, in the latter's ceaseless quest for "more." By the time of the outbreak of the Mexican Revolution in 1910, it had become clear that "the village as a community" had no place in the new economy: their land was to be taken over by the planters and the self-sufficient peasantry turned into agricultural wage workers (Womack, 1968, 15–65).

With this change in the distribution of land came a change in patterns of governance, and a destabilization of consensual elements of rule. Whereas the old hacendados had attempted to supplement force with the appearance of fairness by supporting local governors who at least listened to the grievances of the poor peasants and villagers, by the turn of the century a new plantocracy placed in power governors who made no effort to hide their complete subservience to the planter elite. The legitimacy of planter rule was further undermined in the eyes of the poor (*and* middle classes) by the fact that growing economic and social polarization was accompanied by open displays of lavish and conspicuous consumption on the part of the planter elite. From this point of view, Mexico in the Edwardian era was reproducing a general pattern of the belle epoque. The polarization (and growing grievances of the middle classes) led to a split in the ruling elite over national political succession. In this space, endemic village resistance was able to escalate into armed rebellion in 1910–11 (Womack, 1968).

Some of the same processes are visible in the 1905 Russian Revolution. As in Mexico, a modernization program had opened the country up with railroads and made Russia a major supplier of wheat. But peasants suffered greatly when the world-market price for wheat dropped by half during the late nineteenth-century depression. Peasant rioting, long semidormant, began to revive in 1902. With the final spark of defeat in the Russo-Japanese War and the disintegration of the armed forces, peasant revolts on a massive scale broke out in the Black Earth region, the Volga valley, and parts of the Ukraine (Hobsbawm, 1987, 297; see also Wolf, 1969; Skocpol, 1979).

The Russian Revolution of 1905, however, represented a hybrid case between a peasant-based peripheral revolution and a worker-based core revolution. As a result, it would have enormous international repercussions (a harbinger of the tremendous impact of the 1917 revolution). The hugely successful modernization program had left Russia "with a rapidly growing industrial proletariat, concentrated in unusually large complexes of plants in a few major centres, and consequently with the beginnings of a labour movement which was . . . committed to social revolution." General strikes in Rostov-on-

Don, Odessa, and Baku in 1902–3 broke out as open peasant resistance was resurfacing. "Mass workers' strikes in the capital and sympathetic strikes in most industrial cities in the empire" were crucial in initiating "the government's retreat" in 1905 and later exerting "the pressure which led to the grant of something like a constitution" (Hobsbawm, 1987, 294–97).

Moreover, the role that the rebellions by national minorities played in the 1905 Russian Revolution strengthened its resonance in the multiethnic empires of the world, and especially throughout Asia and the Middle East. The common frontiers shared by the Russian Empire with several Asian countries, the ethnic groups that overlapped on both sides of the frontiers, the large numbers of Persians, Chinese, and Turks who resided, studied, or worked in Russia, all heightened the impact of the Russian Revolution. At the same time, the fact that Russia's minority population of twenty million Muslims participated in the 1905 revolution and held three Muslim Congresses between 1905 and 1907 "had far-reaching repercussions on fellow Muslims beyond Russia's frontiers, especially in Persia and Turkey" (Stavrianos, 1981, 389). The Russian Revolution of 1905 "almost certainly precipitated the Persian and Turkish revolutions, it probably accelerated the Chinese, and by stimulating the Austrian emperor to introduce universal suffrage, it transformed, and made even more unstable, the troubled politics of the Hapsburg Empire" (Hobsbawm, 1987, 297; see also Stavrianos, 1981, 388–409).

These multiple faces of revolution in Russia were seen again in 1917. According to Hobsbawm (1994, 66) the Russian Revolution of 1917 "was universally recognized as a world-shaking event" by both revolutionaries and counterrevolutionaries alike. The immediate international repercussions were even more profound than those of the French Revolution.

> The sheer physical extent and multinationality of an empire which stretched from the Pacific to the borders of Germany meant that its collapse affected a far greater range of countries in two continents. . . . And the crucial fact that Russia straddled the world of conquerors and victims, the advanced and the backward, gave its revolution a vast potential resonance in both. It was both a major industrial economy and a technologically medieval peasant economy; an imperial power and a semi-colony; a society whose intellectual and cultural achievements were more than a match for the most

advanced culture and intellect of the western world, and one whose peasant soldiers gaped at the modernity of their Japanese captors. In short, a Russian revolution could appear to be simultaneously relevant to western labor organizers and to eastern revolutionaries, in Germany and in China. (Hobsbawm, 1987, 300–301; see also Seton-Watson, 1967)

In sum, in the first decades of the twentieth century the combined dislocations caused by the spread of capitalism and great power rivalries created receptivity to examples like the Russian Revolutions of 1905 and 1917. A deep fear of revolution gripped ruling elites in the wake of the Great War. All the defeated powers suffered revolutions and state breakdowns: Germany, Hungary, Turkey, Bulgaria, and Russia. Moreover, even those countries that had won the war faced massive social unrest. In 1919 the British prime minister Lloyd George observed: "[T]he whole of Europe is filled with the spirit of revolution. There is a deep sense not only of discontent, but of anger and revolt among the workmen against prewar conditions. The whole existing order in its political, social and economic aspects is questioned by the masses of the population from one end of Europe to the other" (quoted in Cronin, 1983, 23). Lenin's 1916 prediction that imperialism would intensify all the contradictions of capitalism, and thus would mark "the eve of the social revolution of the proletariat" seemed confirmed (1971, 175).

The Interwar Impasse and the Widening of the Vicious Circle

By the end of the First World War, the United States had surpassed all other states in terms of financial, industrial, and military weight. And at the end of the war, it appeared as if the United States might attempt to lead the world out of the increasing social chaos created by the vicious circle of domestic and international conflict. Woodrow Wilson, recognizing the appeal and the threat represented by Lenin's "summon to world revolution" and call for "the solidarity of the proletariat and the revolt against imperialism," countered with his own internationalist, world-embracing, but *reformist* appeal. Wilson's Fourteen Points and his call for "self-determination and the century of the common man" were a deliberate counterstroke to Lenin's appeals (Barraclough, 1967, 121).

Wilson's program was a harbinger of the reformist and consensual elements of the U.S.-sponsored world-hegemonic order that would emerge after the Second World War. However, the social forces needed to back such a program did not exist in the United States in the 1920s. Congress declined to join the League of Nations and repudiated Wilson's internationalist program. Likewise, Lenin's internationalist program floundered as revolutionary movements failed to gain state power elsewhere in Europe; the failure of the revolution in Germany and the fascist takeover in Italy were decisive blows. In the 1920s, then, neither the revolutionary program of international proletarian solidarity, nor the reformist program of the "century of the common man" prevailed. Instead, proponents of a restorationist program were the victors of the decade.

The restorationists argued that a return to the gold standard and international free trade was necessary in order to reestablish the virtuous circle of international and domestic peace that had characterized the mid-nineteenth century. But a global self-regulating market was an even more utopian project in the 1920s than it had been in the nineteenth century. The mechanisms that, for a short period in the nineteenth century, had absorbed the social tensions produced by laissez-faire policies were no longer there. First, the new center of wealth and power (the largely self-sufficient and protectionist United States) was a poor substitute for the British entrepôt, which had been prepared to absorb a large share of the world's non-industrial exports in the nineteenth century (see chapter 1). Second, the large industrial countries—first and foremost the United States—closed their frontiers to large-scale immigration after the war, thus eliminating "one of the most effective and necessary safety valves of the nineteenth-century international order" (Carr, 1945, 22–23). This change in immigration policy was partly a response to labor movement demands for protection from intense labor market competition. As such, it was related to yet another difference between the mid-nineteenth century environment in which the British-sponsored world-economic liberalization took place, and the environment in which the 1920s restoration was attempted. That is, despite the widespread defeats suffered by labor and socialist movements, the power of working classes to resist laissez-faire policies was far greater in the 1920s than it had been in the 1840s and 1850s. Democratic governments now had to demonstrate concern about the wage levels and living standards of their own workers (and citizens more generally)—something that was of little concern to nineteenth-century economic liberals.

In this highly unpropitious environment, the international gold commission in Geneva began forcing "structural adjustment" policies on countries to promote healthy (convertible) currencies. These policies created immense social dislocations. Governments were forced to choose between sound currency and improved social services, between the confidence of international financial markets and the confidence of the masses, between following the dictates of Geneva and following the results of the democratic ballot box. For those governments tempted to make the wrong choice, the mechanism to punish noncompliance was most effective. "Flight of capital . . . [played] a vital role in the overthrow of the liberal governments of France in 1925, and again in 1938, as well as in the development of a fascist movement in Germany in 1930." In Austria in 1923, in Belgium and France in 1926, in Germany and England in 1931, labor parties were eliminated from government, social services and wages were reduced, and unions busted, in vain attempts to "save the currency" (Polanyi, 1957, 24, 229–33).

Restoring the gold standard became "the symbol of world solidarity" in the 1920s. But within a year or two after the Wall Street crash it became clear that the restorationists' efforts had failed abysmally. Although unsuccessful, the effort to restore the gold standard had important social and political effects: "free markets had *not* been restored though free governments *had* been sacrificed." Democratic forces "which might otherwise have averted the fascist catastrophe" were weakened by the "stubbornness of economic liberals" who had, in the service of deflationary policies, supported the authoritarian policies of (often democratically elected) governments throughout the 1920s (Polanyi, 1957, 26, 233–34).

To be sure, the establishment of a U.K.-centered world market in the 1850s and 1860s also had been built on intense repression—that is, the restoration of the post-Napoleonic years up through the repression of working-class uprisings in 1848. But world capitalism passed safely through "structural adjustments" such as the "Hungry Forties" because the U.K.-centered world market was in its formative/expansive phase in the mid-nineteenth century. Facing a united front of elites who believed that British world hegemony was delivering broad benefits and who were prepared to administer the necessary amount of repression to defend those benefits, there was little room for effective protest by the victims of the structural adjustment. Moreover, most of the burdens of Britain's free-trade world order were borne by Asians whose mid-nineteenth century rebellions were systematically repressed by the strong arm of British imperialism (see chapters 2 and 4). But in the 1920s no amount of repression could reestablish the virtuous circle. The world market was in an advanced stage of disintegration. Even in the colonies, repression would not deliver the goods, and the facade of international elite unity collapsed together with the restorationist effort.

With the political credibility of high finance and liberal governments destroyed in the wake of the crash and the depression, and with no alternative world-hegemonic project on the horizon, internationalism was abandoned in favor of purely national hegemonic projects. The New Deal, the Soviet Five-Year Plan, fascism, and Nazism were different ways of jumping off the disintegrating world market into the life raft of the national economy. These competing national projects shared two common characteristics: first, they discarded laissez-faire principles, and second, they promoted rapid industrial expansion as part of an effort to overcome the social and political crises caused by the failure of the market system, mass unemployment in particular (Polanyi, 1957, chapter 2).

But rapid industrial expansion relieved unemployment only by exacerbating other sources of domestic and international tensions. First and foremost, rapid industrialization increased pressures to seek out new markets and new sources of raw materials. This, in turn, brought about a renewed escalation of interimperialist rivalries. Britain, with its huge head start in overseas territorial expansionism, already controlled a vast empire in Asia and Africa. The United States was itself a continental empire, and was expanding with ease in Latin America by replacing Britain as the center of informal empire. Russia likewise was continental in size, though its eastward expansion would continue to bring it into conflict with both European and Japanese imperialism in Asia. The Axis powers, on the other hand, felt constrained by their relative backwardness as empire builders and their relatively small geographical home bases, and thus began to actively and aggressively challenge the existing distribution of political-economic space (Neumann, 1942).

As interimperialist rivalries reignited, the pressure to industrialize intensified given the now intimate links between industrial and military capabilities. The vicious circle of escalating domestic and international conflict of the Edwardian era resurfaced in the 1930s and 1940s with a vengeance. Thus, figure 7 shows a virtual repeat of the pattern of escalating labor unrest on the eve of the war, declining overt militancy with the outbreak of the war, and a major explosion in the aftermath of the war itself. However, the second round of the vicious circle would be far more massive in both scale and scope. The military-industrial complexes brought into confrontation during the war were of infinitely greater destructive power. Moreover, a much greater proportion of the globe was engulfed by social conflict and political chaos in the period leading up to the war, during the war itself, and in the revolutionary upheavals that followed the war.

The result was a far greater wave of decolonization than the one that had occurred during the transition to British hegemony. The two waves can be seen in figure 8. The number of colonies in the European-centered world system drops sharply in the late eighteenth century (independence of the Americas), only to rise again to new heights in the nineteenth and early twentieth centuries (the colonization of Asia and Africa). Then comes a new and much sharper decline in the mid-twentieth century (Asian and then African independence). Qualitative differences between the waves are even more important. The first wave brought national self-determination and statehood to settlers of European extraction. Haiti, the only exception, was ostracized. The second wave brought national self-determination and statehood to non-Western peoples. The first strengthened Western supremacy in the modern world; the second weakened it. Moreover, the leaders of the independence movements during the first transition were largely successful in keeping the demands of the poor off the agenda; in contrast, the national liberation movement leaders of the second transition would mobilize the masses, wittingly or unwittingly raising the specter of social revolution.

A first cluster of twentieth-century nationalist revolts took place between 1905 and the First World War (in Persia, Turkey, and China). These revolts were largely reactions to the collapse and decay of old systems of rule and the inability of the old power structures to resist the encroachment of Western military and economic power. Their main protagonists were westernized elites, increasingly disillusioned with both the ancien régimes and with Western supremacy. Japan's military victory over Russia in 1905, even more than the 1905 Russian Revolution itself, had an electrifying effect on colonial elites

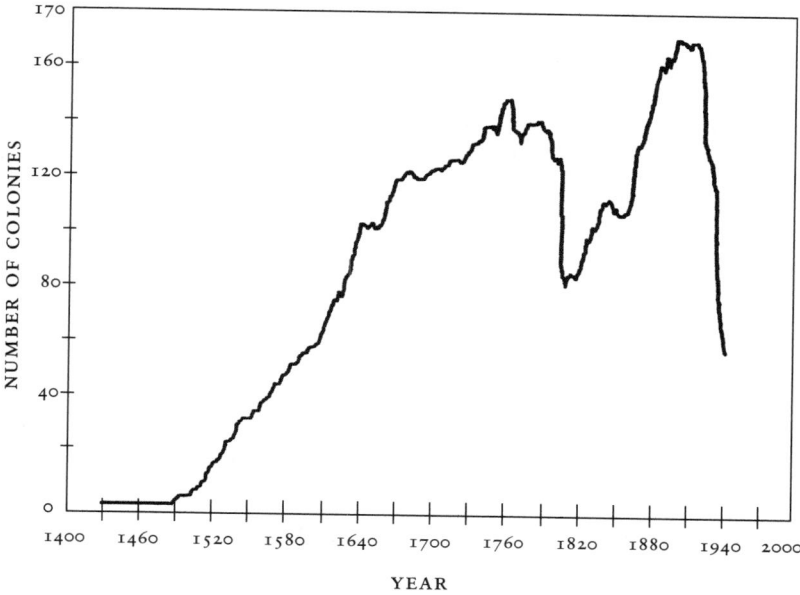

YEAR

Figure 8. Waves of colonization and decolonization. From "Long Waves of Colonial Expansion and Contraction, 1415–1969," by Albert Bergesen and Ronald Schoenberg, in Studies in the Modern World-System, Albert Bergesen, *editor, 1980. Courtesy of Academic Press.*

throughout Asia. According to Sun Zhongshan "the Russian defeat by Japan [was regarded] as the defeat of the West by the East. We regarded the Japanese victory as our own victory." And Jawaharlal Nehru recalled how as a schoolboy in India: "Japanese victories stirred up my enthusiasm . . . Nationalistic ideas filled my mind. I mused of Indian freedom . . . I dreamed of brave deeds of how, sword in hand, I would fight for India and help in freeing her" (quoted by Stavrianos, 1981, 389).

The First World War and the Russian Revolution would have a radicalizing effect on the emergent national liberation movements. The horror and brutality of the First World War—a war that many future Third World nationalist leaders saw firsthand as soldiers in imperial armies—further tarnished the image of "European civilization." And with the Russian Revolution of 1917, one of the major powers raised the banner of anti-imperialism for the first time. The Communist International's "combination of anti-imperialism and socialist internationalism, of national and social revolution, made a powerful appeal during the next decades to the new intellectual elites of the colonial and semicolonial peoples. The appeal was not confined to those who became communist. To a far wider circle, the Soviet Union appeared a land of promise, and the October Revolution a source of inspiration" (Seton-Watson, 1967, 134).

The elites who led the nationalist movements in the years leading up to the First World War made little or no attempt to mobilize the mass of the population into the nationalist struggle. However, in the interwar years, partly in response to the failure of elite-based nationalist movements, and partly in response to the 1917 Russian Revolution and the spread of socialist ideology, the (successful) nationalist leaders— both communist and non-communist—began "broadening . . . the basis of resistance to foreign colonial power by the organization of a mass following among peasants and workers and the forging of links between the leaders and the people" (Barraclough, 1967, 178).

In India, the shift from "nationalist agitation on a relatively narrow middle-class basis" to mass mobilization took place in 1920 when Gandhi launched the first national civil disobedience campaign. Gandhi's "outstanding contribution in the phase immediately following the First World War was to bring Congress to the masses and thus to make it a mass movement" (Barraclough, 1967, 180; see also Chatterjee, 1986). In China an analogous shift was made around 1924 when Sun Zhongshan reorganized the Guomindang (GMD) after a wave of labor militancy in China induced him to rethink the role of the popular classes in the nationalist movement. Prior to 1924, social problems and particularly the agrarian question had played little part in his program. But by 1924 he had made contacts with the Russian Bolsheviks, placed the economic question at the head of his program, allied with the communist party, and reorganized the GMD into a mass party with a revolutionary army as its spearhead (Barraclough, 1967, 182 and chapter 4, below). Likewise, by the 1940s the leading nationalist movements in Africa (e.g., the Gold Coast and Nigeria) had moved from being "middle-class parties with limited popular contacts, to mass parties which mobilized support by combining national with social objectives for the attainment of which the whole people could be stirred to action" (Barraclough, 1967, 189).

Thus, nationalist movements in Asia and Africa increasingly merged with social revolutions. It became clear that a successful independence movement required mass agitation. As Kwame Nkrumah put it, "a middle class elite, without the battering ram of the illiterate masses could never hope to smash the forces of colonialism." But the loyalty of the masses could not be secured without promising that radical social change ("the building of a new society") would be high on the agenda of the nationalist movements (Barraclough, 1967, 190; Nkrumah, 1965, 177).

The disruptive power of mass mobilization was enhanced by the fact that by the eve of the Second World War, the colonies and semi-colonies were tightly interwoven into the supply structures of the imperial powers (as suppliers of both men and material). The Second World War (and the buildup to it) led to rapid urbanization and growth in the size of export enclaves, and provided workers in these enclaves with strong bargaining power. Just as the workers in the armaments industries in the core occupied a strategic position within the military-industrial complexes of the belligerents, so the colonial export enclaves occupied strategic positions within the resource-needs structures of the imperial powers (see Bergquist, 1986; Brown, 1988). In the 1930s and 1940s, as nationalist movements began to hook up with workers movements and as both began to take advantage of the disruptive power of the export workers, strike waves spread in semi-peripheral and peripheral countries (Bergquist, 1986; Brown, 1988; Silver, 1995, 179).

The effectiveness of these strikes is shown by Britain's decision to introduce trade unions and conciliation and arbitration mechanisms throughout its empire during the Second World War. During the First World War tripartite agreements between trade unions, employers, and states only emerged in core countries (and were rapidly eliminated after the war). The tripartite agreements concluded during the Second World War were more permanent, involved far greater concessions to labor in the core, and were much broader in geographical spread (on Britain's colonial trade union policy, see Cooper, 1996; Brown, 1988; Burawoy, 1982).

Thus, by the time of the Second World War it was clear that only a small part of the challenge for the emerging world-hegemonic power came from the nationalist component of the revolt against the West. Indeed, it would be the part of the challenge that was relatively easy to accommodate, for the rising hegemon had little stake in formal colonialism, and much interest in denying exclusive access to the existing colonial powers. Moreover, there was clear past precedence for absorbing a large number of newly independent states into the interstate system—that is, the expansion of the Westphalia system under British hegemony to accommodate the newly independent states of the Americas.

The social revolution posed a different sort of challenge. With the communist victory in China in 1949, the problem of repressing or accommodating the social revolutionary challenge from the non-Western world moved to center stage in the global strategies of the new hegemonic power. Until 1949, attention had been focused on Europe where, as a U.S. undersecretary of commerce reported to President Truman in 1947, "most . . . countries were standing on the very brink [of revolution] and may be pushed over at any time; others are gravely threatened" (quoted in Loth, 1988, 137). By 1949 the social revolutionary threat was unmistakably global. Instead of "a single, weak and isolated USSR, something like a dozen states had emerged, or were emerging, from the second great wave of global revolution . . . Nor was the impetus of global revolution exhausted, for the decolonization of the old imperialist overseas possessions was still in full progress" (Hobsbawm, 1994, 82).

The New Deal Roots of the Cold War World Order

By the end of the Second World War, there was an even more overwhelming concentration of systemic capabilities, both military and financial, within the borders of the United States than at the end of the First World War. The military and financial dominance of the United States was not, however, a sufficient condition for establishing a new world hegemony that could end the ongoing systemic chaos and reestablish favorable conditions for the expanded reproduction of capital on a world scale. The challenge posed by escalating social unrest had to be met. And as the interwar experience made clear, a return to nineteenth century institutions would only exacerbate the underlying tensions.

At the end of the Napoleonic Wars, there was also an (until then) unprecedented and overwhelming concentration of financial and military systemic capabilities within the jurisdiction of a single state. Britain's initial role in the years after 1815 was to carry out a restoration of eighteenth-century political and economic institutions—that is, a restoration of monarchy, colonialism, and slavery. And initially, the main thrust of British rule, both at home and abroad, was repressive. As the nineteenth century progressed, however, new waves of social unrest (e.g., slave uprisings in Jamaica, independence struggles in South America, democratic reform movements at home, and democratic and nationalist movements on the Continent) made it clear that many of the problems that led to the Age of Revolution remained unresolved. By the 1830s and 1840s, Britain began to champion cautious reform at home and abroad. At the same time, the expansion of the British-centered world capitalist system undermined the bargaining power of subaltern groups who had won greater freedom or security in the previous round of struggles.

The same three mechanisms were also central to the establishment of U.S. hegemony; that is, repression, reform, and the undermining of the bargaining power of subaltern groups behind their backs through processes of world-economic expansion. However, in contrast to British hegemony, reform was a leading ingredient in the U.S. hegemonic model from its inception. This was due in part to another contrast between the initial conditions faced by Britain and the United States at the start of their hegemonies. While France (the main great-power embodiment of the revolutionary challenge of the late eighteenth and early nineteenth centuries) suffered a decisive military defeat in 1815, the Soviet Union (the main great-power embodiment of the revolutionary challenge of the first half of the twentieth century) emerged from the Second World War battered, but much stronger politically and militarily. The *counter*revolutionary challenge of the Axis powers was defeated in the war, while the power and prestige of the revolutionary challenge was enhanced.

The continuing revolutionary challenge, combined with the experience of the Great Depression and fascism, convinced the ruling groups of the leading capitalist states that a serious reform of the world capitalist system was required:

> The collapse of capitalism and the rise of fascism convinced people that the systems of peace and progress that had been growing ever since the beginning of the nineteenth century were finally doomed. There was hunger for experimentation with new social and world orders even at the highest levels of interests, while the pessimism was even greater at the bottom. (Schurmann, 1974, 4–5)

The exact nature of the U.S.-sponsored global reform was greatly influenced by the New Deal experience. The core of New Deal "philosophy was that only big, benign and professional government could assure the people order, security and justice" (Schurmann, 1974, 40). In the course of the Depression and the New Deal, U.S. policy makers had come to believe that economic prosperity and political stability were inextricably linked, and that only an activist government could safeguard both. Moreover, there was a widespread perception that "laissez-faire economics and laissez-faire politics" had contributed to the social and political chaos of the interwar and war years. To U.S. policymakers, the lessons of the New Deal seemed relevant to the international sphere:

> Just as the New Deal government increasingly took active responsibility for the welfare of the nation, U.S. foreign policy planners took increasing responsibility for the welfare of the world . . . It could not insulate itself from the world's problems. As at home, moreover, it could not neatly pick and choose among those problems, distinguishing politics from economics, security from prosperity, defense from welfare. In the lexicon of the New Deal, taking responsibility meant government intervention on a grand scale. (Burley, 1993, 125–26, 129–32)

If the image that inspired the founders of the League of Nations was the nineteenth-century night-watchman state, then the supporting image for the United Nations was the twentieth-century welfare state. The United Nations Charter "reflected a newly enlarged conception of the necessary and proper role of international organization in world affairs." It represented "a kind of international New Dealism, an adaptation of the welfare state philosophy to the realm of world affairs." To do the job of keeping the peace, international organizations had to be empowered to deal with "the wide-spreading economic, social, and ideological root structure of the problem of war" (Claude, 1956, 87–89).

The New Deal experience not only taught U.S. policymakers the importance of activist government; it also suggested the kind of governmental institutions that could most effectively diffuse explosive social and political issues. The preferred institutional solution of the domestic New Deal was the "neutral" regulatory agency, which recast social and political conflicts as technical problems of efficiency and productivity. At the global level, likewise, the United States sponsored a proliferation of "neutral" international regulatory agencies to deal with a plethora of potentially explosive social and political problems (Maier, 1978; Burley, 1993, 139–40).

The two most volatile social and political conflicts of the immediate postwar years were the conflict between labor and capital in metropolitan countries and the anti-imperialist revolt in the colonies. These were recast as technical problems of macroeconomic adjustment and economic growth and development—problems that could be overcome using scientific and technical knowledge backed by government planning. We shall deal with these in turn.

The reformist solution to rising labor militancy in the core was reflected in changes in both domestic and international institutions. The "labor-capital accord" or "social contract" that emerged from the 1930s and 1940s wave of labor militancy in the United States called for a truce based on an exchange: government and big business accepted the permanence of unionism, while unions accepted the right of management to make continuing changes in the organization of production to increase productivity. Government promised to use the macroeconomic tools at its disposal to assure full employment, while businesses would pass on a share of the increased profits from rising productivity in the form of rising real wages. This, in turn, assured a mass market for the growing output of industry and allowed for the depoliticization and taming of labor-capital conflict through the promise of "mass consumption"—that is, through the promise of universal access to the "American Dream" (Aglietta, 1979; Gordon et al., 1982; Arrighi and Silver, 1984).

During the postwar decades, the United States actively sought to generalize the mass consumption social contract throughout the core by promoting Keynesianism, economic planning, regional economic integration (without the European Community there would not be a large enough market to support mass production and consumption), and non-communist trade union movements (Maier, 1978, 1981; Arrighi and Silver, 1984). The U.S. economic advisers who fanned "out to the far corners of the U.S.-controlled portion of the globe" preached the Keynesian gospel. Their preaching was "backed up by U.S. power and prestige" in the form of military governments in the defeated countries and Marshall Plan aid for the Allies (Hirschman, 1989, 347–56).

Keynesianism "supplied an attractive third way" between the

Soviet model of centralized planning (which had gained in power and prestige during the 1930s and 1940s) and traditional laissez-faire policies (which had lost all credibility in the course of the Great Depression and the related social-political catastrophes of the era). But Keynesian policies at the national level had no chance of success without corresponding changes in international economic institutions. Indeed, the international economic institutions sponsored by the United States were, in Zolberg's words, "labor-friendly" (see introduction). They were based on the recognition that states have a right and a duty to protect their workers, businesses, and currencies from annihilation by unregulated world market forces. Thus, under the Bretton Woods system it was accepted that governments would use monetary policy as an instrument for reducing unemployment and inflationary pressures. Moreover, there was no attempt to move toward nineteenth-century-style "free trade." Instead, the GATT rounds set up a system of multilateral negotiations designed to promote a controlled process of trade liberalization over time—one that again recognized the "legitimate" interests of governments in protecting the livelihoods of their citizens, both those who earn wages and those who make profits (Ruggie, 1982; Maier, 1987, 121–52; Ikenberry, 1989; Mjöset, 1990).

The cooptation of the "responsible" elements of the labor movement through institutional reforms and mass consumption was supplemented by fierce repression of the "irresponsible" elements. On the home front, the radical and communist left was purged from the ranks of organized labor. The process began in 1947 with the Taft-Hartley Act "loyalty oaths" and culminated in 1949 when communists and alleged sympathizers were excluded from the CIO executive board, and eleven unions representing more than a million workers were purged from the CIO ranks. Thus, while great material rewards awaited union members who stuck to the politics of mass consumption, intense repression, culminating in McCarthyism, awaited those who rejected the parameters of the new hegemonic compromise. In Western Europe, reformism and repression also went hand in hand as "responsible" U.S. labor leaders were invited to assist the U.S. government in the postwar reconstruction of Europe by setting up new noncommunist unions in competition with the existing trade-union movement (McCormick, 1989, 82–84; see also Radosh, 1969; Rupert, 1995).

The defusing of the revolutionary challenge posed by core labor movements was thus accomplished through a combination of repression and cooptation. But neither of these mechanisms would have succeeded without the transformations in the structure of business enterprises described in chapter 2—that is, the global spread of U.S. corporate capitalism. The wave of U.S. corporate investments in Western Europe in the 1950s and 1960s, in combination with the European response to the "American challenge," fostered the rapid spread of Fordist mass production techniques in Western Europe. The result was a weakening of the strongest segments of the labor movement in both Western Europe and the United States. On the one hand, as mass-production techniques spread in Western Europe, craftworkers—who had been the backbone of the militant European labor movement of the first half of the twentieth century—were progressively marginalized from production and their bargaining power undermined. On the other hand, as the geographical relocation and reorganization of U.S. corporate capital proceeded, the semiskilled mass-production workers—who had formed the backbone of the U.S. labor movement in the 1930s and 1940s—were progressively weakened (Arrighi and Silver, 1984; Edwards, 1979; Goldfield, 1987; Moody, 1988).

The combined process of repression, cooptation, and restructuring overcame the anticapitalist challenge of the early twentieth century labor movements of the core (Silver, 1995). By the 1950s and 1960s, this transition was dubbed "the withering away of the strike" by the industrial sociology literature; it was seen as the inevitable and beneficial outcome of "modernization" (Ross and Hartman, 1960; see also figure 7).

This incorporation, cooptation, and eventual weakening of the mass-production workers as junior partners in the hegemonic bloc is analogous to the incorporation of the craft worker elite under British hegemony (the creation of the so-called "labor aristocracy"). Moreover, the attack on these coopted strata of the working class in the 1880s (as in the 1980s) would be one of the opening salvos in the destabilization of the social bases of both world hegemonies. The differences are nonetheless important. Whereas the cooptation of the upper strata of the working class was a late (and short-lived) development in British hegemony, it was one of the foundational elements of U.S. hegemony. That is, U.S. hegemony has been based on efforts to win consent on a deeper (class) basis—reaching out to core working classes with promises of mass consumption. Moreover, whereas British hegemony could shift much of the burden of working-class cooptation onto the non-European world, U.S. hegemony had to confront from the start the escalating demands for independence and social justice in the non-European world.

The victories of national liberation movements in India, and especially in China, eliminated any remaining doubts in the minds of U.S. policymakers about whether reform could be limited to the core. Moreover, it was becoming clear that the longer national liberation struggles dragged on, the more likely they were to precipitate social revolutions. Thus, in his 1949 inaugural address, President Truman emphasized that it was time to bring an end to "the old imperialism" and offer a global "Fair Deal":

> We must embark on a bold new program for making the benefits of our scientific advances and industrial progress available for the improvement and growth of underdeveloped areas. The old imperialism— exploitation for foreign profit—has no place in our plans. What we envisage is a program of development based on the concepts of democratic fair dealing. Greater production is the key to prosperity and peace. And the key to greater production is a wider and vigorous application of modern scientific and technical knowledge. (Quoted in Escobar, 1995, 3; see also Esteva, 1992; McMichael, 1996, 30)

Just as labor-capital conflict was recast as a technical problem of Keynesian pump-priming and increasing growth and productivity, so Truman's global "Fair Deal" recast the North-South conflict as a technical problem amenable to "a wider and vigorous application of modern scientific and technical knowledge." The anticolonial struggles "stimulated thinking about the conditions of economic progress" among policy-oriented economists. This, in turn, led to the emergence of the new subfield of "development economics" and "the conviction, among an influential group of development economists, that they had identified and understood . . . the 'mechanics of development'" and that "a determined effort" should be made "to get those 'mechanics' going" (Hirschman, 1979, 359). The very concept of development was an "invention" of the early post–World War II period—the U.S. response to the need to offer leadership in a world in which the political weight of Asia and Africa suddenly loomed large (Escobar, 1995, 30; cf. Cooper, 1996, on British precursors).

The hegemonic promise—made explicit in Walt Rostow's (1960) "stages of economic growth"—was that all the peoples of the world could achieve the American Dream. Each country had to pass through a set of similar stages before arriving at the "Age of High Mass Consumption," but everyone was on the road to this same (desirable) destination. Also made explicit in the subtitle of Rostow's book—"A Non-Communist Manifesto"—was the reactive nature of U.S. official and semi-official thinking and policy on the Third World.

> In the late 1940s, the real struggle between East and West had already moved to the Third World, and development became the grand strategy for advancing such rivalry and, at the same time, the designs of industrial civilization . . . The fear of communism became one of the most compelling arguments for development. It was commonly accepted in the early 1950s that if poor countries were not rescued from their poverty, they would succumb to communism. To a greater or lesser extent, most early writings on development reflect this preoccupation. (Escobar, 1995, 33–34)

Decolonization and development became the twin pillars of the U.S. hegemonic appeal to the Third World. This appeal was aimed at those segments of the nationalist elite that had not allied themselves with the social revolution (or those segments for whom the alliance was one of only tactical convenience). For while U.S. policymakers supported economic planning in the Third World—again, New Deal experience in the form of the Tennessee Valley Authority would provide a model for what development corporations should look like (Escobar, 1995, 38)—there was to be no Marshall Plan for the Third World as a whole. In contrast to the U.S. role in Western Europe, few public governmental funds were used to support the development project. With the exception of a handful of countries that were built up as showcases of successful capitalist development (Arrighi, 1990a; Grosfoguel, 1996), Third World countries were "instructed to look to private capital, both foreign and domestic." And to attract private capital, it was necessary to create the right investment climate (Walton, 1984). This meant "a commitment to capitalist development; the curbing of nationalism; and the control of the Left, the working class, and the peasantry" (Escobar, 1995, 33; see also Bataille, 1988).

The challenge of the nationalist revolution, on the other hand, was met (and defused) through decolonization and a major expansion of the Westphalia system. Legal sovereignty was extended to all nations—not just those of the West—and enshrined in the charter of the United Nations (see chapter 1). As Inis Claude (1956, 87) remarked: "The United Nations reflected a sharp awareness of the developing significance of non-European peoples as full participants in world affairs. Whereas the League had not represented a decisive break with the tradition of European-focused international politics, the new system was directed toward the problems of a world in which Europe would appear in drastically shrunken, and Asia and Africa in greatly enlarged, proportions."

But the revolutionary potential of this expansion of the system of sovereign states was effectively defused through such safeguards as the great power vetoes and the permanent seats on the Security Council. "In the end" notes Anne-Marie Burley (1993, 145), "all nations were *not* to be treated equally." Just as voting rights were skewed in favor of the Western great powers (the old boy network of the original system), so control over the new institutional guardians of the world economy (the IMF and the World Bank) was weighted in favor of the largest contributors—that is, the rich countries of the world.

Nonetheless, the combined policies of decolonization and development successfully contained the revolutionary anticapitalist challenge rising from the colonial world in the aftermath of the Second World War. As each colony achieved independence, the cross-class alliance of the nationalist movements dissolved. Once nationalist movement leaders controlled state power, workers' and peasants' struggles invariably lost much of their former support from other classes within society (see, for example, Walton, 1984, on Kenya; Post, 1988, on Vietnam; and Beinin and Lockman, 1987, 14–18, on Egypt as well as more generally).

For the nationalist elites who had never embraced social revolution, their central aim of political independence and sovereignty had been achieved. Even those nationalist elites who had believed that the social and national revolutions could not be separated now mostly accepted the idea that "development" (read, industrialization) was a prerequisite for meeting the needs of the people. This, in turn, required a good investment climate, especially a disciplined and hardworking labor force. Moreover, on this front, the Soviet challenge represented no challenge at all. The communist version of "development" also prioritized industrialization as a prerequisite for achieving socialism and thus also emphasized the importance of a disciplined and hardworking labor force. The fruits of this disciplined labor would be reaped in the Age of High Mass Consumption or with the transition to communism. In the meantime, popular movements found themselves politically isolated, and the new power elites found it fairly easy to repress them, usually on their own, sometimes with the help of outside military powers.

The Speeding-Up of Social History?

From the angle of vision of this chapter, past hegemonic transitions appear to be moments of escalating social conflict aimed at reaffirming or challenging established status and class hierarchies—an escalation that is intertwined with intensifying interstate and interenterprise competition. In both transitions, social conflict played a double role. On the one hand, it fed into the escalation of interstate and interenterprise competition, speeding the transition from hegemonic crisis to hegemonic breakdown. On the other hand, the intensity and form of social conflict was decisive in shaping the social compacts that emerged in the midst and aftermath of the hegemonic breakdown, and on which the new hegemony would be based (see figure 6).

As we have seen in chapters 1 and 2, around 1970 the great expansion of world trade and production of the preceding twenty years—the so-called Golden Age of Capitalism—began to taper off amid multiple signs of a hegemonic crisis. By the early 1980s, the diversion of capital from production and trade to finance and speculative activities had gained momentum, giving rise to a new systemwide financial expansion. As in the Dutch-led financial expansion of the mid-eighteenth century and the British-led financial expansion of the late nineteenth century, a rapid and unseemly polarization of wealth signaled that elites were abandoning their efforts to incorporate a broadening "middle class" into the hegemonic bloc. The polarization was a first sign that the basis of social-political stability was breaking down.

In past transitions, crises of legitimacy and social-political unrest grew as conspicuous consumption at the top contrasted sharply with conspicuous poverty at the bottom and widespread insecurity in the middle. In the 1980s, as the financialization of capital accelerated, observers began to point to a growing polarization of wealth both within states and between states, as the North-South gap also widened. And as world politics became increasingly turbulent in the 1990s, observers began not only to make a link between this polarization and growing political instability; they also began to suggest that current dynamics were similar to those that had historically preceded major state breakdowns. Thus, in an opinion piece in the *New York Times*, Russell Baker

(1996) pointed to "the rise of a new American class of super-duper rich," and labels the 1990s "the decadent decade." Baker continued, with marked sarcasm, to draw parallels with other historical periods of decadence:

> As a youth I longed to live in decadent times—in Rome just before the fall, or in France just before the Revolution. In that squalid decadence . . . I would have sinned incessantly—or so I thought. Now, here it is at last: a great age of American decadence, and where, I ask you, where is the joy of it? Most of the Romans probably missed out on it too, and most of the pre-Revolutionary French. It must have soured them. Maybe that's why those antique bouts of delightful decadence were followed by the fall of Rome and the French Revolution.

Likewise, the influential U.S. political analyst, Kevin Phillips, began to hammer away at the corrosive impact that the financialization and polarization of the 1980s was having on the well-being and security of what he terms the "American middle class." (Or, from our perspective, the junior partners of the hegemonic bloc, including the established mass-production working class.) "While speculators and corporate raiders took home huge sums," wrote Phillips, "the average American family wound up fearing for the safety of its bank accounts, insurance coverage, home values and pension coverage." "Across broad swaths of charcoal-grill and lawnmower America, the middle-class was in trouble . . . the American Dream was increasingly at risk." By 1991–92, "the dangerous rise of middle-class frustration politics" could be seen in the popular political success of Pat Buchanan and David Duke, both of whom mixed "an anti-elite and populist message in a confusing package that also included nationalism, anti-immigrant sentiment and economic appeals to the middle-class." Ross Perot's presidential candidacy also tapped into some of the same "middle-class economic apprehensions and status fears" (Phillips, 1993, xxii–xxiii, 5, 232, 237).

However, as in past hegemonic transitions, the declining hegemonic state is not the main site of polarization and rising social-political unrest. Financial expansions have been processes of the world capitalist system as a whole. Thus, in the transition from Dutch to British hegemony, financialization created speculative boom-and-bust cycles that left the port cities of the North American colonies reeling on the eve of the Revolution. Likewise, "capital flight" and speculation during the interwar years shook the political and social systems of Central Europe, preparing the ground for fascism. In the 1980s and 1990s, the effects of financialization and polarization once again have been felt throughout the world capitalist system—a space that is now synonymous with the entire globe. Countries all over the world have been competing ever more intensely for mobile capital by dismantling long-established vehicles for fighting unemployment (Brecher, 1994/95, 33). Likewise, development projects have been abandoned in favor of IMF-imposed structural adjustment and austerity programs aimed at making Third World countries solvent in world financial markets (McMichael, 1996; Bienefeld, 1996).

The result has been both intranational and international polarization of wealth. Looking at the ranking of countries according to GNP per capita, the 1980s and 1990s have seen "the vast majority of the South . . . either slipping backwards, stagnating, or growing slower than the North" (Broad and Landi, 1996, 37). Intranationally, "[w]orkers and communities all over the world are being put into ruinous competition," causing in Jeremy Brecher's (1994/95, 33–34) words, "a 'race to the bottom' in wages and environmental conditions." Brecher links these tendencies to growing "racism and extremist nationalism around the world." Julius Ihonvbere (1992, 8) links these tendencies to the "mounting instability . . . widespread unrest, turmoil, and violence which is now afflicting an unprecedented number of countries in the developing world" (see also Rodrik, 1997).

From the vantage point of the 1990s, then, the current transition seems to be following a familiar path: financialization, polarization of wealth, and the abandonment of the social compact that tied junior partners to the hegemonic bloc are creating widespread legitimation crises for the world's elites. The signs of diffuse and mounting social-political unrest and uncontrollable violence indicate that we may again be entering a period of systemic chaos characterized by widespread social upheavals, state breakdowns, and dysfunctional violence. Indeed, as suggested by Hobsbawm in the passages quoted in the introduction, the revolutions of 1989 and the collapse of the Soviet Union may appear in retrospect to have been the harbinger of a new phase of systemic chaos.

In past transitions, long periods of systemic chaos played a decisive role, not just in destroying the strained social foundations of the collapsing hegemonic order, but also in creating the conditions under which new and more inclusive dominant blocs and social compacts formed and, over time, became hegemonic. New structures of world governance were established only when the ruling groups of the state that emerged with the greatest concentration of global military and financial capabilities succeeded in fashioning an effective *social* response to the challenge posed to the ruling groups of the entire system by the increasingly dysfunctional social conflicts of the transition period. Can we expect the present transition to go through the same trajectory?

Insofar as we can judge from the angle of vision adopted in this chapter, there are several reasons why we should expect the trajectory of present transformations to diverge in some respects from past hegemonic transitions. The first and probably most important reason has to do with the fundamental change that has occurred in the relationship between the interstate power struggle and social conflict from transition to transition. In both past transitions, interstate warfare promoted an escalation of social conflict before and after the breakdown of the old hegemonic order. During the crisis of British hegemony (but not the crisis of Dutch hegemony) the opposite causal relationship also held true; that is, social conflict promoted and inhibited rulers' engagement in warfare. This difference between the two past transitions seems to have been taken to an extreme in the crisis of U.S. hegemony.

The initial crisis of hegemony was signaled by the U.S. defeat in a Third World civil war (Vietnam), and the revolt against the war that flared up at home and around the world. The war and antiwar movements intertwined with the already mobilized black civil rights movements, as well as the growing assertiveness of Third World demands for a new international economic order. Initial attempts to quiet these revolts only intensified the fiscal crisis of the U.S. state. The decline in U.S. power and prestige climaxed in the Iranian revolution of 1979 and the hostage crisis of 1980.

It was in this context of widespread internal and external social-political challenges that the U.S. elite switched strategies. The domestic and global New Deals were abandoned, and the United States sought to reestablish its military prestige. To pay for the military buildup of the Second Cold War, the United States raised interest rates and began to compete actively for internationally mobile capital. The world's surplus was drawn to the United States in the 1980s, precipitating the "debt-crisis" and signaling the abandonment of the hegemonic promise of "development." In abandoning the hegemonic promise of universalizing the American Dream, the U.S. ruling elite was essentially admitting that the promise had been fraudulent. As Wallerstein put it (see introduction), world capitalism as presently constituted cannot accommodate "the combined demands of the Third World (for relatively little per person but for a lot of people) and the Western working class (for relatively few people but for quite a lot per person)."

In sum, whereas in past hegemonic crises the intensification of great power rivalries preceded and thoroughly shaped the intensification of social conflict, in the crisis of U.S. hegemony the intensification of social conflict preceded and thoroughly shaped the intensification of great power rivalries. An analogous speeding-up of social history can also be detected in the relationship between social conflict and interenterprise competition. Whereas in past hegemonic crises, social conflict flared up following the intensification of interenterprise competition, in the crisis of U.S. hegemony a wave of labor militancy preceded and shaped the crisis of Fordism.

The wave of labor militancy that swept through much of the core in the late 1960s and early 1970s both conforms to and diverges from previous patterns of social conflict in hegemonic transitions. On the one hand, as in past transitions, the main protagonists of the wave of unrest were new social groups created during the period of systemic expansion. The backbone of the "resurgence of class conflict in western Europe" (Crouch and Pizzorno, 1978) was the large, new, mass-production working classes created in Western Europe in the 1950s and 1960s as a result of the spread of U.S. multinational corporations and the European response to the American challenge. In the short run, major gains in wages and workers' rights were obtained. In the medium run, the wave of labor militancy (and rising labor costs) touched off a thorough round of restructuring of business enterprises. The crisis of Fordism and the emergence of more decentralized and informal forms of business enterprise during the current crisis of U.S. hegemony (see chapter 2) have thus been driven in important part by social conflict.

This reorganization has transformed the world's working classes and has important implications for the nature of the terrain on which social cohesion and conflict will unfold in the remainder of the hegemonic transition. The global economic restructuring of the past several decades has progressively eliminated the male mass-production worker in the core. But this same restructuring has led to a further increase in the feminization and internationalization (immigration) of the core labor force as employers seek out lower-cost labor. Thus, while a central junior partner of the U.S. hegemonic bloc is literally disappearing as a social force (as Zolberg claims, see introduction), new female and immigrant working classes have grown in size and centrality throughout the core. These transformations have already produced an increase of social conflict along new fault lines with various forms of feminism and "multiculturalism," as well as backlashes against them.

Finally, it cannot be emphasized too strongly that while manufacturing workers may be a disappearing breed in core countries, elsewhere—especially in Asia, and most especially in China—the working class is growing in size and centrality (Silver, 1997). As Hobsbawm (1994, 289) points out, the "most dramatic and far-reaching social change of the second half of [the twentieth] century . . . is the death of the peasantry."

> At the very moment when hopeful young leftists were quoting Mao Tse-Tung's strategy for the triumph of revolution by mobilizing the countless rural millions against the encircled urban strongholds of the status quo, these same millions were abandoning their villages and moving into the cities themselves. (Hobsbawm, 1994, 290)

Thus, the widespread current tendency to dismiss the working class as an important social force may be as premature as late nineteenth and early twentieth century dismissals of the peasantry as a revolutionary force. For just as peasant rebellions from China to Vietnam were fundamental to the formation and crisis of U.S. hegemony, so workers' rebellions in the same region of the world may turn out to be fundamental to an understanding of the social origins of world hegemony in the twenty-first century. But just as the twentieth-century peasant rebellions were enmeshed in a broader revolt against the West, so we can expect future class conflict to be enmeshed in the changing balance of power between the Western and non-Western worlds. It is to this changing intercivilizational balance of power that we now turn to in chapter 4.

Four

Western Hegemonies in World-Historical Perspective

Giovanni Arrighi, Iftikhar Ahmad, and Miin-wen Shih

The first three chapters of the book have focused on the inner structure and dynamic of the expanding European-centered world system as perceived from the angles of vision of the interstate power struggle, interenterprise competition, and social conflict, respectively. Each chapter has underscored how this inner structure and dynamic was profoundly influenced by the changing relationship between the Western and non-Western worlds. But all three chapters remained focused on the structural transformations that enabled the Western system to become global. Chapter 4 recasts the analysis of these transformations in the broader perspective of the encounter and clash of the globalizing Western world with the civilizations of South and East Asia—two civilizations that have played a particularly critical role in shaping the trajectory of the modern world system, both past and present.

The main thrust of the argument is that we can detect a fundamental asymmetry between the transition from Dutch to British hegemony and the transition from British to U.S. hegemony. Dutch and British hegemonies within the Western world were both based, among other things, on a privileged access to Asian resources. And in both hegemonies, this privileged access was based on the coercive incorporation of Asian territories within the jurisdiction of the hegemonic state—the Indonesian archipelago by the Dutch, and the entire Indian subcontinent by the British. The increase in the scale and scope of the hegemonic state within the West was thus associated with an increase in the scale and scope of the hegemonic state's territorial domains in Asia. This increase added an entirely new dimension to the clash of civilizations already entailed by Western intrusions under Dutch hegemony. Western intrusions under Dutch hegemony were and remained interstitial vis-à-vis Asia's world empires and civilizations. They neither needed, nor attempted, to transform the systems of belief and authority on which these civilizations and empires rested. Western intrusions under British hegemony, in contrast, were imperial in scope and, as such, inevitably clashed with indigenous systems of belief and authority.

In this clash, Western systems of belief and authority won at best a partial victory. They did force their way into Asian societies on the basis of a fundamental, and growing, Western superiority in the art of war and related industrial-scientific activities. But Western attempts to persuade the dominant and subordinate strata of Asian societies that this Western superiority was the expression of a more general moral and intellectual superiority never went very far. Claims of moral superiority were made entirely implausible, both by the West's failure to apply Western ideas of rights and liberties to non-Western peoples, and by the West's disregard for the most basic reproductive needs of Asian societies. Western dominance in Asia was thus based overwhelmingly on coercion rather than consent. It was "dominance without hegemony." And it was this dominance without hegemony that in the transition from British to U.S. hegemony spurred and sustained the revolt against the West.

Emancipation from Western dominance did not involve rejection of Western ideas of rights and liberties or of Western scientific-industrial achievements. On the contrary, a large part of the politics of national liberation in Asia turned on a demand for rights and liberties that Western powers had proclaimed abstractly but denied concretely in dealing with Asian peoples and governments. The old and new nations of Asia came to perceive the appropriation of Western scientific-industrial achievements as essential to any attempt to catch up with Western standards of wealth and power. But in upholding Western ideas, and in seeking to appropriate Western achievements, movements of emancipation from Western dominance invariably relied on their own civilizational heritages in those spheres in which they had little or nothing to learn from the West.

Nowhere was the heritage of Western and non-Western civilizations combined more effectively than in East Asia. Western military encroachments on the region's indigenous China-centered world system triggered a process of modernization that posed ever more serious challenges to Western supremacy: the challenge of Japanese military power from 1905 to 1945, the ideological challenge of Communist China from 1949 to 1973, and the economic challenge of the East Asian region as a whole from the late 1970s to the present. Each challenge built on the preceding one and, taken sequentially, the three challenges reflect a downward trajectory in the capacity of the West to exercise dominion globally on the basis of superior military capabilities.

We shall begin by showing how the transition from Dutch to British hegemony was closely associated with the formation of a British empire in India and the deployment of Indian resources to establish Western suzerainty over China. As a result of these endeavors, Western power in the East came to depend on a combination of direct despotic rule and indirect rule through suitably weakened indigenous political structures. The contradictions of this precarious configuration of power are then analyzed as integral aspects of the responses to Western dominance that materialized in the transition from British to U.S. hegemony. We conclude by showing that the East Asian economic renaissance of the last twenty-five years has deep roots in these responses and points to a probable recentering of the global economy on the East.

The Rise of Western Dominance in Asia

The Interstitial Emergence of Western Power in the Far East

The original and most enduring source of Western power in Asia has been the capacity of Western states to disrupt the complex organization that linked Asian societies to one another within and across jurisdictional and civilizational divides. This capacity has been rooted in Western advances in military technology on the one side, and in the vulnerability of Asian societies to the military disruption of their mutual trade on the other. Writing in 1688 during the war against the Mughal emperor Aurangzeb, Sir Josiah Child, director of the East India Company and instigator of the war, captured the essence of this relationship. "The subjects of the Mogul," he noted, "cannot bear a war with the English for twelve months together, without starving and dying by the thousands for want of work to purchase rice; not singly for want of our trade, but because by our war, we obstruct their trade with all the Eastern nations which is ten times as much as ours and all the European nations put together" (quoted in Watson, 1976, 348–49).

Two aspects of this early diagnosis of East-West relations stand out. The first is the incomparably greater size and importance of intra-Asian trade relative to East-West trade. At this time (1688), and for at least another century, the rapidly expanding European world-economy had yet to "catch up" with the size and density of what Fernand Braudel (1984, 523) has called the "super-world-economy" of the Far East.

> The Far East taken as a whole, consisted of three gigantic world-economies: Islam, overlooking the Indian Ocean from the Red Sea and the Persian Gulf, and controlling the endless chain of deserts stretching across Asia from Arabia to China; India, whose influence extended throughout the Indian Ocean, both East and West of Cape Comorim; and China, at once a great territorial power—striking deep into the heart of Asia—and a maritime force, controlling the seas and countries bordering the Pacific. And so it had been for many hundreds of years. But between the fifteenth and eighteenth centuries, it is perhaps permissible to talk of a *single* world-economy broadly embracing all three. (Braudel, 1984, 484; emphasis in the original)

This super-world-economy was "gigantic, fragile, and intermittent." It was intermittent "since the relationship between these huge areas was the result of a series of pendulum movements of greater or lesser strength, either side of the centrally positioned Indian subcontinent." The ebb and flow of these movements redistributed functions, power, and wealth, "favoring by turns the West, that is Islam; and the East, that is China." Sometimes, however, "the pendulum malfunctioned or stopped working altogether: at such times the loose garment of Asia was more than usually divided into autonomous fragments" (Braudel, 1984, 484).

This intermittent formation was also fragile, because it was "structured enough to be penetrated with relative ease, but not sufficiently structured to defend itself." In a sense, it "was asking to be invaded." And so it was repeatedly, both from the north and from the west. The Europeans "were only following in the footsteps of other invaders" (Braudel, 1984, 523).

Unlike their predecessors, however, the European invaders did not seek incorporation within the structures of the Asian super-world-economy. Rather, they sought to incorporate within their own economy centered on Europe the disjointed components of those structures by deploying ever more destructive technologies of war. This brings us to the second aspect of the East-West relationship as diagnosed by Josiah Child: the power that accrued to the West by virtue of the ease with which Western states could disrupt Eastern trade by means of war.

Ever since Roman times, Asia had been a purveyor of valued goods for the tribute-taking classes of Europe and had thereby exercised a powerful pull on Europe's precious metals. This structural imbalance of European trade with the East created strong incentives for European governments and businesses to seek ways and means, through trade or conquest, to retrieve the purchasing power that relentlessly drained from West to East. As Josiah Child's contemporary, Charles Davenant, observed, whoever controlled the Asian trade would be in a position to "give law to all the commercial world" (Wolf, 1982, 125).

The centrality of Asian trade for the intra-European power struggle had been the driving force behind the Iberian discovery of the Americas and of a sea route to the East Indies via the Cape of Good Hope. American silver, in turn, had multiplied the means available to European states in their mutual struggle to appropriate the benefits of trade with the East. Initially, however, the expanded European presence in Asian trade had little impact on the integrity of the Asian super-world-economy.

Religious fervor and intolerance seriously hampered Portuguese expansion in the Indian Ocean. Eventually, the Portuguese found their place in the region, "not as a conquering empire, but as one of many competing and warring maritime powers in the shallow seas of the [Indonesian] archipelago" (Parry, 1981, 244, 242). Their shipping remained "one more thread in the existing warp and woof of the Malay-Indonesian interport trade" (Boxer, 1973, 49). Their inroads in the Asian super-world-economy, "built upon war, coercion and violence," had little effect on Asian trade (van Leur, 1955, 118).

The Spaniards, for their part, concentrated on the development of a direct trade route from America to China via the Philippine Islands. Silver-laden galleons left Acapulco for Manila, where the cargo was transferred to junks for delivery in China, mostly by Chinese merchants.

Although there are no reliable estimates of this traffic, the Manila galleons "seem to have carried as much silver to Asia as the Portuguese *Estado da India* and the Dutch and English Companies combined" (Flynn and Giraldez, 1994, 72, 79–83). Whether larger or smaller, the silver trade via Manila had a more direct impact on the China-centered world-economy than the silver trade via Europe. Like the latter, it contributed toward consolidating China's ongoing transition to a silver standard and toward sustaining the economic expansion of the late Ming era. But its greater reliance on Chinese merchants meant that it probably played a greater role than the silver trade via Europe in reviving the fortunes of the Chinese merchant class, both at home and overseas—a revival that contributed to the instability of the Ming regime in the late sixteenth and early seventeenth centuries (cf. Hamashita, 1994; Flynn and Giraldez, 1994, 84–86).

By and large, the sixteenth-century, Iberian-led wave of European intrusion affected the functioning but not the structures of the Asian super-world-economy. The Dutch-led wave of the seventeenth century, in contrast, initiated the disarticulation of those structures. War, coercion, and violence were as critical to Dutch inroads in Asian trade as they had been to the Portuguese (Parry, 1981, 250–54; Braudel, 1984, 218). Nevertheless, in the century that separated the two intrusions, Europe's art of war had experienced major advances, which the Dutch themselves had pioneered (McNeill, 1982, 125–43). Moreover, in bringing a more advanced military technology to bear on the structures of Asian trade, the Dutch adhered more strictly than the Portuguese to a logic of expansion that gave priority to trade and profit. As a result, they managed to acquire, not just a near-exclusive control over the supply of a commodity (fine spices) that played a critical role in East-West and local trade, but also strategically significant territorial domains in the Indonesian archipelago (see chapter 2).

The impact of this double acquisition on Asia was far less momentous than on Europe. In South Asia, the seventeenth-century arrival of the Dutch and their English and French competitors simply added new merchant communities to the already diverse commercial population of the trading ports. In these ports, European merchants remained wholly dependent on local communities and networks to guide them "through the labyrinth of the 'country trade'" (Braudel, 1984, 496). In East Asia, the company state created by the VOC in the Indonesian archipelago could be perceived as nothing but an addition to the outer fringes of the China-centered world system (cf. Hamashita, 1997, 119–23).

And yet, peripheral as they seemed from an Indocentric or Sinocentric perspective, the VOC's acquisitions drove a wedge at the fault lines between the South and East Asian world-economies. For the East Indies were at a major crossroads of trade, "a network of maritime traffic," in Archibald Lewis's words, "comparable in volume and variety to that of the Mediterranean or of the northern and Atlantic coast of Europe" (quoted in Braudel, 1984, 486–87). This busy crossroads of trade had formed as a result of two developments: the expansion of the East and South Asian world-economies in the thirteenth and fourteenth centuries, and the rise of Malacca and other ports of trade in the fifteenth century. These ports of trade—like the trading towns of medieval Europe—benefited "from not being strictly integrated into any very powerful political units. Despite all the kings and 'sultans' who ruled them . . . these were virtually autonomous towns: wide open to the outside world, they could orient themselves to suit the currents of trade." But their strength was also their weakness, because openness and political fragmentation made them vulnerable to the disruption of their trade and conquest by a superior naval power. And when the Dutch first arrived in the region, they went straight for this vulnerable intersection of Far Eastern trade (Braudel, 1984, 486, 524–30).

The Disarticulation of the Asian "Super-World-Economy"

Dutch power in the seventeenth century thus grew interstitially at the intersection of the South and East Asian world-economies. The eighteenth-century, British-led wave of European intrusion shifted the epicenter of this interstitial growth to the very heart of the South Asian world-economy. The growth remained interstitial, because for most of the eighteenth century the East India Company had little control over the Indian subcontinent's gigantic productive apparatus, and at least until Plassey, it also had little control over the dynamic of the disintegrating Mughal empire. By the end of the century, however, the company was well on its way to becoming the successor of the Mughal court as the redistributive center of the South Asian world-economy and to incorporating Indian trade and production within the structures of the European world-economy.

The story of this double conquest of India, political and economic at the same time, has already been told in chapter 2 and will not be re-told here. Nevertheless, the story must now be recast in the wider context of the clash of civilizations that the British conquest of India entailed. The clash had already begun with the European intrusions of the preceding centuries, but until Plassey, by choice or by necessity, the intrusions had been primarily commercial. In the decades following Plassey, and particularly in the nineteenth century, the intrusion became imperial in scope, and the clash of civilizations thereby moved to the center of the stage in East-West relations.

British imperial rule in the Indian subcontinent was established through an almost uninterrupted series of wars, which constitute the main manifestation of the coercive underside of Britain's world hegemony. From a strictly European-centered perspective, hegemonic Britain could present itself, and be perceived, as having little enthusiasm for wars. As it worked actively to establish and preserve Europe's "hundred years' peace," it cut to the bone its already modest military. According to one estimate, the number of British military personnel shrank from 255,000 in 1816 to 140,000 in 1830; and even by 1880, when the number climbed to 248,000, it was below the numbers at the end of the Napoleonic Wars (Kennedy, 1987, 153–54). According to another estimate, the number of men under arms in Great Britain fell from 292,000 in 1700 to 201,000 in 1850; and troops as percentage of national population fell from 5.4 in 1700 to 1.7 in 1850 (Tilly, 1990, 79).

This downsizing of the British military occurred in the context of what Polanyi (1957, 5) has called "the triumph of a pragmatic pacifism" in Europe. The reverse side of this pragmatic pacifism in Europe was a voracious appetite for military prowess and conquest in the non-Western world. In the Indian subcontinent alone, Britain fought ten wars. These included two Anglo-Maratha wars (1803 and 1818), which brought British control to much of central and parts of northwestern India; one Anglo-Gurkha war (1814–1816), which established British presence in Nepal; two Anglo-Burmese wars (1824 and 1852), which brought parts of Burmese territories under British control; two Anglo-Sikh wars, which extended British control to the borders of Afghanistan; and the infamous Anglo-Afghan wars of 1839–42 and 1878. If we take Asia and Africa together, there were as many as seventy-two separate British military campaigns between 1837 and 1900 (Bond, 1967, 309–11). By a different count, between

1803 and 1901 Britain fought fifty major colonial wars (Giddens, 1987, 223).

Britain could wage all these wars and yet reduce military expenditure and personnel at home because it had the control of the largest European-style army in Asia, manned largely, and paid for entirely, by Indians. By 1880, Indian taxpayers were supporting 130,000 Indian and 66,000 British troops. As Lord Salisbury put it, "India was an English barrack in the Oriental Seas from which we may draw any number of troops without paying for them" (Tomlinson, 1975, 341). This army was not only instrumental in the conquest and control of India and in defending the western frontiers against Russian advances in Central Asia; it was also used to advance British interests around the world. It was sent to China in 1839, 1856, and 1859; to Persia in 1856; to Ethiopia and Singapore in 1867; to Egypt in 1882; to Burma in 1885; to Nyasa in 1893; to Mombasa and Uganda in 1896; to Sudan in 1896 and 1897; to South Africa during the Boer War; and to various places during the First World War (Ambedkar, 1945, 27; Mason, 1974).

The British conquest of the Indian subcontinent thus marked an entirely new stage in the expansion of Western power in Asia. On the one hand, it completed the disarticulation that had begun under Dutch hegemony of the Asian super-world-economy. On the other hand, it endowed Britain with the resources needed to subdue the last bastion of Asian power: the Chinese empire and the East Asian world-economy centered on the empire.

In comparing the different extent of Western dominance in India and China, K. M. Panikkar (1970, 93–94) has pointed out that, "even in the days of her weakness [China] maintained a political unity," whereas "in India by 1740 the Imperial authority had completely broken down." As a result, European companies in India dealt with a fragmented political structure within which one of them (the East India Company) eventually became dominant. In China, by contrast, Europeans had to deal, not just with a unified political structure, but with a unified political structure whose size, wealth, and power were still unmatched in Europe and continued to excite the admiration of most European visitors.

Partly real and partly imagined, the achievements of the Chinese empire in the rising phase of the Qing dynastic cycle were a source of inspiration for leading figures of the Enlightenment. In the first half of the eighteenth century, notes Michael Adas (1989, 79), "the rage for chinoiserie went far beyond latticed garden houses and themes for theatrical works. Some of the most prominent thinkers of the age, including Leibniz, Voltaire, and Quesnay, looked to China for moral instruction, guidance in institutional development, and supporting evidence for their advocacy of causes as varied as benevolent absolutism, meritocracy, and an agriculturally based national economy."

The most striking contrast with European states was the Chinese empire's size and population. In François Quesnay's characterization, the Chinese empire was "what all Europe would be if the latter were united under a single sovereign"—a characterization echoed in Adam Smith's remark that China's "home market" was as big as that of "all the different countries of Europe put together" (Quesnay, 1969, 115; Fairbank, 1983, 170). Equally impressive was the extent to which these huge and populous domains appeared to be, and in comparison with Europe definitely were, ruled by moral persuasion rather than by force. European visitors and residents of China, Jesuit missionaries in particular, contrasted the peace and tranquillity of the Qing empire with Europe's social strife and incessant warfare. The view that European rulers had much to learn from the Chinese in matters of law, government, and morality was greatly enhanced by Jesuit depictions of emperor Kangxi "as a veritable philosopher-king, devoted to his subjects' welfare and deeply interested in the fine arts and sciences, both Chinese and Western" (Adas, 1989, 80–81).

> Kang-xi's so-called edict of toleration in 1692 particularly caught the attention of Bayle, Leibniz, and Voltaire, who like virtually all the philosophes deeply detested religious bigotry and persecution. Even though few dared to make the comparison explicit, the contrast between Kang-xi's religious policies and Louis XIV's revocation of the Edict of Nantes in 1685—with the consequent renewal of religious strife in France and neighboring states—strengthened the arguments of those who sought to defend Chinese political wisdom and ethical probity. (Adas, 1989, 81)

Even the most convinced proponents of China as a model for Europe qualified their enthusiasm by acknowledging the stagnation of scientific learning in China relative to European advances of the preceding century or two. Nevertheless, neither Leibniz and Voltaire, nor the Jesuit writers whose accounts inspired them, saw any contradiction between relative stagnation in the sciences and excellence in the art of government and moral philosophy. After all, European advances in the sciences had occurred in the context of generalized warfare, state breakdowns, and social strife, and had done little to produce stable government and tranquil lives (Adas, 1989, 81–89). And conversely, it was precisely stable government that led Qing China to fall behind the West in the art of war and related scientific activities (Parker, 1989, 98–99).

What tarnished, and eventually completely destroyed, the image of China as a model was not European primacy in the abstract sciences, but European primacy in war and commerce. European merchants and adventurers had long emphasized the military vulnerability of an empire ruled by a scholar-gentry class, while complaining bitterly about the bureaucratic and cultural obstacles met by those who sought to trade with China. Fictionalized in Daniel Defoe's *Farther Adventures of Robinson Crusoe* (1719), and given non-fictional respectability by a travel account attributed to Captain George Anson, *A Voyage around the World* (1748), these indictments and complaints gradually translated into a fundamentally negative view of China as a bureaucratically oppressive and militarily weak empire. This negative view found a receptive ear among such prominent French philosophes as Montesquieu, Diderot, and Rousseau. More important, it contributed to transforming China in the political imagination of the West, from a model to be imitated into the antithesis of the British model of the commercially oriented, liberal state that was becoming hegemonic in Western thought (Adas, 1989, 89–93, 124–25).

Civilization as Proficiency in "The Murderous Art"

This reimagining of "China" as the antithesis of the forming European hegemonic state prepared the way for the rising clash of civilizations that culminated in the Opium Wars of 1839–42 and 1856–58. The Opium Wars were fought primarily to decide whether the British or the Chinese view of law, government, and morality would prevail, not in the abstract, but within the domains of the Chinese empire itself. While the first of these wars was being fought, former U.S. president John Quincy Adams asked whether China or Britain had "the righteous cause" and answered that Britain did. Anticipating some surprise in his audience, he felt "obliged to show that the opium question is not the cause of the war." The cause of the war, he maintained, "is the kowtow!—the arrogant and insupportable pretension of China that she will hold commercial intercourse with the rest of mankind, not on terms of reciprocity, but upon the insulting and degrading forms of lord and vassal" (quoted in Esherick, 1972, 10). Adams's view that the Opium War was not really about opium, but about a general interest in diplomatic equality and commercial opportunity, became standard in Western historiography. Thus, to quote a particularly authoritative source, it has been argued that

> In demanding diplomatic equality and commercial opportunity, Britain represented all the Western states, which would sooner or later have demanded the same things if Britain had not. It was an accident of history that the dynamic British commercial interest in the China trade was centered not only on tea but also on opium. (Fairbank, Reischauer, and Craig, 1965, 318)

This characterization of the Anglo-Chinese conflict is accurate in underscoring the hegemonic function that Britain was exercising vis-à-vis the Western world. In coercing China to open its domains to unregulated trade and proselytizing, Britain did indeed represent the general interest of Western states, as witnessed by John Quincy Adams's support. The characterization, however, misses entirely how central the opium trade was to the more fundamental clash of interests and values that underlay the conflict over trade and diplomacy.

Protocol, as symbolized by the kowtow, was hardly an issue. The famous refusal of George Lord Macartney, head of the 1793 British mission to Beijing, to kowtow to the emperor Qianlong was promptly followed by an agreement that he would not kowtow but only kneel (Peyrefitte, 1992, 203). The diplomatic and commercial aspects of the Anglo-Chinese confrontation were not so easily resolved. They were resolved more than half a century later through the forcible imposition on China of extremely unequal treaties in the name of diplomatic equality and commercial reciprocity. Even trade and diplomacy, however, were not all that was at issue. Underlying all others, there was the issue of whether the East Asian economy should continue to be centered on China or should instead become a subordinate and peripheral component of the increasingly global capitalist system centered on Britain.

From this more fundamental point of view, opium was not just one of two commodities on which the dynamic British commercial interest happened to be focused. It was the one and only commercial means available to Britain in its struggle to oust China from the commanding heights of the East Asian economy. In this struggle, opium was no more "an accident of history" than iron, coal, railways, and steamships were in Britain's successful bid for hegemony within the Western world.

Throughout the first half of the nineteenth century, opium was, in Joseph Esherick's words, "the West's only feasible entree into the China market." As late as 1870, it still accounted for 43 percent of China's imports. By then, local production of opium, particularly in the southwestern provinces of Sichuan and Yunnan, had begun to cut into imports. And yet, import substitution notwithstanding, between 1870 and 1890 imports of opium, varying in value between £8 million and £12 million a year, remained China's largest single import (Esherick, 1972, 10; Hsiao, 1974, tables 2 and 9a; Bagchi, 1982, 101). The main significance of the opium trade for Britain, however, was not strictly commercial. Rather, it lay in the role that sales of Indian opium to China played in the transfer of Indian tribute to Britain. As the head of the statistical department at the East India House put it,

> India, by exporting opium, assists in supplying England with tea. China by consuming opium, facilitates the revenue operations between India and England. England by consuming tea contributes to increase the demand for the opium of India. (Thornton, 1835, 89)

The need to expand the India-China trade by any means in order to facilitate the revenue operations between India and England had been from the start the main stimulus behind the expansion of the opium trade. As early as 1786, Lord Cornwallis, then Governor General of India, saw the expansion of the India-China trade as essential to paying at least in part for Chinese exports to Britain and other European countries and, above all, as the only way in which the vast tribute of Bengal could be transferred to England *without heavy losses through exchange depreciation*. Such was the importance attributed to the expansion of the India-China trade that Cornwallis pleaded with the East India Company to disregard its monopolistic privileges and to extend special facilities to private merchants trading between India and China (Bagchi, 1982, 96; Greenberg, 1951, chapter 2).

Whether the company would have followed Cornwallis's advice of its own accord is a question that was made moot by China's two imperial bans on the opium trade in 1796 and 1800 and by Britain's abrogation of the company's India monopoly in 1813. Before the imperial bans, the opium trade was regulated by the so-called "Canton system," which authorized foreigners to trade with China only through the intermediation of the Co-hong, the guild of Hong merchants. The East India Company's monopoly of the China trade was thus matched by the Co-hong's monopoly of Chinese foreign trade—an arrangement that left little room for private merchants, British or otherwise, to trade in Chinese tea or Indian opium. The rapid increase in the consumption of the habit-forming drug under the Canton system led to the prohibition of further imports by the above mentioned bans. But the bans backfired. Once the Co-hong stopped dealing in opium, the East India Company started encouraging private merchants to smuggle the drug into China.

> The East India Company kept up the polite fiction that its ships could not be used for exporting opium to China. But it did everything in its power to push the sale of the drug, by monopolizing its production in Bengal . . . regulating prices, and assisting the private European smugglers. (Bagchi, 1982, 96)

The abrogation of the India monopoly in 1813 led the company to redouble its efforts to encourage opium smuggling into China—a redoubling of efforts which, as noted in chapter 2, resulted in a more than threefold increase in shipments between 1803–13 and 1823–33.

The soundness of Cornwallis's advice was fully vindicated. As a contemporary account informs us, from the opium trade,

> [t]he Honourable Company has derived for years an immense revenue and through them the British Government and nation have also reaped an incalculable amount of political and financial advantage. The turn of the balance of trade between Great Britain and China in favour of the former has enabled India to increase tenfold her consumption of British manufacture; contributed directly to support the vast fabric of British dominion in the East, to defray the expenses of His Majesty's establishment in India, and by the operation of exchanges and remittances in teas, to pour an abundant revenue into the British Exchequer and benefit the nation to an extent of £6 million yearly. (Quoted in Greenberg, 1951, 106–7)

The "Honourable Company" was soon squeezed out of this highly beneficial branch of British commerce by the abrogation of its China monopoly in 1833. But the abrogation further emboldened the forces of "free trade," which went on to agitate for "the strong arm of

England" to bring down all the restrictions that the Chinese government imposed on their freedom of action.

This mounting pressure was accompanied by a further demeaning of the power and prestige of China in the Western imagination. As tensions increased, China's military vulnerability began to be construed as the sign of a more general civilizational backwardness. Thus, the author of an anonymous essay published in Canton in 1836 claimed that "there is, probably, at the present no more infallible a criterion of the civilization and advancement of societies than the proficiency which each has attained in 'the murderous art,' the perfection and variety of their implements for mutual destruction, and the skill with which they have learned to use them." He then went on to dismiss the Chinese imperial navy as a "monstrous burlesque," to argue that antiquated cannon and unruly armies made China "powerless on land," and to view these weaknesses as symptoms of a fundamental deficiency of Chinese society as a whole (quoted in Adas, 1989, 185).

In reporting these views, Michael Adas adds that the growing importance of military prowess "in shaping European assessments of the overall merit of non-Western peoples boded ill for the Chinese, who had fallen far behind the aggressive 'barbarians' at their southern gates" (1989, 185–86). Worse still, the Chinese government could not just yield to the demands of this new breed of barbarians because the consequences of the opium trade were as baneful for China as they were beneficial for Britain. Beyond the deleterious impact on the fabric of Chinese society of a growing number of addicts, the opium trade had highly disruptive political and economic effects on the Chinese state.

The proceeds of opium smuggling trickled down to Chinese officials whose corruption thereby seriously impaired the execution of official policy in all spheres. At the same time, the trade caused a massive and growing drain of silver from China to India: 1.6 million taels a year in 1814–24, 2.1 million taels a year in 1824–37, and 5.6 million taels a year in the two years preceding the first Opium War (Yen et al., 1957, 34). As the imperial edict of 1838 emphasized in announcing the decision to destroy the trade, the effects of the drain on the financial and fiscal integrity of the Chinese empire were devastating.

> Since opium has spread its baneful influence through China the quantity of silver exported has yearly been on the increase, till its price has become enhanced, the copper coin depressed, the land and capitation tax, the transport of grain and the [salt] gabelle all alike

hampered. If steps not be taken for our defence . . . the useful wealth of China will be poured into the fathomless abyss of transmarine regions. (Quoted in Greenberg, 1951, 143)

Soon after the edict was issued, the vigorous and incorruptible Viceroy for Hunan and Hupei, Lin Zexu, was put in charge of suppressing opium smuggling. Lin's commission was strictly limited to this task and, contrary to John Quincy Adams's opinion, it was not at all aimed at thwarting commercial opportunities in other branches of China's foreign trade, such as silk, tea, and cotton goods, which the Chinese government continued to encourage. Lin himself was careful in drawing a distinction between the illegal opium trade—which he was determined to suppress with or without the British government's cooperation—and other, legal forms of trade, which he invited the British government to encourage as a substitute for the illegal traffic (Waley, 1958, 18, 28–31, 46, 123; Hao, 1986, 113–15).

Having failed to persuade the British government to cooperate in suppressing the traffic in the name of international law and common morality, Lin proceeded to confiscate and destroy smuggled opium and to incarcerate some smugglers. As soon as the news reached Britain, emotions ran high. With the exception of some members of the Tory opposition, Lin's actions were denounced in the British Parliament as "a grievous sin—a wicked offence—an atrocious violation of justice, for which England had the right, a strict and undeniable right," by "the law of God and man," "to demand reparation by force if refused peaceable applications" (quoted in Semmel, 1970, 153; see also Owen, 1934).

Evidently, two quite different views of international law and common morality held sway in Britain and China. But while the Chinese view claimed a right to lay down and enforce the law only at home, the British view claimed a right to lay down and enforce the law not just at home but in China as well. What's more, superior proficiency in "the murderous art" provided Britain with the firepower needed to make its view of right and wrong prevail over the Chinese. Imperial China had no answer to the steam-powered warship that one day in February 1841 destroyed nine war junks, five forts, two military stations, and one shore battery (Parker, 1989, 96). As K. N. Chauduri put it, "When after a disastrous war (1839–42) the Chinese government agreed to open its ports to British opium traders, it did not do so choosing between right and wrong: the choice was between survival and destruction" (1990, 99).

The Subordinate Incorporation of Asian Empires

The Nanjing Treaty of 1842, signed at the end of the first Opium War, is widely held as a watershed event in East-West relations. In comparing this treaty with an earlier treaty, also held as a watershed event in East-West relations—the Balta Limani Treaty of 1838 between Britain and the Ottoman Empire—Resat Kasaba has noted significant differences, as well as similarities, in the premises and outcomes of the two treaties. Both treaties "were 'free trade treaties' in the sense that they sought to provide protection for the activities of foreign merchants, reduced the authority of the Chinese and Ottoman governments to impose unilateral tariffs on the articles of trade, and stipulated the abolition of all kinds of monopolies and other kinds of control that could inhibit the circulation of goods in the two empires" (Kasaba, 1993, 216–18).

Underneath these similarities, however, were important differences. The Nanjing Treaty was more punitive, reflecting China's defeat in the war with Britain. It involved the cession of territory to the British (Hong Kong), the payment of an indemnity of $21 million, amnesty to Chinese subjects imprisoned for illegal dealings with the British, and the presence of the British fleet in Nanjing to enforce the treaty. But the Balta Limani Treaty was far more comprehensive in scope, involving equal treatment of foreign and Ottoman merchants, the prohibition of all government monopolies and locally imposed surcharges, and the specification of the rate and manner of all duties. In the Nanjing Treaty the Chinese made no such concessions. Moreover, while Western diplomatic and consular representatives had resided in the Ottoman Empire for centuries, it took another war to force China to authorize the appointment of a British ambassador to Beijing and consuls in places other than the five ports opened up to trade by the Nanjing Treaty (Kasaba, 1993, 217–218).

As Kasaba (1993, 218–22) underscores, the British obtained a far more comprehensive treaty from the Ottomans than from the Qing, without having to fight the equivalent of the Opium War, primarily because under external and internal pressures of all sorts the Ottomans had already been liberalizing their trade and economy long before 1838. In fact, the Balta Limani Treaty should be seen as a turning point, not so much in Ottoman policies toward free trade, as in British policies toward the Ottoman Empire.

> With this convention, Britain took a firm stand against the expansionist ambitions of France and Russia and declared the preservation of the integrity of the Ottoman empire as the centerpiece of its policy in the Near East. . . . For the Ottomans, being recognized as part of the European state system was a significant step in securing the long-term viability of their empire. From the point of view of the British government, an Ottoman administration that was rationalized, centralized, and secularized was likely to be more effective in maintaining the territorial integrity of the empire and hence in providing unified and friendly access to India. Accordingly, while the Sublime Porte was forthcoming in commercial matters, Britain became the main supporter of Ottoman reforms in the nineteenth century. (Kasaba, 1993, 220–21)

No such convergence of interests existed in Anglo-Chinese relations. At the time of the Nanjing Treaty, no Western state posed a challenge to British dominance in the Far East comparable to that posed by France and Russia in the Near East. Nor did China have any of the strategic significance for Britain that a unified and friendly Ottoman Empire commanded by virtue of its geographical position as a link between continental Europe and British India. The main strategic value of China for Britain remained the role its purchases of Indian opium played in facilitating the revenue operations between India and Britain. For China to play that role, no strong central government was needed, nay, the weaker, the better. Under these circumstances, the Qing government had far more to lose than to gain from its incorporation into the European-centered interstate system, and for that very reason it was far less forthcoming in commercial and diplomatic matters than the Ottoman government. If the problem with the Ottoman Empire on the eve of the Balta Limani Treaty was that it had become "too weak" to serve British interests in the Near East, the problem with the Chinese empire in the wake of the first Opium War was that it remained "too strong" to serve British interests in the Far East.

To be sure, by aggravating the disruptions that the opium trade had been inflicting upon China, the provisions of the Nanjing Treaty sped up the decline of the Qing dynasty. Moreover, once China's capacity to resist Western demands had been tested and found wanting, a breach was opened for more demands to come. Thus, the Treaty of Nanjing was immediately followed by a Supplementary Treaty with

Britain, a treaty with the United States, and one with France. Since the privileges obtained by one foreign power were also claimed by other foreign powers under the so-called "most-favored-nation clause," these treaties reinforced one another. And yet the Western powers, later joined by Japan, kept coming back asking for more.

Through the 1850s and 1860s, however, the progressive weakening of Qing China did not proceed fast enough to satisfy the increasingly unbound imperial will of its British foes. "Just as the Roman in days of old held himself free from indignity, when he could say *Civis Romanus Sum,*" declared Palmerston in 1850, "so also a British subject in whatever land he may be shall feel confident that the watchful eye and the strong arm of England will protect him against injustice and wrong" (quoted in Bourne, 1970, 302). Coming at a time of growing tensions between the Chinese and Western governments over the issues of residence and travel of foreigners and duties on domestic trade, this extraordinary claim of a territorially unrestricted right for all British citizens to be judged by their own code of legality and morality boded ill for China. The following year, a new declaration by Palmerston made it clear that China was indeed in trouble: "I clearly see that the Time is fast coming when we should be obliged to strike another blow in China. . . . These half civilized governments, such as those of China, Portugal, Spain, America require a Dressing every eight or ten years to keep them in order" (quoted in Lowe, 1981, 34).

Two years later, the destruction of the Turkish navy by Russia forced Britain to intervene along with France to protect the integrity of the Ottoman Empire (see chapter 1). But as soon as the Crimean War (1854–56) was over, Britain proceeded without hesitation to give China its long overdue "Dressing." Under the pettiest of excuses—redressing "an insult to a British flag lowered by Chinese police from a Chinese-owned vessel registered at Hong Kong" (Fairbank, Reischauer, and Craig, 1965, 169)—the Anglo-French alliance of the Crimean War was renewed in the second Opium War (1856–58) and in the subsequent military occupation of Beijing in 1860.

As we shall see presently, at the time of the second Opium War the Qing dynasty was in the middle of the most serious upsurge of popular rebellions in its history. Its capacity to resist Western aggression and the imposition of new radical restrictions on its sovereignty was thus even less than in the first Opium War. The Treaty of Tianjin

(1858) and the Convention of Beijing (1860) expanded the so-called treaty-port system by adding nine additional ports to the five already opened to trade by the Nanjing Treaty. They abolished China's tariff autonomy by reducing custom tariffs to a maximum of about 5 percent ad valorem and by handing over Chinese customs to the supervision of foreign powers, represented by a British official. They imposed the payment of a new indemnity of sixteen million taels and granted Western merchants, missionaries, and politicians immunity from Chinese law and freedom of movement throughout China upon the acquisition of passports from their consuls in the ports. They also legalized trade in opium, taxing it at the same rate as other articles of commerce (Zhou, 1986, 15–16; Guo, 1980, 136; Moulder, 1979, 108–10; Rozman, 1981, 101).

Having led the way in imposing upon China yet another unequal treaty in the name of diplomatic equality, Britain turned around to give a helping hand to the newly humiliated Qing government in suppressing the Taiping Rebellion. This turnaround established a pattern that became characteristic of Western relations with the Qing dynasty until its downfall in 1911. In Owen Lattimore's words,

> From time to time one country or another thought it necessary to chasten a too obdurate China. Once chastened, however, China's incompetent Manchu government had to be put back in business again, for it could not be expected that future demands would be carried out if the government was too weak to carry them out. Thus there emerged an interesting principle: for international purposes, the ideal government of China was a government strong enough to carry out orders, but not strong enough to defy orders. (Quoted in Bagchi, 1982, 99)

This "interesting principle" is the same that had inspired Britain's differential treatment of the Ottoman and Qing empires at the time of the Balta Limani Treaty of 1838 and the Nanjing Treaty of 1842. As noted, their similarities notwithstanding, the two treaties performed altogether different functions in the consolidation of British dominance in Asia. The first performed the function of *strengthening* the central government of the Ottoman Empire, while the second performed the function of *weakening* the central government of the Chinese empire. Twenty years later, the central government of the Chinese empire had weakened sufficiently to qualify for the kind of support that Britain had long accorded to the Ottoman Empire.

"Westernism" as Threat to the West

In the combination in space, and alternation in time, of policies aimed at weakening or strengthening the structures of Asian empires to suit Britain's pursuit of world power, "Westernization" as such was never an objective. Suffice it to say that the change in British policy from hostility to friendship toward the central governments of the Ottoman Empire in the late 1830s and the Chinese empire in the early 1860s occurred while these governments were being seriously challenged by rebellions—the revolt of the Egyptian governor Muhammad Ali and the Taiping Rebellion, respectively—that were more strongly oriented toward one form or another of "Westernization" than the central governments with which the British sided. Muhammad Ali had provided the Ottoman government with decisive military assistance in suppressing the Wahhabis Islamic Revival movement in Arabia. When he subsequently turned against the Ottomans, his revolt was part of an attempt to transform Egypt into a modern national state in the European image. In the pursuit of regional hegemony, Britain found nothing appealing in this endeavor and had no qualms in siding with the Ottomans to quell the revolt.

The Taiping Rebellion of 1850–1864 was a far more complex, powerful, and radical movement than the revolts that had shaken the Ottoman Empire twenty years earlier. Coming at the end of a long series of religious/political rebellions, which had marred Qing rule since the apogee of the dynasty's power and prestige under Qianlong (1736–95), the Taiping movement presented features that made it more akin to a social revolution than a mere "rebellion."

> Had it been directed only against the Manchus, like earlier Ming restoration movements or like Sun Yat-sen's Revolutionary party, the gentry might have rallied to it and it might have succeeded. But then it would only have been another of China's many dynastic changes. The Taipings were determined instead to eradicate the most basic elements of traditional Chinese society: the gentry-officials, scholars, landlords—and the Confucian ethos on which their authority rested. (Schurmann and Schell, 1967, 178–79)

Founded by the charismatic leader Hong Xiuquan, and organized militarily by lieutenants drawn from the same ethnic group as Hong (the Hakka, or "guest settlers"—people who had migrated from northern to southern China centuries earlier but had retained a separate ethnic identity), this social-revolutionary movement originated in the Guangzhou region and its hinterland. In 1851 the leadership of the movement gave it the dynastic title *Taiping Tianguo* ("The Heavenly Kingdom of Great Peace") and launched a great northern expedition into the Yangzi valley. By 1853, the Taipings had taken over Nanjing and made it their capital; they had occupied much of central and south China, and they got within thirty miles of Tianjin. Although they failed to oust the Qing from Beijing, the symbol of dynastic authority, they held their own against the imperial forces for another ten years until they were defeated in 1864.

The political and military organization of the Taipings was mostly taken from the ancient classic the *Rites of Zhou*. The primitive communism called for by these and other pre-Confucian texts also informed the Taipings' socialist utopian doctrines. But the most distinctive feature of Taiping ideology was the tying of these doctrines to Christianity, an alien religion with only a short and dubious history in China. In Hong Xiuquan's messianic imagination, Christian beliefs derived mainly from the Old Testament—the uniqueness and omnipotence of God the creator, his spiritual fatherhood of all men, the efficacy of prayer, the Ten Commandments, and so on—were combined with, or replaced by, traditional Chinese beliefs, as in the substitution of the traditional Chinese gloss, "The whole world is one family, and all men are brothers," as the Sixth Commandment, replacing the starker "Thou shalt not kill or injure men" (Franke, 1967, 181, 185–86; Fairbank, 1983, 183–85; 1992, 211).

The result was, in John Fairbank's words, "a unique East-West amalgam of ideas and practices geared to militant action, the like of which was not seen again until China borrowed and sinified Marxism-Leninism a century later." In retrospect, this early amalgam strikes Fairbank "as undoubtedly the best chance Christianity ever had of actually becoming part of the old Chinese culture" (1992, 209, 211). And yet the Western powers did nothing to seize this chance. The only chance they were quick to seize was the one to squeeze more concessions out of the Qing regime, taking advantage of the straits the regime had been put in by the Taiping and other contemporaneous rebellions—the Nian rebellion in the east (1853–68), and the Miao rebellion (1850–72) and various Muslim rebellions (1855–74) in the west. But once they had secured what they wanted in the second Opium War, they threw their lot behind the Qing Restoration for fear of losing what they had just obtained (Franke, 1967, 185).

The logic was not just that, in Jonathan Spence's words, "if the Qing beat back the Taiping, the foreigners would keep their new gains; if the Taipings defeated the Qing . . . then the West would have to start the tiresome process of negotiations—and perhaps wage fresh wars—all over again" (1990, 182). Equally important, adherence to a faith of Western derivation made the Taipings even less accommodating than the Qing toward Western encroachments upon Chinese sovereignty. For their puritanical ardor did not stop at prohibiting gambling, idolatry, adultery, prostitution, and footbinding. It also turned against opium far more firmly than the Qing had ever done, thereby clashing head on with Britain's preeminent interest in the region. Nor did their belief in the equality of all people stop at a general friendliness toward all "foreign brothers" (*wai quo xiongdi*), in sharp contrast with traditional beliefs in the superiority of the Chinese as a chosen people. It translated also into a strong opposition to the restrictions on Chinese sovereignty that the Western powers were forcibly imposing on the debilitated Qing dynasty (Franke, 1967, 187–88).

In short, in the early 1860s in China, as in the late 1830s in the Ottoman Empire, the Western powers under British hegemony showed a distinct preference for dealing and siding with the disintegrating structures of Asia's ancient régimes rather than with the nascent forces of nationalism and "Westernism." Contrary to Western rationalizations, the purpose of the British wars with China, and of most nineteenth-century British wars with the governments and peoples of the non-Western world, was not the establishment of conditions of commercial intercourse on terms of reciprocity and respect for one another's sovereignty. Rather, it was to impose upon China and the non-Western world a condition of political vassalage that utterly contradicted Western ideas of international equality and national sovereignty. In the pursuit of this objective, a partnership with the declining ancient régimes was much safer than a partnership with the forces of nationalism and "Westernism."

Asian Responses to Western Dominance

The Civilizational Foundations of the Revolt against the West in South Asia

A contradiction between Western practices in the non-Western world and Western ideas of rights and liberties characterized, not just interstate relations, but also intrastate relations between rulers and subjects and between dominant and subaltern groups and classes. Nowhere were these social aspects of the contradiction more evident than in India, the main foundation of Britain's own imperial power. Here, implacable champions of democratic reforms and representative government at home—from Jeremy Bentham to James Mill—turned into staunch advocates of coercive rule (Stokes, 1959, 68; Coupland, 1942, 20). Mill's more illustrious son, John Stuart Mill, who joined the East India Company's service in 1823 and eventually replaced his father as the examiner, argued in his *Representative Government* that in backward areas like India, a "vigorous despotism" by a civilized nation, like England, was the only possibility (Bearce, 1961, 289).

Neither during the much lauded "Age of Reform," associated with the administration of the Benthamite friend of James Mill, Lord William Bentick (1828–1835), nor during Britain's "high" hegemony, were any of the democratic institutions characteristic of British hegemony in the West ever applied to India. British India was governed primarily by coercive and bureaucratic institutions—the civil service, the army, and the police. Even these institutions had special characteristics. Unlike civilian bureaucracies in Britain, the Indian Civil Service, proudly known as the "steel frame of India," was not merely executor of policy, but also its maker. Similarly, the army was instrumental in putting down frequent uprisings and coercing recalcitrant landlords. Military men were usually members of ruling institutions, such as the Governor-General's Council, and were often also senior bureaucrats and officials in the civil service and the police. The liberal distinction between the civil and the military was nonexistent (for an extensive bibliography on the Indian army, see Dodwell, 1932, 616–18).

Finally, the role of the police was not confined to maintaining law and order, to ensuring the "rule of law," as preached by liberal democracy. "Police power was often used to circumvent or supplement the legal process because the latter was too dilatory or too scrupulous to satisfy the colonial need for prompt retribution and collective punishment." The coercive character of the police was strengthened by the lack of distinction between political and crime-control functions: "[C]rime and politics were almost inseparable: serious crime was an implicit defiance of state authority and a possible prelude to rebellion; political resistance was either a 'crime' or the likely occasion for it" (Arnold, 1986, 3). Thus, campaigns against highway robbers led not only to laws and institutions for collective and arbitrary punishments, but also to criminalizing all sorts of groups and communities. The Criminal Tribes Act of 1871, replaced by a more sweeping Criminal Tribes Act in 1911, consigned 1,500,000 people in North India alone to 'criminal tribes' and hence subject to confinement (Nigam, 1990a, 131; see also Radhakrishna, 1989; Yang, 1985; Ahmad, 1992).

The centrality of coercive and autocratic institutions in the government of British India reflected the fact that the British did not rule India for the benefit of the Indians.

> As Disraeli pointed out in 1881, the key to India lay in London: British rule was not maintained for the benefit of the Indian, nor simply for the sake of direct British interests in India; the Raj was there to keep firm the foundation on which much of the structure of formal and informal empire rested. For London the twin imperatives of Indian policy were that the Indian empire should pay for itself and that Indian resources should be available in the imperial cause. (Tomlinson, 1975, 338)

The fact that Western ideas of representative government could not be applied to India because India was not ruled for the benefit of the Indians does not mean that coercive rule could dispense completely with an element of persuasion. To this end, coercive rule was rationalized through the construction of a body of "knowledge" about the Indian past and heritage aimed at demonstrating both the unfitness of India for the institutions of representative government and the fitness of Britain to rule India by means of a "vigorous" despotism—a construction now familiar to us as Orientalism (on Orientalist representations of India, see, among others, Inden, 1986; Guha, 1992a; Prakash, 1990). Central to this construction was the portrayal of India as a society composed of implacably hostile communities, castes, cultures, and religions.

The portrayal was used over and over again to deny liberal democratic reforms. In 1892, electoral reforms were restricted because, in the words of then Prime Minister Lord Salisbury, representative government was "not an Eastern idea." It only works well when "all those represented desire the same thing." Its introduction in India would put "an intolerable strain" on a society divided into hostile sections. Even in 1909 only very modest measures were introduced because, in the words of A. J. Balfour,

> representative government . . . is only suitable . . . when you are dealing with a population in the main homogeneous, in the main equal in every substantial and essential sense, in a community where the

minority are prepared to accept the decisions of the majority, where they are all alike in the traditions in which they are brought up, in their general outlook upon the world and in their broad view of national aspiration. (Quoted in Coupland, 1942, 26)

British coercive rule was in turn presented as a continuation of indigenous political traditions. The claim was lent credence by the British adoption of some of the symbols, rituals, and pomp of the Mughal court. But the claim conveniently ignored that behind the glitter of these symbols, rituals, and pomp, the actual power of previous rulers of the Indian subcontinent had been far less centralized and despotic than imagined and practiced by their British successors.

Since at least the tenth century, government in South Asia had rested on the recognition and accommodation of competing and autonomous centers of power, peoples, and cultures. The durability and strength of central power depended on the extent to which the various strains in indigenous civilization were accommodated, not eliminated. Even the Mughals, who like the British were alien conquerors, and whom the British sought to emulate, soon recognized this fundamental principle. Far from running a tightly centralized regime, the Mughals allowed local magnates to continue to function, not only in the marcher regions, but in the heartland of the empire as well (Perlin, 1985; Alam, 1986; Singh, 1988; Bayly, 1988, 1989; Subrahmanyam and Bayly, 1988). Thus, in the crucial sphere of taxation, the sources of revenue on which the central authority depended were largely controlled by a myriad of groups and personal networks around local and regional markets and the surrounding agrarian tracts. In order to get to these,

[the ruler] had to involve himself all the time in local influence and to stake his power in the ever changing alignments of factions jostling for local and regional predominance. By the same token local influence was free to encroach on the imperial center. The integrity of the whole was therefore in the intertwining and overlapping of interests competing for the distribution of power rather than the spectacular use of superior force, which moreover could too easily lead to overextension. The system then was one of a 'balancing of relative weakness,' managed by conflict in which the Mughal could at best be a superior arbiter arranging and rearranging the distribution of power by a judicious and sparing use of resources. (Heesterman, 1978, 42)

More generally, the rulers' absolute power to make laws was in practice limited both by religious laws, which were not in the rulers' power to abrogate or modify, and by customs, which in virtue of their antiquity had the force of law (Rashid, 1979, 139). A fundamental distinction between power and authority was in fact a central aspect of the South Asian political tradition. Different spheres of action had different authority systems, each "divided by counter-weighing authorities." Under these circumstances, an individual had considerable freedom "to choose his authority and follow his own beliefs. . . . The idea of an indigenous, central, public authority exercising political power could not be linked to the traditional ethos" (Nandy, 1972, 119–20).

This highly diffused system of domination did not imply disorganization or fragmentation, as colonial historiography maintained. Economy and culture united the polity. Multiple cultures, communities, and territories were tied in an integrated civilization through extensive and dense networks of trade, which linked innumerable markets to one another and were essential for converting the surplus extracted from land and labor into money and commodities (Heesterman, 1978; Chaudhuri, 1990).

Culturally, numerous popular idioms and codes of ethics provided the moral foundations of the system. Thus, the notion of moral duty embedded in the idiom of *Dharma* was a double-edged concept justifying subordination in the caste hierarchy, but also imposing obligation to promote and support the subordinated. Similarly, the idiom of *Danda,* representing the idea of punishment and authority, served as a source of power, but also of responsibility to provide protection. Indeed, protection was the most important duty of the ruler. For example, the revered epic *Mahabharata* states:

> That king who tells his people that he is their protector but who does not or is unable to protect them, should be killed by his subjects in a body like a dog that is affected with the rabies and has become mad. (Quoted in Guha, 1992a, 268)

To be sure, precolonial systems of rule were highly exploitative and oppressive. But oppression and exploitation were embedded in a civilizational order that rendered their logic flexible, comprehensible, even acceptable. For the peasant, as for other subaltern groups and classes of Indian society,

> Exploitation as such was not unjust. It was inevitable that some ruled and some conducted prayers and some owned the land and some labored, and all lived off the fruits of that labour. But it was

important that everyone in the society made a living out of the resources that were available. (Pandey, 1988, 261)

This was precisely the principle that British rule in India could not
accommodate. For British rule in India was not just alien. It was an
alien rule that, unlike any alien rule previously experienced by India,
continually disrupted established ways of life and, moreover, did so in
the pursuit of objectives that ran counter to all moral principles of the
subcontinent's civilization. As argued in previous chapters, the superexploitation followed by the destruction of the Indian "traditional"
productive apparatus and by its subsequent reconstruction on "modern" foundations made perfect sense in terms of the British national
interest. But it made no sense at all from the standpoint of the reproductive needs of India's subaltern classes. The alternating attraction
and repulsion of their labor by the British system of capital accumulation on a world scale continually disorganized their social life, making
them prey to misery and degradation. To them, this new alien ruler,
who claimed to be the bearer of a superior social order and delivered
instead unprecedented social chaos, must indeed have appeared—to
paraphrase the *Mahabharata*—"like a dog that is affected with the ra-
bies and has become mad."

Here lay the fundamental clash of civilizations that fed popular
insurgency in British India and, in due course, inspired Mohandas
Karamchand Gandhi's utopia of a nonmodern India. As Guha (1992b,
1–2, 13) notes, "agrarian disturbances in many forms and on scales
ranging from local riots to war-like campaigns spread over many districts were endemic throughout the first three quarters of British rule
until the very end of the nineteenth century. At a simple count there
are no fewer than 110 known instances of these even for the somewhat
shorter period of 117 years . . . between the revolt against Deby Sinha
in 1783 and the end of the Birsaite rising in 1900." Often led by "traditional" elites, these popular revolts reached their apogee in the famous Great Rebellion of 1857 (for a comprehensive treatment of elite
and subaltern resistance to British rule, see, among many others,
Chaudhuri, 1955; Guha, 1992b).

The 1857 rebellion induced Britain to abandon the policy of introducing new social and political institutions, and to rely instead on
the restoration of indigenous ones. Just as the contemporaneous
Taiping Rebellion prompted Britain to throw its weight behind the on-

going restoration of the power of the Qing dynasty and of the landlord class in China, so the Great Rebellion of 1857 prompted Britain to restore some of the power and autonomy of landed magnates and petty rulers of "native states" within its own Indian empire (on the latter restoration, see Metcalf, 1964; Bayly, 1988, 11–15). Taken jointly, these parallel shifts in British policy show that British dominance in Asia clashed far more fundamentally with the interests of the lower than with those of the upper social strata. Once the ruling groups of Asia's ancien régimes had been tamed, as in China, or subdued, as in India, they could be turned into useful allies in the reproduction of British dominance over the subaltern strata. But that dominance won little or no allegiance among the subaltern strata themselves.

This fundamental lack of legitimacy of British/Western dominance among the lower strata of Asian societies enabled the nationalist movements that developed in the wake of the "traditional" revolts of the early and mid-nineteenth century to mobilize massive popular support in the revolt against the West. Among the "modernized" indigenous elites who led these movements the central objective was national self-determination—that is, a sovereign national state within the modern Eurocentric interstate system. As Guha (1992a, 266) notes, there was in this respect a curious inversion of roles between colonizers and colonized in upholding Western values and ideals.

> While the colonial regime, which had itself introduced among its subjects the notion of rights and liberties, went on denying these in full or in part in the principles and practice of its government, the disenfranchised subjects went on pressing the rulers to match their administration to their own ideals. Ironically, therefore, a large part of the politics of protest under the raj, especially when initiated by the educated middle-class leadership, turned on the 'un-British' character of British rule.

Western ideas of rights and liberties, however, played only a secondary role in the nationalist mobilization of subaltern strata. "Traditional" beliefs about power, protection, fairness, and protest, inherited from the indigenous civilization and continually violated by "modern" Western civilization as practiced in the East, played a far more important role. Gandhi became mahatma (literally Great Soul) not merely because he opposed and sought to end British rule, like many other figures of the Indian National Congress. Rather, he rose to prominence because he linked the nationalist struggle to a fundamental critique and rejection of modern civilization as a whole and affirmed the continuing validity of a reconstructed indigenous civilization (Amin, 1988; Chatterjee, 1986, chapter 4). As Partha Chatterjee (1993, 201) observes, "the very political strategy of building up a mass movement against colonial rule . . . required the Congress to espouse Gandhi's idea of machinery, commercialization, and centralised state power as the curses of modern civilization, thrust upon the Indian people by European colonialism."

After independence, Gandhi's idea that industrialism itself, rather than the inability to industrialize, was the root cause of Indian poverty was dismissed as "visionary" and "unscientific," in favor of Nehru's idea that modern industrialism was necessary for India to "catch up" with Western countries (Chatterjee, 1993, 201–2). Today, after half a century of strict adherence to Western principles of historical progress without any catching up with the standards of wealth set by Western countries (Arrighi, 1991), it is no longer clear whose ideas were more "visionary" and "unscientific." But whether or not the Gandhi legacy is revived, the future of South Asia is bound to be strongly influenced by developments further east, where the demise of Western dominance followed a very different trajectory.

The Civilizational Foundations of the Revolt against the West in East Asia

In East Asia the demise of British dominance was influenced far more directly and decisively than in South Asia by the escalation of inter-state conflicts and competition. As previously noted, geographical distance sheltered the Chinese empire from the kind of exposure to European rivalries that had shaped British policies toward the Ottoman Empire even at the height of British hegemony. At the time of the first Opium War, no Western state posed a challenge to British dominance in the Far East comparable to that posed by France and Russia in the Near East.

The situation began to change once the mid-nineteenth century transport revolution and the industrialization of war brought the Far East within the reach of a growing number of Western states. As we have seen, France joined Britain in the second Opium War. And in 1857, right after the Anglo-French fleet had attacked, burned, and captured Canton, Tokugawa Japan—a prominent member of the China-centered world system, as we shall see—finally yielded to U.S. pressures to sign a treaty, soon followed by similar treaties with Britain, France, Russia, and the Netherlands. Patterned after the treaties of Nanjing and Tianjin with China, these treaties included the opening of ports to Western trade and residence, extraterritoriality, most-favored-nation clauses, and tariffs fixed at 5 percent ad valorem (So and Chiu, 1995, 63–65; Gibney, 1992, 119–22; Moulder, 1979, 132–33).

In spite of the increasing number of Western powers present in the region, for another twenty years after the second Opium War and the opening up of Japan to Western trade and influence, relationships among Western states in the Far East remained far more cooperative than they had ever been in the Near East. It was as if Western states had to join forces to make significant inroads in the last remaining bastion of the now dismembered Asian super-world-economy. In the 1880s rivalries among European states in East Asia did seem to be gaining momentum. The transformation of Annam (Vietnam)—another important member of the China-centered world system—into a French protectorate following the Sino-French War of 1884–85 led Britain to annex Burma—also a member of the China-centered world system—to balance French influence in the Indo-China peninsula. Soon afterward, Russian advances in Central Asia were countered by the British annexation of Sikkim and the signing of a treaty with Tibet. Nevertheless, the main factor that eventually upset the precarious balance of power on which Qing rule and China's territorial integrity had come to rest were not rivalries among Western states. Rather, it was a conflict internal to the China-centered world system, namely, the Sino-Japanese War of 1894 and the Treaty of Shimonoseki that followed in 1895.

The war and its aftermath—the emergence of Japan as a regional power, the further weakening of Qing rule in China, the threat of the partition of China by the Western powers and Japan, and the nationalist response that this threat provoked in China—constitutes as significant a watershed in East-West relations as did the Opium Wars. From then on, a process of indigenous modernization in the East Asian region posed ever more serious challenges to Western supremacy. As Takeshi Hamashita has suggested, the process of modernization that underlies these challenges was no mere response to the subordinate incorporation of the region within the European-centered interstate system. In his view, this incorporation was partial at best, and the legacy of what he calls the Sinocentric tribute-trade system has continued to shape developments in East Asia right up to the present.

In Hamashita's conceptualization, the regions, countries, and cities located along the perimeter of the several sea zones that stretch from Northeast to Southeast Asia were close enough to influence one another, but too far apart to assimilate or be assimilated. The Sinocentric tribute-trade system provided these territorial entities with a political-economic framework of mutual integration that nonetheless endowed its peripheral components with considerable autonomy vis-à-vis the Chinese center. Within this system, tribute missions performed an "imperial title-awarding" function that was both hierarchical and competitive. Thus, Korea, Japan, the Ryukyus, Vietnam, and Laos, among others, all sent tribute missions to China. But the Ryukyus and Korea sent missions to Japan also; and Vietnam required tribute missions from Laos. Japan and Vietnam, therefore, were both peripheral members of the Sinocentric system and competitors with China in the exercise of the imperial title-awarding function (Hamashita, 1994, 92; 1997, 114–24).

The system of tribute missions was intertwined and grew in symbiosis with extensive trading networks. Indeed, the relationship between trade and tribute was so close that "it is quite legitimate to view tribute exchange as a commercial transaction."

> Even the Chinese court . . . acted as a party to business transactions. The mode of payment was often Chinese currency, whether paper money or silver. Seen from an economic perspective, tribute was managed as an exchange between seller and buyer, with the 'price' of commodities fixed. Indeed, 'price' standards were determined, albeit loosely, by market prices in Peking. Given the nature of this transaction, it can be shown that the foundation of the whole complex tribute-trade formation was determined by the price structure of China and that the tribute-trade zone formed an integrated 'silver zone' in which silver was used as the medium of trade settlement. The key to the functioning of the tribute trade as a system was the huge [foreign] 'demand' for [Chinese] commodities . . . and the difference between prices inside and outside China. (Hamashita, 1994: 96–97)

European expansion in Asia eventually led to the formal dissolution of the Sinocentric tribute-trade system through the subordinate incorporation of its members into the European-centered interstate system as colonies, semisovereign and peripheral, or semiperipheral sovereign states. Substantively, however, the structures and norms of the Sinocentric tribute-trade system continued to shape and influence interstate relations within East Asia. Thus, the formation of national identities among East Asian countries long preceded European impact and was based on their own understanding of Sinocentrism (Hamashita, 1994, 94; 1997, 120–27). Through its seclusion policy in the Edo period (1603–1867), for example, "Japan was trying to become a mini-China both ideologically and materially." And even after the Meiji Restoration, Japanese industrialization "was not so much a process of catching up with the West, but more a result of centuries-long competition within Asia" (Kawakatsu, 1994, 6–7; see also Hamashita, 1988).

Whether formal or substantive, the subordinate incorporation of East Asia within the structures of the European-centered world system transformed its political economy. Three changes were of particular importance for subsequent developments. One was the expansion of what had long been an interstitial formation of the Sinocentric tribute-trade system, the Chinese capitalist diaspora. The second was the adoption of Western military technologies by both China and Japan. And the third was the adoption of a sinified version of Marxism-Leninism by China.

The Expansion of the Chinese Merchant Diaspora

Even after British gunboats had battered down the wall of governmental regulations that enclosed the Chinese domestic economy, the leading branches of the so-called First Industrial Revolution had a hard time outcompeting Chinese products. In 1850, cotton goods accounted for a mere 6 percent of British exports to China and in 1875 for just 8 percent (Woodruff, 1966, 309). As late as 1894, China's indigenous handicraft industry still supplied 86 percent of the Chinese market for cotton cloth (Wu, 1987, 148). By then, foreign imports were rapidly displacing handicraft spinning of cotton yarn, which suffered an estimated 50 percent contraction between 1871–80 and 1901–10. But the use of cheaper, machine-produced foreign yarn gave new impetus to the domestic weaving industry, which managed to hold its own and even expand (Feuerwerker, 1970, 371–75).

The competitiveness of Western firms that set up production in China was even less impressive. Thus, in the silk industry foreign ventures incurred major losses, while local business prospered—the number of plants, workers employed and exports of modern, Chinese-owned filatures increasing by a factor of ten between the 1880s and 1890s. "Foreigners," lamented a British consul in Canton, "had little left to them other than the export trade" (So, 1986, 103–16; So and Chiu, 1995, 47). Western products and businesses did triumph in a few industries, such as cigarettes, which did not compete with any indigenous product, and kerosene, which replaced local vegetable oil. Generally speaking, however, it is hard to dispute Andrew Nathan's observation that "the China market spelled frustration for foreign merchants. Foreign goods made but a superficial mark in Chinese markets" (1972, 5).

Opium, of course, was the great exception, leaving as it did a deep and long-lasting mark. But while the predominance of opium among Chinese imports throughout the nineteenth century may be taken as a measure of the continuing lack of competitiveness of most other foreign goods in the Chinese market, even the opium trade spelled frustration for foreign merchants. Access to the final consumers of the drug could be gained only through Chinese intermediaries organized in groups and networks on the basis of language, residence, kinship, and political patronage. The "squeeze" that these intermediaries exercised on foreign merchants was the subject of recurrent complaints. Self-serving as these complaints undoubtedly were, it was nonetheless the case that Chinese middlemen in all trades, even when formally employed by foreign merchants, often made more money than their Western principals; that they were quick to learn what there was to be learned of Western business techniques; and that in competing with foreign firms they had the great advantage of much lower overheads and of not being "squeezed" by a middleman (Hui, 1995, 91, 96–98; Hao, 1970, 110–11; Murphey, 1977, 192–93).

The result was an unprecedented expansion of the Chinese merchant networks and communities that over the centuries had developed in the coastal regions of China and in the interstices of the Sinocentric tribute-trade system (Hamashita, 1994, 97–103; 1997, 132–35). Chinese merchants had always figured prominently among these interstitial communities (Chang, 1991, 23–24). But at no time had the conditions of their expansion been more favorable than in the nineteenth century, as a direct result of the Western onslaught on the organizational structures of the Sinocentric tribute-trade system. As the capacity of the Qing government to control channels between the Chinese domestic economy and the outer world declined, opportunities increased for Chinese merchants operating around the perimeter of the empire.

Many of these merchants made their "first tank of gold" in the opium trade. But the greatest expansion of the Chinese trading diaspora that connected China to the rest of the region occurred in the "coolie trade," the procurement and transshipment of indentured labor for service overseas. First promoted by the Portuguese in the sixteenth century, the Chinese coolie trade experienced an explosive growth in the second half of the nineteenth century. Between 1851 and 1900, more than two million "contract laborers" were shipped off from China, two-thirds of them to Southeast Asia. The transformation of much of the "periphery" of the China-centered system into a major source of raw materials for European countries created a sudden expansion in the demand for cheap labor in the region. At the same time, the ongoing disintegration of the imperial political economy inflated the surplus population in China and undermined the capacity of the Qing regime to interfere with the resettlement of the surplus overseas (Hui, 1995, 108–9, 115, 138–41; Northrup, 1995).

The ensuing boom in the coolie trade boosted the expansion of the Overseas Chinese trading diaspora in several related ways. Although transportation was in the hands of European shipping companies, most other branches of the trade were controlled by Chinese secret societies in the major ports of China and Southeast Asia. Profits were high and became the foundation of many new fortunes among Chinese merchants. Besides making the fortunes of individual merchants, the coolie trade also made the fortunes of the port cities of Singapore, Hong Kong, Penang, and Macao, all of which became to varying extents major seats and "containers" of the wealth and power of the Chinese business diaspora. Equally important, the coolie trade left a legacy of Chinese settlement throughout Southeast Asia. It is this legacy that, right up to the present, has provided the Overseas Chinese with a highly prolific source of opportunities to profit from one form or another of commercial and financial intermediation within and across jurisdictions in the region (Hui, 1995, 127–38, 142–45, 149–53; Headrick, 1988, 259–303).

The consolidation and expansion of a Chinese capitalist diaspora as the main intermediary and beneficiary of trade between Mainland China and the outer world left a deep and long-lasting mark on the political economy of East Asia. Neither Japanese modernization, nor the Chinese Revolution of 1911, nor indeed the present dynamism of the Chinese economy can be fully understood except in the light of this nineteenth-century development. Focusing on Japanese modernization, Hamashita maintains that Japan's industrialization after the opening of its ports was as much a response to Chinese commercial supremacy in the East Asian region as it was a response to Western military supremacy. Specifically, the production of textiles for export to China—a major component of the process of Japanese industrialization in its early stages—was primarily aimed at breaking the hold of overseas Chinese merchants on Japan's foreign trade (Hamashita, n.d., 18–19). But Sino-Japanese commercial rivalries and the launching of modernization both in Japan and China must be put in the context of a competition that was not just commercial, but political as well.

The Rise and Demise of Japanese Imperialism

This brings us to the second major change that occurred in the China-centered world system as a result of its subordinate incorporation in the European-centered world system—the adoption of Western military technologies by both China and Japan. By brutally revealing the full implications of Western military superiority, the First Opium War awoke the Chinese to the imperatives of modernization much faster and more effectively than cheap Western commodities could have ever done. During the war, Lin Zexu himself had promptly realized that the military equipment at his disposal was no match for that of the British. While trying his best to buy foreign equipment, he also commissioned the translation of foreign texts, and later passed on the material he had collected to the scholar-official Wei Yuan.

Wei used the material to compile *An Illustrated Gazetteer of the Maritime Countries,* which developed the old idea of using the barbarians to control the barbarians into the new idea of using barbarian *armaments* to control the barbarians. The importance of the new idea was not lost on Japanese scholars, who later translated the book to push forward their own reform movement (Tsiang, 1967, 144). In China the idea became central to the Self-Strengthening Movement, which took off after the second Opium War and the defeat of the Taiping Rebellion. In justifying to Beijing the establishment of a machine factory and arsenals to make guns and gunboats, a provincial leader of the movement argued that the foreigners' domination of China was based on the superiority of their weapons, and that China could strengthen itself only by learning to use Western machinery (Fairbank, 1983, 197–98; So and Chiu, 1995, 49–50). A few years later, the Meiji Restoration (1868) propelled Japan along the same path of rapid modernization aimed at using barbarian armaments (and machines) to control the barbarians. The armaments race that had long been a feature of the European-centered world system was thus "internalized" by the China-centered world system.

Launched under the same slogan taken from the ancient text the *Rites of Zhou,* "Enrich the country, strengthen the army," the parallel modernization efforts of China and Japan in military-related industries gave priority to the establishment of modern industrial enterprises in mining, heavy industries, transport, and communications. In both countries, these modern industries were governmental undertakings. In China, government supervision was combined from the start with the capital and management of Chinese merchants experienced in foreign business. In Japan, government enterprises recruited technicians of various nationalities (Dutch, French, English, among others) as managers, assistants, and instructors, and once the enterprises had been put on a sound footing, they were turned over to Japanese merchants at bargain prices. But in both countries, foreign investment and control in the new industries were actively discouraged (Moulder, 1979, 184–87; Thomas, 1984, 17, 64, 81–82; Norman, 1975, 233–34; Hsu, 1983, 278–82; So and Chiu, 1995, 49–53, 74–75).

For about twenty-five years after they were launched, these industrialization efforts yielded similar economic results. On the eve of the Sino-Japanese War of 1894, in Albert Feuerwerker's assessment, "the disparity between the degree of modern economic development in the two countries was not yet flagrant" (1958, 53). Nevertheless, Japan's victory in the war was symptomatic of a fundamental difference in the impact of the modernization drive on the social and political cohesiveness of the two countries. In China, the main agents of the modernization drive were provincial authorities, whose power vis-à-vis the central government had increased considerably during the repression of the rebellions of the 1850s, and who used modernization to consolidate their autonomy in competition with one another. In Japan, by contrast, the modernization drive was an integral aspect of the Meiji Restoration, which centralized power in the hands of the national government and disempowered provincial authorities (So and Chiu, 1995, 53, 68–72).

The advantages Japan came to enjoy vis-à-vis China as a result of these opposite domestic thrusts of their respective modernization efforts were compounded by the geopolitics of the situation, most notably, by Japan's smaller size, insularity, and poverty of resources, all of which oriented Japan's modernization toward overseas expansion at the expense of China and its tributaries. From the start, control over Korea—"a dagger to the heart of Japan" and a "tributary" state of China—was the main goal of this outward thrust of Japanese modernization. By 1876, Japan had already succeeded in opening up Korea to its trade through an unequal treaty, which was immediately followed by similar treaties obtained by the Western powers by virtue of the most-favored-nation clause. Within a few years, Japanese purchases of rice raised prices beyond what ordinary Koreans could afford, precipitating a major rebellion aimed not just at stopping the export of rice, but at reconstituting power in Korea on new social foundations. Unable to quell the rebellion, the Korean government turned to China for help in 1894. As China stepped in, Japanese warships intercepted and destroyed the Chinese fleet (Borthwick, 1992, 145–49; Kim, 1980).

The Japanese victory in the short war that followed turned the underlying divergence in the trajectories of Japanese and Chinese modernization into an unbridgeable chasm. On the one hand, defeat in the war weakened further national cohesion in China, leading to half a century of political chaos marked by further restrictions on sovereignty, the final collapse of the Qing regime, the transformation of provincial governors into semi-sovereign warlords, Japanese invasion, and recurrent civil wars between the forces of nationalism and communism. On the other hand, victory in the war strengthened further national cohesion in Japan, leading over the same half century to the renegotiation and eventual supersession of the unequal treaties with Western powers and Japan's emergence as the paramount economic power and leading imperialist power in East Asia until its defeat in the Second World War.

Japan's victory over China in 1894, followed by its victory over Russia in the war of 1904–5, established Japan—to paraphrase Akira Iriye (1970, 552)—as "a respectable participant in the game of imperialist politics." Economically, victory over China gave a major boost to the resources that Japan could mobilize in the expansion of its military-industrial apparatus. The acquisition of Chinese territory, most notably Taiwan, as well as China's recognition of Japanese suzerainty over Korea, endowed Japan with valuable outposts from which to launch future attacks on China, as well as with more secure overseas supplies of cheap food. At the same time, Chinese indemnities amounting to more than one-third of Japan's GNP helped Japan finance the further expansion of heavy industries and put the currency on the gold standard. This improved Japan's credit rating in London and, therefore, its capacity to tap additional funds for industrial expansion at home and imperialist expansion overseas (Duus, 1984, 143, 161–62; Feis, 1965, 422–23).

Politically, victory over China turned Japan into a respectable participant in the imperialist game, but only after a minor setback. Shortly after the signing of the Treaty of Shimonoseki, France, Germany, and Russia demanded that Japan return to China Port Arthur and the Liandong Peninsula, which the treaty had assigned to Japan, along with Taiwan and the Pescadores Islands. Japan complied only to see the Western powers reap the fruits of its victory through the scramble for exclusive spheres of influence over Chinese territory: Russia leasing Port Arthur and establishing control over the Liandong Peninsula, Germany leasing Kiachow Bay and establishing control over the Shandong Peninsula, France leasing Guangzhou Bay and extending control from northern Indochina to Henan, and Britain leasing Weihaiwei and establishing control over the Yangzi Valley. Worse still, China's recognition of Japanese suzerainty over Korea brought Japan face to face with an increasingly active and influential Russia (Borthwick, 1992, 149–50; Thomas, 1984, 110–11).

Russia's growing activism and influence was nonetheless as upsetting for Britain's balance-of-power policy as it was for Japan's imperialist ambitions. What's more, Britain perceived Japan as strong enough to help counter Russian advances in the Far East, but not strong enough to challenge British dominance in the region. It was thus easy for Japan to persuade Britain to renegotiate their unequal commercial treaty—thereby opening the way to analogous renegotiations with the other Western powers—and to agree to a formal Anglo-Japanese alliance (1902). Emboldened by Britain's commitment to discourage any other power from siding with Russia, in February 1904 Japan launched a surprise attack on the Russian fleet at Port Arthur, sank the entire squadron at anchor, and went on to win the ensuing war.

As Geoffrey Barraclough (1967, 108) observes, in forging an alliance with Japan, Britain seemed to have "pulled off a clever manoeuvre against Russia, but in reality it had called in a force it could not control." The Treaty of Portsmouth (1905) brokered by U.S. President Theodore Roosevelt gave Japan control over Liandong, Port Arthur, the southern half of Sakhalin Island, the southern part of the railway built by the Russians in Manchuria and, most important of all, a free hand in Korea, which Japan formally annexed as a colony five years later. The "dagger to the heart of Japan" was thus transformed into a springboard for furthering expansion in China and into a major source of cheap food with which to support Japan's rapidly increasing industrial population (So and Chiu, 1995, 91, 94; Ho, 1984, 348–50).

These gains were increased during the First World War. Having joined the war on Britain's side, Japan seized German concessions in China and German possessions in the Northern Pacific. It then took advantage of the fact that Britain and Russia were tied down in Europe to seek a sort of Japanese protectorate over China with the aggressive Twenty-One Demands of 1915. The attempt was not successful, but "the effects of the war on the power situation in the Far East—particularly when the Russian revolution in 1917 gave Japan further possibilities of building up its ascendancy—were no less revolutionary than those in Europe. By 1918, even before the end of the European War, Wilson was already girding himself to challenge in earnest the expansion of Japan" (Barraclough, 1967, 108–9, 116–17).

By and large, from Versailles through the Washington Conference of 1920–21 and right up to the Crash of 1929, Japan yielded to U.S. pressure to accept a war fleet significantly smaller than those of Britain and the United States and to restrain its expansionist ambitions in China. This enabled Japan to place a growing share of its exports in the United States and the British empire and to raise money both in London and New York for its own commercial and financial ventures overseas, from loans to Chinese warlord governments to the establishment of the Manchuria Railway Company and the Oriental Development Corporation (Iriye, 1965, 25–26; Duus, 1984, 161–62). But when the Crash of 1929 unplugged Japan from core financial and commodity markets, Japan's imperialist tendencies reemerged with a vengeance. In 1930, Japan demanded parity in warships with the United States and Britain, and when parity was denied, it abrogated all previous agreements controlling the size of the fleet. In 1931–32, it took over the whole of Manchuria under the guise of the puppet state "Manchukuo." In 1934–35, it enlarged its sphere of influence in northern China. In 1937, the Japanese initiated the Second Sino-

Japanese War, leading by late 1938 to the occupation of a vast swath along China's coast from north to south. In 1940, as Germany advanced into France, Japan advanced into French Indochina and signed a treaty of alliance with Germany and Italy (Borthwick, 1992, 203–5, 209–10; So and Chiu, 1995, 105–8).

That was the signal for the United States to intervene to end Japan's bid for regional supremacy by tightening U.S. trade restrictions against Japan, by freezing Japanese assets in the U.S., and by imposing a total embargo on petroleum products to Japan. When Japan responded by doing to the U.S. fleet at Pearl Harbor what it had done to the Russian fleet at Port Arthur in 1904, its career as a respectable military power quickly drew to a close. In the intervening thirty-six years, Japan's advances in "the murderous art" had been truly spectacular. But they had not been sufficient to keep up with further Western advances, as the massive destruction inflicted on Japan by the U.S. strategic bombing campaign demonstrated even before the nuclear holocaust of Hiroshima and Nagasaki.

The Reconstitution of China as a Modern State

As Japan's military challenge to Western dominance in East Asia went up in smoke, a new and more formidable challenge emerged in the region in the form of the reconstitution of China as a modern state by a sinified version of Marxism-Leninism. Once Japan's military challenge was defeated, the challenge posed by this reconstitution became the single most important determinant of Western policies in the Far East. The proximate origins of this new challenge can be traced to the same bifurcation in the trajectories of Chinese and Japanese modernization that occurred in the wake of the Sino-Japanese War of 1894 and propelled Japan on the road to Pearl Harbor and Hiroshima.

Besides imposing a crushing indemnity of 230 million taels on Chinese finances, the Treaty of Shimonoseki forced China to open up several more ports not just to trade but also to "industries and manufactures"—a concession to Japan, which by virtue of the most-favored-nation clause was extended ipso facto to thirteen Western powers. Moreover, as previously noted, Chinese recognition of Japanese suzerainty over Korea and the cession of Chinese territories to Japan triggered a scramble among the Western powers for exclusive spheres of influence over large chunks of Chinese territories. The centrifugal forces that had already characterized Chinese modernization before the war were thus given a tremendous impulse by the war and its aftermath.

Attempts by opposite factions at the Qing court to counter the tendency toward the territorial disintegration of the empire only made things worse. The humiliation of defeat by a former tributary state and the scramble for exclusive spheres of influence that ensued prompted the young and nominal Emperor Guangxu to issue in the summer of 1898 no less than forty decrees aimed at a radical and comprehensive modernization of the Chinese state. The result, however, was a military coup staged by Empress Dowager Cixi, who wielded power behind the scenes. The recovery of Qing fortunes, which Guangxu had sought through a speedup of modernization, Cixi sought through patronage of the anti-foreign Boxer Rebellion, which China fought and lost against all the Western powers combined (Fairbank, 1992, 228–32).

The new indemnity of a staggering 450 million taels and the new restrictions on Chinese sovereignty imposed by the Boxer Protocol of 1901 set the stage for the final downfall of dynastic rule in the Revolution of 1911 and the subsequent breakdown of all semblance of centralized government in the warlord era from 1916 to 1927. Economically, the Boxer Protocol compounded the effects of the Treaty of Shimonoseki in compromising China's modernization efforts for decades to come. Loans contracted to pay the Boxer indemnity more than doubled the annual payments owed on loans contracted to pay the Japanese indemnity of 1895. By 1902, these payments absorbed over 40 percent of the central government revenue (Thomas, 1984, 113).

Between 1895 and 1911, the combined costs of the two indemnities were more than twice the total initial capitalization of all manufacturing enterprises established in China by nationals or foreigners between 1895 and 1913. Foreign investment more than doubled between 1902 and 1914, and again between 1914 and 1931. But over the entire period 1902–30, 75 percent more capital left China as repatriated profit than was invested in China from abroad (Esherick, 1972, 13). As a result of this drain of profit and tribute, China's modern industrial and transport infrastructure on the eve of the Second World War was smaller, more lopsided, and more fragmented than that of India, a colonial country with a smaller population (Bagchi, 1982, 103–7).

Politically, the Qing government "was reduced to little more than a despised tax-collecting agency for the foreign powers" (Esherick, 1972, 14). Prevented by the unequal treaties from raising tariffs, it was forced to raise internal taxes and cut down support for the "self-strengthening enterprises." Worse still, constitutional reforms aimed at introducing some measure of representative government and winning the support of the landed upper classes for the tottering regime through the establishment of provincial assemblies backfired. Provincial interests and authorities quickly turned the assemblies into instruments of consolidation and legitimation of their autonomy from Beijing. And as soon as the occasion arose, the assemblies declared their independence from the central government, precipitating the Revolution of 1911 (So and Chiu, 1995, 115, 117–18; Skocpol, 1979, 79–80).

The Sino-Japanese War thus had opposite legacies for China and Japan. Victory in the war propelled Japan onto the path to full sovereignty and respectability in the Western game of imperialist politics. Defeat plunged China further along the path to imperial disintegration and deepening foreign domination.

Just before the Boxer movement collapsed, Henri Borel, a well-informed Western observer, ventured a prediction that still haunts the West.

> The revolutionary party is likely to do just what the Japanese have done: rid the country of all foreign influences and turn it into an independent power in the East. If the movement succeeds, the West is as good as finished and the future belongs to China and Japan, to the East. (Quoted in Romein, 1978, 50)

The movement did not succeed, and the future has belonged to the West for another century. But as Jan Romein remarks after quoting Borel, merely fifty years after hitting the bottom of national humiliation, China reemerged as a power in its own right. "Behind the rebellious Boxers with their primitive swords, there loomed as in a Chinese shadow play, the gigantic figure of Sun Yat-sen, behind him that of Marshal Chiang Kai-shek, and behind the Marshal that of Mao Tse-tung" (1978, 50).

To this we should add that behind the two main transitions of this Chinese shadow play—from the Boxers to Sun Zhongshan and from Jiang Jieshi to Mao Zedong—the shadow of Japan loomed much larger than that of any Western power. Behind the rise of Sun there loomed the shadow of Japan's victory against Russia in 1905—the same year in which Sun became the head of the Revolutionary Alliance at a meeting of Chinese students in Tokyo. Behind the rise of Mao there loomed the shadow of Japan's takeover of Manchuria in 1931–32, the expansion of its sphere of influence in northern China in 1934, and its takeover of the coastal regions of China in 1937–38. In the period between the rise of Sun and the rise of Mao, there lay the warlord era in China (1916–27) and the transformation of Japan from the main foreign supporter of Chinese nationalism—as it still was on the eve of the Revolution of 1911—into its main foe.

The changing relationship between China and Japan under the impact of their incorporation into the European-centered interstate system thus set the stage for the evolution of China's national liberation movement. But the evolution itself—that is, the nature of the movement's responses to the challenges posed by the rise of Japanese imperialism and the effectiveness of those responses in attaining the movement's goals—was determined primarily by the relationship of the movement to Chinese society on the one side, and to world politics on the other side. For what concerns the movement's relationship to world politics, by far the most important influence was exercised by Marxism-Leninism as instituted by the Russian Revolution of 1917.

In its original Soviet form, Marxism-Leninism was probably more important in reviving the fortunes of Sun's Guomindang (GMD) in the 1920s than in assisting in the subsequent rise to power of Mao's Chinese Communist Party (CCP). When in 1922 Sun joined forces with the Comintern and began to reorganize the GMD on Soviet lines, he had demonstrated his preeminence as China's nationalist leader, but also his incompetence to complete the Revolution.

> The GMD ideology, so necessary to inspire student activists, was nominally Sun Yatsen's Three People's Principles [Nationalism, People's Rights or Democracy, and People's Livelihood], but these were really a party platform (a set of goals) rather than an ideology (a theory of history). The GMD had got no farther than regional warlordism at Guangzhou until in 1923 it allied with the Soviet Union, reorganized itself on Soviet lines, created an indoctrinated Party army, and formed a United Front with the CCP. The four years of Soviet aid and CCP collaboration together with the patriotic Marxist-Leninist animus against the warlords' domestic "feudalism" and the foreign powers' "imperialism" helped the GMD to power. (Fairbank, 1992, 285)

Sun did not live to reap the fruits of the reorganization of the GMD on Leninist lines and the United Front policy with the CCP. Upon his death in 1925, leadership of the GMD passed to the military commander Jiang Jieshi. Under Jiang, the GMD never fully shed the Leninist form of organization, but as soon as it had seized control of the Shangai-Nanjing region, it reversed Sun's United Front policy with the CCP. In a bloody betrayal in April 1927, he attacked and decimated the Communist-led labor unions that had seized control of Shangai, and then proceeded to expel the Chinese Communists from his newly formed Nanjing government and to institute a nationwide terror against the Communists. This reversal of Sun's United Front policy led to the imperialist powers' recognition of Jiang's Nanjing government in 1928, but "tended to dissipate the GMD's revolutionary spirit. Soon it found itself on the defensive against both the CCP and Japan" (Fairbank, 1992, 284–86).

Japan's offensive came soon enough. But before the CCP could effectively displace the GMD at the head of the movement of national liberation, its ideology and organization had to become an organic expression of revolutionary forces within Chinese society itself. This is the transformation that produced a distinct Chinese brand of Marxism-Leninism and eventually led the CCP to power. It began with the formation of the Red Army shortly after Jiang's break with the CCP, but it came to fruition only after Japan took over China's coastal regions.

The transformation had two closely related aspects. First, while the Leninist principle of the vanguard party was retained, the insurrectional thrust of Leninist theory was abandoned. In the deeply fragmented statal structure of warlord-GMD China, there was no "Winter Palace" to be stormed or, rather, there were too many such palaces for any insurrectionary strategy to succeed. The insurrectional aspects of Leninist theory were thus replaced by what Mao later theorized as the "mass line"—the idea that the vanguard party ought to be not just the teacher, but also the pupil of the masses. "This from-the-masses-to-the-masses concept," notes Fairbank (1992, 319) "was indeed a sort of democracy suited to Chinese tradition, where the upper-class official had governed best when he had the true interests of the local people at heart and so governed on their behalf."

Second, and most important, in seeking a social base the CCP gave priority to the peasantry rather than to Marx's and Lenin's revolutionary class, the urban proletariat. As the 1927 massacre of Communist-led workers at Shangai had demonstrated, the coastal regions, where the bulk of the urban proletariat was concentrated, were far too treacherous a ground from which to challenge foreign domination and the GMD's hegemony over the rapidly expanding Chinese bourgeoisie. The foreign powers' recognition of the GMD government the following year made the situation in these regions even more hopeless for the CCP than it had been. Driven ever farther from the seats of capitalist expansion by the Western trained and equipped GMD armies, the CCP and the Red Army were left little choice but to thrust their roots among the peasantry of poor and remote areas. The result was, in Mark Selden's characterization, "a two-way socialization process," whereby the party-army molded the subaltern strata of Chinese rural society into a powerful revolutionary force, and was in turn shaped by the aspirations and values of these strata (1995, 37–38).

The war with Japan gave a powerful impulse to this two-way socialization process, turning it from a force of merely local significance into a force of world significance. By the time of Japan's surrender in 1945, Mao's party-army held sway over almost one hundred million people and was poised to win the subsequent civil war that ended with the defeat of the GMD. The challenge to Western dominance that emerged from the double victory of the CCP against Japan and the GMD was fundamentally different from the Japanese military challenge that had just been terminated by U.S. strategic and nuclear bombing. The Japanese challenge was based on Wei Yuan's idea of using Western military technology to control the West. As previously noted, it failed primarily because Japanese advances in Western military technology could not keep up with the West's own further advances. But it failed also because it called forth in the East Asian region countervailing forces as firmly opposed to Japanese as to Western military supremacy. Once the Japanese challenge collapsed, these countervailing forces remained in place to check the restoration of Western dominance under U.S. hegemony.

This new challenge was not based primarily on Wei Yuan's idea of using Western military technology to control the West. Although minimal proficiency in the use of such technologies was essential to its success, the new challenge was based primarily on Hong Xiuquan's idea of using Western ideology to control the West. Hong had tried with a sinified version of Christianity and had failed. Mao, following in the footsteps of Sun, tried with a sinified version of Marxism-Leninism and succeeded. Between Hong's failure and Mao's success was a century during which the West laid siege to the old center of the East Asian world system, forced upon it a major reorganization, but never succeeded in becoming hegemonic, except in the limited and contradictory sense of drawing Japan onto the path of industrialized warfare and China onto the path of socialist revolution.

This kind of leadership is what we have called leadership against the leader's will because, over time, it tends to intensify competition for power and thereby deflate rather than inflate the power of the hegemon (see introduction). In the intensification of competition that ensued from Japan's strides in acquiring Western military technology, the declining Western hegemon was the first to go under. By the 1930s Japan had for all practical purposes eclipsed Britain as the dominant power in the East Asian region. In the intensified competition that ensued from China's strides in acquiring Western revolutionary ideology, it was Japan itself that went under. That left the rising Western hegemon and a new China facing one another in a struggle for centrality in East Asia that has shaped trends and events in the region ever since.

Beyond Western Hegemonies?

As perceived from the angle of vision adopted in this chapter, past hegemonic transitions within the Western world appear as distinct moments of the process of expansion of Western power in the non-Western world. In the transition from Dutch to British hegemony, the expansionary thrust of the West was the active element that shaped relations among civilizations. In the transition from British to U.S. hegemony, by contrast, the expansionary thrust of the West was held in check by internal rivalries and by the ability of mass nationalism in the non-Western world to exploit these rivalries. The two ideologies that eventually emerged victorious to confront one another in the Cold War era—Americanism and Soviet communism—were first and foremost projects of accommodation of the forces of mass nationalism engendered by the revolt against the West of the preceding half century. As Huntington claims in a passage quoted in the introduction, the Cold War was indeed yet another "Western Civil War." But the main purpose of this civil war was to win the allegiance of the non-Western world to one of the two ideological camps into which the Western world had been divided.

U.S. victory in this new Western Civil War has brought about an almost complete centralization of global military capabilities in the hands of the United States and its closest allies (see chapter 1). This centralization has undoubtedly inflated the power of the capitalist "West" that was born out of the ideological conflicts of the Cold War, in relation to the states of the now defunct "East" centered on the USSR. But it has not increased the collective power of the Western civilization (broadly understood to include Eastern Europe and Russia) in relation to other civilizations. On the contrary, two basic facts of world politics since the crisis of U.S. hegemony suggest that this collective power has declined further, not just from the extraordinary peak it attained under British hegemony in the nineteenth century, but also from the lesser peak it attained under U.S. hegemony in the 1950s and 1960s.

The first basic fact is that, in spite of the unprecedented and unparalleled destructive power of their military-industrial apparatuses, both superpowers of the Cold War era underwent humiliating defeats in the wars they waged on non-Western peoples—the United States in Vietnam in the 1970s and the USSR in Afghanistan in the 1980s. Given the disproportionate military superiority of the two superpowers, the reasons for their respective defeats must be sought on grounds other than strictly military ones. These other grounds are primarily socio-political, first and foremost the fundamental lack of legitimacy of the superpowers' objectives in the two wars, not just among the peoples in whose countries the wars were waged, but also among the superpowers' citizens and allies and in the world community at large. As we have seen in chapter 3, this lack of legitimacy seriously constrained the capacity of the superpowers to mobilize the resources needed to win the confrontations and led to a major erosion of their prestige and power. The fact that each superpower took turns in benefiting from the troubles of the other—the USSR from the troubles of the United States in the 1970s and the United States from the troubles of the USSR in the 1980s—should not conceal the fact that their *joint* power and influence diminished with each confrontation.

The other basic fact of world politics since about 1970 is the tightening of economic constraints on both superpowers' freedom of action. These constraints have had far more devastating effects on the power of the USSR than on that of the United States. Indeed, it is primarily on the terrain of high finance that the United States in the

1980s won the Cold War. Nevertheless, this victory should not make us forget that in the fiscal-financial sphere, as in the socio-political sphere, the crisis of U.S. world power preceded that of the USSR and, in everchanging forms, has outlasted the end of the Cold War. As we have seen in chapter 2, this crisis is deeply rooted in ongoing structural transformations of the relationship between states and capital and, as such, it will probably find no resolution any time soon.

Be that as it may, economically, even more than politically, what one superpower gained from the troubles of the other superpower fell far short of their *joint* losses in relation to the non-Western world. The most conspicuous manifestation of this tendency is the rise of East Asia as the most dynamic center of world-scale processes of capital accumulation. This rise, rather than the demise of Soviet power, may well turn out to have been the most significant event of our age.

The proximate origins of this development can be traced to the peculiar difficulties encountered by the United States in enforcing the Cold War world order in East Asia. As previously noted, the defeat of Japan in the Second World War and the subsequent victory of the CCP over the GMD in Mainland China left the rising Western hegemon, the United States, and the People's Republic of China (PRC) facing one another in a struggle for centrality in the region. At least initially, there was very little that the PRC could do to prevent the United States from gaining the upper hand. The unilateral military occupation of Japan by the United States in 1945 and the division of the region in the aftermath of the Korean War into two antagonistic blocs created, in Bruce Cumings's words, a U.S. "vertical regime solidified through bilateral defense treaties (with Japan, South Korea, Taiwan, and the Philippines) and conducted by a State Department that towered over the foreign ministries of these four countries."

> All became semisovereign states, deeply penetrated by U.S. military structures (operational control of the South Korean armed forces, Seventh Fleet patrolling of the Taiwan Straits, defense dependencies for all four countries, military bases on their territories) and incapable of independent foreign policy or defense initiatives. . . . There were minor demarches through the military curtain beginning in the mid-1950s, such as low levels of trade between Japan and China, or Japan and North Korea. But the dominant tendency until the 1970s was a unilateral U.S. regime heavily biased toward military forms of communication. (Cumings, 1997, 155)

The interpenetration of tribute and trade relations between an imperial center whose domestic economy was of incomparably greater size than those of its vassal states made this unilateral U.S. regime resemble the old Sinocentric tribute-trade system. In this respect, we may well say that U.S. hegemony in East Asia was realized through the transformation of the periphery of the former Sinocentric tribute-trade system into the periphery of a U.S.-centric tribute-trade system. The U.S.-centric system, however, was far more militaristic in structure and orientation than its Sinocentric predecessor. Not only was it based on a military-industrial apparatus of incomparably greater size and technological sophistication; more important, the U.S.-centric system also fostered a functional specialization between the imperial and the vassal states that had no parallel in the old Sinocentric system. While the United States specialized in the provision of protection and the pursuit of political power regionally and globally, its East Asian vassal states specialized in trade and the pursuit of profit.

This division of labor has been particularly important in shaping U.S.-Japanese relations throughout the Cold War era, right up to the present. As Franz Schurmann (1974, 143) wrote at a time when the spectacular economic ascent of Japan had just begun, "[f]reed from the burden of defense spending, Japanese governments have funneled all their resources and energies into an economic expansionism that has brought affluence to Japan and taken its business to the farthest reaches of the globe." Japan's economic expansion, in turn, generated a "snowballing" process of concatenated, labor-seeking rounds of investment in the surrounding region, which gradually replaced U.S. patronage as the main driving force of the East Asian economic expansion (Ozawa, 1993, 130–31; Arrighi, 1996, 14–16).

By the time this snowballing process took off, the militaristic U.S. regime in East Asia had begun to unravel as the Vietnam War destroyed what the Korean War had created. The Korean War had instituted the U.S.-centric East Asian regime by excluding Mainland China from normal commercial and diplomatic intercourse with the noncommunist part of the region through blockade and war threats backed by "an archipelago of American military installations" (Cumings, 1997, 154–55). Defeat in the Vietnam War, by contrast, forced the United States to readmit Mainland China to normal commercial and diplomatic intercourse with the rest of East Asia, thereby broadening the scope of the region's economic integration and expansion (Arrighi, 1996).

This outcome transformed without eliminating the previous imbalance of the distribution of power resources in the region. The evolution of Japan into an industrial and financial powerhouse of global significance transformed the previous relationship of Japanese political and economic vassalage vis-à-vis the United States into a relationship of mutual vassalage. Japan continued to depend on the United States for military protection, but the reproduction of the U.S. protection-producing apparatus came to depend ever more critically on Japanese finance and industry. At the same time, the reincorporation of Mainland China into regional and global markets brought back into play a state whose demographic size, abundance of entrepreneurial and labor resources, and growth potential easily surpassed all other states operating in the region, the United States included. Within less than twenty years after Richard Nixon's mission to Beijing, and less than fifteen after the formal reestablishment of diplomatic relations between the United States and the PRC, this giant "container" of human resources already seemed poised to become again the powerful attractor of means of payments it had been before its subordinate incorporation in the European-centered world system.

If the main attraction of the PRC for foreign capital has been its huge and highly competitive reserves of labor, the "matchmaker" that has facilitated the encounter of foreign capital and Chinese labor is the Overseas Chinese capitalist diaspora.

> Drawn by China's capable pool of low-cost labor and its growing potential as a market that contains one-fifth of the world's population, foreign investors continue to pour money into the PRC. Some 80 percent of that capital comes from the Overseas Chinese, refugees from poverty, disorder, and communism, who in one of the era's most piquant ironies are now Beijing's favorite financiers and models for modernization. Even the Japanese often rely on the Overseas Chinese to grease their way into China. (Kraar, 1993, 40)

In fact, Beijing's reliance on the Overseas Chinese to ease Mainland China's reincorporation into regional and world markets is not the true irony of the situation. As Alvin So and Stephen Chiu (1995, chapter 11) have shown, the close political alliance that was established in the 1980s between the Chinese Communist Party and Overseas Chinese capitalists made perfect sense in terms of their respective pursuits. For the alliance provided the Overseas Chinese with extra-ordinary opportunities to profit from commercial and financial inter-mediation, while providing the Chinese Communist Party with a highly effective means of killing two birds with one stone: to upgrade the domestic economy of Mainland China and to promote national unification in accordance with the "One Nation, Two Systems" model.

The true irony of the situation is that one of the most conspicuous legacies of nineteenth-century Western encroachments on Chinese sov-ereignty is now emerging as a powerful instrument of Chinese and East Asian emancipation from Western dominance. As we have empha-sized, an Overseas Chinese diaspora had long been an integral compo-nent of the indigenous East Asian tribute-trade system centered on im-perial China. But the greatest opportunities for its expansion came with the subordinate incorporation of that system within the structures of the European-centered world system in the wake of the Opium Wars. The diaspora tried to translate its growing economic power into political control over Mainland China by supporting the 1911 revolu-tion and the GMD in the warlord era. But the attempt failed in the face of escalating political chaos, the takeover of China's coastal regions by Japan, and the eventual defeat of the GMD by the CCP.

Under the U.S. Cold War regime, the diaspora's traditional role of commercial intermediary between Mainland China and the surround-ing maritime regions was stifled as much by the U.S. embargo on trade with the PRC as by the PRC's restrictions on domestic and foreign trade. Nevertheless, the expansion of U.S. power networks and Japanese business networks in the maritime regions of East Asia pro-vided the diaspora with plenty of opportunities to exercise new forms of commercial intermediation between these networks and the local networks it controlled. And when restrictions on trade with and within China were relaxed, the diaspora quickly emerged as the single most powerful agency of the economic reunification of the East Asian regional economy (Hui, 1995).

It is too early to tell what kind of political-economic formation will eventually emerge out of this reunification. Nor is it easy to tell how far the rapid economic expansion of the East Asian region can go. Whatever its eventual outcome, the present rise of East Asia as the most dynamic center of world-scale processes of capital accumulation can nonetheless be taken as a sign that the long process of Western intrusion and dominance in Asia has come, or is about to come, full circle. As General Douglas MacArthur predicted in 1951, the expansion of the Western frontier to embrace the trade potentialities of Asia may well be resulting in "the gradual rotation of the epicenter of world trade back to the Far East whence it started many centuries ago" (quoted in Cumings, 1993, 36). But whether or not this is what we are actually observing, the main features of the ongoing East Asian economic renaissance are sufficiently clear to provide us with some insights into its likely future trajectory, as well as its implications for the global political economy.

First, the renaissance is as much the product of the contradictions of U.S. world hegemony as of East Asia's geo-historical heritage. The contradictions of U.S. world hegemony concern primarily the dependence of U.S. power and wealth on a path of development characterized by high protection and reproduction costs—that is, on the formation of a world-encompassing, capital-intensive military apparatus on the one side, and on the diffusion of wasteful and unsustainable patterns of mass consumption on the other. Nowhere have these contradictions been more evident than in East Asia. Not only did the Korean and Vietnam wars reveal the limits of the actual power wielded by the U.S. warfare-welfare state. Equally important, as the global economy became more closely integrated than ever before, East Asia's geo-historical heritage of comparatively low reproduction and protection costs gave the region's governmental and business agencies a decisive competitive advantage vis-à-vis the high protection and reproduction costs of the United States. Whether this heritage will be preserved remains unclear. But if it is preserved, the East Asian expansion may eventually open up for world society as a whole a more economical and sustainable developmental path than the United States did.

Second, the renaissance has been associated with a structural differentiation of power in the region that has left the United States controlling most of the guns, Japan and the Overseas Chinese controlling most of the money, and the PRC controlling most of the labor. This structural differentiation—which has no precedent in previous hegemonic transitions—makes it extremely unlikely that any single state operating in the region, the United States included, will acquire the capabilities needed to become hegemonic regionally and globally. Only a plurality of states acting in concert with one another has any chance of developing a new world order. This plurality may well include the United States and, in any event, U.S. policies toward the region will remain important in determining whether, when, and how such a regionally based new world order would actually emerge.

Third, the process of economic expansion and the integration of the East Asian region is a process structurally open to the rest of the world. In part, this openness is a heritage of the interstitial nature of the process vis-à-vis the networks of power of the United States. In part, it is due to the important role played by informal business networks with ramifications throughout the global economy in promoting the integration of the region. And in part, it is due to the continuing dependence of East Asia on other regions of the global economy for raw materials, high technology, and cultural products. The strong forward and backward links that connect the East Asian regional economy to the rest of the world augur well for the future of the global economy, assuming that the economic expansion of East Asia is not brought to a premature end by internal conflicts, mismanagement, or U.S. resistance to the loss of power and prestige (though not necessarily of wealth and welfare) that the recentering of the global economy on East Asia entails.

Finally, the embedment of the East Asian economic expansion and integration in the region's geo-historical heritage means that the process cannot be replicated elsewhere with equally favorable results. Adaptation to the emergent East Asian economic leadership on the basis of each region's own geo-historical heritage—rather than misguided attempts at replicating the East Asian experience out of context, or even more misguided attempts at reaffirming Western supremacy on the basis of a flawed assessment of the actual power wielded by the U.S. military-industrial apparatus—is the most promising course of action for the states of the Western world. Whether this is a realistic expectation is, of course, an altogether different question to which we shall return in the conclusion of the book.

Conclusion

Giovanni Arrighi and Beverly J. Silver

The story of hegemonic transitions told sequentially in the four chapters of this book highlights different aspects of the process through which the modern system of sovereign states was transformed from being *a* (European) world among other worlds into the historical social system of *the* world. Each chapter has shown that this process of globalization of the European-centered world system has *not* proceeded along a single developmental path within which hegemonic states rose and fell. On the contrary, the systemwide expansions under the leadership of each hegemonic state culminated in a crisis and breakdown of the system. Expansion resumed only when a new hegemonic state opened up a different developmental path, reorganizing the system so as to solve the problems and contradictions encountered along the path opened up by its predecessor.

The globalization of the modern world system has thus occurred through a series of breaks in established patterns of governance, accumulation, and social cohesion, in the course of which an established hegemonic order decayed, while a new order emerged interstitially and, over time, became hegemonic. "The interval between the decay of the old and the formation and establishment of the new," notes John Calhoun, "constitutes a period of transition which must necessarily always be one of uncertainty, confusion, error, and wild and fierce fanaticism" (quoted in Harvey, 1989, 119). Our contention has been that since about 1970 we have been living through yet another one of these periods, as witnessed, among other things, by the difficulties observers have agreeing on the direction and meaning of ongoing transformations of the global political economy. But our contention has been also that by analyzing past hegemonic transitions we can detect patterns of recurrence and evolution that help us better understand the nature and prospective consequences of these transformations. This better understanding can be summed up in five related propositions we put forth as hypotheses to be rejected in the light of the unfolding evidence or, if not rejected, as devices for monitoring ongoing systemic change.

Proposition 1

The global financial expansion of the last twenty years or so is neither a new stage of world capitalism nor the harbinger of a "coming hegemony of global markets." Rather, it is the clearest sign that we are in the midst of a hegemonic crisis. As such, the expansion can be expected to be a temporary phenomenon that will end more or less catastrophically, depending on how the crisis is handled by the declining hegemon.

Our analysis has shown that the particular spatio-temporal combination of circumstances that characterize the crisis of an existing hegemonic order (the intensification of interstate rivalries, interenterprise competition, social conflicts, and the emergence of new configurations of power) has varied from transition to transition. But in all cases, the crises were characterized by systemwide financial expansions. These expansions rest on a massive redistribution of incomes driven by intense interstate competition for mobile capital. Thanks to its continuing centrality in networks of high finance, the declining hegemon could turn this competition to its advantage and thereby experience a reflation of its waning power. This reflation of power came late and was minor in the case of the Dutch; it came early and was major in the case of the British. But in both cases these power revivals and the financial expansions that underlie them ended with the complete breakdown of the decaying hegemonic order some thirty to forty years after they had begun.

Our contention has been that the U.S.-centered financial expansion presents important analogies not just with the British-centered financial expansion of the late nineteenth and early twentieth centuries—as Hirst and Thompson, Soros, and many other observers have noted (see introduction)—but also with the Dutch-centered financial expansion of the mid-eighteenth century. Unlike these earlier expansions, the current one has not yet ended in a breakdown of the decaying U.S. hegemonic order. And as we submit in some of the propositions that follow, there may be grounds for expecting it to end differently than earlier expansions. Nevertheless, there are good reasons to believe that the present expansion and attendant reflation of U.S. power are indeed signs of a hegemonic crisis analogous to those of one hundred and two hundred-fifty years ago.

For one thing, the financial expansion itself seems to rest on increasingly precarious grounds. Even the most enthusiastic supporters of interstate competition in globally integrated financial markets have begun to fear that financial globalization is turning into "a brakeless train wreaking havoc." They worry about a "mounting backlash" against the effects of such a destructive force, first and foremost "the rise of a new brand of populist politicians" fostered by the "mood . . . of helplessness and anxiety" that is taking hold even of wealthy countries (quoted in Harvey, 1995, 8, 12). A backlash of this kind has been a typical feature of past financial expansions (see introduction and chapter 3). It announces that the massive redistribution of income and wealth on which the expansion rests has reached, or is about to reach, its limits. And once the redistribution can no longer be sustained economically, socially, and politically, the financial expansion is bound to end. The only question that remains open in this respect is not whether, but how soon and how catastrophically the present global dominance of unregulated financial markets will collapse.

The apparent blindness of the U.S. elites to the sources, limits, and precariousness of the reflation of U.S. power buttresses this conclusion. It was a blindness of this kind that hastened the destruction of the Dutch Republic under the combined impact of war, revolution, and counterrevolution. It was a blindness of this kind that led Britain to hasten the catastrophic breakdown of its hegemonic order by persisting in a Free Trade Imperialism that had become wholly anachronistic (see chapters 1 and 3). In both transitions, the financial expansions that reflated the power of the declining hegemonic state would have come to an end anyway under the weight of their own contradictions.

But the blindness that led the ruling groups of these states to mistake the "autumn" for a new "spring" of their hegemonic power meant that the end came sooner and more catastrophically than it might otherwise have—mostly for itself in the case of the Dutch Republic, mostly for Europe and the world at large in the case of Britain.

A similar blindness is evident today. The ease with which the United States has succeeded in mobilizing resources in global financial markets to defeat the USSR in the Second Cold War, and then to sustain a long domestic economic expansion and a spectacular boom in the New York stock exchange, has led to the belief that "America's back!" Even assuming that U.S. global power has been reflated as much as this belief implies, it would be a very different *kind* of power than the one deployed at the height of U.S. hegemony. That power rested on the capacity of the United States to rise and raise other states above "the tyranny of small decisions" so as to solve the system-level problems that had plagued the world in the systemic chaos of the war and interwar years. The new power that the United States has come to enjoy in the 1980s and 1990s, in contrast, rests on the capacity of the United States to outcompete most other states in global financial markets. A new tyranny of small decisions has been resurrected, in the context of ever more pressing system-level problems that neither the United States nor any other state seems capable of solving.

Moreover, the *extent* to which U.S. power itself has been reflated is not as great as generally assumed by U.S. elites. Domestic expansion in the United States and contraction in Japan has done little to stop the shift of the global economy's center of gravity to East Asia. As a well-informed observer wrote in 1995,

> Last year the U.S. had its highest level of capital investment in a decade, 12 percent of its GNP, or about $2,500 per capita. "America's back!" we are told. But last year, Japan, in the worst year of the recession, had capital investment of 18.2 percent of its GNP, or $5,700 per capita. (Courtis, 1995, 24)

The spread of the East Asian economic renaissance to greater China—Hong Kong, Taiwan, and now the PRC—adds an entirely new dimension to the shift (Selden, 1997). To be sure, it also adds an entirely new dimension to the problems involved in managing the renaissance, as witnessed by the present turbulence in the region's financial markets. Problems of this kind, however, have been typical of all newly emergent centers of world capitalism. In past hegemonic transitions, as noted by Braudel (see chapter 1), the crises that ushered in the demise of the old financial center were felt earliest and most severely in the *rising* financial centers (London in 1772 and New York in 1929). It follows that the Asian financial crises of the 1990s cannot be taken as proof of long-term weakness. Indeed, no matter how much U.S. power may have been reflated, it is unlikely to have been reflated enough to stop the rotation of the global economy's center of gravity back to where it was in premodern times.

Proposition 2

The most important geopolitical novelty of the present hegemonic crisis is a bifurcation of military and financial capabilities that has no precedent in earlier hegemonic transitions. The bifurcation decreases the likelihood of an outbreak of war among the system's most powerful units. But it does not reduce the chances of a deterioration of the present hegemonic crisis into a more or less long period of systemic chaos.

As argued in chapter 1, the current crisis of state sovereignty is in fact the third such crisis since the formal establishment of the modern interstate system in 1648. Each hegemonic transition resulted in a drastic simplification of the map of world power. In the transition from Dutch to British hegemony, city-states that had been European great powers for centuries, and proto-nation-states like the declining Dutch hegemon itself, were squeezed out of European politics by the emergence of powerful empire-building national states. In the transition from British to U.S. hegemony, it was the turn of the empire-building national states themselves to be squeezed out of world politics by the emergence of two continent-sized superpowers that had formed on the outer perimeter of the European-centered world system.

This process of centralization of systemic capabilities in fewer and fewer hands destroyed the balance of power that originally guaranteed the sovereign equality of the members of the Westphalia system of states. As the system became global through the granting of legal sovereignty to an increasing number and variety of states, most states lost the factual sovereignty that previously had been guaranteed by a more balanced distribution of systemic capabilities. Under British hegemony, such a guarantee became somewhat of a fiction; under U.S. hegemony it was discarded even as a fiction.

In the course of the crisis of U.S. hegemony, this process has been carried one step further by the disintegration of the USSR and the centralization in U.S. hands of global military capabilities. But as the constraints imposed on the United States by the balance of terror with the USSR relaxed, financial constraints on the deployment of these capabilities tightened. Just as victory in the First World War destroyed Britain's status as the leading creditor nation, so victory in the Second Cold War turned the United States into the largest debtor nation. Ever since, the United States' freedom of action as the chief protagonist of world politics has been subject to daunting financial constraints, which the alleged U.S. economic "comeback" of the 1990s has done little to relax. Moreover, this tightening of financial constraints has affected not just the United States, but its closest military allies as well. As a result, fiscal considerations have gradually gained prominence in the management of the awesome U.S. and Western military machine.

Thus, in celebrating the expansion of NATO, President Clinton hailed a new Europe that is "undivided, democratic, and at peace for the first time since the rise of the nation state" (Sanger, 1997b, 4: 5). This may well be the most important legacy of U.S. hegemony and the Cold War world order. In both hegemonic transitions, intra-European divisions and rivalries were the mainspring of the climactic wars that engulfed the world, ushering in unspeakable chaos and human suffering. The fact that many of the divisions and rivalries have been superseded by economic integration into the European Union and a military alliance with the world's greatest military power decreases the likelihood that rivalries among the system's most powerful units will escalate into open war, as happened in past transitions. However, it does not increase the likelihood that the Western military machine will become the foundation of a new world order. Nor does it decrease the likelihood of a disintegration of what is left of the U.S. world order into a new kind of systemic chaos.

As David Sanger reports, the "glow around the celebration of the expansion of NATO . . . lasted for about three days." Even before President Clinton reboarded Air Force One "the carping began." The carping was as much about the purpose of the expansion as about who would pay for it. With the Soviet threat gone, it was hard to find a new mission for NATO, let alone an expanded NATO, that U.S. and European politicians could "sell" to their constituencies as being worth their tax money. Intent on cutting its budget deficit to regain financial flexibility, the Clinton administration announced that the United States would pay only 6 percent of the Pentagon's estimate of the expansion's costs, assuming that the newly admitted members would pay about 50 percent and other current NATO members about 44 percent. Themselves intent on cutting budget deficits that threatened to delay or sink the launching of a common European currency, leading members of the European Union rejected both the Pentagon's estimate and the share they were assumed to pay as too high (Sanger, 1997b, 4: 5; Erlanger, 1997, A1, 10).

The irony of the situation is that on both sides of the equation of NATO expansion—the side of existing members who have been pushing for enlargement and the side of the would-be members who have been pushing for admittance—the primary motive has not been military security, but commercial advantage. Leaving aside the push of arms makers in NATO countries seeking new outlets for expensive, top-of-the-line equipment, the U.S. administration explicitly made the case for NATO expansion as a means of "locking in" privatization and liberalization drives, not just in countries like Hungary, which are actually being admitted, but also in countries like Romania, Estonia, and Bulgaria, which merely hope to be part of a future round of expansion. These countries, for their part, seek NATO admittance primarily as a means to the more ambitious goal of getting into the European Union. But here is where the real problem with the expansion of Western security and prosperity lies:

> It's one thing to pledge that you will defend the nations of Eastern Europe with blood, guts, and missiles. But open markets further to their goods and help subsidize their farm goods? Well, that's serious business. . . . That could mean major transfers of money from West to East. Western Europe is also balking because the new applicants would increase the population of the European Union by 30 percent, but would expand its economic muscle by only about 4 percent—not exactly the kind of great addition China made on July 1 when it added a tiny bit of population and got a world-beater of a business center in Hong Kong. The problem now is that the same three countries that were the first to join NATO are probably also the three in the best shape to join the European Union. That raises the specter of two Europes—one protected and prosperous, one unprotected and struggling. (Sanger, 1997b, 4: 5)

In short, unlike previous hegemonic crises, the present crisis of U.S. hegemony has further concentrated global military resources in the hands of the declining hegemon and its closest allies. Like previous hegemonic crises, however, it has shifted global financial resources to new centers endowed with a decisive competitive edge in world-scale processes of capital accumulation. The declining hegemon is thus left in the anomalous situation that it faces no credible military challenge, but it does not have the financial means needed to solve system-level problems that require system-level solutions.

The obverse side of this anomalous situation is the reemergence of city-states (Hong Kong and Singapore) and semisovereign states (Japan and Taiwan) as the "cash-boxes" of the world capitalist system. Not since the elimination of the Dutch Republic from the high politics of Europe have cash-boxes of this kind exercised as much influence on the politics of the modern world as they do now. Also in this respect— as in the rotation of the center of gravity of the global economy back to East Asia—the present transition seems to be reviving features of early and premodern times. Since all these cash-boxes owe their fortunes to a strict specialization in the pursuit of wealth rather than the pursuit of power, none of them—the biggest one, Japan, included— can be expected to change course by either trying to become a military power of more than local significance, or by trying to provide system-level solutions for system-level problems. This is a further reason for expecting that the present crisis has no inherent tendency to escalate into a war among the system's most powerful units; but it also has no inherent tendency toward the avoidance of a long period of systemic chaos of a new kind.

Proposition 3

Unlike the global financial expansion, the proliferation in the number and variety of transnational business organizations and communities is a novel and probably irreversible feature of the present hegemonic crisis. It has been a major factor in the disintegration of the U.S. hegemonic order and can be expected to continue to shape ongoing systemic change through a general, though by no means universal, disempowerment of states.

Systemwide financial expansions are a recurrent tendency of world capitalism from its earliest origins in late medieval Europe to the present. They are the expression of the continuing and intensifying capitalist nature of the system of states in which world-scale processes of capital accumulation are embedded. But they are also the expression of the instability of world capitalism as instituted at any given time, as well as of its adaptability. While systemwide financial expansions come and go, the transformations in systemic organization that accompany them do not. They constitute successive and distinct stages in the process of formation, widening and deepening of a world market and a world capitalist system.

Thus, as chapter 2 argues, the joint-stock chartered companies that formed and expanded under Dutch hegemony went bankrupt or were phased out of existence in the transition to British hegemony. These government-like organizations had been empowered by their respective chartering states to expand commercially and territorially in environments where it would have been too risky or costly for these states to operate directly. But the chartered companies' activities in the non-Western world created the conditions for the subsequent globalization of the European-centered world system under the leadership of the empire-building British state.

The system of family business enterprise that formed and expanded under British hegemony and withered away or was peripheralized in the transition to U.S. hegemony, was thoroughly embedded in the world-encompassing structures of the British empire. When the British empire collapsed, so did the system of family business enterprise. But the widespread diffusion of mechanization promoted and sustained by the system of family business enterprise lived on as the foundation of the system of multinational corporations that formed and expanded under U.S. hegemony.

In spite of some similarities, the system of multinational corporations is in key respects the mirror image of the system of joint-stock chartered companies. The latter empowered European states to operate globally, but in the process they lost their own functions and power. Multinational corporations, in contrast, were empowered by the United States and its European allies to operate globally, but as they did in ever increasing numbers, they undermined the power of the very states on which they rely for protection and sustenance.

This is one of the reasons why Tilly finds (correctly in our view) that the nineteenth-century wave of globalization was associated with an empowerment of (Western) states, whereas the present wave is associated with their disempowerment (see introduction). This empowerment/disempowerment, however, concerns primarily the states of the Western world on which Tilly's attention is focused. For the nineteenth-century empowerment of Western states was intimately related to the destruction or subordinate incorporation of whatever state structures existed in the non-Western world. Only in East Asia did indigenous state structures survive the Western onslaught, reemerging in the present wave of globalization to challenge Western global supremacy. And it is precisely here that we can also detect important exceptions to the ongoing tendency toward the disempowerment of states.

These exceptions are the city-states and the semisovereign states of the East Asian "capitalist archipelago" that have grown wealthy under the carapace of the unilateral U.S. military regime in the region. These states have consistently and uniformly behaved more like businesses than governmental organizations. They have sought integration with one another and the surrounding region informally (through the transborder expansion of business networks) rather than formally (through interstatal treaties like NAFTA or international institutions like the European Union characterized by sharp boundaries between members and non-members). Two main business networks acting in cooperation and competition with one another have shaped and sustained the economic integration and expansion of the region: the networks of the multilayered subcontracting system of Japanese trading companies and multinational corporations on the one side, and the network of medium-sized, family-owned enterprises of the overseas Chinese on the other. The result has been a form of transnational economic integration that contrasts sharply with the European.

> The European assumption that peace and prosperity can be secured through institutionalization without much regard to the societies located at the European periphery looks in the 1990s like a huge gamble. In sharp contrast, Asian regionalism resists exclusivist institution-building impulses; it favors instead inclusive networks . . . Asia-Pacific is moving to integrate the periphery, currently Burma and Vietnam, and eventually perhaps even North Korea. Kishore Mahbubani put the issue this way: "Europe may be accentuating the contrast between the continent and its neighborhood thus developing potentially destabilizing geopolitical fault lines. By contrast, the geopolitical fault lines in the Asia-Pacific region are gradually being stabilized." In light of the growing crises in the Balkans and in North Africa, recent developments in and around North Korea, Kampuchea, Vietnam, and Burma lend some support to this view. (Katzenstein, 1997, 26–27)

To be sure, the less institutionalized and substantively more open transnational economic integration occurring in East Asia relies on and tends to reproduce interstate inequalities of wealth to a far greater extent than the more institutionalized and substantively less open integration occurring in Europe. Moreover, the ongoing integration of the huge population of the PRC into the regional ensemble presents far greater problems than the integration of any of the region's smaller states has thus far presented. For the time being, however, the main tendency is for at least some of the region's states to be empowered rather than disempowered.

Thus success of U.S. attempts to use its declining but still considerable politico-economic leverage in the region to redirect regional economic integration toward institutionalized forms that would create a more favorable environment for U.S. exports and investments has been limited. U.S. corporations, particularly in high technology industries, have been more successful in finding a place for themselves in the regional economic expansion. But there is little evidence that they can actually serve as powerful wedges to keep East Asian doors open to U.S. influence, as some U.S. government reports suggest (Katzenstein and Shiraishi, 1997, 347). On the contrary, they are more likely to act as wedges that open up Washington to East Asian influence. As Sanger pointed out in reporting the new fear of Asian money that swept the U.S. when donations to the Democratic Party from Taipei, Bangkok, Jakarta, and other outposts of the Chinese diaspora were uncovered,

> it is unclear whether [the donors] are getting their money's worth. Perhaps, like the Japanese in the 80s, they will soon decide this is a bad investment. The reality of life in Washington is that many of the policies sought by Asian business executives—including separating China's human-rights record from trade—are generally also sought by American global giants like Boeing, I.B.M. and Bechtel. (1997a, 4: 4)

Clearly the forces of transnational economy are undermining the power of states. But in the process, some states are actually empowered. Although the extent and intensity of these forces is unprecedented, the empowerment of some states in the midst of a general disempowerment is not. It has been typical of both past hegemonic transitions. The difference is that the states that were being empowered in the past were leaders in state- and warmaking, whereas the ones that are being empowered now are not. The leadership of the latter states is largely invisible because—to borrow an expression that Alan Rix (1993) has coined to describe Japanese leadership—it occurs "from behind." It is analogous to the kind of leadership that city-states, business diasporas, and the Dutch Republic itself exercised in the European world system until empire-building national states eliminated them from world politics (see chapter 1). The leadership of these agencies was so invisible that observers still find it difficult to recognize (see, for example, Hall, 1996). And yet it was precisely under the leadership of one such agency that the Westphalia system was born. We should not rule out the possibility that the eventual supersession or withering away of the Westphalia system will occur under a leadership of the same kind.

Proposition 4

The disempowerment of social movements—the labor movement in particular—that has accompanied the global financial expansion of the 1980s and 1990s is largely a conjunctural phenomenon. It signals the difficulties involved in delivering on the promises of the U.S.-sponsored global New Deal. A new wave of social conflict is likely, and can be expected to reflect the greater proletarianization, increasing feminization, and changing spatial and ethnic configuration of the world's labor forces.

As argued in chapter 3, in both past hegemonic transitions, system-wide financial expansions contributed to an escalation of social conflict. The massive redistribution of rewards and social dislocations entailed by financial expansions provoked movements of resistance and rebellion by subordinate groups and strata whose established ways of life were coming under attack. Interacting with the interstate power struggle, these movements eventually forced the dominant groups to form a new hegemonic social bloc that selectively included previously excluded groups and strata.

In the transition from Dutch to British hegemony, the aspirations of the European propertied classes for greater political representation and the aspirations of the settler bourgeoisies of the Americas for self-determination were accommodated in a new dominant social bloc. But the aspirations of the European non-propertied classes and of the African slaves in the Americas were not, in spite of their respective contributions to the upheavals that transformed the dominant social bloc.

Under British hegemony, slavery was slowly but surely eliminated, but the attendant gains toward racial equality were blunted by European expansion in Asia and Africa, and by new means of effectively subordinating the freed slaves in the Americas. The gradual accommodation of the aspirations of the European non-propertied classes was closely related to both developments. It was at this time more than ever before or since that Europe was truly "enjoying the world" (Goran Therborn's expression). Not only could Britain shift onto Indian workers and taxpayers the burdens of its unilateral free trade, which provided cheap means of livelihood to its growing industrial proletariat and rewarding markets for the settler bourgeoisies of the Americas (see chapter 1 and 2). More important, Europe in general and Britain in particular enjoyed practically unlimited migration outlets for the locally disadvantaged or adventurous. "Even the English center of global industry was an out-migration area. . . . A conservative estimate is that about 50 million Europeans emigrated out of the continent in the period 1850-1930, which corresponds to about 12 percent of the continent's population in 1900" (Therborn, 1995, 40). A major outlet of this exodus was the rapidly industrializing United States, which thereby enjoyed practically unlimited supplies of labor and a highly effective means of keeping its former slave population at the margins of its core working class. And the disruption of livelihoods provoked by European expansion in Asia produced outflows of contract labor that were brought into competition with the newly freed slave populations of the European colonies (Cohen 1997, 57–81).

With the transition from British to U.S. hegemony—under the joint impact of the revolt against the West and working-class rebellions—the hegemonic social bloc was further expanded through the promise of a global New Deal. The working classes of the wealthier countries of the West were promised security of employment and high mass consumption. The elites of the non-Western world were promised the right to national self-determination and development (i.e., assistance in catching up with the standards of wealth and welfare established by Western states). It soon became clear, however, that this package of promises could not be delivered. Moreover, it engendered expectations in the world's subordinate strata that seriously threatened the stability and eventually precipitated the crisis of U.S. hegemony.

Here indeed lies the peculiar social character of this crisis in comparison with earlier hegemonic crises. The crisis of Dutch hegemony was a long, drawn-out process in which a systemwide financial expansion came late and systemwide social conflict came later still. The crisis of British hegemony unfolded more rapidly, but the systemwide financial expansion still preceded systemwide social conflict. In the crisis of U.S. hegemony, by contrast, the systemwide explosion of social conflict of the late 1960s and early 1970s preceded and thoroughly shaped the subsequent financial expansion.

The explosion of social conflict was probably far more important than intensifying intercapitalist competition in provoking the massive flight of capital to extraterritorial financial markets that around 1970 created the supply conditions of the financial expansion. The flight by multinational corporations constituted a vote of "no confidence" in the capacity of the United States and its European allies to protect the profitability of their global operations from the combined demands for high mass consumption in wealthy countries and for national self-determination and development in poor countries. This vote of no confidence, however, backfired because it deepened the crisis of U.S. hegemony, making the global operations of multinational corporations, U.S. corporations in particular, even less profitable.

The situation turned around only in the wake of the Iranian Revolution, the Soviet invasion of Afghanistan, and a new run on the U.S. dollar. Under the impact of these events, the U.S. government started to compete actively in world financial markets for the capital needed to escalate the armaments race with the USSR and simultaneously reduce domestic taxation. This change of strategy contributed decisively to the takeoff of the global financial expansion that in the 1980s and 1990s reflated the power of the U.S. state and capital and correspondingly deflated the power of the movements that had precipitated the crisis of U.S. hegemony. But the underlying problems that had given rise to the movements remain unresolved and can be expected to generate new systemwide waves of social conflict.

At the roots of the present crisis we can detect a fundamental system-level social problem. We concur with Wallerstein's assessment that world capitalism as presently instituted cannot accommodate "the combined demands of the Third World (for relatively little per person but for a lot of people) and the Western working class (for relatively few people but for quite a lot per person)" (see introduction). The financial expansion and the underlying restructuring of the global political economy have undoubtedly succeeded in disorganizing the social forces that were the bearers of these demands in the upheavals of the late 1960s and 1970s. But the process is creating new social forces that the decaying hegemonic order will have even greater difficulties accommodating.

Thus, global restructuring is indeed turning the male mass-production worker in core countries into an "endangered species," as Zolberg claims (see introduction). Nevertheless, the very transformations of the economies of the core countries that are destroying the once powerful "aristocracy of labor" are creating in these same countries new agencies and sources of conflict.

> The greatest movement of the second half of the nineteenth century was the movement of men from the farm to the factory. Out of that movement arose many of the political movements that shaped the history of the time—socialism and anti-socialism, revolutions, and civil wars. . . . The greatest movement of the second half of the twentieth century has been the movement of women from home to the office. Out of that movement there have already arisen political movements that are beginning to shape the history of our own time. One is feminism, with its political demands ranging from equal opportunity to academic deconstructionism to abortion rights. Feminism has in turn produced [a backlash in] a new form of conservatism. These new conservatives speak of "family values"; their adversaries call them the "religious right." (Kurth, 1994, 11; see also Sassen, 1996)

What forms social conflict along these new fault lines will take is hard to tell. To the extent that it will affect the policies of the declining hegemon, as it already does—e.g., in the recent refusal of the U.S. Congress to provide funds to the UN and the IMF as part of a religious anti-abortion campaign—it will profoundly affect the trajectory of the ongoing hegemonic transition. But whatever its forms, social conflict along the new fault lines will not eliminate conflict along familiar lines.

For the movement of women from the home to the office has been the greatest movement of the second half of the twentieth century only in rich countries. In the global economy at large, the greatest movement has been that of men and women from the farm to the factory. For Hobsbawm (1994, 289), the "most dramatic and far-reaching social change of the second half of [the twentieth] century . . . is the death of the peasantry."

> At the very moment when hopeful young leftists were quoting Mao Tse-Tung's strategy for the triumph of revolution by mobilizing the

countless rural millions against the encircled urban strongholds of the status quo, these millions were abandoning their villages and moving into the cities themselves. (Hobsbawm, 1994, 290)

This movement from farm to factory was promoted by a variety of developmentalist states and international agencies, and was given fresh impetus by the worldwide cost-cutting race since the 1970s. The search by multinational corporations for cheap and flexible labor supplies has created new and powerful mass-production working classes. Wherever capital has gone, class conflict has emerged in relatively short order (Silver, 1997).

Since the mid-1980s, China has been the key site of industrial expansion and new working-class formation. Given past experience, we should expect a vigorous workers' movement to emerge in China as well. And given the size and centrality of China—in the East Asian region and globally—the trajectory of this movement will have a tremendous impact on the trajectory of the transition as a whole.

Proposition 5

The clash between Western and non-Western civilizations lies behind us rather than in front of us. What lies in front of us are the difficulties involved in transforming the modern world into a commonwealth of civilizations that reflects the changing balance of power between Western and non-Western civilizations, first and foremost the reemerging China-centered civilization. How drastic and painful the transformation is going to be—and, indeed, whether it will eventually result in a commonwealth rather than in the mutual destruction of the world's civilizations—ultimately depends on two conditions. It depends, first, on how intelligently the main centers of Western civilization can adjust to a less exalted status and, second, on whether the main centers of the reemerging China-centered civilization can collectively rise up to the task of providing system-level solutions to the system-level problems left behind by U.S. hegemony.

As chapter 4 argued, a clash between Western and non-Western civilizations has been a constant of the historical process whereby the modern world system was transformed from a European to a global system. The transition from Dutch to British hegemony was marked by the violent conquest or destabilization of the indigenous world systems of Asia. The transition from British to U.S. hegemony was marked, first, by a further extension of Western territorial empires in Asia and Africa, and then by a general revolt against Western domination.

Under U.S. hegemony, the map of the world was redrawn to accommodate demands for national self-determination. This new map reflected the legacy of Western colonialism and imperialism, including the cultural hegemony that led non-Western elites to claim for themselves more or less viable "nation-states" in the image of the metropolitan political organizations of their former imperial masters. There was nonetheless one major exception to the rule: East Asia. Except for some states on its southern fringes (most notably, Indonesia and the Philippines), the region's map reflected primarily the legacy of the China-centered world system, which the Western intrusion had destabilized and transformed at the margins, but never managed to destroy and recreate in the Western image. All the region's most important nations that were formally incorporated in the expanded Westphalia system—from Japan, Korea, and China to Vietnam, Laos, Kampuchea, and Thailand—had all been nations long before the European arrival. What's more, they had all been nations linked to one another, directly or through the Chinese center, by diplomatic and trade relations and held together by a shared understanding of the principles, norms, and rules that regulated their mutual interactions as a world among other worlds.

This geopolitical relict of the European global cataclysm was as difficult to integrate into the U.S. Cold War world order as into the British world order. The fault lines between the U.S. and Soviet spheres of influence in the region started breaking down soon after they were established—first by the Chinese rebellion against Soviet domination, and then by the U.S. failure to split the Vietnamese nation along the Cold War divide. Then, while the two superpowers escalated their competition in the final embrace of the Second Cold War, the various pieces of the East Asian puzzle reassembled themselves into the most dynamic center of world-scale processes of capital accumulation.

The astonishing speed with which this regional formation has become the new workshop and cash-box of the world under the "invisible" leadership of a businesslike state (Japan) and a business diaspora (the overseas Chinese) has contributed to a widespread "fear of falling" in the main centers of Western civilization. A more or less imminent fall of the West from the commanding heights of the world capitalist system is possible, even likely. But what should be feared about it is not at all clear.

The fall is likely because the leading states of the West are prisoners of the developmental paths that have made their fortunes, both political and economic. The paths are yielding decreasing returns in terms of rates of accumulation relative to the East Asian regional path, but they cannot be abandoned in favor of the more dynamic path without causing social strains so unbearable that they would result in chaos rather than "competitiveness." A similar situation arose in past hegemonic transitions. At the time of their respective hegemonic crises, both the Dutch and the British got themselves ever more deeply into the particular path of development that had made their fortunes, despite the fact that more dynamic paths were being opened up at the margins of their radius of action. And neither got out of the established path until the world system centered on them broke down.

As David Calleo has argued, the "international system breaks down not only because unbalanced and aggressive new powers seek to dominate their neighbors, but also because declining powers, rather than adjusting and accommodating, try to cement their slipping preeminence into an exploitative hegemony" (1987, 142). Our comparison of past transitions shows that the role of aggressive new powers in precipitating systemic breakdowns has decreased from transition to transition, while the role played by exploitative domination by the declining hegemon has increased. Dutch world power was already so diminished in the declining decades of its hegemony that Dutch resistance played only a marginal role in the systemic breakdown in comparison with the role played by the emerging, aggressive, empire-building nation-states, first and foremost Britain and France. By the time of its own hegemonic decline, in contrast, Britain remained powerful enough to transform its hegemony into exploitative domination. Although the emergence of aggressive new powers—first and foremost Germany—still played a major role in the breakdown of the British-centered world system, Britain's resistance to adjustment and accommodation was also crucial (see chapters 1 and 3).

Today we have reached the other end of the spectrum. There are no credible aggressive new powers that can provoke the breakdown of the U.S.-centered world system, but the United States has even greater capabilities than Britain did a century ago to convert its declining hegemony into an exploitative domination. If the system eventually breaks down, it will be primarily because of U.S. resistance to adjustment and accommodation. And conversely, U.S. adjustment and accommodation to the rising economic power of the East Asian region is an essential condition for a non-catastrophic transition to a new world order.

An equally essential condition is the emergence of a new global leadership from the main centers of the East Asian economic expansion. This leadership must be willing and able to rise up to the task of providing system-level solutions to the system-level problems left behind by U.S. hegemony. The most severe among these problems is the seemingly unbridgeable gulf between the life-chances of a small minority of world population (between 10 and 20 percent) and the vast majority. In order to provide a viable and sustainable solution to this problem, the "tracklaying vehicles" of East Asia must open up a new path of development for themselves and for the world that departs radically from the one that is now at a dead end.

This is an imposing task that the dominant groups of East Asian states have hardly begun to undertake. In past hegemonic transitions, dominant groups successfully took on the task of fashioning a new world order only after major wars, systemwide chaos and intense pressure from movements of protest and self-protection. This pressure from below has widened and deepened from transition to transition, leading to enlarged social blocs with each new hegemony. Thus, we can expect social contradictions to play a far more decisive role than ever before in shaping both the unfolding transition and whatever new world order eventually emerges out of the impending systemic chaos. But whether the movements will largely follow and be shaped by the escalation of violence (as in past transitions) or precede and effectively work toward containing the systemic chaos is a question that is open. Its answer is ultimately in the hands of the movements.

Bibliography

Abbott, Andrew, and Stanley DeViney. 1992. "The Welfare State as Transnational Event: Evidence from Sequences of Policy Adoption." *Social Science History* 16, 2: 245–74.

Abendroth, Wolfgang. 1972. *A Short History of the European Working Class.* New York: Monthly Review Press.

Abu-Lughod, Janet. 1989. *Before European Hegemony: The World System A.D. 1250–1350.* New York: Oxford University Press.

———. 1990. "Restructuring the Premodern World-System." *Review* (Fernand Braudel Center) 13, 2: 273–86.

Adams, James Truslow. 1940. *The British Empire, 1784–1939.* New York: Dorset Press.

Adas, Michael. 1989. *Machines as the Measure of Men: Science, Technology, and Ideologies of Western Dominance.* Ithaca: Cornell University Press.

Addington, Larry H. 1984. *The Patterns of War since the Eighteenth Century.* Bloomington: Indiana University Press.

Aglietta, Michel. 1979. *A Theory of Capitalist Regulation: The U.S. Experience.* Trans. David Fernbach. London: New Left Books.

Agnew, John. 1987. *The United States in the World-Economy: A Regional Geography.* Cambridge: Cambridge University Press.

Aguilar, Alonso. 1968. *Pan-Americanism from Monroe to the Present; A View from the Other Side.* New York: Monthly Review Press.

Ahmad, Iftikhar. 1992. "Thugs, Dacoits, and the Modern World-System in Nineteenth-Century India." Ph.D. diss., State University of New York at Binghamton.

Alam, M. 1986. *The Crisis of Empire in Mughal North India: Awadh and the Punjab, 1707–1748.* Delhi: Oxford University Press.

Alker, Hayward R. 1995. "If Not Huntington's 'Civilizations,' Then Whose?" *Review* (Fernand Braudel Center) 18, 4: 533–62.

Ambedkar, B. R. 1945. *Pakistan or Partition of India.* Bombay: Thaacker.

Amin, Shahid. 1988. "Gandhi as Mahatma." In R. Guha, ed., *Subaltern Studies 3,* 1–61. New York: Oxford University Press.

Anderson, Perry. 1979. *Lineages of the Absolutist State.* London: Verso.

———. 1980. *Arguments within English Marxism.* London: New Left Books.

———. 1987. "The Figures of Descent." *New Left Review* 161: 20–77.

Appelbaum, Richard P. 1996. "Multiculturalism and Flexibility. Some New Directions in Global Capitalism." In A. F. Gordon and C. Newfield, eds., *Mapping Multiculturalism,* 297–316. Minneapolis: University of Minnesota Press.

Arnold, David. 1986. *Police Power and Colonial Rule, Madras, 1859–1947.* Delhi: Oxford University Press.

Arrighi, Giovanni. 1990a. "The Developmentalist Illusion: A Reconceptualization of the Semiperiphery." In William G. Martin, ed., *Semiperipheral States in the World-Economy,* 11–42. New York: Greenwood Press.

———. 1990b. "The Three Hegemonies of Historical Capitalism." *Review* (Fernand Braudel Center) 13, 3: 365–408.

———. 1991. "World Income Inequalities and the Future of Socialism." *New Left Review* 189: 39–64.

———. 1994. *The Long Twentieth Century: Money, Power, and the Origins of Our Time.* London: Verso.

———. 1996. "The Rise of East Asia: World-Systemic and Regional Aspects." *International Journal of Sociology and Social Policy* 16, 7: 6–44.

———. 1997. "Financial Expansions in World Historical Perspective: A Reply to Robert Pollin." *New Left Review* 224: 154–59.

Arrighi, Giovanni, and Beverly J. Silver. 1984. "Labor Movements and Capital Migration: The U.S. and Western Europe in World-Historical Perspective." In Charles Bergquist, ed., *Labor in the Capitalist World-Economy,* 183–216. Beverly Hills: Sage.

Arrighi, Giovanni, Satoshi Ikeda, and Alex Irwan. 1993. "The Rise of East Asia: One Miracle or Many?" In R. A. Palat, ed., *Pacific Asia and the Future of the World-System,* 41–65. Westport, Conn.: Greenwood Press.

Attman, Artur. 1983. *Dutch Enterprise in the World Bullion Trade, 1550–1800.* Goteborg: Kungl. vetenskaps-och vitterhets-samhallet.

Aymard, Maurice. 1982. Introduction to M. Aymard, ed., *Dutch Capitalism and World Capitalism* (Capitalisme Hollandais et capitalisme mondial). 1–10. Cambridge: Cambridge University Press.

Bagchi, Amiya Kumar. 1982. *The Political Economy of Underdevelopment.* Cambridge: Cambridge University Press.

Bairoch, Paul. 1976. *Commerce extérieur et développement économique de l'Europe au XIXe siècle.* Paris and The Hague: Mouton.

Baker, Russell. 1996. "The Decadent Decade." *New York Times,* November 16, section 3: 23.

Barbour, Violet. 1950. *Capitalism in Amsterdam in the Seventeenth Century.* Baltimore: Johns Hopkins Press.

Barnet, Richard, and John Cavanagh. 1994. *Global Dreams: Imperial Corporations and the New World Order.* New York: Simon and Schuster.

Barnet, Richard, and Ronald Muller. 1974. *Global Reach: The Power of the Multi-national Corporations.* New York: Simon and Schuster.

Barraclough, Geoffrey. 1967. *An Introduction to Contemporary History.* Harmondsworth: Penguin.

Barrat Brown, Michael. 1963. *After Imperialism.* London: Heinemann.

———. 1974. *The Economics of Imperialism.* Harmondsworth: Penguin.

Bataille, Georges. 1988. *The Accursed Share: An Essay on General Economy.* New York: Zone Books.

Bayly, Christopher A. 1988. *Indian Society and the Making of the British Empire.* Cambridge and New York: Cambridge University Press.

———. 1989. *Imperial Meridian: British Empire and the World, 1780–1830.* London: Longman.

Bearce, George. 1961. *British Attitudes towards India, 1784–1858.* London: Oxford University Press.

Becattini, Giacomo. 1989. "Sectors and/or Districts: Some Remarks on the Conceptual Foundations of Industrial Economics." In E. Goodman, J. Bamford and P. Saynor, eds., *Small Firms and Industrial Districts in Italy,* 123–35. London and New York: Routledge.

———. 1990. "The Marshallian Industrial District as a Socio-Economic Notion." In F. Pyke, G. Becattini, and W. Senenberger, eds., *Industrial Districts and Inter-Firm Cooperation in Italy,* 37–51. Geneva: International Institute for Labor Studies.

Beinin, Joel, and Zachary Lockman. 1987. *Workers on the Nile: Nationalism, Communism, Islam, and the Egyptian Working Class, 1882–1954.* Princeton: Princeton University Press.

Benería, Lourdes. 1995. "Response: The Dynamics of Globalization." *International Labor and Working-Class History* 47 (spring) 45–52.

Bergé, Pierre, Yves Pomeau, and Christian Vidal. 1984. *Order within Chaos: Towards a Deterministic Approach to Turbulence.* New York: John Wiley.

Bergesen, Albert, and Ronald Schoenberg. 1980. "Long Waves of Colonial Expansion and Contraction, 1415–1969." In A. Bergesen, ed., *Studies in the Modern World-System,* 231–77. New York: Academic Press.

Bergquist, Charles. 1986. *Labor in Latin America: Comparative Essays on Chile, Argentina, Venezuela, and Colombia.* Stanford: Stanford University Press.

Bergsten, Fred C. 1987. "Economic Imbalances and World Politics." *Foreign Affairs* 65, 4: 770–94.

Bernstein, Richard, and Ross H. Munro. 1997. "The Coming Conflict with America." *Foreign Affairs* 76, 2: 18–32.

Best, Michael. 1990. *The New Competition: Institutions of Industrial Restructuring.* Cambridge: Harvard University Press.

Bhattacharya, S. 1983. "Regional Economy 1757–1857: Eastern India. Part I." In D. Kumar and D. Meghnad, eds., *The Cambridge Economic History of India.* Vol. 2, c. *1757–c. 1970,* 270–95. Cambridge: Cambridge University Press.

Bienefeld, Manfred. 1993. "Structural Adjustment: Debt Collection Devise or Development Policy?" Paper presented at Sophia University Lectures on "Structural Adjustment: Past, Present and Future," November 24, 1993.

Blackburn, Robin. 1988. *The Overthrow of Colonial Slavery, 1776–1848.* London: Verso.

Blim, Michael. 1990. "Economic Development and Decline in the Emerging Global Factory: Some Italian Lessons." *Politics and Society* 18, 1: 143–63.

Block, Fred L. 1977. *The Origins of International Economic Disorder: A Study of United States International Monetary Policy from World War II to the Present.* Berkeley: University of California Press.

———. 1990. *Postindustrial Possibilities: A Critique of Economic Discourse.* Berkeley: University of California Press.

———. 1996. *The Vampire State: and Other Myths and Fallacies about the U.S. Economy.* New York: The New Press.

Blussé, Leonard, and Femme Gaastra, eds. 1981. *Companies and Trade: Essays on Overseas Trading Companies during the Ancien Régime.* Leiden: Leiden University Press.

Bonacich, Edna, Lucie Cheng, Norma Chinchilla, Nora Hamilton, and Paul Ong, eds. 1994. *Global Production: The Apparel Industry in the Pacific Rim.* Philadelphia: Temple University Press.

Bond, Brian, ed. 1967. *Victorian Military Campaigns.* London: Hutchinson.

Bonnassieux, Pierre. 1969. *Les Grandes Compagnies de commerce, étude pour servir à l'histoire de la colonisation.* New York: Burt Franklin.

Boogman, J. C. 1978. "The *Raison d'État* Politician Johan deWitt." In *The Low Countries History Yearbook 1978*: 55–78.

Borden, William S. 1984. *The Pacific Alliance: United States Foreign Economic Policy and Japanese Trade Recovery, 1947–1955.* Madison: University of Wisconsin Press.

Borthwick, Mark. 1992. *Pacific Century: The Emergence of Modern Pacific Asia.* Boulder, Colo.: Westview Press.

Bourne, Kenneth. 1970. *The Foreign Policy of Victorian England.* Oxford: Clarendon Press.

Boxer, Charles R. 1957. *The Dutch in Brazil, 1624–1654.* Oxford: Clarendon Press.

———. 1965. *The Dutch Seaborne Empire, 1600–1800.* New York: Knopf.

———. 1973. *The Portuguese Seaborne Empire, 1415–1825.* Harmondsworth: Penguin.

———. 1979. *Jan Compagnie in War and Peace, 1602–1799.* Hong Kong and Singapore: Heinemann Asia.

Boyer, Robert. 1979. "Wage Formation in Historical Perspective: The French Experience." *Cambridge Journal of Economics* 3, 2: 99–118.

———. 1988. "Technical Change and the Theory of 'Regulation.'" In G. Dosi, et al., eds., *Technical Change and Economic Theory,* 76–94. London: Pinter.

———. 1990. *The Regulation School: A Critical Introduction.* New York: Columbia University Press.

Braczyk, H. J., G. Schienstock, and B. Stefensen. 1995. "The Region of Baden-Württemberg: A 'Post Fordist' Success Story?" In E. Dittrich, et al., eds., *Industrial Transformation in Europe,* 203–33. London: Sage Publications.

Braudel, Fernand. 1982. *Civilization and Capitalism, Fifteenth–Eighteenth Century,* Vol. 2, *The Wheels of Commerce.* New York: Harper and Row.

———. 1984. *Civilization and Capitalism, Fifteenth–Eighteenth Century,* Vol. 3, *The Perspective of the World.* New York: Harper and Row.

———. 1990. *The Identity of France,* Vol. 2. New York: Harper Collins.

Brecher, Jeremy. 1972. *Strike!* Boston: South End Press.

———. 1994/95. "Global Unemployment at Seven Hundred Million." In *Global Issues 94/95,* 32–35. Guilford, Conn.: Dushkin Publishing.

Brenner, Robert, and Mark Glick. 1991. "The Regulation Approach: Theory and History." *New Left Review* 188: 45–119.

Brewer, John. 1990. *The Sinews of Power: War, Money, and the English State, 1688–1783.* Cambridge: Harvard University Press.

Bridges, Amy. 1986. "Becoming American: The Working Classes in the United States before the Civil War." In I. Katznelson and A. R. Zolberg, eds., *Working-Class Formation,* 157–196. Princeton: Princeton University Press.

Broad, Robin, and Christina Melhorn Landi. 1996. "Whither the North-South Gap?" *Third World Quarterly* 17, 1: 7–17.

Brody, David. 1980. *Workers in Industrial America.* New York: Oxford University Press.

Brown, Alexander Dee. 1971. *Bury My Heart at Wounded Knee: An Indian History of the American West.* New York: Holt, Rinehart, and Winston.

Brown, Carolyn A. 1988. "The Dialectics of Colonial Labour Control: Class Struggles in the Nigerian Coal Industry, 1914–1949." *Journal of Asian and African Studies* 23, 1–2: 32–59.

Brown, William A. Jr. 1940. *The International Gold Standard Reinterpreted, 1914–1934,* Vol. 1. New York: AMS Press.

Brusco, Sebastiano. 1982. "The Emilian Model: Productive Decentralization and Social Integration." *Cambridge Journal of Economics* 6, 2: 167–84.

———. 1986. "Small Firms and Industrial Districts: The Experience of Italy." In D. Keeble and F. Weever, eds., *New Firms and Regional Development,* 184–202. London: Croom Helm.

Burawoy, Michael. 1982. "The Hidden Abode of Underdevelopment: Labor Process and the State in Zambia." *Politics and Society* 11, 4: 123–66.

Burley, Anne-Marie. 1993. "Regulating the World: Multilateralism, International Law, and the Projection of the New Deal Regulatory State." In J. G. Ruggie, ed., *Multilateralism Matters: The Theory and Praxis of an Institutional Form,* 125–56. New York: Columbia University Press.

Burstein, Daniel. 1991. *Euroquake.* New York: Simon and Schuster.

Cain, P. J., and A. G. Hopkins. 1980. "The Political Economy of British Expansion Overseas, 1750–1914," *The Economic History Review,* 2nd ser., 33, 4: 463–90.

Cairncross, A. K. 1953. *Home and Foreign Investment, 1870–1913.* Cambridge: Cambridge University Press.

Calleo, David. 1987. *Beyond American Hegemony: The Future of the Western Alliance.* New York: Basic Books.

Calleo, David P., and Benjamin M. Rowland. 1973. *America and the World Political Economy: Atlantic Dreams and National Realities.* Bloomington: Indiana University Press.

Carr, Edward H. 1945. *Nationalism and After.* London: Macmillan.

Carter, Alice C. 1975. *Getting, Spending, and Investing in Early Modern Times.* Assen, The Netherlands: Van Gorcum & Co.

Castells, Manuel, and Alejandro Portes. 1989. "World Underneath: The Origins, Dynamics, and Effects of the Informal Economy." In A. Portes, M. Castells, and L. A. Benton, eds., *The Informal Economy: Studies in Advanced and Less Developed Countries,* 11–39. Baltimore: Johns Hopkins University Press.

Chandler, Alfred D. Jr. 1977. *The Visible Hand: The Managerial Revolution in American Business.* Cambridge: Harvard University Press.

———. 1978. "The United States: Evolution of Enterprise." In P. Mathias and M. M. Postan, eds., *The Cambridge Economic History of Europe.* Vol. 7, pt. 2, 70–133. Cambridge: Cambridge University Press.

———. 1990. *Scale and Scope: The Dynamics of Industrial Capitalism.* Cambridge, Mass.: The Belknap Press.

———. 1992. *Merchant Enterprise in Britain: From the Industrial Revolution to World War I.* Cambridge: Cambridge University Press.

Chang, Pin-tsun. 1991. "The First Chinese Diaspora in Southeast Asia in the Fifteenth Century." In R. Ptak and D. Rothermund, eds., *Emporia, Commodities, and*

Entrepreneurs in Asian Maritime Trade, c. 1400–1750, 13–28. Stuttgart: Franz Steiner Verlag.

Chapman, Stanley D. 1972. *The Cotton Industry in the Industrial Revolution.* London: Macmillan.

———. 1984. *The Rise of Merchant Banking.* London: Unwin Hyman.

———. 1992. *Merchant Enterprise in Britain: From the Industrial Revolution to World War I.* New York: Cambridge University Press.

Chatterjee, Partha. 1986. *Nationalist Thought and the Colonial World: A Derivative Discourse?* London: Zed Press.

———. 1993. *The Nation and Its Fragments: Colonial and Postcolonial Histories.* Princeton: Princeton University Press.

Chaudhuri, K. N. 1965. *The English East India Company: The Study of an Early Joint-Stock Company 1600–1640.* London: Frank Cass.

———. 1978. *The Trading World of Asia and the English East India Company 1660–1760.* Cambridge: Cambridge University Press.

———. 1990. *Asia before Europe: Economy and Civilization of the Indian Ocean from the Rise of Islam to 1750.* Cambridge: Cambridge University Press.

Chaudhuri, S. B. 1955. *Civil Disturbances during the British Rule in India.* Calcutta: World Press.

Chaussinand-Nogaret, Guy. 1985. *The French Nobility in the Eighteenth Century: From Feudalism to Enlightenment.* Cambridge: Cambridge University Press.

Church, R. A. 1968. "The Effects of the American Export Invasion on the British Boot and Shoe Industry, 1885–1914." *Journal of Economic History* 28, 2: 223–54.

Claude Jr., Inis. 1956. *Swords into Plowshares: The Problems and Progress of International Organization.* 2nd ed. New York: Random House.

Cohen, Benjamin. 1996, "Phoenix Risen: The Resurrection of Global Finance," *World Politics* 48: 268–96.

———. 1971. *The Future of Sterling as an International Currency.* New York: St. Martin's Press.

———. 1977. *Organizing the World's Money.* New York: Basic Books.

Cohen, Robin. 1997. *Global Diasporas.* Seattle: University of Washington Press.

Commission on International Trade and Investment. 1971. *U.S. International Economic Policy in an Interdependent World.* Washington, D.C.: Government Printing Office.

Cooper, Frederick. 1996. *Decolonization and African Society: The Labor Question in French and British Africa.* Cambridge: Cambridge University Press.

Copeland, Melvin T. 1966. *The Cotton Manufacturing Industry of the United States.* New York: Augustus M. Kelley.

Coupland, Reginald. 1942. *The Indian Problem, 1833–1935.* Oxford: Clarendon Press.

Courtis, Kenneth. 1995. "The New Agenda and Its Four Forces." *The National Times,* August/September, 22–25.

Cox, Robert. 1983. "Gramsci, Hegemony, and International Relations: An Essay in Method." *Millennium. Journal of International Relations* 12, 2: 162–75.

———. 1987. *Production, Power, and World Order: Social Forces in the Making of History.* New York: Columbia University Press.

Cronin, James E. 1983. "Labor Insurgency and Class Formation: Comparative Perspectives on the Crisis of 1917–1920 in Europe." In C. Siriani and J. Cronin, eds. *Work, Community, and Power: The Experience of Labor in Europe and America, 1900–1925,* 20–48. Philadelphia: Temple University Press.

Crouch, Colin, and Alessandro Pizzorno, eds. 1978. *The Resurgence of Class Conflict in Western Europe Since 1968.* 2 vols. New York: Holmes and Meier.

Crouzet, François. 1980. "Toward an Export Economy: British Exports during the Industrial Revolution." *Explorations in Economic History* 17, 1: 48–93.

———. 1982. *The Victorian Economy.* New York: Columbia University Press.

Cumings, Bruce. 1987. "The Origins and Development of the Northeast Asian Political Economy: Industrial Sectors, Product Cycles, and Political Consequences." In F. Deyo, ed., *The Political Economy of New Asian Industrialism,* 44–83. Ithaca: Cornell University Press.

———. 1993. "The Political Economy of the Pacific Rim." In R. Palat, ed., *Pacific-Asia and the Future of the World-System,* 12–37. Westport, Conn.: Greenwood Press.

———. 1997. "Japan and Northeast Asia into the Twenty-First Century." In P. J. Katzenstein and T. Shiraishi, eds., *Network Power: Japan and Asia,* 136–68. Ithaca: Cornell University Press.

Curtin, Philip D. 1990. *The Rise and Fall of the Plantation Complex: Essays in Atlantic History.* Cambridge: Cambridge University Press.

Davies, Kenneth G. 1957. *The Royal African Company.* London: Longmans.

———. 1974. *The North Atlantic World in the Seventeenth Century.* Minneapolis: University of Minnesota Press.

Davis, Mike. 1986. *Prisoners of the American Dream.* London: Verso.

Davis, Ralph. 1966. "The Rise of Protection in England, 1689–1786," *Economic History Review* 2nd ser., 19, 306–17.

———. 1969. "English Foreign Trade, 1700–1774." In W. E. Minchinton, ed. *The Growth of English Overseas Trade in the Seventeenth and Eighteenth Centuries,* 99–120. London: Methuen.

———. 1973. *The Rise of the Atlantic Economies.* London: Wiedenfeld and Nicolsen.

———. 1979. *The Industrial Revolution and British Overseas Trade.* Leicester: Leicester University Press.

de Cecco, Marcello. 1984. *The International Gold Standard: Money and Empire.* 2nd ed. New York: St. Martin's Press.

DeGrasse, R. W. 1983. *Military Expansion, Economic Decline.* New York: Council on Economic Priorities.

Dehio, Ludwig. 1962. *The Precarious Balance: Four Centuries of the European Power Struggle.* New York: Alfred A. Knopf.

Dicken, Peter. 1992. *Global Shift: The Internationalization of Economic Activity.* 2d ed. New York: Guilford Press.

Dicken, Peter, and Sture Oberg. 1996. "The Global Context: Europe in a World of Dynamic Economic and Population Change." *European Urban and Regional Studies* 3, 2: 101–20.

Dodwell, H. H., ed. 1932. *The Cambridge History of the British Empire,* Vol. 5. Cambridge: Cambridge University Press.

Drummond, Ian M. 1987. *The Gold Standard and the International Monetary System, 1900–1939.* New York: Macmillan Education.

Du Bois, W. E. B. 1989. *The Souls of Black Folk.* New York: Bantam Books.

Dubofsky, Melvyn. 1983. "Abortive Reform: The Wilson Administration and Organized Labor." In C. Siriani and J. Cronin, eds., *Work, Community, and Power: The Experience of Labor in Europe and America, 1900–1925,* 197–220. Philadelphia: Temple University Press.

Duffy, Michael. 1987. *Soldiers, Sugar, and Seapower: The British Expeditions to the*

West Indies and the Wars against Revolutionary France. New York: Oxford University Press.

Duménil, G., M. Glick, and J. Rangel. 1987. "The Rate of Profit in the United States." *Cambridge Journal of Economics* 11, 4: 331–59.

Dunning, John H. 1983. "Changes in the Level and Structure of International Production: The Last One Hundred Years." In M. Casson, ed., *The Growth of International Business,* 84–139. London: George Allen and Unwin.

Durkheim, Emile. 1964. *The Rules of Sociological Method.* New York: Free Press.

———. 1984. *The Division of Labor in Society.* New York: Free Press.

Duus, Peter. 1984. "Economic Dimensions of Meiji Imperialism: The Case of Korea, 1895–1910." In R. H. Myers and M. R. Peattie, eds. *The Japanese Colonial Empire, 1895–1945,* 128–171. Princeton: Princeton University Press.

Eccleston, Bernard. 1989. *State and Society in Post-War Japan.* Cambridge: Polity Press.

Edwards, Richard. 1979. *Contested Terrain: The Transformation of the Workplace in the Twentieth Century.* New York: Basic Books.

Eichengreen, Barry, and Richard Portes. 1986. "Debt and Default in the 1930s— Causes and Consequences." *European Economic Review* 30, 3: 599–640.

———. 1990. "The Interwar Debt Crisis and Its Aftermath." *The World Bank Research Observer* 5, 1: 69–94.

Elliott, William Y., ed. 1955. *The Political Economy of American Foreign Policy; Its Concepts, Strategy, and Limits.* New York: Henry Holt and Co.

Emmer, P. C. 1981. "The West India Company, 1621–1791: Dutch or Atlantic?" In L. Blussé and F. Gaastra, eds., *Companies and Trade,* 71–95. Leiden: Leiden University Press.

Engels, Friedrich. 1958. *Socialism: Utopian and Scientific.* Moscow: Foreign Languages Publishing House.

Erlanger, Steven. 1997. "Rancorous Debate Emerges over Cost of Enlarging NATO." *New York Times,* October 13, A: 1, 10.

Escobar, Arturo. 1995. *Encountering Development: The Making and Unmaking of the Third World.* Princeton: Princeton University Press.

Esherick, Joseph. 1972. "Harvard on China: The Apologetics of Imperialism." *Bulletin of Concerned Asian Scholars* 4, 4: 9–16.

Esteva, Gustavo. 1992. "Development." In Wolfgang Sachs, ed. *The Development Dictionary,* 6–25. London: Zed Books.

Evans, Peter. 1995. *Embedded Autonomy: States and Industrial Transformation.* Princeton: Princeton University Press.

Ewen, Stuart. 1976. *Captains of Consciousness. Advertising and the Social Roots of the Consumer Culture.* New York: McGraw-Hill.

Fairbank, John K. 1983. *The United States and China.* Cambridge: Harvard University Press.

———. 1992. *China: A New History.* Cambridge, Mass.: The Belknap Press.

Fairbank, John K., Edwin O. Reischauer, and Albert M. Craig. 1965. *East Asia: The Modern Transformation.* Vol. 2. Boston: Houghton Mifflin.

Farnie, D.A. 1979. *The English Cotton Industry and the World Market, 1815–1896.* Oxford: Clarendon Press.

Fearon, Peter. 1979. *The Origins and Nature of the Great Slump, 1929–1932.* New Jersey: Humanities Press.

Feis, Herbert. 1965. *Europe: The World's Banker, 1870–1914.* New York: Norton.

Feldman, Gerald. 1966. *Army, Industry, and Labor in Germany, 1914–1918*. Princeton: Princeton University Press.

Feuerwerker, Albert. 1958. *China's Early Industrialization: Sheng Hsuan-Huai 1844–1916 and Mandarin Enterprise*. Cambridge: Harvard University Press.

———. 1970. "Handicraft and Manufactured Cotton Textiles in China, 1871–1910." *Journal of Economic History* 30, 2: 338–78.

Flynn, Dennis O., and Arturo Giraldez. 1994. "China and the Manila Galleons." In A. J. H. Latham and H. Kawakatsu, eds. *Japanese Industrialization and the Asian Economy*, 71–90. London: Routledge.

Franke, Wolfgang. 1967. "The Taiping Rebellion." In F. Schurmann and O. Schell, eds., *Imperial China*, 180–92. New York: Vintage.

Frieden, Jeffry. 1987. *Banking on the World*. New York: Harper and Row.

Friedman, David. 1988. *The Misunderstood Miracle*. Ithaca: Cornell University Press.

Fries, Russell I. 1975. "British Response to the American System: The Case of the Small Arms Industry after 1850." *Technology and Culture* 16, 3: 377–403.

Fröbel, Folker, Jürgen Heinrichs, and Otto Kreye. 1980. *The New International Division of Labour: Structural Employment and Industrialization in Developing Countries*. Cambridge: Cambridge University Press.

Fukuyama, Francis. 1989. "The End of History?" *The National Interest* 16: 3–18.

———. 1992. *The End of History and the Last Man*. New York: Free Press.

Furber, Holden. 1976. *Rival Empires of Trade in the Orient 1600–1800*. Minneapolis: University of Minnesota Press.

Furtado, Celso. 1970. *Economic Development of Latin America: Historical Background and Contemporary Problems*. New York: Cambridge University Press.

Galbraith, John S. 1974. *Crown and Charter: The Early Years of the British South Africa Company*. Berkeley: University of California Press.

Gamble, Andrew. 1985. *Britain in Decline: Economic Policy, Political Strategy, and the British State*. London: Macmillan.

Gattrell, V. A. C. 1977. "Labour, Power, and the Size of Firms in Lancashire Cotton in the Second Quarter of the Nineteenth Century." *Economic History Review,* 2nd ser., 30, 1: 95–139.

Genovese, Eugene D. 1979. *From Rebellion to Revolution: Afro-American Slave Revolts in the Making of the Modern World*. Baton Rouge: Louisiana State University Press.

Gibney, Frank. 1992. "Introduction: Arrival of the Black Ships." In M. Borthwick, *Pacific Century: The Emergence of Modern Pacific Asia*, 119–27. Boulder, Colo.: Westview.

Giddens, Anthony. 1987. *The Nation-State and Violence*. Berkeley: University of California Press.

———. 1990. *The Consequences of Modernity*. Cambridge: Polity Press.

Gilder, George. 1989. *Microcosm: The Quantum Revolution in Economics and Technology*. New York: Simon and Schuster.

Gill, Stephen. 1986. "Hegemony, Consensus, and Trilateralism," *Review of International Studies* 12: 205–21.

———. 1990. *American Hegemony and the Trilateral Commission*. Cambridge: Cambridge University Press.

———, ed. 1993. *Gramsci, Historial Materialism, and International Relations*. Cambridge: Cambridge University Press.

Gill, Stephen, and David Law. 1988. *The Global Political Economy: Perspectives, Problems, and Policies*. Baltimore: Johns Hopkins University Press.

Gill, Stephen, and James H. Mittelman, eds. 1997. *Innovation and Transformation in International Studies.* Cambridge: Cambridge University Press.

Gilpin, Robert. 1975. *U.S. Power and the Multinational Corporation.* New York: Basic Books.

———. 1981. *War and Change in World Politics.* Cambridge: Cambridge University Press.

———. 1996. "The Prospects for a Stable International Political Order." Paper presented at the conference "Plotting Our Future: Technology, Environment, Economy, and Society: A World Outlook." Fondazione Eni Enrico Mattei, Milan, Italy, October.

Godfrey, Walter. 1986. *Global Unemployment: The New Challenge to Economic Theory.* Sussex: Harvester Press.

Goldfield, Michael. 1987. *The Decline of Organized Labor in the United States.* Chicago: University of Chicago Press.

Goldstein, Joshua, and David P. Rapkin. 1991. "After Insularity: Hegemony and the Future of World Order." *Futures* 23, 9: 935–59.

Goodman, John, and Louis W. Pauly. 1993. "The Obsolescence of Capital Controls? Economic Management in an Age of Global Markets." *World Politics* 66, 1: 50–82.

Gordon, David M. 1996. *Fat and Mean: The Corporate Squeeze of Working Americans and the Myth of Managerial "Downsizing."* New York: Martin Kessler Books.

Gordon, D. M., R. Edwards, and M. Reich. 1982. *Segmented Work, Divided Workers: The Historical Transformation of Labor in the United States.* Cambridge: Cambridge University Press.

Gramsci, Antonio. 1971. *Selections from the Prison Notebooks.* New York: International Publishers.

Greenberg, Michael. 1951. *British Trade and the Opening of China, 1800–1842.* Cambridge: Cambridge University Press.

Grosfoguel, Ramón. 1996. "From Cepalismo to Neoliberalism: A World-System Approach to Conceptual Shifts in Latin America." *Review* (Fernand Braudel Center) 19, 2: 131–54.

Gross, Leo. 1968. "The Peace of Westphalia, 1648–1948." In R. A. Falk and W. H. Hanrieder, eds. *International Law and Organization,* 45–67. Philadelphia: Lippincott.

Guha, Ranajit. 1992a. "Dominance without Hegemony and Its Historiography." In R. Gupta, ed. *Subaltern Studies 4,* 210–305. New York: Oxford University Press.

———. 1992b. *Elementary Aspects of Peasant Insurgency in Colonial India.* Delhi: Oxford University Press.

Guo, Tingyi. 1980. *Jindai zhongguo shigang* (Contemporary Chinese History). Hong Kong: Zhongwen daxue chubanshe.

Hale, David H. 1995. "Is It a Yen or a Dollar Crisis in the Currency Market?" *Washington Quarterly* 18 4: 145–71.

Hall, John A. 1996. *International Orders.* Cambridge: Polity Press.

Halliday, Fred. 1986. *The Making of the Second Cold War.* London: Verso.

Hamashita, Takeshi. n.d. "Japan and China in the Nineteenth and Twentieth Centuries." Tokyo: Institute of Oriental Culture, University of Tokyo.

———. 1988. "The Tribute Trade System of Modern Asia." *The Memoirs of the Toyo Bunko* 46: 7–25.

———. 1994. "The Tribute Trade System and Modern Asia." In A. J. H. Latham and

H. Kawakatsu, eds. *Japanese Industrialization and the Asian Economy,* 91–107. London and New York: Routledge.

———. 1997. "The Intra-regional System in East Asia in Modern Times." In P. J. Katzenstein and T. Shiraishi, eds. *Network Power: Japan and Asia,* 113–35. Ithaca: Cornell University Press.

Hao, Yen-p'ing. 1970. *The Comprador in Nineteenth-Century China: Bridge between East and West.* Cambridge: Harvard University Press.

———. 1986. *The Commercial Revolution in Nineteenth-Century China.* Berkeley: California University Press.

Harrison, Bennett. 1994. *Lean and Mean: The Changing Landscape of Corporate Power in the Age of Flexibility.* New York: Basic Books.

Harvey, David. 1989. *The Condition of Postmodernity: An Enquiry into the Origins of Cultural Change.* Oxford: Basil Blackwell.

———. 1995. "Globalization in Question." *Rethinking Marxism* 8, 4: 1–17.

Haudrere, Philippe. 1989. *La Compagnie française des Indes au XVIIIe siècle 1719–1795.* Vol. 1. Paris: Librairie de l'Inde.

Haupt, Georges. 1972. *Socialism and the Great War: The Collapse of the Second International.* Oxford: Clarendon Press.

Headrick, Daniel R. 1988. *The Tentacles of Progress: Technology Transfer in the Age of Imperialism, 1850–1940.* London: Oxford University Press.

Heesterman, J. C. 1978. "Was There an Indian Reaction? Western Expansion in Indian Perspective." In H. L. Wesseling, ed. *Expansion and Reaction: Essays on European Expansion and Reaction in Asia and Africa,* 31–58. Leiden: Leiden University Press.

Held, David. 1995. *Democracy and the Global Order: From the Modern State to Cosmopolitan Governance.* Stanford: Stanford University Press.

Helleiner, Eric. 1992. "Japan and the Changing Global Financial Order." *International Journal* 47, 2: 420–44.

———. 1994. *States and the Reemergence of Global Finance: From Bretton Woods to the 1990s.* Ithaca: Cornell University Press.

———. 1997. "A Challenge to the Sovereign State? Financial Globalization and the Westphalian World Order." Paper presented at the Conference on States and Sovereignty in the World Economy, University of California, Irvine, February.

Henderson, W. O. 1975. *The Rise of German Industrial Power, 1834–1914.* Berkeley: University of California Press.

Hettne, Bjorn. 1995. *International Political Economy: Understanding Global Disorder.* London: Zed Books.

Hibbs, Douglas A. 1978. "On the Political Economy of Long-Run Trends in Strike Activity." *British Journal of Political Science* 7, 2: 153–75.

Hilferding, Rudolf. 1981. *Finance Capital: A Study of the Latest Phase of Capitalist Development.* London: Routledge and Kegan Paul.

Hirschman, Albert O. 1979. *Essays in Trespassing: Economics to Politics and Beyond.* Cambridge: Cambridge University Press.

———. 1989. "How the Keynesian Revolution Was Exported from the United States, and Other Comments." In Peter A. Hall, ed. *The Political Power of Economic Ideas: Keynesianism across Nations,* 347–59. Princeton: Princeton University Press.

Hirst, Paul, and Grahame Thompson. 1992. "The Problem of 'Globalization': International Economic Relations, National Economic Management, and the Formation of Trading Blocs." *Economy and Society* 21, 4: 357–96.

―――. 1996. *Globalization in Question: The International Economy and the Possibilities of Governance.* Cambridge: Polity Press.

Ho, S. P. S. 1984. "Colonialism and Development: Korea, Taiwan, and Kwantung." In R. Myers and M. Peattie, eds. *The Japanese Colonial Empire,* 348–98. Princeton: Princeton University Press.

Hobsbawm, Eric. 1962. *The Age of Revolution, 1789–1848.* New York: Mentor.

―――. 1968. *Industry and Empire: An Economic History of Britain since 1750.* London: Weidenfeld and Nicolson.

―――. 1969. *Industry and Empire: From 1750 to the Present Day.* Harmondsworth: Penguin Books.

―――. 1979. *The Age of Capital, 1848–1875.* New York: New American Library.

―――. 1987. *The Age of Empire, 1875–1914.* New York: Pantheon Books.

―――. 1994. *The Age of Extremes: A History of the World, 1914–1991.* New York: Vintage.

Hopkins, Terence K. 1990. "Note on the Concept of Hegemony." *Review* 13, 3: 409–11.

Horsman, M., and A. Marshall. 1994. *After the Nation State.* London: HarperCollins.

Hossain, Hameeda. 1979. "The Alienation of Weavers: Impact of the Conflict between the Revenue and Commercial Interests of the East India Company, 1750–1800." *Indian Economic and Social History Review* 16, 3: 323–45.

―――. 1988. *The Company Weavers of Bengal: The East India Company and the Organization of Textile Production in Bengal, 1750–1813.* Delhi: Oxford University Press.

Hounshell, David A. 1984. *From the American System to Mass Production, 1800–1932: The Development of Manufacturing Technology in the United States.* Baltimore: Johns Hopkins University Press.

Howard, Michael. 1976. *War in European History.* New York: Oxford University Press.

Howell, David. 1997. "East Comes West." *Foreign Affairs* 76, 2: 164.

Hsiao, Liang-lin. 1974. *China's Foreign Trade Statistics, 1864–1949.* Cambridge: Harvard University Press.

Hsu, Immanuel C. Y. 1983. *The Rise of Modern China.* New York: Cambridge University Press.

Hugill, Peter J. 1993. *World Trade Since 1431: Geography, Technology, and Capitalism.* Baltimore: Johns Hopkins University Press.

Hui, Po-keung. 1995. "Overseas Chinese Business Networks: East Asian Economic Development in Historical Perspective." Ph.D. diss., State University of New York at Binghamton.

Huntington, Samuel P. 1993. "The Clash of Civilizations?" *Foreign Affairs* 73, 3: 22–49.

―――. 1996. *The Clash of Civilization and the Remaking of World Order.* New York: Simon and Schuster.

Huntington, Samuel, et al. 1993. *The Clash of Civilizations? The Debate.* New York: Council on Foreign Relations.

Hymer, Stephen. 1972. "The Multinational Corporation and the Law of Uneven Development." In J. N. Bhagwati, ed. *Economics and World Order: From the 1970s to the 1990s,* 113–40. New York: Macmillan.

Hymer, Stephen, and Robert Rowthorn. 1970. "Multinational Corporations and International Oligopoly: The Non-American Challenge." In C. P. Kindleberger, ed. *The International Corporation: A Symposium.* Cambridge: MIT Press.

Ihonvbere, Julius. 1992. "The Third World and the New World Order in the 1990s."

In *Annual Editions 1996/97 Developing World*, 6–15. Guilford, Conn.: Dushkin Publishing.

Ikeda, Satoshi. 1996. "World Production." In T. K. Hopkins, I. Wallerstein, et al. *The Age of Transition: Trajectory of the World-System, 1945–2025*, 38–86. London: Zed Books.

Ikenberry, John G. 1989. "Rethinking the Origins of American Hegemony." *Political Science Quarterly* 104, 3: 375–400.

———. 1997. "The West: Precious, Not Unique." *Foreign Affairs* 76, 2: 162–65.

Inden, Ronald. 1986. "Orientalist Constructions of India." *Modern Asian Studies* 20, 3: 401–46.

Ingham, Geoffrey. 1984. *Capitalism Divided? The City and Industry in British Social Development*. London: Macmillan.

———. 1994. "States and Markets in the Production of World Money: Sterling and the Dollar." In S. Corbridge, R. Martin, N. Thrift, eds., *Money, Power, and Space*. Oxford: Blackwell.

———. 1995. "British Capitalism: Empire, Merchants, and Decline." *Social History* 20, 3: 339–54.

Iriye, Akira. 1965. *After Imperialism: The Search for a New Order in the Far East, 1921–1931*. Forge Village, Mass.: Harvard University Press.

———. 1970. "Imperialism in East Asia." In J. Crowley, ed. *Modern East Asia*, 122–50. New York: Harcourt.

Israel, Jonathan I. 1989. *Dutch Primacy in World Trade, 1585–1740*. Oxford: Clarendon Press.

Jackson, Robert. 1990. *Quasi-States: Sovereignty, International Relations, and the Third World*. Cambridge: Cambridge University Press.

James, C. L. R. 1989. *The Black Jacobins: Toussaint L'Ouverture and the San Domingo Revolution*. New York: Vintage Books.

Japan Almanac. Various years. Tokyo: Asahi Shimbum Publishing Co.

Jenks, Leland H. 1938. *The Migration of British Capital to 1875*. New York and London: Knopf.

Johnson, Chalmers, and E. B. Keehn. 1995. "The Pentagon's Ossified Strategy." *Foreign Affairs* 74, 4: 103–14.

Kahn, Herman. 1970. *The Emerging Japanese Superstate*. Englewood Cliffs, N.J.: Prentice Hall.

Kasaba, Resat. 1993. "Treaties and Friendships: British Imperialism, the Ottoman Empire, and China in the Nineteenth Century." *Journal of World History* 4, 2: 215–41.

Katzenstein, Peter. 1987. *Policy and Politics in West Germany: The Growth of a Semisovereign State*. Philadelphia: Temple University Press.

———. 1997. "Introduction: Asian Regionalism in Comparative Perspective." In Peter J. Katzenstein and Takashi Shiraishi, eds. *Network Power: Japan and Asia*, 1–44. Ithaca: Cornell University Press.

Katzenstein, Peter, and Takashi Shiraishi. 1997. "Conclusion: Regions in World Politics, Japan and Asia—Germany in Europe." In Peter J. Katzenstein and Takashi Shiraishi, eds. *Network Power: Japan and Asia*, 341–81. Ithaca: Cornell University Press.

Kawakatsu, Heita. 1994. "Historical Background." In A. J. H. Latham and H. Kawakatsu, eds. *Japanese Industrialization and the Asian Economy*, 4–8. London and New York: Routledge.

Kennedy, Paul. 1976. *The Rise and Fall of British Naval Mastery*. New York: Charles Scribner's Sons.

———. 1980. *The Rise of the Anglo-German Antagonism, 1860–1914*. London: Allen and Unwin.

———. 1987. *The Rise and Fall of the Great Powers: Economic Change and Military Conflict from 1500 to 2000*. New York: Random House.

Keohane, Robert. 1984a. *After Hegemony: Cooperation and Discord in the World Political Economy*. Princeton: Princeton University Press.

———. 1984b. "The World Political Economy and the Crisis of Political Liberalism." In J. H. Goldthorpe, ed. *Order and Conflict in Contemporary Capitalism*, 15–38. New York: Oxford University Press.

Keohane, Robert, and Joseph Nye. 1987. "*Power and Interdependence* Revisited." *International Organization* 41, 4: 725–53.

Kim, K-H. 1980. *The Last Phase of the East Asian World Order: Korea, Japan, and the Chinese Empire, 1860–1882*. Berkeley: University of California Press.

Kindleberger, Charles. 1969. *American Business Abroad*. New Haven: Yale University Press.

———. 1973. *The World in Depression, 1929–1938*. Berkeley: University of California Press.

———. 1978. *Economic Response: Comparative Studies in Trade, Finance, and Growth*. Cambridge: Harvard University Press.

———. 1984. *A Financial History of Western Europe*. Boston: Allen and Unwin.

———. 1988. *The International Economic Order*. Cambridge: Massachusetts Institute of Technology Press.

———. 1989. *Manias, Panics, and Crashes. A History of Financial Crises*. Rev. ed. New York: Basic Books.

Kissinger, Henry. 1964. *A World Restored: European after Napoleon: The Politics of Conservatism in a Revolutionary Age*. New York: Grosset and Dunlap.

Knapp, J. A. 1957. "Capital Exports and Growth." *Economic Journal* 67, 267: 432–44.

Kocka, Jürgen. 1986. "Problems of Working-Class Formation in Germany: The Early Years, 1800–1875." In Ira Katznelson and Aristide R. Zolberg, eds. *Working-Class Formation*, 279–351. Princeton: Princeton University Press.

Kraar, Louis. 1993. "The New Power in Asia." *Fortune*, October 31, 38–44.

Krasner, Stephen. 1988. "A Trade Strategy for the United States." *Ethics and International Affairs* 2: 17–35.

Krugman, Paul. 1994. "The Myth of Asia's Miracle." *Foreign Affairs* 73, 6: 62–78.

Kurth, James. 1994. "The Real Clash." *The National Interest* 37: 3–15.

LaFeber, Walter. 1963. *The New Empire; An Interpretation of American Expansion, 1860–1898*. Ithaca: Cornell University Press.

Landes, David S. 1966. "The Structure of Enterprise in the Nineteenth Century." In D. S. Landes, ed. *The Rise of Capitalism*, 99–111. New York: Macmillan.

———. 1969. *The Unbound Prometheus: Technological Change and Industrial Development in Western Europe from 1750 to the Present*. Cambridge: Cambridge University Press.

Lane, Frederic C. 1979. *Profits from Power: Readings in Protection Rent and Violence-Controlling Enterprises*. Albany: State University of New York Press.

Lazonick, William. 1991. *Business Organization and the Myth of the Market Economy*. New York: Cambridge University Press.

Le Roy Ladurie, Emmanuel. 1974. "Revoltes et contestations rurales en France de 1675 à 1788." *Annales E.S.C.* 1: 6–22.

———. 1975. "De la crise ultime a la vraie croissance, 1660–1789." In George Duby, dir., *Histoire de la France rurale*, 2: E. Le Roy Ladurie, dir., *L'Age classique des paysans, 1340–1789*, 355–599. Paris: Seuil.

Lenin, V. I. 1971. "Imperialism, the Highest Stage of Capitalism." In *V. I. Lenin: Selected Works*. New York: International Publishers.

Lim, Linda. 1983. "Capitalism, Imperialism, and Patriarchy: The Dilemma of Third-World Women Workers in Multinational Factories." In June Nash and Maria Patricia Fernandez-Kelly, eds. *Women, Men, and the International Division of Labor*, 70–91. Albany: State University of New York Press.

———. 1990. "Women's Work in Export Factories: The Politics of a Cause." In I. Tinker, ed. *Persistent Inequalities: Women and World Development*, 101–119. New York: Oxford University Press.

Loth, Wilfried. 1988. *The Division of the World, 1941–1955*. London: Routledge.

Lowe, Peter. 1981. *Britain in the Far East: A Survey from 1819 to the Present*. London: Longman.

Mahan, A. T. 1957. *The Influence of Sea Power upon History*. New York: Sagamore Press.

Maier, Charles. 1978. "The Politics of Productivity: Foundations of American Economic Policy after World War II." In P. Katzenstein, ed. *Between Power and Plenty: Foreign Economic Policies of Advanced Industrial States*. Madison: University of Wisconsin Press.

———. 1981. "The Two Postwar Eras and the Conditions for Stability in Twentieth-Century Europe." *American History Review* 86: 327–52.

———. 1987. *In Search of Stability: Explorations in Historical Political Economy*. Cambridge: Cambridge University Press.

Mann, Michael. 1986. *The Sources of Social Power*. Vol. 1, *A History of Power from the Beginning to A.D. 1760*. Cambridge: Cambridge University Press.

———. 1993. *The Sources of Social Power*. Vol. 2, *The Rise of Classes and Nation-States, 1760–1914*. Cambridge: Cambridge University Press.

Marichal, Carlos. 1989. *A Century of Debt Crises in Latin America—From Independence to the Great Depression, 1820–1830*. Princeton: Princeton University Press.

Markoff, John. 1996. *Waves of Democracy: Social Movements and Political Change*. Thousand Oaks, Calif.: Pine Forge Press.

Marshall, Alfred. 1919. *Industry and Trade*. London: Macmillan.

Marshall, P. J. 1987. *Bengal: The British Bridgehead: Eastern India, 1740–1828*. Cambridge: Cambridge University Press.

Marx, Karl. 1959. *Capital*. Vol. 1. Moscow: Foreign Languages Publishing House.

———. 1976. "Results of the Immediate Process of Production." In *Capital*. Vol. 1, 948–1084. Harmondsworth: Penguin Books, in association with New Left Review.

Marx, Karl, and Friedrich Engels. 1967. *The Communist Manifesto*. Harmondsworth: Penguin.

Mason, Philip. 1974. *A Matter of Honour: An Account of the Indian Army, Its Officers and Men*. New York: Holt, Rinehart and Winston.

Mathias, Peter. 1969. *The First Industrial Nation: An Economic History of Britain, 1700–1914*. London: Methuen.

Mayer, Arno. 1981. *The Persistence of the Old Regime: Europe to the Great War*. New York: Pantheon.

McCormick, Thomas J. 1989. *America's Half-Century: United States Foreign Policy in the Cold War*. Baltimore: Johns Hopkins University Press.

McElwee, William L. 1974. *The Art of War: Waterloo to Mons*. London: Weidenfeld and Nicolson.

McMichael, Philip. 1996. *Development and Social Change: A Global Perspective.* Thousand Oaks, Calif.: Pine Forge Press.

McNeill, William. 1982. *The Pursuit of Power: Technology, Armed Force, and Society since A.D. 1000.* Chicago: Chicago University Press.

———. 1997. "Decline of the West?" *New York Review of Books* 64, 1: 18–22.

Mendelsohn, M. S. 1980. *Money on the Move.* New York: Praeger.

Metcalf, Thomas. 1964. *The Aftermath of Revolt: India, 1857–1870.* Princeton: Princeton University Press.

Minchinton, Walter E., ed. 1969. *The Growth of English Overseas Trade in the Seventeenth and Eighteenth Centuries.* London: Methuen.

———. 1973. "Patterns of Demand 1750–1914." In C. M. Cipolla, ed. *The Fontana Economic History of Europe,* Vol. 3, *The Industrial Revolution,* 77–186. Glasgow: Fontana/Collins.

Mintz, Sidney W. 1985. *Sweetness and Power: The Place of Sugar in Modern History.* New York: Penguin Books.

———. 1989. *Caribbean Transformations.* New York: Columbia University Press.

Mittelman, James H., ed. 1996. *Globalization: Critical Reflections.* Boulder, Colo.: Lynne Rienner.

Mjöset, Lars. 1990. "The Turn of Two Centuries: A Comparison of British and U.S. Hegemonies." In D. P. Rapkin, ed. *World Leadership and Hegemony,* 21–47. Boulder, Colo.: Lynne Reinner.

Modelski, George. 1987. *Long Cycles in World Politics.* Seattle: University of Washington Press.

Modelski, George, and William R. Thompson. 1995. *Leading Sectors and World Powers: The Coevolution of Global Economics and Politics.* Columbia: University of South Carolina Press.

Montgomery, David. 1979. *Workers' Control in America.* Cambridge: Cambridge University Press.

———. 1987. *The Fall of the House of Labor: The Workplace, the State, and American Labor Activism, 1865–1925.* Cambridge: Cambridge University Press.

Moody, Kim. 1988. *An Injury to All: The Decline of American Unionism.* London: Verso.

———. 1997. *Workers in a Lean World.* London: Verso.

Moore, Jr., Barrington. 1966. *The Social Origins of Dictatorship and Democracy: Lord and Peasant in the Making of the Modern World.* Boston: Beacon Press.

Morris, Morris D. 1965. *The Emergence of an Industrial Labor Force in India: A Study of the Bombay Cotton Mills, 1854–1947.* Berkeley: University of California Press.

———. 1982. "The Growth of Large-Scale Industry to 1947." In D. Kumar and D. M. Desai, eds. *The Cambridge Economic History of India.* Vol. 2, *c. 1757–c. 1970,* Cambridge: Cambridge University Press.

Moss, D. J. 1976. "Birmingham and the Campaigns against the Orders-in-Council and East India Company Charter, 1812–13." *Canadian Journal of History* (Annales Canadiennes d'Histoire). 11, 2: 173–88.

Moulder, Frances. 1979. *Japan, China, and the Modern World-Economy.* Cambridge: Cambridge University Press.

Mumford, Lewis. 1934. *Technics and Civilization.* New York: Harcourt, Brace and World.

Murphey, R. 1977. *The Outsiders: The Western Experience in India and China.* Ann Arbor: University of Michigan Press.

Nakao, Shigeo. 1995. *The Political Economy of Japanese Money.* Tokyo: University of Tokyo Press.

Nandy, Ashis. 1972. "The Making and Unmaking of Political Cultures in India." In S. N. Eisenstadt, ed. *Post-Traditional Societies,* 115–38. New York: Norton.

———. 1984. "Culture, State, and the Rediscovery of Indian Politics." *Economic and Political Weekly,* 19, 49: 2078–83.

Nash, Gary B. 1986. *The Urban Crucible: The Northern Seaports and the Origins of the American Revolution.* Abridged edition. Cambridge: Harvard University Press.

Nathan, Andrew J. 1972. "Imperialism's Effects on China." *Bulletin of Concerned Asian Scholars* 4, 4: 3–8.

Nathan, Andrew, and Robert Ross. 1997. *The Great Wall and the Empty Fortress: China's Search for Security.* New York: Norton.

Neal, Larry. 1990. "The Dutch and English East India Companies: Evidence from the Stock and Foreign Exchange Markets." In J. D. Tracy, ed. *The Rise of Merchant Empires,* 195–223. Cambridge: Cambridge University Press.

Nef, John U. 1943. "The Industrial Revolution Reconsidered." *Journal of Economic History* 3, 3: 1–31.

Neumann, Franz. 1942. *Behemoth: The Structure and Practice of National Socialism.* London: Victor Gollancz.

Nigam, Sanjay. 1990a. "Disciplining and Policing the 'Criminals by Birth,' Part 1: The Making of a Colonial Stereotype—The Criminal Tribes and Castes of North India." *The Indian Economic and Social History Review* 27, 2: 131–64.

———. 1990b. "Disciplining and Policing the 'Criminals by Birth,' Part 2: The Development of a Disciplinary System, 1871–1900." *The Indian Economic and Social History Review* 27, 3: 257–87.

Nkrumah, Kwame. 1965. *Autobiography.* New York: Nelson.

Norman, E. H. 1975. *Origins of the Modern Japanese State: Selected Writings of E. H. Norman.* Edited by J. W. Dower. New York: Pantheon.

Northrup, David. 1995. *Indentured Labor in the Age of Imperialism, 1834–1922.* Cambridge: Cambridge University Press.

Nye, Joseph S. 1990. *Bound to Lead: The Changing Nature of American Power.* New York: Basic Books.

———. 1995. "The Case for Deep Engagement." *Foreign Affairs* 74, 4: 90–102.

O'Connor, James. 1973. *The Fiscal Crisis of the State.* New York: St. Martin's Press.

Offer, A. 1985. "The Working Classes, British Naval Plans, and the Coming of the Great War." *Past and Present* 107, 204–26.

Ohmae, K. 1990. *The Borderless World.* New York: Harper Business.

Okimoto, Daniel I., and Thomas P. Rohlen. 1988. *Inside the Japanese System: Readings on Contemporary Society and Political Economy.* Stanford: Stanford University Press.

Ong, Aihwa. 1987. *Spirits of Resistance and Capitalist Discipline: Factory Women in Malaysia.* Albany: State University of New York Press.

Orrù, Marco, Nicole Woolsey Biggart, and Gary G. Hamilton. 1997. *The Economic Organization of East Asian Capitalism.* Thousand Oaks, Calif.: Sage.

Owen, D. E. 1934. *British Opium Policy in China and India.* New Haven: Yale University Press.

Ozawa, Terutomo. 1993. "Foreign Direct Investment and Structural Transformation: Japan as a Recycler of Market and Industry." *Business and the Contemporary World* 5, 2: 129–50.

Padfield, Peter. 1982. *Tide of Empires: Decisive Naval Campaigns in the Rise of the West, 1654–1763*, Volume 2. London: RKP.

Palmer, R. R. 1959. *The Age of Democratic Revolution*, Vol. 1. Princeton: Princeton University Press.

Pandey, Gyanendra. 1988. "Peasant Revolt and Indian Nationalism: The Peasant Movement in Awadh, 1919–1922." In R. Guha, ed. *Subaltern Studies 1*, 143–97. New York: Oxford University Press.

Panikkar, Kavalam Madhava. 1970. *Asia and Western Dominance. A Survey of the Vasco Da Gama Epoch of Asian History*. London: Allen and Unwin.

Pares, R. 1950. *A West-India Fortune*. London: Longmans, Green.

Parker, Geoffrey. 1989. "Taking Up the Gun." *MHQ: The Quarterly Journal of Military History* 1, 4: 88–101.

———. 1991. "Europe and the Wider World, 1500–1700: The Military Balance." In James D. Tracy, ed. *The Political Economy of Merchant Empires: State Power and World Trade, 1350–1750*, 161–95. London: Cambridge University Press.

Parry, J. H. 1981. *The Age of Reconnaissance: Discovery, Exploration, and Settlement*. Berkeley: University of California Press.

Parsons, Talcott. 1960. "The Distribution of Power in American Society." In *Structure and Process in Modern Societies*. New York: Free Press.

———. 1964. "Some Reflections on the Place of Force in Social Process." In H. Eckstein, ed. *Internal War*, 33–70. Glencoe, Ill.: The Free Press.

Passell, Peter. 1997. "The Downside of Europe's One-Size-Fits-All Monetary Policy." *New York Times*, June 19, D2.

Pateman, Carole. 1989. "The Fraternal Social Contract." In C. Pateman, *The Disorder of Women*. Stanford: Stanford University Press.

Pauly, Louis W. 1995. "Capital Mobility, State Autonomy, and Political Legitimacy." *Journal of International Affairs* 48, 2: 369–88.

Payne, P. L. 1974. *British Entrepreneurship in the Nineteenth Century*. London: Macmillan.

Pemsel, Helmut. 1977. *A History of War at Sea: An Atlas and Chronology of Conflict at Sea from the Earliest Times to the Present*. Annapolis: Naval Institute Press.

Perlin, Frank. 1985. "State Formation Reconsidered." *Modern Asian Studies* 19, 3: 415–80.

Peterson, Erik R. 1995. "Surrendering to Markets." *Washington Quarterly* 17, 4: 103–15.

Peyrefitte, A. 1992. *The Immobile Empire*. New York: Knopf.

Phelps Brown, Henry, and M. H. Browne. 1968. *A Century of Pay*. New York: Macmillan.

Phillips, Kevin. 1993. *Boiling Point: Republicans, Democrats, and the Decline of Middle-Class Prosperity*. New York: Random House.

Piore, Michael J., and Charles F. Sabel. 1984. *The Second Industrial Divide: Possibilities for Prosperity*. New York: Basic Books.

Piven, Frances, ed. 1992. *Labor Parties in Postindustrial Societies*. New York: Oxford.

———. 1995. "Is It Global Economics or Neo-Laissez-Faire?" *New Left Review* 213: 107–14.

Piven, Frances, and Richard A. Cloward. 1979. *Poor People's Movements: Why They Succeed, How They Fail*. New York: Vintage.

Polanyi, Karl. 1957. *The Great Transformation: The Political and Economic Origins of Our Time*. Boston: Beacon Press.

Pollard, Sidney. 1965. *The Genesis of Modern Management: A Study of the Industrial Revolution in Great Britain*. Cambridge: Harvard University Press.

Portes, Alejandro. 1994. "The Informal Economy and Its Paradoxes." In N. J. Smelser and R. Swedberg, eds. *Handbook of Economic Sociology*, 426–49. Princeton: Princeton University Press.

Post, Ken. 1988. "The Working Class in North Viet Nam and the Launching of the Building of Socialism." *Journal of Asian and African Studies* 23, 1–2: 141–55.

Postma, Johannes Menne. 1990. *The Dutch in the Atlantic Slave Trade, 1600–1815*. Cambridge: Cambridge University Press.

Prakash, Gyan. 1990. "Writing Post-Orientalist Histories of the Third World: Perspectives from Indian Historiography." *Comparative Studies in Society and History* 32, 2: 383–408.

Prakash, Om. 1987. "The Dutch East India Company in the Trade of the Indian Ocean." In A. Das Gupta and M. N. Pearson, eds. *India and the Indian Ocean, 1500–1800*, 185–200. Calcutta and Delhi: Oxford University Press.

Quesnay, François. 1969. "From *Despotism in China*." In F. Schurmann and O. Schell, eds. *Imperial China*, 115–120. New York: Vintage.

Radhakrishna, Meena. 1989. "The Criminal Tribes Act in Madras Presidency: Implications for Itinerant Trading Communities." *The Indian Economic and Social History Review* 26, 3: 269–95.

Radosh, Ronald. 1969. *American Labor and United States Foreign Policy*. New York: Random House.

Rashid, Shaikh Abdur. 1979. "The Mugal Imperial State." In R. J. Moore, ed. *Tradition and Politics in South Asia*, 128–50. New Delhi: Vikas Publishing House.

Rasler, Karen A., and William R. Thompson. 1989. *War and State Making: The Shaping of the Global Powers*. Boston: Unwin Hyman.

Raychaudhuri, Tapan. 1982. "Non-Agricultural Production: Mughal India." In T. Raychaudhuri and I. Habib, eds. *The Cambridge Economic History of India*, Vol. 1, c. 1200–c. 1750, 261–307. Cambridge: Cambridge University Press.

Rediker, Marcus. 1987. *Between the Devil and the Deep Blue Sea: Merchant Seamen, Pirates, and the Anglo-American Maritime World, 1700–1750*. Cambridge: Cambridge University Press.

Reich, Robert. 1992. *The Work of Nations: Preparing Ourselves for Twenty-First-Century Capitalism*. New York: Random House.

Rix, Alan. 1993. "Japan and the Region: Leading from Behind." In Richard Higgott, Richard Leaver, and John Ravenhill, eds. *Pacific Economic Relationships*, 62–82. Boulder, Colo: Lynne Reinner.

Robertson, Priscilla. 1967. *Revolutions of 1848: A Social History*. Princeton: Princeton University Press.

Robinson, William. 1996. *Promoting Polyarchy: Globalization, U.S. Intervention, and Hegemony*. Cambridge: Cambridge University Press.

Rodrik, Dani. 1997. *Has Globalization Gone Too Far?* Washington, D.C.: Institute for International Economics.

Romein, Jan. 1978. *The Watershed of Two Eras: Europe in 1900*. Middletown, Conn.: Wesleyan University Press.

Ropp, Theodore. 1962. *War in the Modern World*. New York: Collier Books.

Rosenau, James N. 1990. *Turbulence in World Politics: A Theory of Change and Continuity*. Princeton: Princeton University Press.

Rosenberg, Hans. 1943. "Political and Social Consequences of the Great Depression of 1873–1896 in Central Europe." *Economic History Review* 13: 58–73.

Ross, Arthur M. and Paul T. Hartman. 1960. *Changing Patterns of Industrial Conflict.* New York: Wiley.

Ross, Robert J. S. and Kent Trachte. 1990. *Global Capitalism: The New Leviathan.* Albany: State University of New York Press.

Rostow, Walt W. 1960. *The Stages of Economic Growth: A Non-Communist Manifesto.* Cambridge: Cambridge University Press.

Rowen, Herbert H. 1978. *John de Witt: Grand Pensionary of Holland, 1625–1672.* Princeton: Princeton University Press.

Rozman, G. 1981. *The Modernization of China.* London: The Free Press.

Rubinstein, W. D. 1977. "Wealth, Elites, and the Class Structure of Modern Britain." *Past and Present* 76: 99–126.

Ruggie, John G. 1982. "International Regimes, Transactions, and Change: Embedded Liberalism in the Postwar Economic Order." *International Organization* 36, 2: 379–415.

———. 1983. "Continuity and Transformation in the World Polity: Toward a Neorealist Synthesis." *World Politics* 35, 2: 261–85.

———. 1994. "Third Try at World Order? America and Multilateralism after the Cold War." *Political Science Quarterly* 109, 4: 553–70.

Rupert, Mark. 1995. *Producing Hegemony: The Politics of Mass Production and American Global Power.* Cambridge: Cambridge University Press.

Sabel, Charles, and Jonathan Zeitlin. 1985. "Historical Alternatives to Mass Production: Politics, Markets, and Technology in Nineteenth-Century Industrialization." *Past and Present* 107: 133–76.

Sanger, David E. 1997a. "Paper Tiger: 'Asian Money,' American Fears." *New York Times,* January 5, 4: 1, 4.

———. 1997b. "European Integration: Guns, Yes; Butter, Maybe." *New York Times,* July 13, 4: 5.

Sassen, Saskia. 1996. *Losing Control? Sovereignty in an Age of Globalization.* New York: Columbia University Press.

———. 1997. "Towards a Feminist Analytics of the Global Economy." *Indiana Journal of Global Legal Studies* 4, 1: 7–42.

Saul, S. B. 1968. "The Engineering Industry." In D. H. Aldcroft, ed. *The Development of British Industry and Foreign Competition, 1875–1914: Studies in Industrial Enterprise,* 186–237. London: Allen and Unwin.

———. 1969. *The Myth of the Great Depression, 1873–1896.* London: Macmillan.

Saville, John. 1987. *1848: The British State and the Chartist Movement.* Cambridge: Cambridge University Press.

Saxenian, AnnaLee. 1990. "Regional Networks and the Resurgence of Silicon Valley." *California Management Review* 33, 1: 89–112.

———. 1993. *Regional Networks: Culture and Competition in Silicon Valley and Route 128.* Cambridge: Harvard University Press.

Sayers, R. S. 1990. "The Return to Gold, 1925." In B. Eichengreen, ed. *Monetary Regime Transformations,* 282–95. Aldershot, England: E. Elgar.

Schama, Simon. 1989. *Citizens: A Chronicle of the French Revolution.* New York: Vintage Books.

———. 1992. *Patriots and Liberators: Revolution in the Netherlands, 1780–1813.* 2nd ed. London: Fontana Press.

Schoffer, Ivo. 1985. "Did Holland's Golden Age Coincide with a Period of Crisis?"

In G. Parker and L. N. Smith, eds. *The General Crisis of the Seventeenth Century.* London: Routledge and Kegan Paul.

Schumpeter, Joseph. 1963. *The Theory of Economic Development.* New York: Oxford University Press.

Schurmann, Franz. 1974. *The Logic of World Power: An Inquiry into the Origins, Currents, and Contradictions of World Politics.* New York: Pantheon.

Schurmann, Franz, and Orville Schell, eds. 1967. *Imperial China.* New York: Vintage.

Seidman, Gay W. 1994. *Manufacturing Militance: Workers' Movements in Brazil and South Africa, 1970–1985.* Berkeley: University of California Press.

Selden, Mark. 1995. "Yan'an Communism Reconsidered." *Modern China* 21, 1: 8–44.

———. 1997. "China, Japan, and the Regional Political Economy of East Asia, 1945–1995." In Peter J. Katzenstein and Takashi Shiraishi, eds. *Network Power: Japan and Asia,* 306–40. Ithaca: Cornell University Press.

Semmel, Bernard. 1970. *The Rise of Free Trade Imperialism.* Cambridge: Cambridge University Press.

Servan-Schreiber, J. J. 1968. *The American Challenge.* New York: Athaeneum.

Seton-Watson, Hugh. 1967. "Nationalism and Imperialism." In *The Impact of the Russian Revolution, 1917–1967: The Influence of Bolshevism on the World Outside Russia,* 134–205. London: Oxford University Press.

Sewell Jr., William H. 1986. "Artisans, Factory Workers, and the Formation of the French Working Class, 1789–1848." In Ira Katznelson and Aristide R. Zolberg, eds. *Working-Class Formation,* 45–70. Princeton: Princeton University Press.

Shefter, Martin. 1986. "Trade Unions and Political Machines: The Organization and Disorganization of the American Working Class in the Late Nineteenth Century." In Ira Katznelson and Aristide R. Zolberg, eds. *Working-Class Formation,* 197–276. Princeton: Princeton University Press.

Sheth, D. L. 1989. "State, Nation, and Ethnicity: Experience of Third World Countries." *Economic and Political Weekly* March 25, 24, 12: 619–26.

Silver, Beverly J. 1995. "World-Scale Patterns of Labor-Capital Conflict: Labor Unrest, Long Waves, and Cycles of World Hegemony." *Review* (Fernand Braudel Center) 18, 1: 155–92.

———. 1997. "Turning Points in Workers' Militancy in the World Automobile Industry, 1930s–1990s." In *Research in the Sociology of Work.* Vol. 6, 41–69. Greenwich, Conn.: JAI Press.

Sinha, Narendra K. 1953. "East India Company Investment Policy in the Eighteenth Century." *Bengal Past and Present* 73, 1: 25–44.

———. 1965. *The Economic History of Bengal.* Vol. 1. *From Plassey to the Permanent Settlement.* Calcutta: Firma K. L. Mukhopadhyay.

Singh, C. 1988. "Center and Periphery in the Mughal State: The Case of Seventeenth-Century Punjab." *Modern Asian Studies* 22, 2: 299–318.

Sklair, Leslie. 1991. *Sociology of the Global System.* Baltimore: Johns Hopkins University Press.

Sklar, Martin J. 1988. *The Corporate Reconstruction of American Capitalism, 1890–1916: The Market, the Law, and Politics.* Cambridge: Cambridge University Press.

Sklar, Richard. 1976. "Postimperialism: A Class Analysis of Multinational Corporate Expansion." *Contemporary Politics* 9, 1: 75–92.

Skocpol, Theda. 1979. *States and Social Revolutions.* Cambridge: Cambridge University Press.

Smith, Adam. 1961. *An Inquiry into the Nature and Causes of the Wealth of Nations.* 2 Vols. London: Methuen.

So, Alvin Y. 1986. *The South China Silk District.* Albany: State University of New York Press.

So, Alvin Y., and Stephen W. K. Chiu. 1995. *East Asia and the World-Economy.* Newbury Park, Calif.: Sage.

Sobel, Andrew C. 1994. *Domestic Choices, International Markets: Dismantling National Barriers and Liberalizing Securities Markets.* Ann Arbor: University of Michigan Press.

Soros, George. 1997. "The Capitalist Threat." *Atlantic Monthly,* 279, 2: 45–58.

Spence, Jonathan D. 1990. *The Search for Modern China.* New York: Norton.

Stavrianos, L. S. 1981. *Global Rift: The Third World Comes of Age.* New York: William Morrow and Company.

Steensgaard, Niels. 1974. *The Asian Trade Revolution of the Seventeenth Century: The East India Companies and the Decline of the Caravan Trade.* Chicago: University of Chicago Press.

———. 1981. "The Companies as a Specific Institution in the History of European Expansion." In L. Blussé and F. Gaastra, eds. *Companies and Trade,* 245–64. Leiden: Leiden University Press.

———. 1982. "The Dutch East India Company as an Institutional Innovation." In M. Aymard, ed. *Dutch Capitalism and World Capitalism,* 235–57. Cambridge: Cambridge University Press.

Stivers, William. 1982. *Supremacy and Oil: Iraq, Turkey, and the Anglo-American World Order, 1918–1930.* Ithaca: Cornell University Press.

Stokes, Eric. 1959. *The English Utilitarians and India.* London: Oxford University Press.

Stopford, John M., and John H. Dunning. 1983. *Multinationals: Company Performance and Global Trends.* London: Macmillan.

Subrahmanyam, S., and C. A. Bayly. 1988. "Portfolio Capitalists and the Political Economy of Early Modern India." *Indian Economic and Social History Review* 25, 4: 401–24.

Tabb, William. 1997. "Globalization Is *an* Issue, the Power of Capital Is *the* Issue." *Monthly Review* 49, 2: 20–30.

Taylor, Peter. 1994. "Ten Years That Shook the World? The United Provinces as First Hegemonic State." *Sociological Perspectives* 37, 1: 25–46.

———. 1996. *The Way the Modern World Works: World Hegemony to World Impasse.* Chichester: John Wiley and Sons.

Therborn, Goran. 1977. "The Rule of Capital and the Rise of Democracy." *New Left Review* 103: 3–41.

———. 1995. *European Modernity and Beyond: The Trajectory of European Societies, 1945–2000.* London: Sage Publications.

Thomas, S. C. 1984. *Foreign Intervention and China's Industrial Development, 1870–1911.* Boulder, Colo.: Westview.

Thompson, E. P. 1966. *The Making of the English Working Class.* New York: Vintage Books.

Thompson, William R. 1992. "Dehio, Long Cycles, and the Geohistorical Context of Structural Transition." *World Politics* 65, 1: 127–52.

Thornton, Edward. 1835. *India: Its State and Prospects.* London: Parbury, Allen and Co.

Thurow, Lester. 1992. *Head to Head: The Coming Economic Battle among Japan, Europe, and America.* New York: William Morrow.

Tilly, Charles. 1989. "Introduction: The Effects of Short-Term Variation." In L. Haimson and C. Tilly, eds. *Strikes, Wars, and Revolutions in International Perspective,* 433–48. Cambridge: Cambridge University Press.

———. 1990. *Coercion, Capital, and European States, A.D. 990–1990.* Cambridge, Mass.: Basil Blackwell.

———. 1995. "Globalization Threatens Labor's Rights." *International Labor and Working-Class History* 47: 1–23.

Tilly, Richard. 1967. "Germany, 1815–1870." In R. Cameron, ed. *Banking in the Early Stages of Industrialization: A Study in Comparative Economic History,* 151–82. New York: Oxford University Press.

Tomlinson, B. R. 1975. "India and the British Empire, 1880–1935." *The Indian Economic and Social History Review* 12, 4: 337–80.

Toussaint, Auguste. 1966. *History of the Indian Ocean.* London: Routledge and Kegan Paul.

Tracy, James D., ed. 1990. *The Rise of Merchant Empires: Long-Distance Trade in the Early Modern World, 1350–1750.* Cambridge: Cambridge University Press.

Trevor-Roper, H. R. 1967. "The General Crisis of the Seventeenth Century." In T. Aston, ed. *Crisis in Europe, 1560–1660,* 59–96. Garden City, N.Y.: Doubleday Anchor.

Trouillot, Michel-Rolph. 1995. *Silencing the Past: Power and the Production of History.* Boston: Beacon Press.

Tsiang, Ting-fu. 1967. "The English and the Opium Trade." In F. Schurmann and O. Schell, eds. *Imperial China,* 132–45. New York: Vintage.

Tyson, R. L. 1968. "The Cotton Industry." In D. H. Aldcroft, ed. *The Development of British Industry and Foreign Competition, 1875–1914: Studies in Industrial Enterprise,* 100–27. London: George Allen and Unwin.

Unger, W. S. 1982. "Essay on the History of the Dutch Slave Trade." In M. A. P. Meilink-Roelofsz and M. J. L. van Yperen, eds. *Dutch Authors on West Indian History: A Historiographical Selection,* 46–98. The Hague: Martinus Nijhoff.

Union Bank of Switzerland. 1996. "The Asian Economic Miracle." *UBS International Finance* 29: 1–8. Zurich: UBS.

U.S. Department of Commerce. Various years. *Survey of Current Business.* Washington, D.C.: Government Printing Office.

van der Pijl, K. 1984. *The Making of an Atlantic Ruling Class.* London: Verso.

van Leur, Jacob C. 1955. *Indonesian Trade and Society: Essays in Social and Economic History.* The Hague: W. van Hoewe.

Vernon, Raymond. 1971. *Sovereignty at Bay: The Multinational Spread of U.S. Enterprises.* New York: Basic Books.

Vogel, Ezra. 1979. *Japan as Number One: Lessons for America.* Cambridge: Harvard University Press.

Waley, Arthur. 1958. *The Opium War through Chinese Eyes.* London: Allen and Unwin.

Wallerstein, Immanuel. 1974. *The Modern World-System.* Vol. 1, *Capitalist Agriculture and the Origins of the European World-Economy in the Sixteenth Century.* New York: Academic Press.

———. 1980. *The Modern World-System.* Vol. 2, *Mercantilism and the Consolidation of the European World-Economy, 1600–1750.* New York: Academic Press.

———. 1982. "Crisis as Transition." In S. Amin, G. Arrighi, A. G. Frank, and I. Wallerstein. *Dynamics of Global Crisis,* 11–54. New York: Monthly Review Press.

———. 1984. *The Politics of the World-Economy: The States, the Movements, and the Civilizations*. Cambridge: Cambridge University Press.

———. 1989. *The Modern World-System*. Vol. 3, *The Second Era of Great Expansion of the Capitalist World-Economy, 1730s–1840s*. New York: Academic Press.

———. 1995a. *After Liberalism*. New York: The New Press.

———. 1995b. "Evolution of the Modern World-System." *Proto-Soziologie* 7: 4–10.

———. 1995c. "Response: Declining States, Declining Rights?" *International Labor and Working-Class History* 47: 24–27.

———. 1996. "The Global Possibilities, 1990–2025." In T. K. Hopkins, I. Wallerstein, et al., *The Age of Transition*, 226–43. London: Zed Books.

Walton, John. 1984. *Reluctant Rebels: Comparative Studies of Revolution and Underdevelopment*. New York: Columbia University Press.

Waltz, Kenneth. 1979. *Theory of International Politics*. Reading, Mass.: Addison-Wesley.

Washbrook, David. 1990. "South Asia, the World System, and World Capitalism." *The Journal of Asian Studies* 49, 3: 479–508.

Waters, Malcolm. 1995. *Globalization*. New York: Routledge.

Watson, Bruce I. 1976. "The Establishment of English Commerce in Northwestern India in the Early Seventeenth Century." *The Indian Economic and Social History Review* 13, 3: 375–91.

Weber, Max. 1961. *General Economic History*. New York: Collier.

———. 1978. *Economy and Society*. Berkeley: University of California Press.

Weigall, David. 1987. *Britain and the World, 1815–1986: A Dictionary of International Relations*. New York: B.T. Batsford.

Weiss, Linda. 1997. "Globalization and the Myth of the Powerless State." *New Left Review* 225: 3–27.

Wilkins, Mira. 1970. *The Emergence of Multinational Enterprise: American Business Abroad from the Colonial Era to 1914*. Cambridge: Harvard University Press.

Williams, Eric. 1964. *Capitalism and Slavery*. London: Andre Deutsch.

Williams, William A. 1969. *The Roots of the Modern American Empire: A Study of the Growth and Shaping of Social Consciousness in a Marketplace Society*. New York: Random House.

Williamson, James A. 1922. *A Short History of British Expansion*. London: Macmillan.

Wilson, Charles. 1965. *England's Apprenticeship, 1603–1763*. London: Longmans, Green.

———. 1966. *Anglo-Dutch Commerce and Finance in the Eighteenth Century*. Cambridge: Cambridge University Press.

———. 1976. *The Transformation of Europe, 1558–1648*. London: Weidenfeld and Nicolson.

Wolf, Eric. 1969. *Peasant Wars of the Twentieth Century*. New York: Harper and Row.

———. 1982. *Europe and the People without History*. Berkeley: University of California Press.

Womack Jr., John. 1968. *Zapata and the Mexican Revolution*. New York: Vintage Books.

Wood, George Henry. 1910. "The Statistics of Wages in the Nineteenth Century. Part 19—The Cotton Industry." *Journal of the Royal Statistical Society*. n.s., 73, pt. 6: 585–626.

Woodruff, William. 1966. *Impact of Western Man: A Study of Europe's Role in the World Economy, 1750–1960*. New York: St. Martin's Press.

Wu, Chengming. 1987. *Zhongguo zibenzhuyi yu guoneishichang* (Chinese Capitalism and Domestic Market). Taipei: Ku-pheng Publishers.

Yang, A., ed. 1985. *Crime and Criminality in British India.* Tucson: University of Arizona Press.

Yen, Zhongping, et al. 1957. *Zhongguo jindai jingjishi tongji* (Collections of Statistical Data of Modern Chinese Economic History). Beijing: Scientific Publishers.

Zevin, Robert. 1992. "Our World Financial Market Is More Open? If So, Why and with What Effect?" In T. Banuri and J. B. Schor, eds. *Financial Openness and National Autonomy: Opportunity and Constraints.* New York: Oxford University Press.

Zhou, Gucheng. 1986. *Zhongguo shehuei zhi bianhua* (Change of Chinese Society). Taipei: Gufong chubanshe.

Zolberg, Aristide R. 1995. "Response: Working-Class Dissolution." *International Labor and Working-Class History* 47: 28–38.

Index

Abbott, Andrew, 184
Abendroth, Wolfgang, 181
Abu-Lughod, Janet, 20–21
Acapulco, 221
Adams, James Truslow, 175
Adams, John Quincy, 227–28, 232
Adas, Michael, 226–27, 231
Addington, Larry H., 57
Afghanistan, 224, 264, 284
Africa, 15, 44, 63, 93, 105, 197–98,
    200–1, 283, 287. *See also* colonization/
    decolonization, social movements,
    trade, and individual places
Aglietta, Michel, 137, 205
Agnew, John, 77
agriculture, 111, 113, 129, 184, 191
Aguilar, Alonso, 59
Ahmad, Iftikhar, 217–70
Alam II, Shah, 110
Alam, M., 242
Ali, Muhammad, 237
Alker, Hayward R., 17
Ambedkar, B. R., 225
Americas, 93, 96, 100–5, 198, 221–22,
    280. *See also* colonization/decoloniza-
    tion, Latin America, revolutions, social
    movements, wars, and individual places

Amin, Shahid, 246
Amsterdam, 41–42, 51, 99, 102; finan-
    cial market, 41, 43, 52–55, 74, 101,
    103
Anderson, Perry, 45, 81, 173
Appelbaum, Richard P., 10
Argentina, 70
Arnold, David, 240
Arrighi, Giovanni, 22, 32, 41, 48, 61, 89,
    149, 205, 207, 209, 246, 266–67
Asia: contract labor, 283; "country
    trade" and European merchants, 222;
    Dutch and British intrusions compared,
    223; European "invasion," pecularity
    of, 221; Portuguese and Dutch intru-
    sions compared, 222; "super-world-
    economy" (Braudel), 220–23; "three
    departments of government" (Marx),
    113; vulnerability to Western military
    disruptions, 219–20, 223, 286–87;
    Western dominance, 15, 197, 218–19,
    225, 236, 239, 245, 247, 257, 262–63,
    270, 283; "Westernization," 237, 239.
    See also colonization/decolonization,
    East Asia, rebellions, revolutions,
    social movements, wars, and individual
    places

Atlantic Ocean, 77, 101, 103
Attman, Artur, 52
Aurangzeb, emperor, 219
Australasia, 62
Austria, 70, 109,
Aymard, Maurice, 99

Bagchi, Amiya Kumar, 111, 113, 115,
    229–30, 236, 258
Bainey, Geoffrey, 3
Bairoch, Paul, 119
Baker, Russell, 211
Balfour, A. J., 241
Bangkok, 281
Barbour, Violet, 41
Barnet, Richard, 6
Barr, Kenneth, 97–150
Barraclough, Geoffrey, 15, 183, 194,
    200, 255–56
Barrat-Brown, Michael, 60
Bataille, Georges, 209
Batavia, 103, 107
Bayle, Pierre, 226
Bayly, Christopher A., 110, 112, 114,
    242, 245
Bearce, George, 240
Becattini, Giacomo, 142
Beijing, 228, 233, 238, 248, 267
Beinin, Joel, 210, 213
Belgium, 70, 77
Benería, Lourdes, 13–14
Bengal, 108, 111, 113
Bentham, Jeremy, 240
Bentick, William, Lord, 240
Bergé, Pierre, 22
Bergesen, Albert, 199
Bergquist, Charles, 201
Bergsten, Fred C., 7, 95–96
Bernstein, Richard, 17
Best, Michael, 142
Bhattacharya, S., 110
Bienefeld, Manfred, 213
Biggart, Nicole Woolsey, 149
Bihar, 108
Birmingham, 114
Birnbaum, Eugene, 146
Bismarck, Otto von, 124
Blackburn, Robin, 154–59, 161–63,
    167–72, 174
Blim, Michael, 148

Block, Fred L., 8, 11, 87
Blussé, Leonard, 100
Bolivar, Simon, 171
Bonacich, Edna, 10
Bond, Brian, 224
Bonnassieux, Pierre, 100
Boogman, J. C., 48
Borden, William S., 87
Borel, Henri, 259
Borthwick, Mark, 254–55, 257
Bourne, Kenneth, 235
Boxer, Charles R., 50–52, 99, 104–5,
    164–65, 221
Boyer, Robert, 137, 181
Braczyk, H. J., 148
Braudel, Fernand, 31–32, 40–42, 48–49,
    51, 53–55, 68, 74–75, 81, 95, 99,
    101–3, 154, 166, 220, 222–23, 275
Brazil, 13, 47, 104–5
Brecher, Jeremy, 10, 183, 213
Brenner, Robert, 137
Bretton Woods, 12, 80, 87–88, 94, 98,
    206
Brewer, John, 43
Brezhnev, Leonid, 18
Bridges, Amy, 182
British world hegemony: and Asian re-
    sources, 217–18, 283; and Asian em-
    pires, 239; coercive aspects, 111, 172,
    174–76, 183–84, 196–97, 202–3, 224,
    240–42, 282–83; emulation of Britain,
    175–76, 227; exploitative domination
    in decline, 288; and general western in-
    terest, 59–61, 184, 228; global reach,
    22, 37, 279; "Hundred Years' Peace,"
    58, 60, 64, 224; and industrial capa-
    bilities, 84; and mastery of balance of
    power, 58–59, 86; and restoration of
    slavery, 172, 176, 202–3; social foun-
    dations, 152–53, 172–78, 181, 185,
    202–3, 207–8, 282–83; and state sov-
    ereignty, 93, 239; and territorial ex-
    pansion, 83, 176, 178, 203, 282–83;
    and world entrepot functions, 82–86;
    and world-scale division of labor,
    60–61. See also hegemonic transitions,
    hegemony, United Kingdom, world
    hegemony
Broad, Robin, 213
Brody, David, 188

Brown, Alexander Dee, 178
Brown, Carolyn A., 201
Brown, William A., Jr., 73
Browne, M. H., 181
Brusco, Sebastiano, 142
Brussels, 20
Buchanan, Pat, 212
Bulgaria, 277
Burawoy, Michael, 201
Burley, Anne-Marie, 204–5, 210
Burma, 225, 280
Burstein, Daniel, 5
Bush, George, 3
business enterprises: and armament race, 70–71, 125; competition, 30, 32–33, 97, 119–20, 123–24, 130, 140–41, 144–45, 147, 151–52, 215, 284, 286; "concentration without centralization", 148–49; corporate, 117, 128, 149; crisis of U.S. system, 141–43, 147; diaspora, 32, 51, 108, 149, 250–52, 267–68, 280, 282, 287; differentiation of management from ownership, 125; diversification of operations, 135, 137, 147; family, 99, 102, 115–16, 121, 125, 128, 149, 279–80; and high value-added activities, 97, 132; horizontal combination, 123–25, 129; "industrial districts", 127, 142–43, 148; "informalization," 141–43, 147–49; integration of mass production and distribution, 138; "lean" production, 148; manufacturers, 8, 98, 106, 114, 127; merchants, 100, 105–6, 115, 143, 222, 250–53; multi-unit, 123, 134; multidivisional, 135, 137, 139; "multilayered subcontracting system," 148–49, 280; networks of, 98, 102, 127–28, 141–43, 148, 222, 242, 250–52, 268, 280; privatization, 277; and scientific management, 135; single-unit, 134; transition from Dutch to British system of, 121; transition from British to U.S. system of, 121, 124, 128–29, 133–34; transnational, 38, 146, 278; vertical integration/disintegration, 123–24, 126–31, 134, 147; Western techniques in China, 250. *See also* capital, capitalism, chartered companies, firms and

companies, industries, multinational corporations and trade

Cain, P. J., 63
Cairncross, A. K., 133
Calhoun, John, 271
Calleo, David P., 87, 288
Cambodia (Kampuchea), 19, 280, 287
Canada, 58, 80, 87
Canning, Charles J., 175
Canton, 246, 249
Cape of Good Hope, 99, 103, 221
capital: accumulation as end in itself, 48; commodity vs. money form, 32; over-accumulation, 31–32, 66, 89; relationship to hegemonic state, 97–99; spatial mobility, 7, 10–11, 74, 133, 153, 196, 284, 286; surplus, 68, 89. *See also* business enterprises, capitalism, chartered companies, financial entries
capitalism: Asian, 19; corporate, 121, 131; corporate, Dutch style, 99, 102–26, 143; corporate, German style, 124–25; corporate, U.S. style, 129–30, 132–40; 143–46; corporate, U.S. and Dutch style compared, 144–46; family, 130–31, 134; family, British-style, 125–29, 133, 143, 279; and financial expansions, 31–33, 151, 278–79; "golden age," 88, 211; industrial, 12, 63, 117–20; laissez faire, 9; "last stage," 66; liberal, 1–3; as logic of power, 48–49; and mechanization of production, 117–20, 279; national variants, 130–31; "organized," 124; "state monopoly," 131; and states, 6–10, 31, 79. *See also* business enterprises, capital, chartered companies, financial entries, firms and companies, multinational corporations, and world system
Carr, Edward H., 39, 154, 177, 187, 195
Carter, Alice C., 52–53
Castells, Manuel, 141
Castlereagh, Lord, 75, 172, 175
Catherine II, czarina, 53
Cavanagh, John, 6
Ceylon, 103, 111
Chandler, Alfred D., Jr., 124, 129, 130, 134–35, 138–40, 143

Chang, Pin-tsun, 250
chaos theory, 21–22
Chapman, Stanley D., 119, 127, 133
Charles II, king, 44
chartered companies: competition, 101,
    106, 109; displacement by family en-
    terprises, 102, 106, 115–17; and Dutch
    hegemony, 97–100, 279; as instru-
    ments of European expansion, 115–17,
    143–44; and multinational corpora-
    tions compared, 144–46, 149–50; and
    relationship between power and profit,
    111–12. *See also* Dutch East India
    Company, English East India Com-
    pany, firms and companies, Royal
    African Company, and West Indische
    Compagnie
Chatterjee, Partha, 200, 246
Chaudhuri, K. N., 107–8, 232, 243
Chaudhuri, S. B., 244
Chaussinand-Nogaret, Guy, 167–68
Cheng, Lucie, 10
Chicago, 77
Child, Josiah, Sir, 219, 221
Chile, 70
China: the "agrarian question," 200; and
    American silver, 222; and Asian trade,
    220; Boxer Protocol, 258; and British
    goods and capital, 70, 133, 249–50;
    and British-Indian army, 225; "Canton
    system," 230; Communist Party (CCP),
    260–62, 265, 267–68; conflicts with
    Britain, 227–36; Confucian ethos, 237;
    and "Confucian-Islamic connection,"
    16; "coolie trade," 251; and East Asian
    economy, 228–29, 266–67; and Europe
    compared, 226–27; and European
    Enlightenment, 225–27; foreign capital
    in, 258, 267–68; Guomindang (GMD),
    200, 260–62, 265, 268; ideological
    challenge to the West, 219, 262–63; in-
    demnities, 233, 236, 257–58; Hong
    Kong takeover, 277; integration in East
    Asian region, 281; Japan invades, 254,
    268; Japan's Twenty-One Demands,
    256; labor militancy, 200, 216, 286;
    labor reserves, 267–68; lack of demand
    for European goods, 114, 229,
    249–50; landed upper classes, 237,
    259; merchant class, 222; military ca-

pabilities, 16, 18; military vulnerabili-
    ty, 227, 231–33; modernization and
    development, 17–18, 219, 252–53,
    257–58, 267–68; and "most-favored
    nation clause," 235, 257; Nanjing gov-
    ernment, 261; national identity, 287;
    "One Nation, Two Systems" model,
    268; opium trade, regulation impact
    of, 229–32, 236, 250; and Ottoman
    Empire compared, 233–36; and over-
    seas Chinese, 267–68, 280–81, 287;
    proletarianization, 286; Qing, achieve-
    ments in state-making, 226–27; Qing,
    demise of, 234–35, 247, 254, 258–59;
    Qing Restoration, 238; reintegration
    into global economy, 149, 266–67;
    Revolutionary Alliance, 260; scholar-
    gentry class, 227; self-strengthening
    movement, 252, 259; sovereignty, en-
    croachments on, 239, 258, 268; split
    with Soviet Union, 287; treaty-port
    system, 236; warlord era, 258–60; and
    United States, 17, 88, 235, 266–68. *See
    also* China-centered world system,
    communism, East Asia, English East
    India Company, opium, rebellions,
    revolutions, wars
China-centered world system ("Sino-
    centric tribute-trade system"): arma-
    ment race, 253; Chinese merchants'
    role, 221, 250–52, 268; Hamashita's
    conceptualization, 248–49; incorpora-
    tion into the European-centered world
    system, 248–49, 287; Japan's position/
    role, 246, 248; peripherality of VOC,
    222–23; re-emergence of, 286–87; rela-
    tionship between trade and tribute,
    248; responses to Western military en-
    croachments, 219; Sino-Japanese rival-
    ries, 247, 252–3, 257; US- and Sino-
    centric tribute-trade systems compared,
    266; Vietnam's position/role, 247–48.
    See also East Asia
Chinchilla, Norma, 10
Chiu, Stephen W. K., 149, 247, 250,
    252–53, 256–57, 259, 267
Church, R. A., 132
civilizations: Asian/Eastern, 19, 103,
    218–19, 242–44; balance of power, 4,
    16, 21, 216, 263–64, 286–89; com-

monwealth of, 286; conflicts and interaction, 16, 19, 21, 217–18, 224, 227, 286–89; "modern," curses of (Gandhi), 245–46; non-Western, 4, 16, 150, 218; as "proficiency in the murderous art," 231–32; Western, 4, 16–17, 58, 199, 218–19, 245–46

Cixi, Dowager, empress, 258

Claude, Inis, Jr., 209

Clay, Henry, 78

Clinton, William J., 276–77

Cloward, Richard A., 183

Cohen, Benjamin, 7–8, 73, 86, 283

Colbert, Jean Baptiste, 45, 100

Cold War, 4, 15–18, 21, 66, 87, 92, 94, 138, 147, 266; new, 17; Second, 89, 91, 214, 274, 276, 284, 287; legacy of, 276; as "Western Civil War," 16, 263–64; world order, 38, 79, 202, 265, 276, 287

colonization/decolonization, 93, 104–5, 191, 197–98, 200–1, 283, 287, colonization and decolonization waves, 198–202. *See also* Africa, Americas, Asia, chartered companies, nationalism, social movements, and individual countries

commodities: canned meat, 129; cigarettes, 129, 250; cultural, 270; electronics, 142; grain, 40–41, 104, 184; high technology, 270; kerosene, 250; raw materials, 62–63, 67, 114, 117, 120, 126, 129, 133, 135, 270; rice, 254; spices, 102–4, 107–8, 112, 222; sugar, 100, 151, 155–56, 157; tea, 114, 230, 232; tobacco, 155; vegetable oil, 250. *See also* firms and companies, industries, opium, trade, precious metals

communism (Marxism-Leninism): Chinese, 17, 219, 257, 261–63; combining of national and social revolution, 200–2; demise of, 1–2, 4–5; and East Asian capitalism, 19; Soviet, 260–1, 263; anti-imperialism 200; vanguard party, 261; Vietnamese, 19; and indusrializaiton, 210. *See also* revolutions and state-breakdowns, social movements, and individual countries

Concert of Europe, 59

consumerism, 135–36, 138, 205–10,

284. *See also* social compacts and U.S. world hegemony

Cooper, Frederick, 201, 208

Copeland, Melvin T., 127–28

Cornwallis, Charles, Lord, 229–30

Coromandel, 108

Coupland, Reginald, 240, 242

Courtis, Kenneth, 274

Cox, Robert, 12, 26

Craig, Alert M., 228, 235

Cronin, James E., 189, 194

Crouch, Colin, 215

Crouzet, François, 118–19, 127

Cumings, Bruce, 94, 265–66, 269

currencies: copper coin, 231; U.S. dollar, 5, 73, 86, 88, 284; euro, 5, 277; pound sterling, 67, 73, 86; yen, 5. *See also* precious metals

Curtin, Philip D., 154–55

Davenant, Charles, 221

Davies, Kenneth G., 100, 104–5, 115

Davis, Mike, 188

Davis, Norman, 79, 84

Davis, Ralph, 50, 55, 57, 158

de Cecco, Marcello, 64, 73

de Gaulle, Charles, 91

De la Court, Peter, 48, 50, 62

Defoe, Daniel, 227

DeGrasse, R. W., 137

Dehio, Ludwig, 47–48, 57–58, 90–91

Delaware, 44

Denmark, 51, 53, 70, 109

DeViney, Stanley, 184

Dicken, Peter, 5–6

Diderot, Denis, 227

Dodwell, H. H., 240

Drummond, Ian M., 74

Du Bois, W. E. B., 15

Dubofsky, Melvyn, 188

Duffy, Michael, 57

Duke, David, 212

Dulles, John Foster, 139

Duménil, G., 136

Dunning, John H., 138, 145

Durkheim, Emile, 30

Dutch East India Company (VOC), 8, 99, 101–3, 107–8, 111–12; 143, 222–23

Dutch world hegemony: beneficiaries, 154–59; and chartered companies,

97–101; and coercion, 156–59; decline, 273; emulation of Dutch republic, 153–54; and financial power, 40–41; as "leadership from behind," 282; and military power, 39–40; and modern system of sovereign states, 22, 28, 37, 39, 43, 92; and privileged access to Asian resources, 217–18; and slavery, 154, 156–59; social foundations, 152–63; 177–78. *See also* hegemony, hegemonic transitions, world hegemony, United Provinces

Duus, Peter, 155, 256

East Asia: advance in global finance, 18, 38, 96, 287; British dominance, 234, 246, 255–56, 263, 267–68, 278; and Chinese business diaspora, 149, 268–69, 280–81, 287; "concentration without centralization," 150; dependence on global economy, 270; economic challenge to Western supremacy, 20, 219, 268–69, 275, 278, 280, 288; economic expansion, 17–18, 89, 96, 149, 265, 269–70, 274–75, 281, 287; and Indian military manpower, 63; and Japanese capital, 96, 148–49, 269, 287; low protection and reproduction costs, 269, 288; national identities, formation of, 249; as new workshop of world, 287; regional integration, 280–81; structural differentiation of power, 269; survival of indigenous state structures, 280, 287; U.S.-Chinese struggle for centrality, 265; U.S. dominance, 265–70, 280; Western rivalries, 247, 255–57; world hegemonic leadership (future), 289. *See also* China-centered world system, financial crises, individual places

East Indies 59–60, 103, 109, 116, 221, 223. *See also* Dutch East India Company, English East India Company, India and Indonesia

Eccleston, Bernard, 149

Edwardian *belle époque*, 66, 179, 185, 198

Edwards, Richard, 181–83, 207

Egypt, 225, 237

Eichengreen, Barry, 73–74

Elliott, William Y., 83

Emmer, P. C., 100, 103

Engels, Friedrich, 62, 125

England. *See* United Kingdom

English East India Company: and British finances, 101, 113; and British power, 98, 110; campaigns against, 114; China monopoly, 102, 114–15, 230; China trade, 111, 113–15, 222, 229–30; as "company state," 110–11; comparison with Dutch East India company, 112; comparison with Mughal rule, 113–14; and demise of Dutch commerical supremacy, 109; dissolution, 115; and Dutch capital, 52; establishment, 100; and European imperialism in Asia, 143; and European trade in Asia, 107–8; "factories," 108; growing debt, 114; and Indian economy, 112–14; India monopoly, 102, 114, 119, 230; initial difficulties, 107; and Indian textile industry, 108, 110–11; military activities, 110–11; Mughal court, as successor of, 223; territorial expansion, 109–11, 114; as winner among chartered companies, 101–2, 112

Enlightenment, 2, 225–27

Erlanger, Steven, 277

Escobar, Arturo, 208–9

Esherick, Joseph, 228–29, 258–59

Estado da India, 102, 108, 111–12, 222

Esteva, Gustavo, 208

Estonia, 277

Ethiopia, 225

Europe: and Asian markets, 103; Asian trade, centrality of, 221; and Atlantic triangular trade, 100; and China compared, 226–27; Coal and Steel Community, 140; colonialism, 15; and East Asian economic model, 19; fascism, 213; Marshall Plan, 205–6; mercantilism, 45; military organization, 20; overseas expansion, 100–1, 115–17; Payments Union, 140; revolution, 202; trade, 62; trade imbalance with the East, 221; Union and Common Market, 4–5, 138–40, 276–77, 280. *See also* world system and individual places

Evans, Peter, 13
Ewen, Stuart, 135–36, 138

Fairbank, John K., 226, 228, 235, 238, 252, 258, 260–61
Farnie, D. A., 114, 127
Fearon, Peter, 74
Feis, Herbert, 255
Feldman, Gerald, 188
Feuerwerker, Albert, 249, 253
financial crises: Dutch/British (1763, 1772–73, 1780), 53–54, 74, 95, 275; East Asian (1997–98), 74, 96, 274–75; "Great Crash" (1929–31), 74, 80, 95–96, 121, 136, 196, 256, 275; Japanese (1990–92), 6, 74, 95–96; Mexican (1994–95), 7
financial expansions: British- and Dutch-led compared, 68, 272; current, 211–13, 272–74, 278, 284; and hegemonic crises, 31–33, 272–74, 282, 284; and polarization of wealth, 151, 153, 179, 211–13, 282; U.S.- and British-led compared, 88–89
financial/money markets, 7, 21, 32–3, 81, 89, 101, 196, 274, 284. *See also* Amsterdam, Hong Kong, London, New York, Tokyo
firms and companies: Armstrong Co., 70; Bank of England, 46, 52–53, 73; Bechtel, 281; Boeing, 281; British South Africa Company, 116–17; Chase Manhattan Bank, 146; Compagnie des Indes Occidentales, 100; Compagnie des Indes Orientales, 100; Credit Anstalt, 74; Donatbank, 74; Ford Motor Company, 135; Fuggers, 8; General Motors Company, 139; IBM, 281; Jardine Mathieson, 133; Krupp, 70–71; Moody's Investor Services, 7, 9; South Sea Company, 52; Whitworth, 70; Wisselbank, 52–54. *See also* chartered companies
Flynn, Dennis O., 222
France: achievements in state-making, 45–46; alliance with U.K., 44, 235; and American War of Independence, 56–57; as aspiring continental hegemon, 90; and Atlantic trade, 104–5; and British capital, 77; chartered companies, 100, 109; colonies, 156; and Concert of Europe, 59; conflicts with the Dutch, 44–45, 54; Conseil des Indes, 100; and Dutch capital, 53–54; eclipse as world power, 81; Edict of Nantes, 226; as empire-building national state, 34–42, 288; expansion in Asia, 234–35, 247, 255; Germany invades, 77, 257; and industrialization of war, 69–71, 84; and Japanese industrialization, 253; labor and socialist movement, 182; mercantilism, 45–51; sea power, 57, 75; and U.S. multinationals, 139. *See also* Napoleon, revolutions, wars
Franke, Wolfang, 238–39
Franklin, Benjamin, 158
Frieden, Jeffry, 79, 87, 146
Friedman, Thomas, 7
Friedman, David, 142
Fries, Russell, 132
Fröbel, Folker, 10
Fukuyama, Francis, 3, 16
Furber, Holden, 112
Furtado, Celso, 48

Gaastra, Femme, 100
Galbraith, John Kenneth, 143
Galbraith, John S., 117
Gamble, Andrew, 72
Gandhi, M. K., 200, 244–46
Gattrell, V. A. C, 127
General Agreement on Tariffs and Trade (GATT), 14, 206
Genoa, 38, 41–42, 48–49, 55
Genovese, Eugene D., 158–59, 170
George, Lloyd, 194
Germany/Prussia: banks, 125; bid for mastery in Europe, 81, 90, 288; and corporate capitalism, 121, 124–25; fascism and Nazism, 80, 196–97; industrialization, 68, 72, 125–26, 132; and industrialization of war, 70–71, 84, 125; invasion of Belgium and France, 77; mercantilism, 51; national unification, 124–25; rivalry with U.K., 72, 75, 131–32; Social Democratic Party, 183–84; social insurance schemes, 184; sphere of influence in China, 255–56; territorial expansionism, 197; working

classes, 124, 181; and U.S. multinationals, 139. *See also* capitalism, revolutions, wars, and individual cities
Ghana (Gold Coast), 200
Gibney, Frank, 247
Gibraltar, 47
Giddens, Anthony, 10, 93, 188, 225
Gilder, George, 142
Gill, Stephen, 8, 12–3, 26
Gilpin, Robert, 4, 27, 140, 145
Giraldez, Arturo, 222
Glick, Mark, 136–37
globalization, 3, 6, 9; of armaments business, 71; definition, 10; financial, 9; of interstate system, 93; of revolutionary processes, 190–91, 202–3; waves, 10
Godfrey, Walter, 10
gold. *See* precious metals
Goldfield, Michael, 207
Goldstein, Joshua, 57, 77
Goodman, John, 8
Gordon, David M., 11, 181–83, 205
Gould, Stephen J., 131
Gramsci, Antonio, 26–27
Great Britain. *See* United Kingdom
great depression: Great Depression of 1873–96, 64, 66–67, 120–21, 125, 128, 130, 181, 184–85, 191; Interwar (1930s), 9, 66, 121, 136–37, 147, 203–4
Greenberg, Michael, 115, 229–30, 232
Grosfoguel, Ramón, 209
Gross, Leo, 39
Group of Seven (G-7), 5, 7–8
Guangxu, emperor, 258
Guangzhou, 238, 255
Guha, Ranajit, 27, 241, 243–45
Guo, Tingyi, 236

Habsburgs, 41, 153
Haiti (Saint Domingue), 168–73, 198
Hale, David H., 6
Hall, John A., 3, 282
Halliday, Fred, 89
Hamashita, Takeshi, 222–23, 247–50, 252
Hamilton, Gary G., 149
Hamilton, Nora, 10
Hao, Yen-p'ing, 232, 250
Harrison, Bennett, 142–43, 147–48

Hartman, Paul T., 207
Harvey, David, 75, 272–73
Haudrere, Philippe, 100
Haupt, Georges, 187
Headrick, Daniel R., 251
Heesterman, J. C., 242–43
hegemonic transitions: and balance of class forces, 160, 178–79, 191, 211, 213–16, 283–86; bifurcation of military and economic power, 275–78, 281–82; British to U.S., 64–66, 72–73, 79, 86, 121, 143–44, 152–53, 176–77, 179, 181, 186, 189–91, 195–98, 263, 272–75, 279, 283–84, 287–88; and centralization of financial capabilities, 277; and centralization of military capabilities, 91–92, 275–8; and clash with Asian civilizations, 217–19, 286–89; conceptualization, 29–30; current, 38, 141, 143, 153, 211–16, 269–70; 272–78, 283–89; and decolonization, 198; Dutch to British, 42–43, 47–48, 51–52, 54–58, 60, 100–2, 106, 143–44, 152–53, 159, 178–79, 186, 189–90, 198, 271, 272–75, 277–79, 282–84, 286, 288; exploitative domination by declining hegemon, 288–89; and interstate balance of power, 90–91, 275, 287–89; overviews, 3–4, 33–35, 38–39, 151, 180, 271–72; and path dependency, 288; and polarization of wealth, 164–66, 185–86, 211, 273; and reorganization of interstate system, 74–75, 275–78, 281, 287–89; and social conflict, 151–53, 179–80, 189–91, 197–98, 211, 273, 282–86, 289; and transformation of business enterprise, 98–99, 101, 121–22, 141, 143–44, 278–79; U.S. to non-western, 286–89; and war, 189–90, 197–98, 211, 278, 289; and western power in the non-western world, 263, 269–70, 286–89. *See also* world hegemony
hegemony: and domination, 26–27, 218; and general interest, 26–28; of global markets, 10; of governmental-business complexes, 22, 34; Gramsci's conception, 26–27; and leadership, 26–27, 30, 45, 263; and leadership from behind, 282; "national" projects, 197; as

"power inflation," 27, 45; and social
compacts, 151–53, 289. *See also* hege-
monic transitions, power, states, world
hegemony, British world hegemony,
Dutch world hegemony, U.S. world
hegemony
Heinrichs, Jürgen, 10
Held, David, 93
Helleiner, Eric, 8
Henan, 255
Henderson, W. O., 125
Hettne, Bjorn, 13
Heyn, Piet, 104
Hibbs, Douglas A., 188
Hilferding, Rudolf, 124
Hiroshima, 18, 80, 257
Hirschman, Albert O., 205, 208
Hirst, Paul, 8, 273
Hisaeda, Shuji, 97–150
Ho, S. P. S., 256
Hobsbawm, Eric, 1–2, 21, 36, 61–62,
    66–67, 95, 120, 127, 134, 155, 172,
    175–76, 181, 184, 186, 189, 192–94,
    202, 213, 216, 285–86
Holland. *See* United Provinces
Holy Alliance, 59, 175
Hong, Xiuquan, 237–38, 262–63
Hong Kong, 233, 235, 251, 274, 277–78;
    financial market, 96
Hopkins, A. G., 63
Hopkins, Terence K., 22
Horsman, M., 6
Hossain, Hameeda, 110–11
Hounshell, David A., 78, 135–37
Howard, Michael, 45–46
Howell, David, 19
Hsiao, Liang-lin, 229
Hsu, Immanuel C. Y., 253
Hugill, Peter J., 44, 67
Hui, Po-keung, 37–96, 250–51, 268
Hungary, 277
Huntington, Samuel P., 16–17, 19–20,
    263
Hussein, Saddam, 3
Hymer, Stephen, 6, 130

Ihonvbere, Julius, 213
Ikeda, Satoshi, 18, 145, 149
Ikenberry, John G., 17, 206
Inden, Ronald, 241

India: and Asian trade, 220; British auto-
    cratic rule, 240–44; and British hege-
    mony, 218, 283; buoyant markets,
    112–13; burdens of "free trade," 283;
    caste hierarchy, 243–44; competition
    of British machinofactures, 115–19;
    contribution to British wealth, 55–56,
    63–64, 229–39; Criminal Tribes Act
    (1871), 241; disintegration of Mughal
    empire, 109–10; finances, 63–64; fi-
    nancial support of British army, 225;
    incorporation in European world-
    economy, 223; indigenous civilization,
    222–24; interstate system, 110; mili-
    tary manpower, 63, 110, 225; National
    Congress, 200, 245–46; Orientalist
    representations of, 241; piece-goods
    trade, 112; Plassey plunder, 63, 167;
    trade with the U.K., 62. *See also*
    English East India Company, Mughal
    Empire, and individual places
Indian Ocean, 99, 101–4, 107, 220
Indochina, 95
Indonesia, 218, 222, 287. *See also* Dutch
    East India Company and East Indies
industrialization: and interimperialist ri-
    valries, 197; and national development,
    246; as response to interwar collapse
    of market system, 197; spread, 67–68,
    71–72, 126, 133; and territorial expan-
    sion, 197; and war- and state-making,
    37, 61, 68–71, 125. *See also* industries
    and warfare
industries: "American system of manu-
    facture," 69–70, 78; armament, 69–70,
    132, 138, 188–89, 252–53, 277;
    artisanal/craft production, 69, 110,
    118–19, 142, 249; automation, 69;
    capital goods, 69, 120, 125, 253; cot-
    ton, 117, 119, 126–28, 249; *dadni* sys-
    tem, 108, 110; engineering, 131–32;
    export processing zones, 14; high
    technology, 281; iron, 61, 119–20;
    machinofacture/factory system,
    118–19, 127, 249; manufacturing,
    117, 119; mass production, 69,
    135–38, 142, 253; national, 62; steel,
    Bessemer, 70; transport and communi-
    cation, 61–62, 71, 75, 77, 83, 117,
    119, 246, 253; shoe, 132; silk, 249. *See*

also business enterprises, chartered companies, commodities, firms and companies, machinery, railways, ships/shipbuilding and textiles

Ingham, Geoffrey, 85, 87, 126, 146

International Bank for Reconstruction and Development (IBRD, World Bank), 8, 210

international law, 8, 39, 232, 235–36

International Monetary Fund (IMF), 8, 11, 87, 210, 285

Iran (Persia) 95, 214, 225, 284. *See also* revolutions

Iriye, Akira, 254, 256

Irwan, Alexander, 149

Islam: 16, 193, 220, 237. *See also* Ottoman Empire, rebellions and individual countries

Israel, Jonathan I., 43–44, 48, 51, 101, 109

Italy: 31–32, 37, 41–42, 71, 77, 81, 195, 197. *See also* individual cities

Jackson, Robert, 94

Jakarta, 281

Jamaica, 203

James, C. L. R., 171

Japan: alliance with Germany and Italy, 257; alliance with U.K., 255; banks, 5, 18; bid for mastery in the Far East, 81; as businesslike state, 287; and Chinese nationalism, 259–60; competitive advantage, 142; and East Asian economic expansion, 266; economic expansion, 266, 274, 287; emulation of China, 249; financial strength, 96, 255, 278; foreign assets/investments, 96, 274; global power, 5–6, 95, 267; imperialism, 197; industrialization, 249, 253–55; and industrialization of war, 70, 253; invasion of China, 254, 256–57; leadership from behind, 282, 287; military challenge to the West, 198–98, 219, 256–57, 262–63; national identity, 287; opening to western trade and influence, 246–47; Meiji Restoration, 249, 253; modernization, 251–54; "multilayered subcontracting system," 148–49, 280; relations with U.S., 17, 246–47, 257, 265–67; sea power, 75; as semisovereign state, 278; take-over of Korea, 254–56; take-over of Chinese territories, 255–56, 260, 268. *See also* financial crises, wars, and individual cities

Jaques, Martin, 5

Jefferson, Thomas, 172

Jenks, Leland H., 120

Jiang, Jieshi, 259, 261

Johnson, Chalmers, 18–19

Kahn, Herman, 5

Kangxi, emperor, 226

Kasaba, Resat, 233–34

Katzenstein, Peter J., 94, 149, 280–81

Kawakatsu, Heita, 249

Keehn, E. B., 18–19

Kennedy, Paul, 47, 57, 60, 68, 71, 75, 77, 81, 104, 224

Keohane, Robert, 23, 26

Kiachow bay, 255

Kim, K-H., 254

Kindleberger, Charles, 6, 52–54, 74, 80

Kissinger, Henry, 59

Knapp, J. A., 133

Kocka, Jürgen, 176, 181

Korea: 13, 248, 254–56, 265, 280, 287. *See also* wars

Kraar, Louis, 267

Krasner, Stephen, 94

Kreye, Otto, 10

Krugman, Paul, 18

Kurth, James, 285

Kuwait, 3, 6

labor: agency system, 110–11; agricultural, 192; in armaments industry, 188; coal mining, 187–88; and commercial supremacy, 49–51; "deskilling," 182–83, 207; female, 14, 282, 285; and First World War, 188; global scope of proletarianization, 282, 285–86; internationalism, 187; international migration, 195, 283; maritime, 159, 187; mass production 207, 216, 285–86; and mechanization 118; and "postindustrial society," 12, 142; "race to bottom"/cost-cutting race, 213, 286; racial and ethnic composition of, 14–15, 282; and racism, 14–15; rail-

way, 187–88; repression, 206–7; restructuring of, 207, 215–16; and scientific management, 181; subordination
to capital, 117–18; superexploitation,
113; tripartite agreements, 188, 201;
unemployment, 124, 181, 197; wages
and working conditions, 10, 136, 181,
196, 213; welfare, 12; workers' rights,
11–12, 14. *See also* business enterprises, rebellions, social classes and
groups, social compacts, social conflict,
social movements
LaFeber, Walter, 184
Lancashire, 119, 126–28
Landes, David S., 66, 68, 71–72, 117,
129, 131–32
Landi, Christina Melhorn, 213
Lane, Frederic C., 103
Laos, 248, 287
Latin America, 59, 62, 73, 78, 87, 93,
100, 197. *See also* Americas and indi-
vidual places
Lattimore, Owen, 236
Law, David, 12, 26
Lazonick, William, 135
Le Roy Ladurie, Emmanuel, 166
League of Nations, 195, 204
Lebanon, 95
Leibniz, Gottfried von, 226
Lenin, V. I., 194–95, 261
Lewis, Archibald, 223
Liandong peninsula, 255–56
Lim, Linda, 14
Lin, Zexu, 232, 252
Liverpool, 127
Lockman, Zachary, 210, 213
London, 42, 53, 55, 69–70; financial
market, 5, 43, 53–55, 64, 73–74, 85,
87, 95
Loth, Wilfried, 202
Louis XIV, king, 44–45, 47, 226
Lowe, Peter, 235
Lyon, Leverett, 136

Macao, 251
MacArthur, Douglas, 269
Macartney, George, Lord, 228
machinery, 61, 69, 118, 129, 142, 252.
See also industries
Mackinder, Halford, 67

Madras, 108
Mahan, A. T., 40, 47–48, 57
Mahbubani, Kishore, 280
Maier, Charles, 205–6
Malabar, 103
Malacca, 103, 223
Malay archipelago, 107, 112
Manchester, 8, 128
Manchuria, 256, 260
Mann, Michael, 22, 174, 178, 182
Mao, Zedong, 216, 259–63, 285
Marichal, Carlos, 74
Markoff, John, 11, 13
Marshall, Alfred, 142
Marshall, P. J., 6, 110
Marx, Karl, 52, 62, 117, 261
Marxism-Leninism. *See* communism
Mason, Philip, 225
Mathias, Peter, 120, 133
Maurice of Nassau, 39
Mayer, Arno, 184, 191
Mazur, Paul, 136
McCormick, Thomas J., 79, 81, 87, 139,
206
McElwee, William L., 71
McMichael, Philip, 208, 213
McNeill, William, 19, 39, 46, 57, 61, 63,
69–71, 78, 92, 110, 120, 190, 222
Meade, Edward S., 123
Mendelsohn, M. S., 146
Metcalf, Thomas, 245
Mexico. *See* financial crises, revolutions,
wars
Mill, James, 240
Mill, John Stuart, 240
Minchinton, Walter E., 51, 120
Minorca, 47
Mintz, Sidney W., 156–58, 170
Mittelman, James H., 13
Mjöset, Lars, 206
Modelski, George, 27
Mombasa, 225
Montesquieu, Baron, 227
Montgomery, David, 181, 183
Moody, Kim, 13, 207
Moore, Barrington, Jr., 166
Morgenthau, Henry, 87
Morris, Morris D., 119
Moss, D. J., 114
Moulder, Frances, 236, 247, 253

Mughal Empire, 109–10, 113–14, 220, 223, 242–43. *See also* India
Muller, Ronald, 6
multinational corporations, 6, 8, 12, 21; and cheap labor, 286; and chartered companies compared, 144–46, 279; emergence, 121–30; expansion after Second World War, 138–40; and extraterritorial/offshore money markets, 89, 98, 146, 284; increase in number, 145, 149; and small business, 148; and state power, 146–47, 278–82; U.S. government support, 139–40; and U.S. hegemony, 97–99, 145–47 ,279, 281, 284. *See also* business enterprises, capitalism
Mumford, Lewis, 137
Munro, Ross H., 17
Murphey, R., 250

Nagasaki, 18, 80, 257
Nakao, Shigeo, 5–6
Nandy, Ashis, 243
Naples, 47
Napoleon Bonaparte, 42, 57–58. *See also* wars
Nash, Gary B., 156, 158, 160–62
Nathan, Andrew J., 18, 250
nationalism: in Asia, 198–201; of citizen armies, 190; and democracy, 190, 245; in East Asia, 19, 239, 260; in nonwestern world, 79, 208–11, 245, 263, 287; and racism, 14; and Russian revolutions, 193–94; in West Asia, 237, 239. *See also* social movements
navies: Anglo-French 246; British/ English, 46–47, 69, 75; Chinese, 231–32; 254; French 46, 69; German, 75; Japanese, 254–55; Russian, 69, 255, 257; trade in stores for, 40–41, 104; Turkish, 69, 235; U.S., 257, 265. *See also* ships and shipbuilding
Neal, Larry, 109
Nef, John U., 61
Nehru, Jawaharlal, 199, 246
Nepal, 224
Netherlands. *See* United Provinces
Neumann, Franz, 197
New Jersey, 44

New York, 44; financial market, 5, 74, 77, 86–87, 95–96, 274
Newfoundland, 47
Nigam, Sanjay, 241
Nigeria, 200
Nixon, Richard, 267
Nkrumah, Kwame, 201
Norman, E. H., 253
North Sea, 40, 75, 100
Northup, David, 251
Norway, 51
Nyasa, 225
Nye, Joseph S., 18, 23, 60, 75

Oberg, Sture, 5
O'Connor, James, 137
Offer, A., 190
Ohmae, K., 6
Okimoto, Daniel I., 148
Ong, Aihwa, 14
Ong, Paul, 10
opium, 114–15, 227–32, 234. *See also* wars
Orissa, 108
Orrù, Marco, 149
Ottoman Empire, 62, 69–70, 233–36. *See also* Islam, revolutions, individual places
Owen, D. E., 232
Ozawa, Terutomo, 266

Pacific Ocean, 77, 99
Padfield, Peter, 44, 46
Palmer, R. R., 163, 165, 167
Palmerston, Lord, 235
Pandey, Gyan, 244
Panikkar, K. M., 225
Pares, R., 157
Parker, Geoffrey, 227, 232
Parry, J. H., 102–3, 221
Parsons, Talcott, 26–28
Passell, Peter, 5
Pauly, Louis W., 8
Payne, P. L., 126, 128
Pearl Harbor, 257
Pemsel, Hellmut, 44
Penang, 251
Perlin, Frank, 242
Perot, Ross, 212
Persia. *See* Iran

Persian Gulf, 220
Peterson, Erik R., 7, 10
Pétion, Alexandre, 171
Peyrefitte, A., 228
Phelps Brown, Henry, 181
Philippines, 19, 221, 287
Phillips, Kevin, 165, 212
Piore, Michael J., 142
Piven, Frances Fox, 11, 183
Pizzorno, Alessandro, 215
Poincaré, Henri, 21
Pol Pot, 19
Polanyi, Karl, 12–13, 58–59, 66–67, 80, 85, 117, 174–75, 183, 185, 196–97, 224
Pollard, Sidney, 118
Pomeau, Yves, 22
Port Arthur, 255–57
Port Mahon, 47
Portes, Alejandro, 141–42
Portes, Richard, 73–74
Portugal: 47, 56, 107, 102–4, 221. *See also* Brazil, Estado da India
Post, Ken, 210
Postma, Johannes Menne, 100
power: balance of, 3–4, 39, 47, 56–59, 90–91, 93–94; capitalist vs. territorialist logic, 48–49, 62–63; "deflation"/ "inflation," 26–27, 30, 45; distributive and collective aspects, 28; "island," 46, 57, 77; land/sea, 46–47, 54, 71, 90–91, 223; military and financial, fusion/fission of, 38, 94–96; money as source of, 49, 92; and precious metals, 221; and profit, 102–3, 111–12, 117, 266; Weber's definition, 28; world configuration of, 81, 95. *See also* hegemony, states, world hegemony
Prakash, Gyan, 241
Prakash, Om, 107
precious metals, 52; American silver 40–41, 221; Brazilian gold, 47; gold standard, 9, 47–48, 73–74, 80, 87, 195–96, 255; Manila silver galleons, 221–22; silver standard, 47–48, 222, 248; silver trade with China, 114, 221–22
Prussia. *See* Germany

Qianlong, emperor, 228, 237

Quesnay, François, 226

Radhakrishna, Meena, 241
Radosh, Ronald, 206
railways, 61, 66, 71, 78, 120, 125, 129, 131–33, 184, 191–92, 256
Rangel, J., 136
Rapkin, David P., 57, 77
Rashid, Shaikh Abdur, 243
Rasler, Karen A., 40
Ray, Krishnendu, 37–96
Raychaudhuri, Tapan, 108, 110
Reagan, Ronald, 3, 7
rebellions and insurrections: agrarian (India), 244; anti-Qing, 237; Boxer Rebellion (1900–1901) 258–59; Captain Swing riots, 174; Great Rebellion (India, 1857–58), 70, 102, 178, 244–45; Hidalgo and Morales (1810), 171; Kiel, 189; Kronstadt, 189; Miao (1850–72), 238; Muslim (China, 1855–74), 238; Native Americans, 161, 163, 178; Nian (1853–74), 238; peasant, 154, 191–92, 216; Peterloo Massacre (1819), 173; Shanghai (1927), 261; slave, 158–59, 169–73, 203; Taiping (1850–64), 178, 236–39; 244, 252; Tupac Amaru (1780–82), 171; working class, 174–78, 188, 192–94, 196, 205–7; 216, 261, 283
Red Sea, 220
Rediker, Marcus, 155, 159
Reich, M., 181–83
Reich, Robert, 6
Reifer, Thomas Erlich, 37–96
Reischauer, Edwin O., 228, 235
revolutions, 151–54, 159–60, 195, 285; Algerian, 191; American, 53, 56, 159–64, 173, 185, 189; American Revolution's effect on Europe, 163–64; Americas, 153, 203; Chinese (1911), 198, 259–60, 268; Chinese (1949), 191, 208, 216; Dutch Patriots, 54, 164–67, 185; Eurasia, 87; Europe, 153; Europe (1848), 176–77; French (1789), 2, 57, 164, 166–68, 172–73, 185, 193–94; French (1830), 174; "general crisis of the seventeenth century," 153; geographical scope, 190; Germany, 195; global, 153, 179, 202;

impact of French and Russian compared, 193–94; Iran, 214, 284; Maoist strategy, 216; Mexican (1910), 191; Persian, 193; Russian (1905), 189, 191–94, 198; Russian (1917), 38, 188, 191, 193–94, 199–200, 256, 260; Saint Domingue (Haiti), 168–73; Spanish America, 171–73; systemwide, 153, 194; Turkish, 193; Vietnamese, 191, 216; and war, 172, 188, 190

Rix, Alan, 282

Robertson, Priscilla, 175–76

Robinson, William, 13, 26

Rodrik, Dani, 213

Rohlen, Thomas P., 148

Romania, 277

Romein, Jan, 259

Roosevelt, Franklin D., 85–87, 93

Ropp, Theodore, 75

Rosenau, James N., 2, 21

Rosenberg, Hans, 125

Ross, Arthur M., 207

Ross, Robert J. S., 10, 18

Rostow, Walt. W., 208–9

Rousseau, Jean Jacques, 227

Rowen, Herbert H., 45

Rowland, Benjamin M., 87

Rowthorn, Robert, 6

Royal African Company, 101, 105–6, 116, 143

Rozman, G., 236

Rubinstein, W. D., 126

Ruggie, John G., 4, 22–24, 206

Rupert, Mark, 13, 26, 206

Russia/USSR: Afghanistan invasion, 264, 284; and British capital, 77; and Chinese nationalism, 260; demise of Soviet regime, 4–5, 8, 88, 91–92, 274, 276; and European states, 37–39; Five Year Plans, 80, 197; general strikes, 192–93; grain exports, 184; industrial mercantilism, 51; industrial proletariat, 192–93; industrial supremacy, 18; and industrialization of war, 69–71, 84; influence on U.S. vision of world hegemony, 87–88, 206; launch of Sputnik, 84, 91; multiethnic empire, 193; and Napoleonic wars, 58; Soviet empire, 66; and "spheres of influence," 93–94; territorial expansion in Asia, 197, 225,

247, 255; and western European unification, 140; and western power, 264. *See also* communism, Cold War, revolution, wars

Ryukyus, 248

Sabel, Charles, 130–31, 142

Sakhalin island, 265

Salisbury, Lord, 225, 241

Salter, Arthur, Sir, 80

San Francisco, 81

Sanger, David E., 5–6, 276–77

Sassen, Saskia, 8–9, 285

Saul, S. B., 120, 131, 181

Saville, John, 174

Saxenian, AnnaLee, 142

Sayers, R. S., 73

Schama, Simon, 164–65, 167

Schell, Orville, 237

Schienstock, G., 148

Schoenberg, Ronald, 199

Schoffer, Ivo, 41

Schumpeter, Joseph, 27

Schurmann, Franz, 85–86, 88, 203–4, 237, 266

Seidman, Gay W., 13

Selden, Mark, 262, 274

Semmel, Bernard, 232

Servan-Schreiber, J. J., 140

Seton-Watson, Hugh, 194, 200

Sevastopol, 69–70

Sewell, William H., Jr., 182

Shandong peninsula, 255

Shanghai, 261–62

Shefter, Martin, 182

Shih, Miin-wen, 217–270

ships/shipbuilding: 40, 61, 66, 69–71, 120, 232, 252. *See also* navies

Shirashi, Takashi, 281

Sichuan, 229

Sicily, 47

Sikkim, 247

silver. *See* precious metals

Silver, Beverly J., 13, 187, 201, 205, 207, 216, 286

Singapore, 96, 251, 278

Singh, C., 242

Sinha, Deby, 244

Sinha, Narendra K., 108

"Sino-centric tribute-trade system"

(Hamashita). *See* China-centered world system

Sklair, Leslie, 6, 8

Sklar, Martin J., 123

Sklar, Richard, 6

Skocpol, Theda, 57, 192, 259

Slater, Eric, 151–216

slaves and slavery. *See* rebellions, Royal African Company, social classes and groups, trade, West Indische Compagnie

Sloan, Alfred, 139

Smith, Adam, 116, 121, 226

So, Alvin Y., 149, 247, 250, 252–53, 256–57, 259, 267

Sobel, Andrew C., 8

social classes and groups: agrarian (European), 184; aristocracy/nobility, 164, 167; balance of class forces, 160, 215–16; financiers, 155, 165; industrialists, 175; landowners, 154–55, 175, 192, 237, 245, 259; merchants and shippers, 155, 162; "middle" classes, 151–53, 157–60, 164, 185, 212–13; national bourgeoisie (European), 184, 282; national minorities, 193–94; peasantry, 191–92, 210–11, 216, 261, 285; people of color, 153, 169; planters (Caribbean), 106, 155–56, 177; settlers, 156–59, 160, 167, 177–79, 282; slaves, 156–59, 162, 170, 172, 179, 203, 282–83; subaltern (China), 262; subaltern (India), 243–44; traditional elites, 244–45; urban proletariat, 261–62; westernized elites, 152, 198–201, 209–11, 245, 283; women, 14, 153, 216, 282; working classes, 152–53, 181, 210–11, 215–16, 282–86. *See also* business enterprises and individual countries

social compacts: and British hegemony, 152, 172–78, 282–83; and colonial outlets for surplus population, 283; and Dutch hegemony, 153–59, 176–78; "global New Deal," 282–84; and hegemony, 151–53, 211, 214, 282, 284, 289; racist underpinnings, 14–15, 178; and territorial expansion, 185, 283; undermined by capital flight, 196, 213–15, 284; and U.S. hegemony, 153,

205–11, 214, 282–84; and war, 187–88, 201–2; and workers, 182, 195, 201–2, 205–7, 210–22, 285

social conflict: and decolonization, 200–2, 208–11, 283; and economic depression, 161–62, 164, 185, 191; and First World War, 186, 199; future, 282, 284–86; geographical scope, 153, 198, 202, 212–13; and hegemonic crisis, 29–30, 151–53, 178–80, 197–203, 211–16, 282–86, 289; and interenterprise competition, 124, 152, 179–80, 215; and interstate conflict, 152, 179–80; intra-elite, 152, 155, 160, 167–69, 179, 192; and military strategy, 189–90; and polarization of wealth, 160–62, 164–66, 178, 192, 211–13; "racialized" class conflict, 15–16, 212–13; and Second World War, 201–2; and taxation, 178, 186; workplace, 181–83; and workers in arms industry, 188–89, 201; and war, 160–61, 172, 185–90, 197–98, 201–4, 211, 215, 282; "withering away of strike," 207

social movements: abolition, 172; anti-abortion, 285; antiwar, 188, 214; British reform movement, 175; black civil rights, 214; Chartists, 174; democratic, 11, 203, 245; fascist, 213, 285; feminism, 216, 285; labor, 12–15, 176, 181–89, 192–96, 198, 200–1, 205–11, 215–16, 282; Luddism, 114; mass civil disobedience (India, 1920), 200; merging of national and social, 200–2, 208; "multiculturalism," 216; national liberation, 15, 198–202, 205, 208–11; 245–46, 260–63, 283, 287; "new," 13–14; socialist, 124, 184–85, 187–88, 193, 195, 200, 285; "religious right," 285; suffrage, 176, 184; "Third World," 214–15, 284; weakening of, 282, 284; working class internationalism, 187, 195. See also labor, nationalism, rebellions, revolutions, social conflict

Sonthonax, Léger Felicité, 170

Soros, George, 9, 273

South Africa, 13, 225

Soviet Union. *See* Russia/USSR

Spain, 39–41, 43–44, 47, 56, 58, 70, 104
Spence, Jonathan D., 239
Spice Islands, 103
states: absolutist, 41, 49; and charter
    companies, 144–46; city- and proto-
    nation-, 31–32, 37–38, 41–42, 75, 96,
    275, 278, 280, 282; "company,"
    110–11, 222; competition among,
    30–33, 52, 72, 83, 89, 130, 151, 246;
    conflict/struggle among, 16, 38, 52,
    64–66, 68, 83, 85, 89–91, 96, 121,
    152; continent-sized, 37–39, 75, 77,
    131, 197, 275; cooperation among, 28,
    34, 60, 247; empire-building, 42, 275,
    279, 282; European system of, 22, 37,
    39, 42–43, 59, 90–91; and globaliza-
    tion, 10–11; "half-civilized" (Palmer-
    ston), 235; hegemonic, 3–4, 28, 30,
    33–34, 45; liberal, 15, 227; maritime,
    90; and mobility of capital, 7, 10, 38,
    52; and multinational corporations,
    144–47; national, 1–2, 6, 32, 37, 42,
    75, 237, 245, 275, 287; and national
    economy-making, 42, 67, 131; "na-
    tive" (British India), 245; "nightwatch-
    man," 184, 204; power (and disem-
    powerment) of, 4, 6, 8, 27, 30, 94–95,
    146–47, 149–50, 246, 278–82;
    "quasi-," 94; "semisovereign," 94, 96,
    265–66, 277; settler-, 93; South Asian,
    109–10; sovereignty, 37, 39, 79,
    92–94, 198, 239, 245, 275, 287; terri-
    torial, 42, 45–46, 48–49, 90, 105, 109;
    "warfare-welfare," 137–38, 146–47,
    269; welfare, 12, 14, 184, 204. See
    also hegemony, power, revolutions,
    world system, world hegemony entries
Stavrianos, L. S., 51, 193, 199
Steensgaard, Niels, 100, 102
Stefensen, B., 148
Stivers, William, 79
Stokes, Eric, 240
Stopford, John M., 145
Strait of Magellan, 99
Subrahmanyam, S., 242
Sudan, 225
Sun, Zhongshan, 199–200, 237, 259–61
Surat, 108
Surinam, 100
Sweden, 44, 51, 53, 70, 109

Tabb, William, 11
Taipei, 281
Taiwan (Formosa), 96, 103, 274, 278.
    See also individual cities
Taylor, Peter, 22, 27, 39, 49, 154
Temple, Sir William, 40
textiles, 51, 63, 107–8, 110–12, 114,
    117–20, 156, 232, 249. See also com-
    modities, industries, machinery
Thailand, 287
Thatcher, Margaret, 7
Therborn, Goran, 184, 283
Thomas, S. C., 253, 255, 258
Thompson, E. P., 173–74
Thompson, Grahame, 8, 273
Thompson, William R., 27, 40, 46
Thornton, Edward, 229
Thurow, Lester, 4–5
Tibet, 247
Tilly, Charles, 10–13, 188, 190, 224,
    279–80
Tilly, Richard, 125
"time-space compression," 75–76, 83
Tokyo, 20, 260; financial market, 5–6,
    74, 95–96
Tomlinson, B. R., 225, 241
Toussaint, Auguste, 100
Toussaint Louverture, François
    Dominique, 170–71
Trachte, Kent, 10
Tracy, James D., 100
trade: agriculture, 184; Atlantic, 154;
    Baltic, 40–41, 99–102, 104; contra-
    band, 100, 229–32; "coolie," 251,
    283; East Asian, 281; Indian Ocean,
    102–4; intra-Asian, compared to East-
    West, 220; liberalization, 123, 277;
    Malay-Indonesia inter-port, 221–22;
    "protection costs," 48, 60, 67, 103,
    115, 269; protectionism, 184–85;
    slave, 40, 44, 47, 104, 154, 157, 172;
    "transaction costs", 123, 127; triangu-
    lar (Atlantic), 50, 100–1, 104–5, 116,
    143. See also business enterprises and
    commodities
Treaties: Anglo-French treaty of "mutual
    guarantee," 48; Balta Limani Treaty,
    233–34, 236; Beijing Convention, 236;
    Congress of Berlin, 184; Congress of
    Vienna, 59; Methuen Treaties, 47;

Nanjing Treaty, 233–34, 236, 247; North American Free Trade Agreement (NAFTA), 280; North Atlantic Treaty Organization (NATO), 17, 140, 276–77; Ottawa Agreement, 80; Paris Convention, 170; Peace of Utrecht, 50,154; Peace of Vienna, 42, 58; Peace/Treaties of Westphalia, 2, 16, 22, 37, 39, 43–44, 50, 54, 58, 60, 92–93, 154; Strategic Arms Limitation Treaty (SALT), 92; Treaty of Portsmouth, 256; Treaty of Rijswijk, 46; Treaty of Shimonoseki, 247, 255, 257; Treaty of Tianjin, 247; Treaty of Utrecht, 47, 52, 58; Versailles Conference, 256; Warsaw Pact, 18; Washington conference, 256

Trevor-Roper, H. R., 153
Truman, Harry S., 87, 202, 208
Tsiang, Ting-fu, 252
Turkey. *See* Ottoman empire
Tyson, R.L., 128

Uganda, 225
Unger, W. S., 100
United Kingdom (Britain, England, Great Britain): alliance with Dutch, 44–47; alliance with France, 44, 235; alliance with Japan (1902), 255; and Atlantic trade, 50, 57, 104–6; autocratic rule in India, 240–42; and balance of power, 56–61, 72, 77, 255; "Blue Water" strategy, 46; centrality in world trade, 60–61, 72, 82–83, 85; colonies, 79, 83, 104–5, 156, 197; competition from rising industrial nations, 126, 128, 131–32; competitive disadvantage, 142; conflicts with China, 227–36; control over European commerce, 46; Corn Law, 60, 173–74; currency, 47–48, 80; and diffusion of mechanization, 118–20, 279; domestic repression, 173–74; and Dutch capital, 47, 52–56; entrepot trade/functions, 50, 60–62, 82, 126, 128, 130, 132, 177, 195; foreign investment, 132–33; Free Trade Imperialism, 109, 112, 131, 178; "free trade treaties," 233; as imperial power/organization, 9, 37–38, 42, 56–57, 62–63, 75, 83, 102, 288; and

Indian economy, 244; and Indian military manpower, 63, 110; industrial restructuring, 126–27; and industrialization of war, 69–72, 84; and Japanese industrialization, 253; military prowess in non-Western world, 224–25; national debt, 52, 55, 63; Navigation Acts, 43, 60, 105; and North American settlers, 50, 56, 105, 156, 160–62; Poor Laws, 174; relationships with Chinese and Ottoman Empires compared, 223–26; rivalry with Germany, 72, 75, 131–32; sea power, 54, 72, 232; social insurance schemes, 184; surplus capital, 68, 72, 133; tariffs, 50–51; territorial expansion, 116, 173, 225; trade unions, 182; "Two Power Standard," 75; unilateral free trade, 60, 67, 79; and U.S. capital, 77, 131; wealth/liquidity from India, 55–56, 63–64, 114; as "workshop of the world," 61–62, 67, 82, 126; as world financial center, 67, 73, 77, 81–83, 85, 126, 132. *See also* British world hegemony, English East India Company, hegemonic transitions, rebellions, Royal African Company, wars, and individual cities

United Nations, 8, 81, 86–87, 93, 204, 209–10, 285
United Provinces (Dutch, Holland, Netherlands): alliance with British, 44–47; and American silver, 40–41, 104; and American War of Independence, 53, 56; Atlantic trade, 44, 104–5; Baltic trade, 40–41, 109; banks and money-lenders, 53, 55; and British finances, 47, 52–56; and capitalist logic of power, 48–49, 62–63, 105; carrying and entrepot trades, 43, 61; commercial supremacy, contradictions of, 108–9; conflicts with France, 44–45; and European mercantilism, 45, 49–51, 60; financial supremacy, terminal crisis of, 54–56; and Japanese industrialization, 253; labor shortage, 49–52; military innovations, 39–40; national debt, 47; sea power, 54; as semisovereign organization, 37–38, 278; struggle for sovereignty, 43–44,

56, 153; surplus capital, 67–68, 109. See also Dutch East India Company, Dutch world hegemony, revolutions, wars, West Indische Compagnie, and individual cities

United States: and British capital, 132–33; and competition for mobile capital, 7, 89, 264–65; as continental system/empire, 78, 82–83, 197; and corporate capitalism, 121; Declaration of Independence, 163; East Asian donations to US political parties, 281; employment policy, 137, 205; European immigration, 138; and European integration, 139–40; and European states and balance of power, 37–39, 59, 77–78, 81–82, 85; financial strength, 73–74, 77, 86, 94–96, 147; fiscal crisis, 146, 276; foreign assets and investment, 73–74, 79, 87, 130, 139–40; global power of, 4, 16, 21, 78–79, 81, 85, 89, 145–46, 202, 264, 269–70, 284; grain exports, 184; industrial working class, 182; industrialization, 68, 126; and industrialization of war, 69–70; 78, 84; and Latin America, 59, 78, 197; "labor-capital accord," 205, 211; law firms, 8; loans to GI families, 138; McCarthyism, 206; militaristic regime in East Asia, 265–67, 269–70; military capabilities and expenditures, 18–20, 85, 91, 94–95, 137–38, 264; national debt, 133, 276; New Deal, 80, 85–86, 137, 197; Open Door Policy, 79; productive capabilities, 78, 85; protectionist policies, 136, 195; relationship of domestic to world economy, 82–83, 85–86, 134, 136; sea power, 75; Sherman Antitrust Act, 129; space program, 91; "spheres of influence," 93–94; State Department, 3, 265; strike waves, 205; surplus capital, 87; Taft-Hartley Act, 206; tariffs, 80, 84, 134, 136; territorial expansion, 77, 185; trade unions, 182, 205; wartime deficit spending, 137; war with Spain, 185. See also hegemonic transitions, revolution, U.S. world hegemony, wars

U.S. world hegemony: application of New Deal experience, 204–6, 209; Bretton Woods system, 206; challenge of social revolutions in non-Western world to, 202–3, 205, 283; and changing balance of class forces, 207; coercive aspects, 203, 206–7, 210–11; compared to British world hegemony, 202–3, 214; compared to Dutch world hegemony, 214; and concentration of systemic capabilities, 81–82, 194, 202, 264, 276; contradictions, 269; and decolonization, 202, 209–11, 283; European Community, 205–6; exploitative domination in decline, 288–89; full employment, 205–6, 283; General Agreement on Tariffs and Trade (GATT), 206; general features, 8, 22, 37–38, 80–81; global "Fair Deal," 208; impact of counter-revolutionary challenge of Axis powers, 203; impact of Great Depression, 203–4, 206; Keynesianism as third way, 205–6; "labor-friendly" institutions, 206; and leadership in industrialization of war, 84; Marshall Plan, 205–6; mass consumption in core, 205–6, 283–84; and multinational corporations, 145–47, 284; and non-Western world, 202, 205–11, 263, 283, 287; "power reflation" in 1980s and 1990s, 284; promise of "development," 208–9, 214–15, 283–84; reformist appeal, 194–95, 203–11, 283; and regional integration in East Asia, 281; rejection of laissez-faire, 204–6; and relationship of U.S. to global economy, 82–83; social foundations, 152–53, 194–95, 203–11, 283; Soviet challenge, 203, 206, 210; and state sovereignty, 93–94; and territorial configuration of the U.S., 83; and world-income inequalities, 289; and world monetary institutions, 86–8. See also Cold War, hegemonic transitions, United States

van der Pijl, K., 12
van Leur, Jacob C., 221
Venice, 38, 41–42, 48–49
Vernon, Raymond, 6, 143
Vidal, Christian, 22

Vietnam, 19, 88, 95, 247–48, 264, 280, 287. *See also* revolutions and wars
VOC. *See* Dutch East India Company
Vogel, Ezra, 5
Voltaire, 226

Waley, Arthur, 232
Wallerstein, Immanuel, 2, 8, 11, 14–15, 23–26, 30, 154–55, 161, 166, 168, 172, 215, 284
Walton, John, 209–10
Waltz, Kenneth, 22–24, 28
warfare: armaments race, 69–70, 84, 89, 92, 138, 185–86, 252–53, 284; and balance of power, 58–59; "citizens armies," 190; civil, 285; colonial, 56, 58, 224–25; and demise of British family capitalism, 133–34; dependence on colonial supplies, 201; Dutch innovations, 39–40, 154; and European scientific achievements, 227; link with imperialism and industrialization, 197–98; industrialization of, 69–71, 75, 83–84, 91, 190, 198, 246; land vs. sea, 46–47, 56–7, 90–1, 104; and mass production, 137; "military-industrial complexes", 198; and non-combatants, 154; and polarization of wealth, 186; and redistribution of world purchasing power, 134; and scientific discovery of new weapons systems, 92; and social conflict, 160–1, 172, 185–90, 197–8, 201–4, 211, 215, 282; and trade, 49–50, 154, 220–3; and United Nations, 204; and Westphalia system, 39. *See also* industries, navies, revolutions, wars
wars: American Independence, 45, 54, 57; American Civil, 70, 78, 84, 182; Anglo-Afgan (1839–42, 1878), 224; Anglo-Burmese (1824, 1852), 224; Anglo-Dutch, First (1652–54), 43; —, Second (1665–67), 44; —, Third (1672–74) 44–45; —, Fourth (1781–84) 54; Anglo-Gurkha (1814–16), 224; Anglo-Maratha (1803, 1818), 224; Anglo-Sikh, 224; Austrian Succession, 51; Battle of Buxar (1764), 110; Battle of Trafalgar, 57; Boer (South African), 189, 225;

Crimean, 58, 69, 70, 71, 235; First World War, 9, 16, 64, 66–68, 72–73, 78, 81, 85, 121, 131–34, 138, 186, 188–89, 190, 194, 198–200, 225, 256, 276; Gulf, 3, 6, 95; Korean, 18, 265–66, 269; Mexican-American (1846–48), 177; Napoleonic, 23, 42–43, 59, 61, 63, 81–82, 118–19, 126, 173, 190, 202, 224; Nine Years' (1688–97), 46, 50; Opium, 227–28, 231–35, 238, 246–47, 252; Plassey (Battle), 55, 110, 223–24; Russo-Japanese (1904–5), 192, 198–99, 254–55, 259; Second World War, 9, 12, 16, 66, 80–82, 86, 91, 121, 134, 137–38, 140, 145, 147, 195, 201–3, 210, 254, 258, 265; Seven Years' (1756–63), 53–54, 56, 110, 154, 158, 160, 189; Sino-French (1884–85), 247; Sino-Japanese, 247, 253, 257, 259; Spanish-American, 189; Spanish Succession (1701–13), 42, 47, 50; Thirty Years' (1618–48), 23, 104; Vietnam, 18, 146, 214, 266, 269, 287. *See also* Cold War
Washbrook, David, 63
Washington, 20, 87
Waters, Malcolm, 6
Watson, Bruce, 220
Weber, Max, 28, 31, 103
Wei, Yuan, 252, 262
Weigall, David, 59, 75
Weihaiwei, 255
Weiss, Linda, 8
West: and Asia's ancien régimes, 239, 245; decline, 286–89; dominance in India and China compared, 225; expansion, 19–20; global dominance, 16, 20, 198, 280; path dependency, 288; practices vs. ideas, 239–40; "revolt against," 15–16, 20, 218, 245, 262–63, 283. See also capitalism, civilizations, states, and individual places
West Indies, 57, 59–60, 109, 116, 126
West Indische Compagnie (WIC): 100–1, 103–5, 143
Wilkins, Mira, 130–31
William III, king, 44, 46, 174
Williams, William A., 184–85
Williams, Eric, 157

Williamson, James A., 46
Wilson, Charles, 41, 53–54
Wilson, Woodrow, 79, 93, 194–95, 256
Wolf, Eric, 101, 190–92, 221
Womack, John, Jr., 192
Wood, George Henry, 118
Woodruff, William, 249
world hegemony: breakdown, 29–30,
    32–34, 85–92, 271–72; crisis, 29–30,
    32–33, 88–89, 271–72; cultural, 287;
    cycle, 24–25, 30, 34; definition, 26–28;
    and "leadership from behind," 282; so-
    cial foundations, 151–52, 271; and sys-
    temic chaos, 2, 32–33, 274, 276, 278,
    286, 289; as systemic governance, 28,
    33–34, 271, 274, 278, 286; and sys-
    tems of business enterprise, 97–98,
    271; Wallerstein's conceptualization,
    23–26; western, end of, 288–89. *See
    also* British world hegemony, Dutch
    world hegemony, hegemony, hege-
    monic transitions, U.S. world hege-
    mony, world system/economy
world system/economy: Afro-Eurasian,
    20; Asian, 220–23; capitalist/modern,
    2, 19, 28, 31, 37–38, 88, 117; crisis,
    1–2, 20; European, 22, 37, 39, 42–43,

90–91; expansion of world trade and
    production, 30, 34, 67, 71–72, 88–89,
    120, 128, 151–52; globalization of,
    271, 279, 286; organizational break-
    down, 33–34, 84–85, 95–96, 197; the-
    ories of, 22–24; transformation, 3,
    21–22, 24, 30, 32, 34–36, 92–94,
    133–34, 141, 217, 271–72, 279; "self-
    regulating world market," 185, 195;
    "volume and dynamic density," 30, 34.
    See also China-centered world system
World Trade Organization (WTO), 8
World Bank. *See* International Bank of
    Reconstruction and Development
Wu, Chengming, 249

Yang, A., 241
Yangzhi valley, 238, 255
Yen, Zhongping, 231
Yunnan, 229

Zeitlin, Jonathan, 130–31
Zevin, Robert, 9
Zhou, Gucheng, 236
Zolberg, Aristide R., 12–13, 206, 216,
    285

Giovanni Arrighi is professor of sociology at the Johns Hopkins University and executive board member of the Fernand Braudel Center, Binghamton University. He is the author or coauthor of many books, including *Essays on the Political Economy of Africa* (with J. S. Saul), *The Geometry of Imperialism, Dynamics of Global Crisis* (with S. Amin, A. G. Frank, and I. Wallerstein), and *Antisystemic Movements* (with T. K. Hopkins and I. Wallerstein). His latest book, *The Long Twentieth Century: Money, Power, and the Origins of Our Times,* won the Distinguished Scholarship Award of the Political Economy of the World System section of the American Sociological Association.

Beverly J. Silver is associate professor of sociology at the Johns Hopkins University, senior research associate at the Fernand Braudel Center at Binghamton University, and a member of the Faculty Advisory Council for the Institute for Global Studies in Culture, Power, and History at Johns Hopkins. She is coauthor of *Labor Unrest in the World-Economy, 1870–1990* (a special issue of *Review*) and has written articles and book chapters on labor, development, and world-historical social change.